THE BLESSINGS OF LIBERTY

Leading legal scholar John Witte, Jr. explores the role religion played in the development of rights in the Western legal tradition and traces the complex interplay between human rights and religious freedom norms in modern domestic and international law. He examines how US courts are moving toward greater religious freedom, while recent decisions of the pan-European courts in Strasbourg and Luxembourg have harmed new religious minorities and threatened old religious traditions in Europe. Witte argues that the robust promotion and protection of religious freedom is the best way to protect many other fundamental rights today, even though religious freedom and other fundamental rights sometimes clash and need judicious balancing. He also responds to various modern critics who see human rights as a betrayal of Christianity and religious freedom as a betrayal of human rights.

John Witte, Jr. is Woodruff University Professor, McDonald Distinguished Professor, and Director of the Center for the Study of Law and Religion at Emory University. A world-class scholar of legal history, human rights, and law and religion, he has published 300 articles and 40 books. Recent works include *The Western Case for Monogamy over Polygamy* (Cambridge, 2015), *Christianity and Family Law* (Cambridge, 2017), and *Church, State, and Family* (Cambridge, 2019).

LAW AND CHRISTIANITY

The Law and Christianity series publishes cutting-edge work on Catholic, Protestant, and Orthodox Christian contributions to public, private, penal, and procedural law and legal theory. The series aims to promote deep Christian reflection by leading scholars on the fundamentals of law and politics, to build further ecumenical legal understanding across Christian denominations, and to link and amplify the diverse and sometimes isolated Christian legal voices and visions at work in the academy. Works collected by the series include groundbreaking monographs, historical and thematic anthologies, and translations by leading scholars around the globe.

Books in the series

The Blessings of Liberty: Human Rights and Religious Freedom in the Western Legal Tradition
John Witte, Jr.

Christianity and International Law: An Introduction
edited by Pamela Slotte and John D. Haskell

Christianity and Market Regulation: An Introduction
edited by Daniel A. Crane and Samuel J. Gregg

Christianity and the Laws of Conscience
edited by Jeffrey B. Hammond and Helen M. Alvaré

Infidels and Empires in a New World Order: Early Modern Spanish Contributions to International Legal Thought
David M. Lantigua

The Possibility of Religious Freedom: Early Natural Law and the Abrahamic Faiths
Karen Taliaferro

Catholic Social Teaching: A Volume of Scholarly Essays
edited by Gerard V. Bradley and E. Christian Brugger

The Immortal Commonwealth: Covenant, Community, and Political Resistance in Early Reformed Thought
David P. Henreckson

Great Christian Jurists in American History
edited by Daniel L. Dreisbach and Mark David Hall

Great Christian Jurists and Legal Collections in the First Millennium
edited by Philip L. Reynolds

The Profession of English Ecclesiastical Lawyers: An Historical Introduction
R. H. Helmholz

Law, Love and Freedom: From the Sacred to the Secular
Joshua Neoh

Great Christian Jurists in French History
edited by Olivier Descamps and Rafael Domingo

Church Law in Modernity: Toward a Theory of Canon Law Between Nature and Culture
Judith Hahn

Common Law and Natural Law in America: From the Puritans to the Legal Realists
Andrew Forsyth

Care for the World: Laudato Si' and Catholic Social Thought in an Era of Climate Crisis
edited by Frank Pasquale

Church, State, and Family: Reconciling Traditional Teachings and Modern Liberties
John Witte, Jr.

Great Christian Jurists in Spanish History
edited by Rafael Domingo and Javier Martínez-Torrón

Under Caesar's Sword: How Christians Respond to Persecution
edited by Daniel Philpott and Timothy Samuel Shah

God and the Illegal Alien: United States Immigration Law and a Theology of Politics
Robert W. Heimburger

Christianity and Family Law: An Introduction
edited by John Witte, Jr. and Gary S. Hauk

Christianity and Natural Law: An Introduction
edited by Norman Doe

Great Christian Jurists in English History
edited by Mark Hill, QC and R. H. Helmholz

Agape, Justice, and Law: How Might Christian Love Shape Law?
edited by Robert F. Cochran, Jr. and Zachary R. Calo

Calvin's Political Theology and the Public Engagement of the Church: Christ's Two Kingdoms
Matthew J. Tuininga

God and the Secular Legal System
Rafael Domingo

How Marriage Became One of the Sacraments: The Sacramental Theology of Marriage from Its Medieval Origins to the Council of Trent
Philip L. Reynolds

Christianity and Freedom (Volume I: Historical Perspectives, Volume II: Contemporary Perspectives)
edited by Timothy Samuel Shah and Allen D. Hertzke

The Western Case for Monogamy over Polygamy
John Witte, Jr.

The Distinctiveness of Religion in American Law: Rethinking Religion Clause Jurisprudence
Kathleen A. Brady

Pope Benedict XVI's Legal Thought: A Dialogue on the Foundation of Law
edited by Marta Cartabia and Andrea Simoncini

The Blessings of Liberty

HUMAN RIGHTS AND RELIGIOUS FREEDOM IN THE WESTERN LEGAL TRADITION

JOHN WITTE, JR.
Emory University

CAMBRIDGE
UNIVERSITY PRESS

University Printing House, Cambridge CB2 8BS, United Kingdom

One Liberty Plaza, 20th Floor, New York, NY 10006, USA

477 Williamstown Road, Port Melbourne, VIC 3207, Australia

314–321, 3rd Floor, Plot 3, Splendor Forum, Jasola District Centre, New Delhi – 110025, India

103 Penang Road, #05–06/07, Visioncrest Commercial, Singapore 238467

Cambridge University Press is part of the University of Cambridge.

It furthers the University's mission by disseminating knowledge in the pursuit of education, learning, and research at the highest international levels of excellence.

www.cambridge.org
Information on this title: www.cambridge.org/9781108429207
DOI: 10.1017/9781108652841

First published 2022

A catalogue record for this publication is available from the British Library.

Library of Congress Cataloging-in-Publication Data
NAMES: Witte, John, Jr., 1959– author.
TITLE: The blessings of liberty : human rights and religious freedom in the western legal tradition / John Witte, Jr.
DESCRIPTION: Cambridge, United Kingdom ; New York, NY : Cambridge University Press, 2021. | Series: Law and christianity | Includes index.
IDENTIFIERS: LCCN 2021015819 (print) | LCCN 2021015820 (ebook) | ISBN 9781108429207 (hardback) | ISBN 9781108652841 (ebook)
SUBJECTS: LCSH: Human rights. | Civil rights – Religious aspects – Christianity. | Magna Carta – Influence. | Christianity – Influence. | Christianity and law. | Freedom of religion – United States – History. | Freedom of religion – European Union countries. | European Court of Human Rights.
CLASSIFICATION: LCC K3240 .W58 2021 (print) | LCC K3240 (ebook) | DDC 341.4/832–dc23
LC record available at https://lccn.loc.gov/2021015819
LC ebook record available at https://lccn.loc.gov/2021015820

ISBN 978-1-108-42920-7 Hardback
ISBN 978-1-108-45326-4 Paperback

For Johan D. van der Vyver,
Friend, Brother, and Colleague

[N]o free government, or the blessings of liberty, can be preserved to any people but by a firm adherence to justice, moderation, temperance, frugality, and virtue and by frequent recurrence to fundamental principles.

Virginia Declaration of Rights, sec. XV (June 12, 1776)

We, the people of the United States, in order to form a more perfect Union, establish justice, insure domestic tranquility, provide for the common defense, promote the general welfare, and secure the blessings of liberty to ourselves and our posterity, do ordain and establish this Constitution for the United States of America.

Preamble to the US Constitution (1789)

Every Circumstance in our present Situation must lead us to reflect, with the deepest Gratitude, on . . . the inestimable Blessings of Liberty and Order, which we consider as being, under the Favor of Providence, the principal Source of all our present Advantages.

Address of Parliament to King George IV of England (1792)

Contents

Preface and Acknowledgments

For the past thirty plus years, I have been writing on the history, theory, and law of human rights and religious freedom. My main arguments have been (1) that religion has long been a critical foundation and dimension of human rights; (2) that religion and human rights still need each other for each to thrive; and (3) that robust promotion and protection of religious freedom is the best way to protect many other fundamental rights today, even though religious freedom and other fundamental rights sometimes clash and need judicious balancing. I have defended these propositions with various historical, legal, and theological arguments, and have learned much from deep conversations with Christian, Jewish, and Muslim scholars as well as self-professed secular and postreligious scholars who variously defend, deride, and demur on the value and validity of human rights and religious freedom.

This volume presses further on all three of these main arguments. It includes nine studies on human rights and religious freedom historically and today – ranging from the earliest urtexts on liberty in the Bible and classical sources to the latest machinations of the American and European high courts. The first chapters explore the foundational role of Christianity in the development of rights and liberties in the Western tradition, particularly in the Anglo-American common-law tradition. Other chapters show how the protection of religion and religious freedom proved critical to the development of domestic and international protection of human rights. Several chapters analyze closely and critically the efforts of the American and European high courts to protect religious freedom and other fundamental rights and liberties. The "Concluding Reflections" respond to criticisms of human rights and religious freedom offered by various scholars and defends these rights and freedoms, particularly against various Christian critics.

These chapters are drawn in part from various articles that have gone to press since the publication of several earlier volumes of mine in this field. Those earlier volumes included *The Reformation of Rights* (Cambridge University Press, 2007), *Christianity and Human Rights* (Cambridge University Press, 2010), *Religion and Human Rights* (Oxford University Press, 2012), *No Establishment of Religion*

(Oxford University Press, 2012), and *Religion and the American Constitutional Experiment*, 4th ed. (Oxford University Press 2016). I am grateful to the *Journal of Law and Religion*, the *Journal of Church and State*, the *Emory Law Journal*, the *Southern California Law Review*, and the *Texas Journal of International Law* for permission to publish updated excerpts from articles that first appeared in them.

I am deeply grateful to the McDonald Agape Foundation, particularly its great founder, the late Ambassador Alonzo McDonald, and his successor and son, Peter McDonald, for their continued generous support of my work on this and other volumes and projects. My warm thanks to my colleague Dr. Justin Latterell, who provided and coordinated research support for this volume and coauthored an article with me, which is excerpted in part of Chapter 1. I am most grateful as well to my friend Professor Andrea Pin of the University of Padua, who first inspired me to look carefully at the new religious freedom jurisprudence of the pan-European courts, and who coauthored two law review articles with me that are revised and reworked here. I am also grateful for the excellent research tips and guidance into several specialty literatures offered by my friends Silas Allard, Nathan Chapman, Norman Doe, Rafael Domingo, Daniel Dreisbach, Richard Garnett, Christy Green, Dick Helmholz, Mark Hill, Russell Hittinger, Patrick Judd, Douglas Laycock, David Little, Martin Marty, Alexander Rudofsky, Jan Stieverman, Christoph Strohm, Eric Wang, and Michael Welker.

For the past thirty-five years, I have been privileged to serve as director of the Center for the Study of Law and Religion at Emory University. For much of this time, the Center has been home to two stalwart professional staff members and friends, Amy Wheeler and Anita Mann, who have again generously supported the production of this volume. In recent years, the Center has also been privileged to engage the brilliant services of Dr. Gary S. Hauk as senior editor, whose editorial handiwork has greatly improved all these pages.

Several of my Center colleagues have been kind enough to engage me in ongoing conversations about human rights and religious freedom – particularly Professors Frank S. Alexander, Abdullahi Ahmed An-Na'im, Michael J. Broyde, Rafael Domingo, Timothy P. Jackson, Michael J. Perry, and Johan D. van der Vyver. I have benefited greatly from interactions with them and with the hundreds of scholars who have worked on our Center's international research projects on religion, human rights, and religious freedom over the years, and the thousands of students since 1985 who took my courses on the History of Church–State Relations in the West; First Amendment: Religious Freedom; Comparative Religious Freedom; and Advanced Religious Liberty.

Finally, I am grateful to John Berger, Beatrice Rehl, and Jackie Grant at Cambridge University Press for taking on this volume and applying their usual standards of excellence in their editing, production, and marketing. It is a special joy to appear in the Cambridge Studies in Law and Christianity book series.

I dedicate this volume to my distinguished friend, brother, and colleague, Professor Johan D. van der Vyver. Johan serves as the I. T. Cohen Professor of International Law and Human Rights at Emory Law School, Senior Fellow in our Law and Religion Center, and former Senior Fellow for Human Rights at the Carter Center of Emory University. Johan's lifelong devotion to human rights and religious freedom have been an inspiration to me since my early college days, when he kindly sent me a copy of his sterling book, *Seven Lectures on Human Rights* (Juta, 1976). We have worked side by side from the start of our Center's work on democracy, human rights, and religious freedom. Johan contributed a brilliant lecture and chapter to our first conference and volume on *Christianity and Democracy in Global Context* (Westview, 1993). We ran several more conferences together and coedited two massive volumes on *Religious Human Rights in Global Perspective* (Martinus Nijhoff, 1996), and several later journal symposia and anthologies on religious freedom, church–state relations, proselytism, children's rights, and more.

Johan began teaching law in 1958 at his alma mater, the University of Potchefstroom, South Africa, where he soon became a chaired professor and then dean of the law faculty. He taught and wrote at length in the fields of property law, family law, the law of persons, church–state relations, legal science, and legal philosophy. He produced several leading texts, in multiple editions, some of which are still in print.

In the 1970s, he added human rights to his scholarly repertoire. He studied human rights as a visiting scholar and lecturer at Columbia, Michigan, Harvard, and the Institute for Advanced Legal Studies in London, yielding his LL.D. dissertation on "The Juridical Meaning of the Doctrine of Human Rights." This new accent in his work soon landed Johan in trouble with both the conservative churches of his community and the apartheid state of South Africa. Many local Protestant churches thought human rights to be a dangerous product of Enlightenment liberalism and individualism, which Bible-believing Christians should firmly reject. Johan argued powerfully and patiently to the contrary, that human rights are God's gifts to human nature, which should be enjoyed and exercised by every human being, regardless of color, class, confession, or sexual orientation. The apartheid state, in turn, reserved human rights to the white elite, leaving vast portions of South African society trapped in dire poverty, illiteracy, and oppression with little legal recourse or protection. Johan risked much in speaking out against these racist and apartheid policies using the spotlight of human rights to expose the grave injustices that these state policies inflicted. He was soon rejoined, rebuked, censored, demoted, and then dismissed from his deanship at Potchefstroom, and eventually forced to leave the university and take up a position at the University of Witwatersrand, in Johannesburg.

While now a pariah in some conservative religious and political communities, Johan became a powerful antiapartheid voice in South Africa and a champion of human rights and democratic reform, which he defended on Christian philosophical and jurisprudential terms. He wrote several pathbreaking books and articles in this field and led workshops and lectures around South Africa and well beyond. In 1976, he flew to New York City and walked in without appointment to the Ford Foundation offices, asking them to support the burgeoning human rights movement in South Africa. They supported this effort generously, and in 1979 Johan organized the first great international human rights conference in South African history, hosting it in the glorious city of Cape Town. There he helped introduce the world to a still regional hero at the time, Archbishop Desmond Tutu. Throughout this time, he argued constitutional cases in the South African courts on behalf of racial and religious minorities. And he remained one of the legal architects, along with his many students and a growing body of coworkers, of the antiapartheid efforts and then the constitutional reform movements of South Africa in the later 1980s and early 1990s.

Johan's work attracted the attention of the leading human rights scholar at Emory Law School at the time, Thomas Buergenthal, as well as President Jimmy Carter, who had established the Carter Center of Emory University. In the early 1990s, they invited him to make regular visits to Emory, where, in 1995, he became senior fellow at the Carter Center and was appointed to the law school in the I. T. Cohen Professorship, which he still holds. My colleagues and I in the field of law and religion saw the power of his mind, heart, and work, too, and we drew him into our Center's projects.

After moving permanently to Emory, Johan added yet another thick layer to his scholarly work. While retaining his earlier legal specialties, he now took on the new subjects of public international law, international humanitarian law, the laws of military conflict, and international criminal law. He followed his trademark method of learning by doing, as he took each of these topics and wrote voluminously on each of them while creating new courses, seminars, and public lectures. He is now bringing this new phase of scholarship into a capstone multivolume work on the International Criminal Court.

Johan remains a quiet giant in the legal academy today with high standing around the globe for his brilliant contributions to many fields of legal study, captured in a score of books in multiple editions and languages and 300 plus articles. He has stood at distinguished lecterns on every continent, save Antarctica, and in the last few years alone has traveled to India, China, Morocco, Belgium, Bulgaria, Singapore, Chile, and various cities in North America and South Africa to give lectures and lead conferences. He still teaches full time at Emory, while flying back and forth to South Africa between semesters.

On some of these recent trips back to his native land, Johan has finally gotten his just due from his native South Africa as well. He has now been decorated with all manner of academic awards, tributes, and citations, including an appointment as Professor of Law Extraordinaire at the University of Pretoria. In sublime acts of sweet justice, the University of Zululand gave him an honorary doctorate for his courageous advocacy for black South Africans, and eventually his own alma mater, the University of Potchefstroom, gave him an honorary doctorate for his courageous prophecy to white South Africans.

I dedicate this volume to Johan van der Vyver with all admiration, appreciation, and affection. May his remarkable life, work, and example long continue to the edification of us all.

Introduction

A half century ago, the world welcomed some of the most remarkable human rights documents it had ever seen. The US Congress passed the Civil Rights Act of 1964 and the Voting Rights Act of 1965. These were America's strongest statutory rebukes to its long and tragic history of racism, chauvinism, nativism, and religious and cultural bigotry. Born of the civil rights movement and inspired especially by Black churches, these two acts declared anathema on all manner of discrimination in the voting booth, public accommodations, schools, and the workplace. They called American courts and citizens to give full and faithful protection to the rights of everyone regardless of race, color, religion, sex, or national origin. And they called America back not only to the high promise of the Thirteenth to Fifteenth Amendments, ratified in the aftermath of the Civil War, but also to the founding ideals set out in the nation's ur text, the 1776 Declaration of Independence: "that all men [now persons] are created equal, that they are endowed by their Creator with certain unalienable Rights, that among these are Life, Liberty and the pursuit of Happiness."[1] The 1789 US Constitution and several state constitutions repeated and elaborated these "unalienable rights," repeatedly calling them "the blessings of liberty."[2]

1 US Declaration of Independence (1776), para. 2.

2 US Const. (1789), Preamble. Six original state constitutions also spoke of "the blessings of liberty": Virginia (1776), art. XV; North Carolina (1776), sec. XXI (under "A Declaration of Rights"); Pennsylvania (1776), art. XIV; Vermont (1786), art. XX; Alabama (1861), Preamble; Illinois (1870), Preamble and art. II. Twelve current constitutions repeat the phrase: North Carolina Const., art. I, § 35; New Hampshire Const., pt. first, art. 38; West Virginia Const., art. III, § 20; Vermont Const., ch. I, art. 18; Colorado Const., Preamble; Alabama Const., Preamble; Virginia Const., art. I, § 15; Ohio Const., art. VIII, § 18 and Ohio Const., Preamble; Illinois Const., art. I, § 23; Maine Const., Preamble; New Mexico Const., Preamble; South Dakota Const., Preamble. It also appears in six foreign constitutions influenced by the United States: Argentina, Bhutan, Colombia, Ghana, Japan, and Panama. "Blessings of liberty" also appears in Federalist Papers Nos. 45 (Madison) and 84 (Hamilton), and was a commonplace in presidential proclamations (Law Day, National Day of Prayer, Independence Day, Flag Day, and Thanksgiving Day), and in numerous presidential speeches across the political spectrum. See, for example, John Adams, Inaugural Address, Mar. 4, 1797; James Madison, Seventh Annual Message, Dec. 5, 1815; John Quincy Adams, Inaugural Address, Mar. 4, 1825; Andrew Jackson, Second Annual Message, Dec. 6, 1830; Andrew Jackson, Farewell Address, Mar. 4, 1837; James K. Polk, Inaugural

A half century ago, the Second Vatican Council, speaking to and for a half billion Catholics at the time, opened up a new chapter in the church's mission and ministry with a series of sweeping new papal and conciliar declarations – *Pacem in Terris*, *Dignitatis Humanae*, *Gaudium et Spes*, and *Lumen Gentium*.[3] The Council firmly rejected the church's antidemocratic and antirights posture of the 1864 *Syllabus of Errors*,[4] and instead returned to Pope Leo XIII's clarion call in 1880 for *Libertas*[5] and for a new "social teachings" movement to transform the church.[6] The church now taught that every human being is created by God with "dignity, intelligence and free will . . . and has rights flowing directly and simultaneously from their very nature."[7] Such rights include the right to life and adequate standards of living, to moral and cultural values, to religious activities, to assembly and association, to marriage and family life, and to various social, political, and economic benefits and opportunities. The church emphasized the religious rights of conscience, worship, assembly, and education, calling them the "first rights" of any civic order.[8] It also stressed the need to balance individual and associational rights, particularly those involving the church, family, and school, which stood as important bulwarks between the individual and the state. The church urged the abolition of discrimination on grounds of

Address, Mar. 4, 1845; Andrew Johnson, Third Annual Message, Dec. 3, 1867 and Andrew Johnson, Fourth Annual Message, Dec. 9, 1868; Franklin D. Roosevelt, Inaugural Address, Jan. 20, 1937; John F. Kennedy, Annual Message to the Congress on the State of the Union, Jan. 30, 1961; Lyndon B. Johnson, Annual Message to the Congress on the State of the Union, Jan. 14, 1969; George H. W. Bush, Address Before a Joint Session of the Congress on the State of the Union, Jan. 29, 1991; William J. Clinton, Inaugural address, Jan. 20, 1997.

3 Collected in W. Abbott and J. Gallagher, eds., *The Documents of Vatican II* (New York: Guild Press, 1967).

4 In Philip Schaff, ed., *Creeds of Christendom with a History and Critical Notes*, 3rd enlarged ed. (New York: Harper, 1881), 218–33 (paras. 20, 24–35, 41–44, 53–54, 75–80). See also *Mirari Vos* (On Liberalism and Religious Indifferentism) (1832), in www.papalencyclicals.net/greg16/g16mirar.htm (paras. 14–23), with discussion in John Witte, Jr., "That Serpentine Wall of Separation," *Michigan Law Review* 101 (2003), 1869–905.

5 See Pope Leo XIII, *Libertas: On the Nature of Human Liberty*, repr. ed. (West Monroe, LA: St. Athanasius Press, 2016), 3–4: "Liberty, the highest of natural endowments, being the portion only of intellectual or rational natures, confers on man this dignity – that he is 'in the hand of his counsel' and has power over his actions. But the manner in which such dignity is exercised is of the greatest moment, inasmuch as on the use that is made of liberty the highest good and the greatest evil alike depend. Man, indeed, is free to obey his reason, to seek moral good, and to strive unswervingly after his last end. Yet he is free also to turn aside to all other things; and, in pursuing the empty semblance of good, to disturb rightful order and to fall headlong into the destruction which he has voluntarily chosen." See, further, Russell Hittinger, "Pope Leo XIII (1810–1903)," in John Witte, Jr. and Frank S. Alexander, eds., *The Teachings of Modern Roman Catholicism on Law, Politics, and Human Nature* (New York: Columbia University Press, 2007), 39–105. See further the prototypes in Mary Elsbernd, "Papal Statements on Rights: A Historical Contextual Study of Encyclical Teaching from Pius VI–Pius XI (1791–1939)" (PhD Dissertation, Catholic University of Louvain, 1985).

6 See, e.g., Gerard V. Bradley and E. Christian Brugger, eds., *Catholic Social Teaching* (Cambridge: Cambridge University Press, 2019).

7 "Pacem in Terris," para. 9 (1963), reprinted in Joseph Germillion, ed., *The Gospel of Peace and Justice: Catholic Social Teaching Since Pope John* (Maryknoll, NY: Orbis, 1976), 203.

8 Ibid., 203–18.

sex, race, color, social distinction, language, and religion. And it called on clergy and laity alike to be ambassadors and advocates for the rights and liberties of all persons, especially the "least" of God's children, as the Bible called them – the poor, needy, sick, and handicapped; widows, orphans, sojourners, and refugees; the incarcerated and incapacitated; and children, born and unborn.[9] The robust advocacy of Vatican II for the rights and liberties of all helped to drive a new "third wave of democracy" around the world thereafter.[10]

Finally, a half century ago, the United Nations, embracing almost all 186 nation-states around the world at the time, passed the International Covenant on Civil and Political Rights (1966) and the International Covenant on Economic, Social, and Cultural Rights (1966).[11] Only two decades before passage of these twin covenants, the world had stared in horror into Hitler's death camps and Stalin's gulags, where all sense of humanity and dignity had been viciously sacrificed. It had witnessed the slaughter of sixty million people around the world in six years of unprecedented brutality during World War II. In response, the world had seized anew on the ancient concept of human dignity, claiming this as the ur-principle of a new world order.[12] The Universal Declaration of Human Rights (1948) opened its preamble with classic words: "recognition of the inherent dignity and of the equal and inalienable rights of all members of the human family is the foundation of freedom, justice, and peace in the world."[13] The two 1966 international covenants sought to translate the general principles of the Universal Declaration into more specific precepts. The International Covenant on Economic, Social, and Cultural Rights posited as essential to human dignity the rights to self-determination, subsistence; work, welfare, security, education, and cultural participation. The International Covenant on Civil and Political Rights set out a long catalogue of rights to life and to security of person and property; freedom from slavery and cruelty; basic civil and criminal procedural protections; rights to travel and pilgrimage; freedoms of religion, expression, and assembly; rights to marriage and family life; and freedom from discrimination on grounds of race, color, sex, language, and national origin. These documents are binding on the nations that have ratified them.

9 Ibid.

10 Samuel P. Huntington, *The Third Wave of Democracy: Democratization in the Late Twentieth Century* (Norman: University of Oklahoma Press, 1991); Larry J. Diamond, *Consolidating the Third Wave Democracies* (Baltimore, MD: Johns Hopkins University Press, 1997); John Witte, Jr., ed., *Christianity and Democracy in Global Context*, repr. ed. (London: Routledge, 2020).

11 See Ian Brownlie and Guy S. Goodwin-Gill, eds., *Basic Documents on Human Rights*, 6th ed. (Oxford: Oxford University Press, 2010), 370–79; 388–404. See also International Covenant on Civil and Political Rights, www.ohchr.org/en/professionalinterest/pages/ccpr.aspx; and International Covenant on Economic, Social, and Cultural Rights, www.ohchr.org/EN/ProfessionalInterest/Pages/CESCR.aspx.

12 The term "ur-principle" is from Louis Henkin et al., *Human Rights* (New York: Foundation Press, 1999), 80.

13 In Brownlie and Goodwin-Gill, eds., *Basic Documents* 39–44; and www.ohchr.org/EN/UDHR/Pages/Language.aspx?LangID=eng.

Several regional instruments also proved critical to this rights development, including the European Convention on Human Rights (1950)[14] and the [Inter-]American Convention on Human Rights (1969).

These landmark human rights documents of the mid-twentieth century echoed and elaborated two millennia of rights developments in the Western legal tradition[15] – among other traditions around the world.[16] Western jurists have long talked about rights and liberties and applied them in their legal systems. Classical Roman jurists called them *iura* and *libertates*.[17] Anglo-Saxon laws first translated these Roman law terms into the early English language of *ryhtes* and *rita(e)*, *freoles* and *freo-dom*.[18] Early modern jurists translated medieval canon law and civil law discussions of *iura humana* into the now familiar vernacular terms of human rights, *droits de l'homme*, *Menschenrechte*, *derechos humanos*, *diritti umani*, and others.[19]

All these terms had wide and shifting definitions, interpretations, and applications over time and across cultures.[20] At its core, however, this Western language of rights and liberties enabled jurists to map in ever greater detail the proper interactions between private parties in society and between private parties and the reigning authorities, whether political, religious, feudal, or economic. Rights defined the claims that one legal subject could legitimately make against another to protect their person, property, business, reputation, and interest, or to compel another to live up to their contracts, promises, and other obligations. Rights and liberties also defined limits to the actions, duties, or charges that authorities could legitimately impose upon their individual and corporate subjects. And rights and liberties language set out the procedures and principles that were to be followed in all of these legal interactions, sometimes casting them in terms of justice, equity, liberty, equality, due process, and other ideals.[21]

14 See Chapter 8.

15 While the terms "West" and "Western" now have strong ideological connotations in some circles, I am using the phrase "Western legal tradition" as a conventional historical description of the law that emerged out of ancient Jewish, Greek, and Roman sources and spread throughout Latin Christendom and its extension overseas to the Americas. See Harold J. Berman, *Law and Revolution: The Formation of the Western Legal Tradition* (Cambridge, MA: Harvard University Press, 1983).

16 For contributions of other world religions and philosophical traditions, see John Witte, Jr. and M. Christian Green, eds., *Religion and Human Rights: An Introduction* (Oxford: Oxford University Press, 2012).

17 See Chapter 1, p. 23–25.

18 See Chapter 1, p. 26 and Chapter 2, p. 45–46.

19 See Chapters 3–5.

20 For a quick summary of various definitions of rights and liberties historically and today, see, e.g., M. N. S. Sellers, *The Sacred Fire of Liberty: Republicanism, Liberalism, and the Law* (New York: NYU Press, 1998). The taxonomy and classification of rights and liberties are highly contested questions these days. Some interesting recent efforts include Winston P. Nagan, John A. C. Cartner, and Robert J. Munro, *Human Rights and Dynamic Humanism* (Leiden: Brill, 2017); James Griffin, *On Human Rights* (Oxford: Oxford University Press, 2008); Roger Crisp, ed., *Griffin on Human Rights* (Oxford: Oxford University Press, 2014).

21 See, further, "Concluding Reflections," pp. 290–300.

While Western jurists sometimes treated vaunted documents like Magna Carta (1215)[22] or the US Bill of Rights (1791)[23] with reverence, they usually thought of rights in simpler instrumental and utilitarian terms. After all, as Justice Oliver Wendell Holmes, Jr. once quipped, a right is "only the hypostasis of a prophecy," a mere prediction of what might happen to "those who do things said to contravene it."[24] That prediction depends very much on the ability of a legal subject to press a rights claim, the willingness of the authorities to vindicate those rights, and the capacity of the society to develop a human rights culture. Human rights "declarations are not deeds," John T. Noonan Jr. reminds us; "a form of words by itself secures nothing." Human rights language "pregnant with meaning in one cultural context may be entirely barren in another."[25] That was true throughout Western history and can be seen today in many Western lands marked by new forms of nativism, populism, tribalism, and authoritarianism.

The human rights instruments of the mid-twentieth century did add measurably to this long tradition of rights. The 1964 Civil Rights Act echoed the norms of due process and equal protection found in the Fifth and Fourteenth Amendments and their common law antecedents going back to Magna Carta and other medieval and Anglo-Saxon charters. But the act also added more specific and expansive protections of rights and helped trigger a massive wave of rights litigation in the American federal courts that is still going on today. The Second Vatican Council's decrees confirmed the rich teachings about rights by the medieval canonists and early modern Spanish neoscholastics and their retrieval by Pope Leo XIII's social teachings movement. These conciliar documents, however, also offered a more universal defense of the rights and freedoms of all humanity, not just Christians or Catholics, and they helped to render the pope and clergy effective agents and allies in the global struggle for human rights. The 1948 Universal Declaration and the 1966 UN covenants drew on and distilled many earlier national and international rights statements, going back as early as the Religious Peace of Westphalia (1648).[26] Yet these new human rights instruments now called further for every state party worldwide to enforce these rights at the risk of international shame and rebuke, if not censure and reprisal. These international documents also grounded human rights and liberties on a more universal theory of human dignity, equality, and fraternity, in place of earlier Christian rights theories based on the Golden Rule, the Decalogue, biblical love commands, or Christian anthropologies of the image of God or the imitation of Christ. Later international human rights instruments added further specificity to rights concerning religion, race, laborers, migrants, refugees, prisoners

22 See Chapter 2.

23 See Chapter 5.

24 Oliver Wendell Holmes, Jr., "Natural Law," *Harvard Law Review* 32 (1918), 42.

25 John T. Noonan, Jr., "The Tensions and the Ideals," in Johan D. van der Vyver and John Witte, Jr., eds., *Religious Human Rights in Global Perspective: Legal Perspectives* (The Hague: Martinus Nijhoff, 1996), 594.

26 See Chapter 4, p. 86.

of war, indigenous peoples, women, and children, and new protections against genocide and torture. Even so, the vast majority of human rights of today are the natural, constitutional, conciliar, customary, and treaty rights of earlier centuries now writ larger and rooted more widely.

THE CORNERSTONE – RELIGIOUS FREEDOM

The right to religious freedom has long been a foundational part of this gradual development of human rights in the Western tradition, and today it is regarded as a cornerstone in the edifice of human rights. In its most basic sense today, the right to religious freedom is the freedom of individuals and groups to make their own determinations about religious beliefs and to act upon those beliefs peaceably without incurring civil or criminal liabilities. More fully conceived, freedom of religion embraces a number of fundamental principles of individual religious liberty – freedom of conscience, exercise, speech, association, worship, diet, dress, and evangelism; freedom from religious discrimination, coercion, and unequal treatment; freedom of religious and moral education; and freedom of religious travel, pilgrimage, and association with coreligionists abroad. It also involves a number of fundamental principles of corporate religious liberty – freedom of religious groups to organize their own polity and leadership; to hold and use corporate property; to define their own creed, cult, confessional community, and code of conduct; to establish institutions of worship, education, charity, and outreach; and to set standards of admission, participation, and discipline for their members and leaders.[27] These are now standard principles of religious freedom in modern instruments of international and regional human rights, and in many national constitutions, not least the First Amendment to the US Constitution.[28]

The Western legal tradition came to this robust understanding of religious freedom only after many centuries of hard and cruel experience to the contrary, and only as the tradition gradually developed many other human rights and liberties to make these religious rights and freedoms ever more real. The phrase "freedom of religion" (*libertas religionis*) first emerged at the turn of the third century in Tertullian's plea against Roman persecution. The classic Roman law phrase "right to freedom" (*ius libertatis*) first emerged prominently in the twelfth century in reference to religious freedom, including Pope Gregory VII's clarion call for "freedom of the church" (*libertas ecclesiae*). This language was part of the church's attempt to establish individual and corporate religious freedom against overreaching political and feudal authorities. It took until the seventeenth century, however, for

27 See, e.g., W. Cole Durham, Jr. and Brett G. Scharffs, *Law and Religion: National, International, and Comparative Perspectives* (New York: Wolters Kluwer, 2019); Tad Stahnke and J. Paul Martin, *Religion and Human Rights: Basic Documents* (New York: Columbia University Center for the Study of Human Rights, 1998). See further Chapter 1, p. 38–44.

28 See Chapters 5–7.

"the right to religious freedom" (*ius libertatis religionis*) to become a common phrase in religious and legal circles, and for the abridgment of this right to trigger a cause of action in court, rather than a reason to flee or revolt.[29] While guarantees of religious freedom became more common in treaties and constitutions after the seventeenth century, they were still often honored in the breach by leaders of religious establishments and secular states alike. And while the nineteenth and twentieth centuries brought powerful new guarantees of religious freedom in both national and international human rights instruments and court cases, vicious religious persecution remains a commonplace of modern life around the globe, including in many Western lands.[30] Even the US Supreme Court and the pan-European courts sitting in Strasbourg and Luxembourg have decidedly mixed records on individual and corporate religious freedom in recent decades.[31]

Historically and today, however, the protection of religion and religious freedom has proved critical for the protection of many other individual and associational rights. Religion is a dynamic and diverse, but ultimately ineradicable, condition and form of human community. Religions help to define the meanings and measures of shame and regret, restraint and respect, responsibility and restitution that a human rights regime presupposes. Religions help to lay out the fundamentals of human dignity and human community, and the essentials of human nature and human needs upon which rights are built. Moreover, religious institutions often stand alongside the state and other institutions in helping to implement and protect the rights of a community – especially in transitional societies, or at times when a once-stable state becomes weak, distracted, divided, or cash-strapped. Religions can create the conditions (sometimes the prototypes) for the realization of first-generation civil and political rights of speech, press, assembly, and more. They can provide a critical (sometimes the principal) means to meet second-generation rights of education, health care, child care, labor organizations, employment, and artistic opportunities. And they can offer some of the deepest insights into norms of creation, stewardship, and servanthood that lie at the heart of third-generation rights.

Many social scientists and human rights scholars today have thus come to see that providing strong protections of rights and liberties for religious individuals and religious institutions enhances, rather than diminishes, human rights for all, even if there are inevitable conflicts at the margins. Already in 1895, German jurist Georg Jellinek called religious freedom "the mother of many other rights."[32] Many other scholars now repeat the American founders' declaration that religious freedom is "the first freedom," from which other rights and freedoms evolve. Several recent comprehensive studies of the state of religious freedom in the world today have

29 See Chapter 1, p. 33–36 and Chapter 3, p. 87–104.

30 See Chapter 1, p. 36–44 and Chapters 8–9.

31 See Chapters 5, 8, and 9.

32 Georg Jellinek, *Die Erklärung der Menschen- und Bürgerrechte: ein Beitrag zur modernen Verfassungsgeschichte* (Liepzig: Duncker and Humblot, 1895), 42.

shown that proper protection of religious freedom in a country is strongly associated with other freedoms, including civil and political liberty, press freedom, and economic freedom, as well as with multiple measures of well-being. … [W]herever religious freedom is high, there tend to be fewer incidents of armed conflict, better health outcomes, higher levels of earned income, prolonged democracy, and better educational opportunities "for Women."[33] Religious freedom, writes leading Catholic scholar Richard Garnett, "is a crucial aspect of the common good, one in which – like clean air and safe roads – everyone has a stake."[34]

THE STORY AND ARGUMENT TOLD HERE

This volume offers nine interlinked studies of these intertwined developments and guarantees of human rights and religious freedom. The chapters range from analysis of rights and liberties in the earliest ur texts of the Western tradition to the latest machinations of the high courts of Europe and the United States. Chapter 1 retrieves and reconstructs the gradual emergence of rights and liberties in the teachings of the Bible, classical Roman law, medieval canon law and civil law, the Protestant Reformation, the Anglo-American common law tradition, and modern national constitutions and international human rights documents. It focuses especially on the contributions of Christian ideas and institutions to rights and liberties throughout much of this historical development, as well as the contributions of Enlightenment liberal and republican thought in more recent times.

Chapter 2 zeroes in more closely to offer a lengthy study of the development of rights and liberties in the Anglo-American legal tradition from Magna Carta, in 1215, to seventeenth-century England and its colonies leading up to the American Revolution. Since the fourteenth century, Parliament and the English courts treated Magna Carta as a source of due-process rights as well as sundry other religious and civil freedoms. In the sixteenth and seventeenth centuries, English Puritans and American colonists gradually developed expansive new Magna Cartas in the forms of written bills and bodies of rights that were eventually echoed in American state and federal constitutions.

Chapter 3 retrieves the long-deprecated teachings of the Protestant Reformation regarding natural law and natural rights, and reconstructs the reformers' role in the development of human rights, religious freedom, and democratic revolution in early modern Protestant lands. Lutherans, Anabaptists, and Calvinists alike made notable contributions to the expansion of public, private, penal, and procedural rights and liberties, which they eventually enumerated in written declarations, charters, and

33 Brian J. Grim, "Restrictions on Religion in the World: Measures and Implications," in Allen D. Hertzke, ed., *The Future of Religious Freedom: Global Challenges* (Oxford: Oxford University Press, 2013), 101. See further Chapter 5, p. 167–69, 295–96.

34 Richard W. Garnett, "Religious Freedom and the Churches: Contemporary Challenges in the United States Today," *Studies in Christian Ethics* 33 (2020), 200.

constitutions. The pervasive and persistent breach of these fundamental rights and liberties by a political tyrant, some Protestants further insisted, triggered the fundamental rights of resistance, revolt, and, if necessary, wholesale democratic revolution, as took place in the Netherlands, England, Scotland, France, and America.

Chapter 4 offers a close study of the 1780 Massachusetts Constitution and its amendments to illustrate the tension between inherited European political traditions of establishing one form of Christianity by law, and the emerging American experiment of granting religious freedom for all faiths. The chapter further shows that in early America, the disestablishment of religion did not necessarily mean the secularization of society or the erection of a high and impregnable wall of separation between church and state, religion and politics. Even after outlawing religious tithes and oaths and ending bald discrimination against religious minorities, the Massachusetts Constitution retained strong established forms of virtue, morality, religious education, and public ceremony, all of which the state's founders considered essential to the protection of constitutional rights and liberties for all.

Chapter 5 places this Massachusetts story within the fuller context of the American founding era of 1760 to 1820. In this period, the American founders developed six essential principles of religious freedom – liberty of conscience, free exercise of religion, religious pluralism, religious equality, separation of church and state, and no establishment of religion. They wove these principles into the new state constitutions as well as into the First Amendment to the US Constitution. The founders treated religious freedom as the "first freedom," which helped ground correlative constitutional freedoms of speech, press, and assembly as well as other enumerated rights to property and household, civil and criminal procedural rights, due process of law, and more. They also set forth a constitutional and cultural ideal, albeit often breached, that all persons of any faith and of no faith must enjoy religious freedom and other constitutional rights as fully as possible, with courts and legislatures alike tasked to resolve conflicts between rights.

Chapters 6 and 7 offer two studies of this American experiment of religious freedom in action, illustrating some of the trends in the US Supreme Court's 240 plus cases on religious freedom, most of them since 1940. Chapter 6 studies the complex and shifting run of seventy-five US Supreme Court cases dealing with the role of religion in public schools, the role of government in religious schools, and the rights of parents and children to religion, speech, press, assembly, and tax benefits in education. Questions about religion and education have provided the most active laboratory for Supreme Court religious freedom jurisprudence and have produced many of the Court's strongest opinions on separation of church and state, religious neutrality, free exercise of religion, and equal access and treatment of religion and nonreligion. This topic will remain a perennial frontier of litigation about religious freedom and human rights.

Chapter 7 takes up the nitty-gritty issue of tax exemption of religious property, an ancient privilege in the Western tradition going to biblical and Roman times, but now under growing attack in America. The current fight over the constitutionality of religious property-tax exemptions illustrates the tension between federal and state laws, free exercise and no establishment of religion, and treatment of traditional and new religions. It also tests concretely the costs and benefits to the individual and society of granting religious exemptions from general laws, and tests the ancient teaching of the common law and equity law that religious property exemptions relieve the state of burdens it would otherwise have to discharge at taxpayers' expense.

The final two chapters study the parallel religious freedom and broader human rights jurisprudence of the two pan-European courts: the European Court of Human Rights, in Strasbourg, which has poured out more than 170 cases on religious freedom in the past three decades, and the Court of Justice of the European Union, in Luxembourg, which is rapidly emerging as the new boss of religious freedom. The religious landscape of Europe has changed dramatically in the past two generations. Traditional Christian establishments have been challenged by the growth of religious pluralism and strong new movements of *laïcité* and secularism. Massive new migrations have created tense local intermixtures of old and new religions. Old constitutions, concordats, and customs that privileged local forms and forums of Christian identity and morality have come under increasing attack. These changes have radically reshaped the law of religious freedom not only in individual European states but also as determined by these two pan-European Courts. Interpreting the norms of religious freedom laid out in the European Convention of Human Rights (1950) and the Charter on Fundamental Rights of the European Union (2010), these two courts have been notably churlish of late in their treatment of Muslim, Jewish, and conservative Christian claimants, while often privileging self-professed atheists and secularists. The two courts have repeatedly held against Eastern European Orthodox state policies on religion, even while granting wide margins of appreciation to Western European states that blatantly target religious minorities in the name of secularization and *laïcité*. In particular, the Luxembourg Court has begun to second-guess norms of religious autonomy and longstanding constitutional forms of church–state relations, even though EU laws formally protect them. While many other cases in these two courts do offer ample protection, their most recent cases pose troubling signs for religious freedom and other fundamental human rights.

Throughout these chapters, I have addressed some of the sharp criticisms of religion, human rights, and religious freedom that are now widely in vogue in the Western academy and media. Chapters 1 and 3 take up the rights skepticism of several modern Christian theologians. Chapters 5 through 7 analyze several recent attacks on the historical pedigree and current protections of religious freedom. Chapters 8 and 9 address the escalating attacks on the rights of religious and cultural minorities and the judicial erosion of religious autonomy claims.

The final chapter titled "Concluding Reflections" collects further criticisms of rights and freedoms, especially those offered by leading Christian scholars today, and then outlines my own defense of human rights and religious freedom. My choice of book title, *The Blessings of Liberty*, underscores my starting belief, widely shared, that freedom is an inherent human quality and claim. Indeed, in my view freedom is a unique gift of God to all human creatures.[35] But I support the positive law of rights and liberties today more out of utility than ideology. In my view, rights laws over time and across cultures have proved to be useful instruments to promote and protect the good life and the good society; to impose and enforce limits on the power of states, churches, and other authorities; and to enable and equip persons to carry out their vocations and duties to God, neighbor, and self. I do not consider human rights to be a "fundamental belief system." To the contrary, I argue that rights and liberties depend upon fundamental beliefs for grounding, limitation, and direction. I also do not consider rights talk to be a substitute for many other richer forms of moral and communal expression and discourse.[36] I regard rights talk as a useful grammar and vocabulary of human life and interaction, not a language in and of itself. It is a legal means to the fuller ends of justice, peace, order, and happiness, not an end in itself.

I come to this discussion about human rights and religious freedom as a Christian jurist and legal historian, not a Christian theologian or philosopher. Folks in my legal discipline operate closer to the ground than many high-flying human rights theorists at work today. We lawyers deal with the routine corners and concerns of public and private life – of authority and liberty, of relationships and their rupture, of promises and their breach, of harms and their remedies, of crimes and their punishment. The chapters on religious freedom cases help illustrate that kind of nitty-gritty, concrete complexity of the law on the books and law in action. We legal historians, in turn, dig out and document how, over many centuries, our legal forebearers gradually developed, by fits and starts, an ever wider set of rights categories, concepts, terms, distinctions, and limitations to map and deal with the complex interactions between and among persons, associations, and authorities. This growing collection of legal rights and liberties instruments was gradually pushed under the legal canopy of what are now regularly called human rights and liberties.[37] Like many legal institutions, legal rights and liberties have emerged out of an evolving spectrum of legal normativity: acts become behaviors; behaviors become habits; habits yield customs; customs produce rules; rules beget statutes; statutes

35 See, e.g., Michael Welker, ed., *Quests for Freedom: Biblical, Historical, Contemporary*, 2nd ed. (Eugene, OR: Cascade Books, 2019).

36 See, e.g., Mary Ann Glendon, *Rights Talk: The Impoverishment of Political Discourse*, repr. ed. (New York: Free Press, 2014); Nigel Biggar, *What's Wrong with Rights* (Oxford: Oxford University Press, 2020).

37 Early and diverse examples of this kind of developmental accounts include Roscoe Pound, *The Development of Constitutional Guarantees of Liberty* (New Haven, CT: Yale University Press, 1957); Glanville Williams, "The Concept of Legal Liberty," *Columbia Law Review* 56 (1956), 1129–50.

require procedures; procedures guide cases; statutes, procedures, and cases get systematized into codes; and all these forms of legality are eventually confirmed in national constitutions, if not regional conventions and international covenants.

This bottom-up approach to our topic sometimes produces blurrier lines of reasoning; more slippage between principles, precepts, and practices; provisional and sometimes messier recommendations and prescriptions for church, state, and society.[38] But I hope it also makes for an account and defense of human rights and religious freedom that is more realistic, rigorous, and resilient over time and perhaps even across cultures. This developmental and eclectic historical approach to modern rights talk, however, is quite different from that offered by many philosophers and theologians. Modern critics of human rights often have one or two key definitions or forms of rights in mind – sometimes with labels such "natural," "universal," "human," "fundamental," or "unalienable" rights – and then engage in critical or constructive reflection on rights based on that specific vision or definition. From such lofty theoretical heights, I submit, much of the reality of rights gets blurry, even sometimes lost from view.

Finally, I come to this project as a North American Protestant, interested in some of the Protestant and broader Christian foundations of the Western legal tradition of human rights and religious freedom. While noting the contributions of the Latin Church Fathers, medieval Catholics, and the Second Vatican Council, I focus in these chapters more on Protestant contributions to the development of modern human rights and religious freedom in the history of the West.[39] While gesturing to the Greek Fathers and to the rich potential of Eastern Orthodox theology for the development of human rights, I have not given this third branch of Christianity its due – let alone all the other religious and philosophical traditions that have contributed to our understanding of rights.[40] While touching on various Western legal traditions on both sides of the Atlantic, I accent Anglo-American common law and American constitutional law, without corresponding attention to the rich civil law traditions of Europe and Latin America, or the constitutional developments of individual states in Europe and the global British Commonwealth.[41]

38 See a comparable perspective in Seth D. Kaplan, *Human Rights in Thick and Thin Societies: Universality without Uniformity* (Cambridge: Cambridge University Press, 2018).

39 For more Catholic contributions, see John Witte, Jr. and Frank S. Alexander, eds., *Christianity and Human Rights: An Introduction* (Cambridge: Cambridge University Press, 2012); and Witte and Alexander, *The Teachings of Modern Catholicism.*

40 I do a bit more with Orthodox rights talk in John Witte, Jr. and Michael Bourdeaux, eds., *Proselytism and Orthodoxy in Russia: The New War for Souls* (Maryknoll, NY: Orbis Books, 1999) and John Witte, Jr. and Frank S. Alexander, eds., *The Teachings of Modern Orthodox Christianity* (New York: Columbia University Press, 2007).

41 For these developments see further the volumes in our series on "Great Christian Jurists in World History": Paul Valliere and Randall Poole, eds., *Law and the Christian Tradition in Modern Russia* (London: Routledge, 2021); Wim Decock and Janwillem Oosterhuis, eds., *Great Christian Jurists in the Low Countries* (Cambridge: Cambridge University Press, 2021); Geoffrey Lindsay and Wayne A. Hudson, eds., *Great Christian Jurists in Australian History* (Alexandria, Australia: The Federation Press, 2021); Franciszek Longchamps de Bérier and Rafael Domingo, eds., *Law and Christianity in*

All these accents are functions of my scholarly competence, such as it is, not products of denominational, religious, or geographical chauvinism. Scholars of other Christian denominations and other world religions have happily made many profound contributions to our understanding of rights, liberties, and religious freedom, and these efforts deserve far more recognition than I have given them. Scholars from the many other parts of the Western world – especially in the global south and in southern and eastern Europe – have mined their legal traditions for further insights into human rights and religious freedom. My colleagues at the Center for the Study of Law and Religion and I are taking some account of these developments in an emerging fifty-volume series, Great Christian Jurists in World History, as well as in our *Journal of Law and Religion*, which offers broader comparative law and religion analysis. But the vast story of the development and protection of human rights and religious freedom in the Western legal tradition, let alone in the global-law tradition, is still being written. And the global struggle for human rights and religious freedom for all must and will long continue.

Poland: The Legacy of the Great Jurists (London: Routledge, 2021); M. C. Mirow and Rafael Domingo, eds., *Law and Christianity in Latin America: The Work of Great Jurists* (London: Routledge, 2021); Kjell Å Modéer and Helle Vogt, eds., *Law and the Christian Tradition in Scandinavia: The Writings of Great Nordic Jurists* (London: Routledge, 2020); Orazio Condorelli and Rafael Domingo, eds., *Law and the Christian Tradition in Italy: The Legacy of the Great Jurists* (London: Routledge, 2020); Olivier Descamps and Rafael Domingo, eds., *Great Christian Jurists in French History* (Cambridge: Cambridge University Press, 2019); Rafael Domingo and Javier Martínez Torrón, eds., *Great Christian Jurists in Spanish History* (Cambridge: Cambridge University Press, 2018); Allen Hertzke and Timothy Samuel Shah, eds., *Christianity and Freedom*, 2 vols. (Cambridge: Cambridge University Press, 2016).

1

Christian Contributions to the Development of Rights and Liberties in the Western Legal Tradition

It will come as a surprise to some human rights lawyers to learn that Christianity was a deep and enduring source of human rights and liberties in the Western legal tradition. Our elementary textbooks have long taught us that the history of human rights began in the later seventeenth and eighteenth centuries. Human rights, many of us were taught, were products of the Western Enlightenment – creations of Grotius and Pufendorf, Locke and Rousseau, Montesquieu and Voltaire, Hume and Smith, Jefferson and Madison. Rights were the mighty new weapons forged by American and French revolutionaries who fought in the name of political democracy, personal autonomy, and religious freedom against outmoded Christian conceptions of absolute monarchy, aristocratic privilege, and religious establishment. Rights were the keys forged by Western liberals to unchain society from the shackles of a millennium of the church's oppression of society and domination of the state. Human rights were the core ingredients of the new democratic constitutional experiments of the later eighteenth century forward. The only Christians to have much influence on this development, the conventional story goes, were a few early Church Fathers who decried pagan Roman persecution, a few brave medieval writers who defied papal tyranny, and a few early modern Anabaptists who debunked Catholic and Protestant persecution.[1] But these exceptions prove the rule, according to many human rights scholars: Christianity as a whole, they argue, was an impediment to the development and expansion of human rights – doubly so in our day when religious freedom and other fundamental rights are often counterposed.[2]

It will come as an equal surprise to some Christian readers to learn that their forebearers proved so critical to the development of rights in the Western tradition and beyond. A number of Christian theologians and philosophers today – Catholic,

[1] See representative literature analyzed in Victoria Kahn, "Early Modern Rights Talk," *Yale Journal of Law and the Humanities* 13 (2001), 391; Lynn Hunt, *Inventing Human Rights: A History* (New York: W. W. Norton, 2007); Samuel Moyn, "Substance, Scale, and Salience: The Recent Historiography of Human Rights," *The Annual Review of Law and Social Science* 8 (2012), 123–40.

[2] See discussion in John Witte, Jr. and Joel A. Nichols, *Religion and the American Constitutional Experiment*, 4th ed. (Oxford: Oxford University Press, 2016), 279–88 and further in Chapter 5, p. 160–70.

Orthodox, and Protestant alike – view human rights with suspicion, if not derision.[3] Yes, these critics acknowledge that Christians from the start embraced the right to religious freedom, at least for the Christian church and its members.[4] Many Christians today lament the myriad persecutions of Christians and others around the world,[5] and the growing tension between religious freedom and sexual freedom in late modern liberal democracies.[6] But many serious Christians today question seriously whether their spiritual predecessors really had much to do with rights, and whether modern human rights ideas faithfully express the moral norms and narratives of the Bible and the Christian tradition. Many view human rights as a dangerous invention of Enlightenment liberalism, predicated on a celebration of reason over revelation, of greed over charity, of nature over scripture, of the individual over the community, of the pretended sovereignty of humanity over the absolute sovereignty of God. These scholars call for better ideas and language to emphasize core virtues like faith, hope, and love and core goods like peace, order, and community.[7]

Such Christian skeptics about rights are not isolated and eccentric cranks. They include leading theologians like Stanley Hauerwas,[8] Oliver O'Donovan,[9] John Milbank,[10] Alasdair McIntyre,[11] Orthodox Ecumenical Patriarch Bartholomew,[12]

3 See such critics discussed in Nigel Biggar, *What's Wrong with Rights* (Oxford: Oxford University Press, 2020).

4 See Robert Louis Wilken, *Liberty in the Things of God: The Christian Origins of Religious Freedom* (New Haven, CT: Yale University Press, 2019).

5 See Timothy Samuel Shah and Allen Hertzke, eds., *Christianity and Freedom: Historical and Contemporary Perspectives* (Cambridge: Cambridge University Press, 2016); Daniel Philpott and Timothy Samuel Shah, *Under Caesar's Sword: How Christians Respond to Persecution* (Cambridge: Cambridge University Press, 2018).

6 See Helen Alvaré, "Religious Freedom versus Sexual Expression: A Guide," *Journal of Law and Religion* 30 (2015), 475–95.

7 See, for example, Mary Ann Glendon, *Rights Talk: The Impoverishment of Political Discourse* (New York: Free Press, 1991); Marta Cartabia, "Europe and Rights: Taking Dialogue Seriously," *European Constitutional Law Review* 5 (2009), 5–31.

8 Stanley Hauerwas, "How to Think Theologically About Rights," *Journal of Law and Religion* 30 (2015), 402–13, and further discussion, p. 291–93.

9 See Oliver O'Donovan, "The Language of Rights and Conceptual History," *Journal of Religious Ethics* 37 (2009), 193–207; and broader political theology in Oliver O'Donovan, *The Ways of Judgment* (Grand Rapids, MI: Eerdmans, 2005); Oliver O'Donovan, *The Desire of the Nations: Rediscovering the Roots of Political Theology* (Cambridge: Cambridge University Press, 1996).

10 John Milbank, "Against Human Rights: Liberty in the Western Tradition," *Oxford Journal of Law and Religion* 1 (2012), 203–34; John Milbank, "The History of Natural Right," *Church Life Journal* (January 18, 2019), https://churchlifejournal.nd.edu/articles/the-history-of-natural-right/.

11 See Alasdair MacIntyre, *After Virtue: A Study in Moral Theory* (Notre Dame, IN: University of Notre Dame Press, 1984), 69–70; and Mark D. Retter, "The Road Not Taken: On MacIntyre's Human Rights Skepticism," *The American Journal of Jurisprudence* 63 (2018), 189–219.

12 See Patriarch Bartholomew's remarks in John Witte, Jr. and Michael Bourdeaux, eds., *Proselytism and Orthodoxy in Russia: The New War for Souls* (Maryknoll, NY: Orbis Books, 1999), 19–20; and further Orthodox critique in Vigen Guroian, *Rallying the Really Human Things* (Wilmington, DE: ISI Press, 2005), 189–232. For a good summary of and response to Orthodox skepticism about rights, see John McGuckin, *The Ascent of Christian Law: Patristic and Byzantine Formulations of a New Civilization* (Yonkers, NY: St. Vladimir's Seminary Press, 2012).

and scores of mainline Protestant and Evangelical scholars influenced by Karl Barth's early "Nein!" to natural law and natural rights talk.[13] While many human rights lawyers today dismiss premodern Christian rights talk as a betrayal of Enlightenment liberalism, many Christians today dismiss modern Enlightenment rights talk as a betrayal of traditional Christianity.

Whatever the philosophical and theological merits of these respective positions might be, the historical readings and narratives that conventionally supported them can no longer be sustained. Over the past few decades, a veritable cottage industry of important new scholarship has emerged dedicated to the history of rights talk in the Western tradition prior to the Enlightenment. We now know a great deal more about classical Roman understandings of rights (*iura*), liberties (*libertates*), capacities (*facultates*), powers (*potestates*), and related concepts, and their elaboration by medieval and early modern civilians. We can now pore over an intricate latticework of arguments about individual and group rights and liberties developed by medieval Catholic canonists and moralists. We can now trace the ample expansion and reform of this medieval handiwork by neoscholastic writers in early modern Spain and Portugal and by Lutheran, Anglican, and Calvinist Protestants on the Continent and in Great Britain and their later colonies. We now know a good deal more about classical republican theories of liberty developed in Greece and Rome, and their transformative influence on early modern common lawyers and political revolutionaries on both sides of the Atlantic. We now know, in brief, that the West knew ample "liberty before liberalism"[14] and had many fundamental rights in place before there were modern democratic revolutions fought in their name. It is a telling anecdote that by 1650 almost every right listed 150 years later in the French Declaration of the Rights of Man and of the Citizen (1789) and the US Bill of Rights (1791) had already been defined, defended, and died for by Christians on both sides of the Atlantic.

The history of Western rights is still very much a contested work in progress, however, with scholars still sharply divided over the roots and routes of rights and liberties. Every serious new historian of human rights over the past century has tended to focus on a favorite period or person. Leo Strauss picked Hobbes and Locke as the founders of modern subjective rights talk, Perry Miller the New England Puritans, Lord Acton the English revolutionaries, Bernard Bailyn the American revolutionaries. Otto von Gierke picked German jurist Johannes Althusius as the rights founder; for Josef Bohatec it was John Calvin; and for R. R. Palmer it was the later Calvinist monarchomachs. Michel Villey and Richard Tuck saw deep sources of human rights in late medieval nominalist philosophy, Brian Tierney and R. H. Helmholz in high medieval canon law, F. W. Maitland and John C. Holt in

[13] Karl Barth, *Nein! Antwort an Emil Brunner* (Munich: C. Kaiser, 1934), translated in Karl Barth and Emil Brunner, *Natural Theology: Comprising "Nature and Grace"* (Eugene, OR: Wipf and Stock, 2002). See detailed sources in the recent study in Stephen J. Grabill, *Rediscovering the Natural Law in Reformed Theological Ethics* (Grand Rapids, MI: Eerdmans, 2006), 21–53.

[14] Quentin Skinner, *Liberty Before Liberalism* (Cambridge: Cambridge University Press, 2012).

Magna Carta. Max Kaser, Charles Donahue, and Tony Honoré saw sources of subjective rights in Roman law, while Nicholas Wolterstorff and Pope Benedict XVI pointed to key biblical and patristic texts as foundational.

A decade ago, scholars seemed to be settling on a story of a gradual and escalating two-millennia development of Western rights and liberties, with disputes focused on the novelty and influence of the contributions of individuals and texts in this evolution. But Yale historian Samuel Moyn has challenged this settlement anew by arguing that human rights were invented only in the last half of the twentieth century. He further dismissed the historical contribution of Christianity to human rights as a fiction and myth, designed to elevate the church as the nurturing mother of human rights throughout its history, while conveniently ignoring all the ways the church has betrayed basic rights and liberties.[15] While a number of historians have challenged Moyn's arguments, his influential work forces us to reconsider the history of rights anew. A brief sketch follows, with some parts of this picture filled in by subsequent chapters.

BIBLICAL FOUNDATIONS

The Bible has long been used as the anchor text for Christian teachings on human rights. Of course, the Bible is no textbook of human rights, but both the Hebrew Bible and the New Testament are filled with critical passages that have long inspired Christian writers in their reflections on the origin, nature, and purpose of human rights.[16]

Foremost among the Hebrew Bible texts is the Genesis account of the creation of man and woman. Genesis 1 rehearses God's creation of the world, and then comes to the apex:

> Then God said, "Let us make man in our image, after our likeness; and let them have dominion over the fish of the sea, and over birds of the air, and over the cattle, and over all the earth, and over every creeping thing that creeps upon the earth." So

15 See Samuel Moyn, *The Last Utopia: Human Rights in History* (Cambridge, MA: Belknap Press, 2012); Samuel Moyn, *Christian Human Rights* (Philadelphia: University of Pennsylvania Press, 2015). See my review of the latter volume in John Witte, Jr., "The Long History of Human Rights," *Books and Culture* 22, no. 2 (March/April, 2016), 22–24. See further Sara Shortall and Daniel Steinmetz-Jenkins, *Christianity and Human Rights Reconsidered* (Cambridge: Cambridge University Press, 2020).

16 Various scholars, however, have drawn rights, liberties, and related teachings on the strength of the Bible. See, for example, Jonathan Burnside, *God, Justice, and Society: Aspects of Law and Legality in the Bible* (New York: Oxford University Press, 2011); Michael Welker, ed., *Quests for Freedom: Biblical, Historical, Contemporary*, 2nd ed. (Eugene, OR: Cascade Books, 2019); Robert F. Cochran and David VanDrunen, eds., *Law and Bible: Justice, Mercy and Legal Institutions* (Downers Grove, IL: InterVarsity Press, 2013); Brent A. Strawn et al., eds., *The Oxford Encyclopedia of the Bible and Law*, 2 vols. (New York: Oxford University Press, 2015); Richard H. Hiers, *Women's Rights and the Bible: Implications for Christian Ethics and Social Policy* (Eugene, OR: Pickwick Publications, 2012); David Novak, *Covenantal Rights: A Study in Jewish Political Theory* (Princeton: Princeton University Press, 2000).

> God created man in his own image, in the image of God he created him; male and female he created them. And God blessed them, and God said to them, "Be fruitful and multiply, and fill the earth and subdue it; and have dominion over the fish of the sea and over the birds of the air and over every living thing that moves upon the earth."[17]

Archbishop Desmond Tutu has underscored how the idea of humans created in the image of God forms the deep ontological foundation of a Christian theory of human dignity, human freedom, and human rights. Every human being is created as a "God-carrier," Tutu writes, and as such deserves the utmost respect of their neighbors because of that inherent dignity.[18] Every human being is created with reason, will, and conscience and has the inherent right, duty, and freedom to make choices guided by the law written on their heart and rewritten in scripture, tradition, and experience. Such freedom of choice includes religious freedom. Tutu puts it memorably: "God, who alone has the perfect right to be a totalitarian, has such a profound reverence for our freedom that He had much rather we went freely to hell than compel us to go to heaven."[19]

The creation story continues with God's command to the first man and the first woman to join together "in one flesh" and to "be fruitful and multiply."[20] This primal teaching about the first family was amplified in many later biblical passages that modeled marriage on Yahweh's enduring love for his chosen people[21] and on Christ's eternal love for his church,[22] and that called parents and kin networks to nurture, care for, and educate children. Scripture provided Jews and Christians alike with foundations on which to build their systems of family law and the special rights and duties of spouses, parents, children, and kin.[23]

The creation story ends by recounting that humans are called to be caretakers and cultivators of nature, tasked to dress and keep the beauties of the Garden of Paradise even as they build toward the splendors of a Golden City in the eschaton.[24] In this primal command of stewardship, medieval monks and modern Christian environmentalists alike have found the warrants for what we now call the third-generation rights pertaining to the environment and to orderly and sustainable development.[25]

17 Genesis 1:26–28 (RSV); I have used the RSV throughout unless otherwise noted.

18 Desmond M. Tutu, "The First Word: To Be Human Is to Be Free," *Journal of Law and Religion* 30 (2015), 386–90.

19 Ibid.

20 Genesis 1:28.

21 See biblical texts in John Witte, Jr., "The Covenant of Marriage: Its Biblical Roots, Historical Influence, and Modern Uses," *INTAMS Review: Journal for the Study of Marriage and Spirituality* 18 (2012), 147–65.

22 Ephesians 5:32.

23 See John Witte, Jr., *Church, State, and Family: Reconciling Traditional Teachings and Modern Liberties* (Cambridge: Cambridge University Press, 2019), 238–73.

24 Genesis 2:15.

25 See, e.g., Bron Taylor, ed., *The Encyclopedia of Religion and Nature* (New York: Oxford University Press, 2010); John Chryssavgis and Bruce V. Foltz, eds., *Toward an Ecology of Transfiguration:*

Also fundamental to later Christian teachings were the many reciprocal rights and duties embedded in the Mosaic law and its amplification by both the prophets of the Hebrew Bible and the rabbis of the Talmud.[26] This early Judaic understanding of rights and duties inspired the Church Fathers, medieval Catholics, and early modern Protestants alike. Particularly the Ten Commandments, or Decalogue, set out in Exodus 20 and Deuteronomy 5, proved important to later Christian rights theorists. The First Table of the Decalogue defined religious duties to God, the Second Table duties toward neighbors. Later Christian writers used this template to set out the correlative religious rights and freedom that each person can claim to do the religious duties of the First Table, and the corollary civil rights of life, property, marriage, family, and reputation that each neighbor can claim against others.[27]

The Mosaic law governed a "covenanted" people who were bound together in community with each other and with God.[28] Already with Noah in the aftermath of the Flood, the Bible tells us that God entered into a covenant with all humanity and nature.[29] Both Jews and Christians would later see in this Noahide covenant the foundation of a new order of natural law and natural rights.[30] Thereafter, God entered into a more particular covenant with the chosen people of Israel, repeating the terms of the covenant to their leaders Moses, Joshua, Hezekiah, Josiah, and Ezra.[31] This covenant obliged every member of the community to live by the law of God and to obey the central commandments to love God and neighbor. Various Mosaic laws called for special care, protection, and provisions for widows, orphans, debtors, the poor, sojourners, and other needy persons. As the late chief rabbi Lord Jonathan Sacks wrote, the "fate" of a covenant community "is dependent on its treatment of the most vulnerable and marginal members. Ultimately, how a society fares in history is dependent on its commitment to justice, to compassion, to caring for the poor and the widow and the orphan and the stranger."[32] The later Hebrew prophets returned to these themes repeatedly in calling the people of Israel to their

Orthodox Perspectives on Environment, Nature, and Creation (New York: Fordham University Press, 2013); Noah J. Toly and Daniel I. Block, eds., *Keeping God's Earth: The Global Environment in Biblical Perspective* (Downers Grove, IL: InterVarsity Press, 2010); Willis J. Jenkins, *Ecologies of Grace: Environmental Ethics and Christian Theology* (Oxford: Oxford University Press, 2008).

26 David Novak, "The Judaic Foundations of Rights," in John Witte, Jr. and Frank S. Alexander, eds., *Christianity and Human Rights: An Introduction* (Cambridge: Cambridge University Press, 2010), 47–63.

27 See Chapter 3.

28 See, e.g., Daniel J. Elazar, *Covenant and Polity in Biblical Israel: Biblical Foundations and Jewish Expressions* (New Brunswick, NJ: Transaction Publishers, 1995); Novak, *Covenantal Rights*.

29 Genesis 9:1–17.

30 See David Novak, *Natural Law in Judaism* (Cambridge: Cambridge University Press, 1998); David VanDrunen, *Divine Covenants and Moral Order: A Biblical Theology of Natural Law* (Grand Rapids, MI: Eerdmans, 2014).

31 See Deuteronomy 29–31; Joshua 24; 2 Chronicles 29; 34; 2 Kings 22–23; Nehemiah 8.

32 Jonathan Sacks, "The Great Covenant of Liberties: Biblical Principles and Magna Carta," in Robin Griffith-Jones and Mark Hill QC, eds., *Magna Carta, Religion, and the Rule of Law* (Cambridge: Cambridge University Press, 2015), 301–13.

covenant obligations. Many Christian scholars used these Hebrew Bible passages and their echoes in the New Testament to defend an array of social welfare rights.[33]

Finally, the Hebrew Bible's account of the "covenant" between King David and the people of Israel proved critical for later Western constitutionalism. 2 Samuel 5:1–3 recounts how all the tribes of Israel came to David at Hebron, and said, "Behold we are your bone and flesh," and that they wanted him as their ruler in place of the abusive King Saul or some dynastic successor. In response, the passage continues, "David made a covenant with them at Hebron before the Lord, and they anointed David king over Israel." These same political covenant ceremonies were repeated anew on the appointment of biblical kings Solomon, Rehoboam, and others to the throne.[34] These passages became critical starting points for later discussions of political covenants, contracts, and constitutions, as well as popular sovereignty and the right to vote in and for a constitutional government.

The New Testament offered several strong pronouncements on freedom (*eleutheria; libertas*). "For freedom, Christ has set us free."[35] "You were called to freedom."[36] "Where the Spirit of the Lord is, there is freedom."[37] "For the law of the Spirit of life in Christ has set [you] free from the law of sin and death."[38] "You will know the truth, and the truth will make you free."[39] "You will be free indeed,"[40] for you all have been given "the glorious liberty of the children of God."[41] You must all now "live as free men."[42] "Freedom" meant three main things in these passages – freedom from "slavery" to sin and earthly temptation and the condemnation it brought;[43] freedom from following Mosaic laws, particularly the ceremonial laws, as a means to salvation;[44] and freedom to follow the rules of right Christian conduct before God, even if never perfectly, before gaining full communion with God in heaven.[45]

These passages have long inspired Christians to work out the meaning and means of attaining spiritual and political freedom. Already in the first centuries after Christ, the Church Fathers and church councils used these texts as the foundation for increasingly detailed canon laws that defined Christian responsibility within the

33 See, e.g., George M. Newlands and Allen P. Smith, *Hospitable God: The Transformative Dream* (Burlington, VT: Ashgate, 2010); George M. Newlands, *Christ and Human Rights: The Transformative Engagement* (Burlington, VT: Ashgate, 2006).
34 1 Kings 1:34–40; 12:1–20.
35 Galatians 5:1.
36 Galatians 5:13.
37 2 Corinthians 3:17.
38 Romans 8:2.
39 John 8:32.
40 John 8:36.
41 Romans 8:21.
42 1 Peter 2:16.
43 John 8:36; Romans 8:21, 33; Galatians 2:4; 5:1, 13; 1 Corinthians 7:21–22; 1 Peter 2:16.
44 Galatians 3:28; 4:26; 6:8; 2 Corinthians 3:17; Romans 6:20.
45 Gerhard Kittel et al., *Theological Dictionary of the New Testament*, 10 vols. (Grand Rapids, MI: Eerdmans, 1964), s.v. "eleutheria/freedom."

church and shaped rallying cries for liberty within the state.[46] In later centuries, Catholic, Protestant, and Orthodox Christians alike turned to these biblical texts as starting points for their theories of rights and liberties. These texts also proved to be powerful rhetorical tropes for early modern Christian democratic revolutionaries and political sermonizers on both sides of the Atlantic.[47]

The New Testament also called for equality. Saint Paul's manifesto to the Galatians famously declared: "There is neither Jew nor Greek, there is neither slave nor free, there is neither male nor female; for you are all one in Christ Jesus."[48] This radical Christian message of human equality trumped conventional Greco-Roman hierarchies based on birth, nationality, social status, gender, and more. Saint Peter amplified this call to equality with his admonition that all Christian believers are called to be prophets, priests, and kings of God: "You are a chosen race, a royal priesthood, a holy nation, God's own people."[49] These New Testament passages were critical to the gradual development of the understanding of equal protection and treatment of all persons before the law, and to domestic and international guarantees of freedom of all from discrimination based on gender, race, culture, ethnicity, and social or economic status.

The New Testament was even more radical in its call to treat the "least" members of society with love, respect, and dignity. Jesus took pains to minister to the social outcasts of his day – Samaritans, tax collectors, prostitutes, thieves, traitors, lepers, the lame, the blind, the adulteress, and others.[50] "He who is without sin, cast the first stone," he instructed a stunned crowd ready to stone a convicted adulteress.[51] "Today you will be with me in Paradise," he told the contrite thief nailed on the cross next to his.[52] The point was that even duly convicted criminals deserve mercy and love. Echoing the Hebrew Bible, Jesus called his followers to feed and care for the poor, widows, and orphans in their midst, to visit and comfort the sick, imprisoned, and refugee. "As you did it to one of the least of these my brethren, you did it to me," he told them.[53] And Jesus paid special attention to the care, nurture, and protection of children, and warned that it would be better to be cast into the sea with a millstone around one's neck than to

46 See several textual examples and a good literature summary in Julia Crick, "*Pristina Libertas*: Liberty and the Anglo-Saxons Revisited," *Transactions of the Royal Historical Society* 14 (2003), 47–71.

47 For American examples, see Ellis Sandoz, ed., *Political Sermons of the American Founding Era, 1730–1805* (Indianapolis, IN: Liberty Fund, 1998); John Wingate Thornton, *The Pulpit of the American Revolution*, repr. ed. (New York: De Capo Press, 1970). On European parallels, see sources and discussion in John Witte, Jr., *The Reformation of Rights: Law, Religion, and Human Rights in Early Modern Calvinism* (Cambridge: Cambridge University Press, 2007).

48 Galatians 3:26–28; see also Colossians 3:11; Ephesians 2:14–15.

49 1 Peter 2:9; cf. Revelation 5:10; 20:6.

50 See, e.g., Luke 10:25–37; Matthew 9:10; Luke 7:36–50; Matthew 21:31; Mark 15:27; Matthew 8:3; Mark 2:1–12; Mark 8:22–25; John 8:1–15.

51 John 8:7.

52 Luke 23:43.

53 Matthew 25:40.

mislead a child. Few texts of the day would prove stronger foundation for the later development of children's rights in the Christian tradition.[54]

Jesus and Saint Paul also called believers to share their wealth, to shore up those in need, to give up their extra clothes and belongings even to their creditors.[55] They even called believers to love their enemies,[56] to give them food and water,[57] to turn their cheeks to those who strike them,[58] to forgo lawsuits, vengeance, and retributive measures,[59] to be peacemakers in expression of the radical demands of Christian discipleship.[60] Many Christians over the centuries – monks and nuns, ascetics and Anabaptists, missionaries and peacemakers and various others – have sought to live out these Christian ideals, often in highly structured Christian communities. These biblical passages and historical exemplars, too, provide strong foundations for the rights of the poor and needy in society as well as the rights of conscientious objectors against military participation.[61]

Finally, the New Testament called Christians to "render to Caesar the things that are Caesar's and to God the things that are God's"[62] and reminded them that God has appointed "two swords"[63] to rule this life, the spiritual and the temporal. Christian scripture called believers to "remain separate" from worldly temptations, to be "in the world, but not of it," and not "conformed" to its secular ways.[64] For Christians are, at heart, "strangers and exiles on the earth," and have their true "commonwealth in heaven."[65] The Bible also spoke frequently about building and rebuilding "walls" to foster this basic separation between believers and the outside world. In the Hebrew Bible, these walls separated the city of Jerusalem from the outside world, and the temple and its priests from the commons and its people.[66] In the New Testament, Saint Paul spoke literally of a "wall of separation" or "partition

54 See Marcia Bunge, *Children in the Bible* (Grand Rapids, MI: Wm. B. Eerdmans Publishing Co., 2008); Marcia Bunge, ed., *The Child in Christian Thought* (Grand Rapids, MI: Wm. B. Eerdmans Publishing Co., 2001).

55 See, e.g., Matthew 18:5–9; 19:13–15; Mark 7:24–30; 9:14–27; 10:13–16; Luke 8:40–56; John 4:46–52.

56 Matthew 5:43–48.

57 Matthew 25:31–46.

58 Matthew 5:38–40.

59 Matthew 5:25.

60 Matthew 5:21–26; Romans 12:9–21.

61 See, e.g., Brian Tierney, *Medieval Poor Law: A Sketch of Canonical Theory and Its Application in England* (Berkeley: University of California Press, 1959); Walter Rauschenbusch, *A Theology for the Social Gospel* (Louisville, KY: Westminster John Knox Press, 1997); United States Catholic Bishops, *Economic Justice for All: Pastoral Letter on Catholic Social Teaching and the U.S. Economy* (1986) and other papal encyclicals, http://w2.vatican.va/content/francesco/en/encyclicals/index.html; and analysis in Gerard V. Bradley and E. Christian Brugger, *Catholic Social Teaching: A Volume of Scholarly Essays* (Cambridge: Cambridge University Press, 2019).

62 Matthew 22:21; Mark 12:17; Luke 20:25.

63 Luke 22:38.

64 2 Corinthians 6:17; Romans 12:2.

65 Hebrews 11:13; Philippians 3:20; see also Romans 12:2; 2 Corinthians 6:14–18; Colossians 3:1.

66 1 Kings 3:1; Jeremiah 1:18–19; 15:19–21; Ezekiel 42:1; Nehemiah 3:1–32; 4:15–20; 12:27–43.

wall" interposed by the law of God.[67] These passages and others have inspired Christians over the centuries to develop dualistic theories of religion and politics, church and state – two ways, two cities, two powers, two swords, two kingdoms, two realms, and two institutions of religion and politics, of spiritual and temporal life. Today such images are captured in constitutional injunctions to separate church and state, and to protect the rights and autonomy of churches and their leadership.[68]

CLASSICAL ROMAN LAW

While the Bible provided ample inspiration for the later development of rights in the Western tradition, classical Roman law offered equally ample illustration of how rights worked in a sophisticated legal system.[69] Both before and after the Christian conversion of Emperor Constantine in the fourth century CE, classical Roman jurists used the Latin term *ius* to identify a "right" in both its objective and subjective senses. (*Ius* also meant law or legal order more generally.) The objective sense of *ius* – to be in proper order, to perform what is right and required, "to give to each his due" (*ius suum cuiuque tribuere*) – dominated the Roman law texts. But these texts also sometimes used *ius* subjectively, in the sense of a subject or person having a right that could be defended and vindicated. Many of the subjective rights recognized by classical Roman law involved property: the right to own or co-own property, the right to possess, lease, or use property, the right to build or prevent building on one's land, the right to gain access to water, the right to be free from interference with or invasion of one's property, the right or capacity to alienate property, the right to bury one's dead, and more. Several texts dealt with personal rights: the rights of testators and heirs, the rights of patrons and guardians, the rights of fathers and mothers over children, the rights of masters over slaves. Other texts dealt with public rights: the right of an official to punish or deal with subjects in a certain way, the right to delegate power, the right to appoint and supervise lower officials. Other texts dealt with procedural rights in criminal and civil cases.[70]

67 Ephesians 2:14. This is the literal meaning of the Latin *paries maceriae* in the Vulgate, which the KJV translated as "partition wall."

68 See John Witte, Jr., "Facts and Fictions About the History of Separation of Church and State," *Journal of Church and State* 48 (2006), 15–46.

69 See Charles A. Donahue, "*Ius* in the Subjective Sense in Roman Law: Reflections on Villey and Tierney," in Domenico Maffei, ed., A *Ennio Cortese*, 3 vols. (Rome: Il Cigno Ed., 2001), 1:506–35; Max Kaser, *Ius Gentium* (Cologne: Böhlau, 1993); Max Kaser, *Ausgewählte Schriften*, 3 vols. (Naples: Jovene, 1976–77) and summary in Max Kaser, "Zum 'Ius'-Begriff der Römer," *Acta Juridica* 63 (1977), 63–81; Tony Honoré, *Ulpian: Pioneer of Human Rights*, 2nd ed. (Oxford: Oxford University Press, 2002); Chaim Wirszubski, *Libertas as a Political Idea at Rome During the Late Republic and Early Principate* (Cambridge: Cambridge University Press, 1950).

70 Harvard legal historian Charles Donahue has recently identified 191 texts on subjective rights in the Digest alone (one of the four books of Justinian's sixth-century *Corpus Iuris Civilis*) and speculates that hundreds, if not thousands, more such texts can be found in other books of classical Roman law. See Donahue, "*Ius* in the Subjective Sense in Roman Law." See further Peter Garnsey, "Property and

The *Corpus Iuris Civiliis*, which collected the main texts of classical Roman law, also referred more than two thousand times to *libertas*.[71] The primary meaning of *libertas* in these ancient texts was that a person was not enslaved, owned, or under the mastery, rightful claim, or power of another (*alieni iuris; in aliena potestate*).[72] One's *libertas* at Roman law turned in part on one's status. Citizens had more *libertas* than noncitizens, freedmen more than those conditionally manumitted. Men had more *libertas* than women, married women more than concubines, adults more than children. But Roman law gave each person a basic freedom from subjection or undue restraint or actions from others who had no right to (*ius*) or possessory claim (*dominium*) over them. Think of Saint Paul, who claimed the *libertas* of a Roman citizen to be free from whipping or capital punishment without a hearing before the emperor, who alone had such ultimate authority over him.[73] Similarly, a free wife had *libertas* from others besides her husband. A natural or adopted child had *libertas* from others save his or her paterfamilias or an assigned guardian or tutor. While all persons, regardless of their status and *libertas*, were subject to the rule of the emperor, he ruled not as "an absolute monarch, but as a protector of republican liberty, institutions, and practices."[74]

Libertas also meant the "power (*potestas*) to live as you choose,"[75] "the natural ability (*facultas*) to do anything one pleases, unless it is prohibited by force or law."[76] Roman jurists and philosophers linked this positive idea of *libertas* with the concept of rights (*iura*) and sometimes spoke of the "right of liberty" (*ius libertatis*) which should not be "impaired" (from *integrum*), "abridged" (*imminutum*), "violated" (*infringitur*), or "dismissed" (*amittant*).[77] They also spoke more generally of the "rights of the people" (*iura populi*) to exercise their liberties (*libertates*).[78] A good example is the religious freedom guarantees offered by the so-called Edict of Milan (313) passed by Emperor Constantine to end Roman persecution of Christians. The

Its Limits: Historical Analysis," in B. Winiger, et al., eds., *La propriété et ses limites/Das Eigentum und seine Grenzen* (Stuttgart: Franz Steiner, 2017), 13–38.

71 *The Corpus Iuris Civilis* mentions *libertas* and its derivatives 2,078 times (483 in the Code, 80 in the Institutes, 1,446 in the Digest, and 69 in the Novellae). For earlier formulations in the Roman Republic, see the distillation in Gaius, *Institutes*, bk. 1, chap. 3 (on the conditions of men), bk. 1, chap. 7, 48–56 in Gaius, *The Institutes of Gaius. Parts One and Two. Text with Critical Notes and Translation*, ed. Francis de Zulueta, 2 vols. (Oxford: Clarendon Press, 1946); see discussion in Valentina Arena, *Libertas and the Practice of Politics in the Late Roman Republic* (Cambridge: Cambridge University Press, 2012), 14–44.

72 Jed W. Atkins, *Roman Political Thought* (Cambridge: Cambridge University Press, 2018), 37–63.

73 Acts 22:22–29.

74 Rafael Domingo, *Roman Law* (London: Routledge, 2018), 21–22.

75 Cicero, *Paradoxa stoicorum* 5.1.34, quoted in Domingo, *Roman Law*, 21.

76 Florentinus (second century) in the Digest, 1.5.4, repeated in Justinian, *Institutes*, 1.3.

77 See, e.g., Cicero, *Pro Rabiro perduellionis reo*, 11; Sallust, *Bellum Catilinae*, 37; Digest 35.1.71.2; see also fifth-century Christian writer Salvian, *De gubernatione Dei*, 5, 8, 9. I am grateful to my colleague Rafael Domingo for guiding me through these Roman law texts, and to Alexander Rudofsky for painstakingly extracting all references to *libertas* and its derivatives in the *Corpus Iuris Civilis*, a vast database that will require its own separate study.

78 Domingo, *Roman Law*, 21–22.

Edict spoke of "the freedom (*libertas*) to follow whatever religion each one wished"; "a public and free liberty to practice their religion or cult"; and a "free capacity" (*facultas*) to follow their own religion "and worship as befits the peacefulness of our times." The Edict also recognized the rights (*iura*) of Christian groups to restitution of property and places of worship, "which belonged by right to their body – that is, to the churches not to individuals," and the right to restitution of properties confiscated in earlier times of persecution.[79]

This language reflected a century or more of calls by Church Fathers for religious freedom. Tertullian of Carthage (ca. 160–220), a theologian with some legal training, was the first (in surviving sources) to introduce the term "freedom of religion" (*libertas religionis*) into Western Christian thought.[80] After decrying the Roman persecution of Christians in his day, he wrote famously: "It is only just and a privilege inherent in human nature that every person should be able to worship according to his own convictions; the religious practice of one person neither harms nor helps another. It is not part of religion to coerce religious practice, for it is by choice not coercion that we should be led to religion." "To take away freedom of religion (*libertas religionis*) and forbid free choice with respect to divine matters" only "fosters irreligion."[81] This passage was often repeated in medieval and early modern texts, and quoted by Thomas Jefferson and James Madison alike in their arguments for the new American experiment in religious freedom.[82]

MEDIEVAL CATHOLICISM

Early medieval texts echoed and elaborated these biblical and classical Roman discussions of rights and liberties. The biblical passages on liberty (*eleutheriá; libertas*) attracted hundreds of references and glosses among Christian writers in the later first millennium.[83] So did the Roman texts on *ius* and *iura*. Spanish encyclopedist Isidore of Seville (560–636), for example, ascribed to the *ius naturale* "the union of men and women, the procreation and raising of children, the common possessions of all persons, the equal liberty of all persons (*omnium una libertas*), the acquisition of things that are taken from the heavens, earth, or sea, the return of property or money that has been deposited or entrusted. This also includes the right to repel violence with force."[84]

79 See Sidney Z. Ehler and John B. Morrall, *Church and State through the Centuries: A Collection of Historic Documents with Commentaries* (Westminster, MD: Newman Press, 1954), 4–6; original in Lactantius, *De Mortibus Persecutorum [c. 315]*, 48.2–12, ed. and trans. J. L. Creed (Oxford: Clarendon Press, 1984), 71–73.

80 The first reference is in Tertullian, *Apollogeticum* (197 CE), in E. Dekkers, ed., *Corpus Christianorum: Series Latina – Tertullianus* (Turnhout: Brepols, 1954), 234.

81 Wilken, *Liberty in the Things of God*, 1, 11–13.

82 Ibid., 189–92.

83 *Patrologia Latina*, s.v. "libertas" and derivatives. See English examples in Crick, "*Pristina Libertas*."

84 *Etymologies*, 5.4 with discussion in Kenneth Pennington, "Rights," in George Klosko, ed., *Oxford Handbook of the History of Political Philosophy* (Oxford: Oxford University Press, 2011), 535; Kenneth Pennington, "Lex naturalis and Ius naturale," *The Jurist* 68 (2008), 581. See further

Anglo-Saxon laws usually translated the Roman term *ius/iura* as "law(s)" or "justice,"[85] but also occasionally as "*rihtae*" and "*ryhtes*" in the subjective sense. King Edward, for example, ordered that "no man shall withhold from another his ryhtes" to property, compensation for injury, and contractual performance.[86] King Edgar II declared that "God's churches shall be entitled to all their *rihtes*" to tithes, alms, cemeteries, festivities, feasts, fasts, and sanctuary.[87] Furthermore, several Anglo-Saxon charters of monasteries, abbeys, churches, and towns from the later eighth century on used the Roman term *libertas*, which they sometimes translated as *freoles* or *freo-dom*.[88] "Some 15 percent of original pre-Conquest charters deployed the rhetoric of liberty," writes Julia Crick: "grants of liberty, privileges of liberty … *ecclesiastica libertas, libertas ecclesiarum*, even the Gregorian formulation, *libertas ecclesiae* [and] *ius ecclesiasticae libertatis*."[89] Here *libertas* meant at least freedom of the church or religious freedom from secular taxes, dues, and military service as well as from the secular lord's jurisdiction over the chartered land and its members.[90] Sometimes *libertas* also entailed "a bundle of rights" and freedom to do something with, on, or about the chartered land and its improvements. Some of these charters also translated *libertas* into terms like "*sondor-freodom*," meaning a special right over land, and "*freoles*" and "*freolboc*," meaning freedom from the jurisdiction or dues of another, and "freedom to exercise rights without the control of another."[91] All these Anglo-Saxon terms and texts became important prototypes for the hundreds of high medieval English charters of rights and liberties that emerged, including the most famous of these, the Magna Carta of 1215 and the Forest Charter of 1216, which became anchor texts for Anglo-American constitutionalism.[92]

Philip Reynolds, "Isidore of Seville," in Rafael Domingo and Javier Martínez Torrón, eds., *Great Christian Jurists in Spanish History* (Cambridge: Cambridge University Press, 2018), 31–49.

85 See the well-indexed collection in Felix Liebermann, *Die Gesetze der Angelsachsen*, 3 vols. (Halle: Niemeyer, 1903–16).

86 II Edward (ca. 900–25), item 2, in F. L. Attenborough, ed., *The Laws of the Earliest English Kings*, repr. ed. (Cambridge: Cambridge University Press, 2015), 118–19. See also I Edward (899–924), sec. 2 in ibid., 117, prescribing penalties for anyone "who withholds from another his rights (*ryhtes*)" in various lands.

87 II Edgar (ca. 946–61), item 1, and item 5(3) in A. J. Robertson, *The Laws of the Kings of England from Edmund to Henry* (Cambridge: University Press, 1925), 20–23. For other examples of subjective rights held by kings or lords and delegated to selected subjects, see Stefan Jurasinski, Lisi Oliver, and Andrew Rabin, eds., *English Law Before Magna Carta: Felix Liebermann and Die Gesetze der Angelsachsen* (Leiden: Brill, 2010), esp. 157–60, 173–74, 211–13, 225–27; Alfred Kiralfky, "Law and Right in English Legal History," in *La formazione storica de diritto moderno in Europa* (Florence: Leo S. Olschki, 1977), 3:1069–86.

88 See the dozens of volumes collecting these documents in the ongoing series Anglo-Saxon Charters (Oxford: Oxford University Press, 1973–).

89 Crick, "*Libertas Pristina*," 59–60.

90 Ibid. 61.

91 Ibid., 62, citing charters in David A.E. Pelteret, *Slavery in Early Mediaeval England from the Reign of Alfred until the Twelfth Century* (Woodbridge: Boydell, 1995), 47–48, 276–78, 383–84, 303–04.

92 See Chapter 2.

The rediscovery and new study of Roman law texts in the late eleventh century forward triggered a fuller renaissance of rights theories and laws. Leading medieval historians Brian Tierney and Kenneth Pennington have shown that, already in the twelfth century, the civilians and canonists (the jurists who worked on the church's laws, which were called canon laws) differentiated all manner of rights (*iura*) and liberties (*libertates*).[93] They grounded these rights and liberties in the law of nature (*lex naturae*) or natural law (*ius naturale*), in customs and treaties, as well as in moral principles like the Golden Rule ("Do unto others as you would have done to you").[94] Medieval jurists associated rights variously with a power (*facultas*) inhering in rational human nature, with the property (*dominium*) of a person, or the power (*potestas*) of an office of authority (*officium*).[95]

The early canonists repeated and glossed many of the subjective rights and liberties set out in Roman law, starting with the rights to property, marriage, self-defense, and criminal procedural protections,[96] and more broadly the "rights of liberty" (*iura libertatis*) enjoyed by persons of various stations in life and offices of authority.[97] The medieval canonists also began to weave earlier Roman and Germanic texts into a whole complex latticework of what we now call rights, freedoms, powers, immunities, protections, and capacities for different groups and persons.[98]

Most important to the medieval canonists were the rights needed to protect the "freedom of the church" (*libertas ecclesiae*). "Freedom of the church" from civil and feudal control and corruption was the rallying cry of Pope Gregory VII (r. 1073–85)  that inspired the Papal Revolution of 1075 and ultimately established the church as an independent legal and political authority for all of Western Christendom.[99] In defense of this revolution, medieval canonists specified in increasing detail the rights of the church to make its own laws, to maintain its own courts, to define its own doctrines and liturgies, to elect and remove its own clergy. Canonists stipulated the exemptions of church property from civil taxation and takings, and the right of the clergy to control and use church property without interference or encumbrance from secular or feudal authorities. They guaranteed the immunity of the clergy from

93 For this section, see Brian Tierney, *The Idea of Natural Rights: Studies on Natural Rights, Natural Law, and Church Law, 1150–1625* (Grand Rapids, MI: Wm. B. Eerdmans, 2001), 34–70; see further Peter Landau, "Zum Ursprung des 'Ius ad Rem' in der Kanonistik," in *Proceedings of the Third International Congress of Medieval Canon Law* (1971), 81–102.

94 See texts gathered in Pennington, "Rights," 535–38.

95 Tierney, *Idea of Natural Rights*, 8.

96 Pennington, "Rights," 538–39, and, more generally, Kenneth Pennington, *The Prince and the Law, 1200–1600: Sovereignty and Rights in the Western Legal Tradition* (Berkeley: University of California Press, 1993).

97 C. 16, q. 3, dictum post c. 15, quoted in Tierney, *Idea of Natural Rights*, 57.

98 See R. H. Helmholz, *The Privilege Against Self-Incrimination: Its Origins and Development* (Chicago: University of Chicago Press, 1997); James Q. Whitman, *The Origins of Reasonable Doubt: Theological Roots of the Criminal Trial* (New Haven, CT: Yale University Press, 2008).

99 This is the main theme of Berman, *Law and Revolution*.

secular prosecution, military service, and compulsory testimony; and the rights of church entities like parishes, monasteries, charities, and guilds to form and dissolve, to accept and reject members, and to establish order and discipline. They defined the rights of church councils and synods to participate in the election and discipline of bishops, abbots, and other clergy. They defined the rights of the lower clergy vis-à-vis their superiors. They defined the rights of the laity to worship, evangelize, maintain religious symbols, participate in the sacraments, travel on religious pilgrimages, and educate their children. They defined the rights of the poor, widows, and needy to seek solace, succor, and sanctuary within the church. They defined the rights of husbands and wives, parents and children, masters and servants within the household. They defined the (truncated) rights that Orthodox Christians, Jews, Muslims, and heretics had in Christian society. Rights and liberties laid out in canon law texts were enforced by a hierarchy of church courts and other administrative church offices, each with distinctive and complex rules of litigation, evidence, and judgment, and each providing the right to appeal, ultimately to Rome.[100]

These formulations of rights yielded increasingly sophisticated reflections in the writings not only of medieval jurists but also of medieval theologians and philosophers like John Duns Scotus (1266–1308) and William of Ockham (1285–1307), political thinkers like Marsilius of Padua (1275–1342), Jean Gerson (1363–1429), and Conrad Summenhart (1455–1502), and sundry Spanish sages gathered at the University of Salamanca.[101] This last group included Francisco de Vitoria (1483–1546), Bartolomé de las Casas (d. 1566), Fernando Vázquez de Menchaca (1512–69), Francisco Suarez (1548–1617), and many others.[102] Vitoria, in particular, made pathbreaking advances in defending "the rights of the Indians" and others in the newly conquered Latin American world.[103] Las Casas was a brilliant apostle for

[100] Tierney, *The Idea of Natural Rights*; Brian Tierney, *Rights, Law, and Infallibility in Medieval Thought* (Aldershot, UK: Variorum Reprints, 1997); Brian Tierney, *Religion, Law, and the Growth of Constitutional Thought, 1150–1650* (Cambridge: Cambridge University Press, 1982); Udo Wolter, "Amt und Officium in mittelalterlichen Quellen vom 13. bis 15. Jahrhundert: Ein begriffsgeschichtliche Untersuchung," ZSS KA 78 (1988), 246; Charles J. Reid, Jr., "Rights in Thirteenth Century Canon Law: An Historical Investigation" (PhD Dissertation, Cornell, 1994); Charles J. Reid, Jr., "Thirteenth Century Canon Law and Rights: The Word *ius* and its Range of Subjective Meanings," *Studia Canonica* 30 (1996), 295; Charles J. Reid, Jr., "Roots of a Democratic Church Polity in the History of the Canon Law," *Canon Law Society of America Proceedings* 60 (1998), 150; Charles J. Reid, Jr., *Power over the Body, Equality in the Family: Rights and Domestic Relations in Medieval Canon Law* (Grand Rapids, MI: Eerdmans, 2004).

[101] Tierney, *The Idea of Natural Rights*, 93–206; Richard Tuck, *Natural Rights Theories: Their Origins and Development* (Cambridge: Cambridge University Press, 1979); Michel Villey, *La formation de la pensée juridique moderne* (Paris: Presses Universitaires de France, 1968); Michey Villey, *Le droit et les droits de l'homme* (Paris: Presses Universitaires de France, 1983).

[102] Domingo and Torrón, *Great Christian Jurists in Spanish History*, 84–239; Annabel S. Brett, *Liberty, Right, and Nature: Individual Rights in Later Scholastic Thought* (Cambridge: Cambridge University Press, 1997). See the emerging virtual library at www.rg.mpg.de/research/academy_project_mainz.

[103] Francisco de Vitoria, *De Indis et de jure belli relectiones*, ed. Ernst Nys, trans. John P. Bate, rev. Herbert F. Wright (Washington, DC: Carnegie Institution, 1917).

religious freedom and the rights of the poor whose writings influenced key figures on both sides of the Atlantic.[104]

Medieval canon law formulations of rights and liberties had parallels in the common law and civil law texts of the Middle Ages. Particularly notable sources were the hundreds of treaties, concordats, charters, and other constitutional texts issued in the eleventh to sixteenth centuries by various religious and secular authorities. These were often detailed – and sometimes very flowery and elegant – statements of the rights and liberties to be enjoyed by defined groups of clergy, nobles, barons, knights, urban councils, citizens, universities, guilds, fraternities, hospitals, orphanages, monasteries, cloisters, and others. Such charters were often highly localized instruments, but occasionally they applied to whole territories and nations.[105] A famous example was Magna Carta (1215), the great charter issued by the English Crown at the insistence of the restive barons of England and drafted under the guidance of the archbishop of Canterbury, Stephen Langton. Magna Carta guaranteed that "the Church of England shall be free (*libera*) and shall have all her whole rights (*iura*) and liberties (*libertates*) inviolable." The charter also provided that all "free-men" (*liberis hominibus*) were to enjoy sundry "liberties" (*libertates*), including rights to property, marriage, and inheritance, to freedom from undue military service, and to freedom to pay one's debts and taxes from the property of one's own choosing. Magna Carta also set out various rights and powers of towns and local justices and their tribunals, various rights and prerogatives of the king and the royal courts, and various criminal procedural rights which, by the fourteenth century, were called the "rights of due process."[106]

Magna Carta and other medieval charters of rights became important prototypes on which later revolutionaries would call to justify their revolts against arbitrary and tyrannical authorities. Among others, early modern Protestant revolutionaries in France, Scotland, the Netherlands, England, and America all reached back to these chartered rights to help justify their revolutions against tyrants, and eventually reached beneath these charters to the natural laws and rights and the classical and biblical teachings on which they were founded.[107] And Magna Carta itself provided the foundation for an ever expanding system of rights at Anglo-American common law. When William Blackstone sat down to write his famous *Commentaries on the Laws of England* (1765), he opened his first volume with a lengthy list of public,

[104] See Bartolomé de las Casas, *In Defense of the Indian*, trans. Stafford Poole (DeKalb: Northern Illinois University Press, 1992), with analysis in David Lantigua, "The Image of God, Christian Rights Talk, and the School of Salamanca," *Journal of Law and Religion* 31 (2016), 19–41; David Lantigua, "Faith, Liberty, and the Defense of the Poor: Bishop Las Casas in the History of Human Rights," in Shah and Hertzke, eds., *Christianity and Freedom*, 1:176–209.

[105] R. H. Helmholz, "Magna Carta and the Law of Nations," in Robin Griffith-Jones and Mark Hill, eds., *Magna Carta, Religion, and the Rule of Law* (Cambridge: Cambridge University Press, 2015), 70–80.

[106] See Chapter 2.

[107] See Witte, *The Reformation of Rights*.

private, penal, and procedural rights taught variously by the common law, civil law, canon law, Roman law, natural law, and law of nations.[108]

EARLY MODERN PROTESTANTISM

While "freedom of the church" was the manifesto of the twelfth-century Papal Revolution, "freedom of the Christian" was the manifesto of the sixteenth-century Protestant Reformation. Martin Luther (1483–1546), John Calvin (1509–64), Thomas Cranmer (1489–1556), Menno Simons (1496–1561), and other leading sixteenth-century reformers all began their Protestant movements with a call for freedom from the medieval Catholic Church – freedom of the individual conscience from intrusive canon laws and clerical controls, freedom of political officials from ecclesiastical power and privileges, and freedom of the local clergy from central papal rule and oppressive princely controls. Spurred by the cry of "freedom of the Christian," theologians and jurists, clergy and laity, princes and peasants alike denounced canon laws and ecclesiastical authorities with unprecedented alacrity and urged radical reforms in church, state, and society. Books of canon law were burned and church courts closed. Monastic institutions were confiscated, endowed benefices dissolved, and church lands seized. Clerics were stripped of their privileges, and mandatory celibacy was suspended. Indulgences were condemned. Annates to Rome were outlawed, ties to the pope severed, and appeals to the papal rota barred. Each nation, church, and Christian was to be free.[109]

Left in such raw and radical forms, the early Protestant call for freedom was a recipe for lawlessness and license, as Luther learned the hard way during the Peasants' Revolt of 1525. He and other Protestants soon realized that structures of law and authority were essential to protecting order and peace, even as guarantees of liberties and rights were essential to preserving the message and momentum of the Reformation. The challenge for early Protestants was to strike new balances between authority and liberty, order and rights on the strength of principal biblical teachings.

One important Protestant contribution to the Western rights tradition was their effort to define constitutionally the nature and authority of the family, the church, and the state vis-à-vis each other and their subjects. Most Protestant reformers regarded these three institutions as fundamental orders of creation, equal before God and each other, and vested with certain natural duties and qualities that the other authorities could not trespass. Defining these institutions and their respective offices in clear new constitutions, covenants, and codes of conduct served to check the natural appetite of the *paterfamilias*, *patertheologicus*, and *paterpoliticus* for tyranny and abuse. It also helped to clarify the rights and liberties of those subject

108 William Blackstone, *Commentaries on the Laws of England*, 4 vols. (Oxford: Oxford University Press, 1765), bk. 1, chap. 1. See further Chapter 2 of this book.

109 See Martin Luther, *The Freedom of a Christian*, in Timothy Lull and William Russell, eds., *Martin Luther's Basic Theological Writings*, 3rd ed. (Minneapolis, MN: Fortress Press, 2012), 403–27.

to their authority and to specify the grounds on which they could protest or disobey in the event of chronic abuse or tyranny.[110]

A second major contribution was the Protestant reformers' habit of grounding rights in the duties of the Decalogue and other biblical moral teachings. The First Table of the Decalogue, they argued, prescribes duties owed to God – to honor God and God's name, to observe the Sabbath and to worship, to avoid false gods and false swearing. The Second Table prescribes duties owed to others – to honor one's parents and other authorities, and not to kill, commit adultery, steal, bear false witness, or covet. The reformers cast duties toward God as a set of rights that others could not obstruct – the right to religious exercise, to honoring God and God's name, to rest and worship on the Sabbath, and to be free from false gods and false oaths. They cast duties toward neighbors, in turn, as the neighbors' right to have that duty discharged. One person's duties to honor parents and not to kill, commit adultery, steal, bear false witness, or covet thus gives rise to another person's rights to the marital household, life, property, fidelity, and reputation.[111]

The third contribution of the Protestant Reformation was the permanent shattering of the unity of Western Christendom, from whose rubble arose the foundations for the modern constitutional system of confessional pluralism – at the territorial, national, community, or congregational levels. The Lutheran Reformation *territorialized* the faith through the principle of *cuius regio, eius religio* ("whosever's region, his religion"), established by the Religious Peace of Augsburg in 1555.[112] Princes or city councils could prescribe the forms of Lutheran or Catholic doctrine and practice for their polities, while religious dissenters gained the right to worship privately or emigrate peaceably. The Peace of Westphalia (1648) extended this right to Reformed Calvinists as well, creating a veritable honeycomb of religious pluralism in Germany and beyond.[113]

The Anglican Reformation *nationalized* the faith through the famous Supremacy Acts and Acts of Uniformity passed by the English Parliament between 1534 and 1559.[114] Although citizens of the Commonwealth of England initially were required to be communicants of the Church of England, subject to the ecclesiastical and political authority of the monarch, the Toleration Act of 1689 extended a modicum of rights and liberties to some Protestant dissenters,[115] and the Catholic and Jewish Emancipation Acts of 1829 and 1833 granted all non-Anglicans the full rights of citizenship.[116]

110 John Witte, Jr., *Law and Protestantism: The Legal Teachings of the Lutheran Reformation* (Cambridge: Cambridge University Press, 2002).

111 Ibid., 121–68; Witte, *The Reformation of Rights*, 81–142, 209–76. See further Chapter 3 of this book.

112 In Ehler and Morrall, *Church and State*, 164–73.

113 Ibid., 189–192.

114 In Carl Stephenson and Frederick B. Markham, *Sources of English Constitutional History*, rev. ed. (New York: Harper and Row, 1972), 303–21.

115 Ibid., 607–8.

116 In Ehler and Morrall, *Church and State*, 254–71.

The Anabaptist Reformation *communalized* the faith by introducing what Menno Simons once called the *Scheidingsmaurer* – "the wall of separation" between the redeemed realm of religion and the fallen realm of the world. Anabaptist religious communities were ascetically withdrawn from the world into small, self-sufficient, intensely democratic communities, governed internally by biblical principles of discipleship, simplicity, charity, and Christian obedience. When such communities grew too large or divided, they colonized themselves and spread their principles and practices of self-governance from Russia to the farthest frontiers of North America.[117]

The Calvinist Reformation *congregationalized* the faith by introducing rule by an elected consistory of pastors, elders, and deacons. In John Calvin's day, the Geneva consistory was still appointed and held broad personal and subject matter jurisdiction over all members of the city. By the seventeenth century, however, most Calvinist communities in Europe and North America had reduced the consistory to an elected, representative system of government within each congregation. Consistories featured separation among the offices of preaching, discipline, and charity, and a fluid, dialogical form of religious polity and policing centered on collective worship and the congregational meeting.

The fourth contribution of the Protestant Reformation was the erosion of the primacy of corporate Christianity and a new emphasis on the individual. The Protestant Reformation did not invent the individual, as too many exuberant commentators still maintain. But sixteenth-century Protestant reformers gave new emphasis to the (religious) rights and liberties of individuals at both religious law and civil law.

A central feature of this new emphasis surfaced with the Anabaptist doctrine of adult baptism, which stressed a voluntarist understanding of religion, as opposed to conventional notions of a birthright or predestined faith. The adult individual now had to make a conscientious choice to accept the faith – metaphorically, to scale the wall of separation between the fallen world and the realm of religion and come into the garden of religion which God cultivated. Later Free Church followers converted this central image into a powerful platform of liberty of conscience and free exercise of religion not only for Christians but also eventually for all peaceable religious practitioners.

The Great Awakening in America (ca. 1720–80) built on this early Anabaptist vision. Various evangelical denominations and movements that emerged from the Great Awakening emphasized Christian conversion, the "warmed heart," the necessary spiritual rebirth of each sinful individual. On that basis, they strongly advocated the liberty of conscience of each individual along with the rights of free speech and press and the missionary duties to proselytize, both on the American frontier and abroad. Evangelicals, moreover, had a high view of the Christian Bible as the

117 Walter Klaassen, ed., *Anabaptism in Outline: Selected Primary Sources* (Scottdale, PA: Herald Press, 1973); Robert M. Friedmann, *The Theology of Anabaptism* (Scottdale, PA: Herald Press, 1973).

infallible textbook for human living. On that basis, they celebrated the use of the Bible in chapels, classrooms, prisons, and elsewhere. Evangelicals also emphasized sanctification, the process of each individual becoming holier before God, neighbor, and self. Evangelicals thus underscored a robust ethic of spiritual and moral progress, education, and improvement of all. These views helped shape the norms of religious liberty in the early American republic and eventually in countries around the world shaped by American missionaries.

Calvinist reformers set out an ever more expansive theory and law of individual rights. Many early Calvinist leaders were trained in both theology and law, and they embraced the traditional law of subjective rights. John Calvin, for example, spoke about the "the common rights of mankind" (*iura commune hominum*), the "natural rights" (*iura naturali*) of persons, the "rights of a common nature" (*communis naturae iura*), or the "the equal rights and liberties" (*pari iura et libertates*) of all.[118] Half a century later, Calvinist jurist Johannes Althusius (1557–1638) laid out a comprehensive system of what he called, first, spiritual or religious rights and liberties and, second, temporal or civil rights and liberties, drawn variously from the Bible, the Talmud, Roman law, the medieval *ius commune*, and the Spanish neoscholastics in Salamanca.[119] In 1641, New England jurist and theologian, Nathaniel Ward (1578–1652), drew all these insights together into the *Body of Liberties* for the new colony of Massachusetts Bay.[120]

Early modern Calvinists also grounded these rights in the signature Protestant teaching first made famous by Luther, that every person is both saint and sinner (*simul iustus et peccator*).[121] On the one hand, they argued, the individual is created in the image of God and justified by faith in God. Called to a distinct vocation that stands equal in dignity and sanctity to all others, the individual is prophet, priest, and sovereign and is responsible to exhort, minister, and rule in the community. Each person, therefore, stands individually and equally before God. Each person is vested with a natural liberty to live, believe, and serve God and neighbor. Each is entitled to the vernacular scripture, to education, and to work in a vocation. On the other hand, human beings are sinful and prone to evil and egoism. All persons, therefore, need the restraint of the law to deter them from evil and to drive them to repentance. All need the natural association of others to exhort, minister, and rule them with law and with love. All therefore are inherently communal creatures, symbiotically bonded with families, churches, and political communities.

These Protestant teachings helped to inspire many of the early modern revolutions fought in the name of human rights and democracy. They were the driving ideological forces behind the revolts of the French Huguenots, Dutch Pietists, and

[118] See detailed sources in Witte, *The Reformation of Rights*, 56–59.

[119] Ibid., 169–81.

[120] See Chapter 2.

[121] See sources in John Witte, Jr., *God's Joust, God's Justice: Law and Religion in Western Tradition* (Grand Rapids, MI and Cambridge: Wm. B. Eerdmans Publishing Co, 2006), 49–62.

Scottish Presbyterians against their monarchical oppressors in the later sixteenth and seventeenth centuries. They were critical weapons in the arsenal of the revolutionaries in England, America, and France. They were important sources of the great age of democratic construction in later eighteenth- and nineteenth-century America and Western Europe.[122]

ENLIGHTENMENT REFORMS

While medieval Catholics grounded rights in natural law and ancient charters, and while early modern Protestants grounded them in biblical texts and theological anthropology, Enlightenment writers in Europe and North America grounded rights in human nature and the social contract. Building in part on the ancient ideas of Cicero, Seneca, and other Stoics about a prepolitical state of nature, as well as on Calvinist ideas of covenant community, John Locke (1632–1704), Jean Jacques Rousseau (1712–78), Thomas Jefferson (1743–1826), and others argued for a new contractarian theory of human rights and political order. Each person, they argued, was created equal in virtue and dignity and vested with inherent and unalienable rights of life, liberty, and property. Each was naturally capable of choosing his or her own means and measures of happiness without necessary external references or divine commandments. All persons in their natural state were free to exercise their natural rights fully. But life in this "state of nature" was, at minimum, "inconvenient," as Locke put it – if not "solitary, poor, nasty, brutish, and short," in the phrase of Thomas Hobbes (1588–1679). For there was no means to balance and broker disputes between one person's rights and all others; no incentive to invest or create property or conclude contracts when one's title was not sure; no mechanism for dealing with the needs of children, the weak, the disabled, or the vulnerable. Consequently, rational persons chose to move from the state of nature into societies with stable governments. They did so by entering into social contracts and ratifying constitutions to govern their newly created societies. By these instruments, persons agreed to sacrifice or limit some of their natural rights for the sake of creating social order and peace, and they agreed to delegate their natural rights of self-rule to elected officials who would represent and exercise executive, legislative, and judicial authority on their behalf. At the same time, however, these social and political contracts enumerated the various "unalienable" rights and liberties that all persons were to enjoy without derogation, and the conditions of due process of law under which alienable rights could be abridged or taken away. These contracts also stipulated the right of the people to elect and change their representatives in government, and to be tried in all cases by a jury of peers.

122 John Witte, Jr., ed., *Christianity and Democracy in Global Context*, repr. ed. (London: Routledge, 2020).

Enlightenment views helped shape the American and French constitutions, in particular. The Virginia Declaration of Rights (1776), for example, provided in Section 1: "That all men are by nature equally free and independent, and have certain inherent rights, of which, when they enter into a state of society, they cannot, by any compact, deprive or divest their posterity; namely, the enjoyment of life and liberty, with the means of acquiring and possessing property, and pursuing and obtaining happiness and safety." The Declaration went on to specify the rights of the people to vote and to run for office, their "indubitable, unalienable, and indefeasible right to reform, alter or abolish" their government if necessary, various traditional criminal procedural protections, the right to jury trial in civil and criminal cases, freedom of press, and various freedoms of religion. But the Declaration also reflected traditional Christian sentiments in Sections 15 and 16: "[N]o free government, or the blessings of liberty, can be preserved to any people but by a firm adherence to justice, moderation, temperance, frugality, and virtue and by frequent recurrence to fundamental principles." Further, "it is the mutual duty of all to practice Christian forbearance, love, and charity towards each other."[123] In this formulation, subjective rights were qualified and complemented by traditional moral virtues and duties. Even stronger traditional qualifications stood alongside Enlightenment views in the 1780 Massachusetts Constitution and other New England state constitutions.[124]

The 1791 Bill of Rights, comprising ten amendments to the 1789 US Constitution, provided a new set of rights of national citizenship to be enforced by the federal courts. While the Constitution itself had spoken generically of the "blessings of liberty" and specified a few discrete "privileges and immunities" in Articles I and IV, it was left to the Bill of Rights to enumerate these blessings and privileges. The Bill of Rights guaranteed citizens freedoms of religion, speech, assembly, and press; the right to bear arms; freedom from forced quartering of soldiers; freedom from illegal searches and seizures; various criminal procedural protections; the right to jury trial in civil cases; the guarantee not to be to be deprived of life, liberty, or property without due process of law; and protection against eminent domain without just compensation. This set of rights was later augmented by other amendments, the most important of which prohibited slavery, guaranteed equal protection and due process, and gave all adults the right to vote.[125] Contemporary defenders of the Bill of Rights used a variety of arguments – Enlightenment reason being among the best remembered today – but many of these rights had earlier Christian roots, too, and plenty of Christian champions and advocates across the denominational spectrum of the later eighteenth century.

123 In Francis N. Thorpe, ed., *The Federal and State Constitutions, Colonial Charters, and Other Organic Laws*, 7 vols. (Washington, DC: Government Printing Office, 1909), 7:3813.

124 See Chapter 4.

125 US Constitution, preamble; Arts. 1.9, 1.10, IV; Amendments 1–8, 13–15, 19, 24, 26, reprinted with many prototypes and defenses in Philip B. Kurland and Ralph S. Lerner, eds., *The Founders' Constitution*, 5 vols. (Indianapolis: Liberty Fund, 2000).

Enlightenment arguments proved more singularly decisive in shaping the French Declaration of the Rights of Man and of the Citizen (1789). This signature instrument, which eventually helped to revolutionize a good deal of Western Europe, enumerated various "natural, unalienable, and sacred rights," including liberty, property, security, and resistance to oppression; "the freedom to do everything which injures no one else"; the right to participate in the foundation and formulation of law; equality of all citizens before the law, and equal eligibility to all dignities and all public positions and occupations according to one's abilities. The Declaration also included basic criminal procedural protections, freedom of (religious) opinions, freedoms of speech and press, and rights to property.[126] Both the French and American constitutions and declarations were essential prototypes for a whole raft of constitutional and international documents on rights and liberties forged in the next two centuries, culminating in the Universal Declaration of Human Rights (1948) and the many declarations, covenants, and treaties that it inspired.

INTERNATIONAL NORMS OF HUMAN RIGHTS AND RELIGIOUS FREEDOM TODAY

The Universal Declaration of Human Rights was forged in the tragic aftermath of World War II by the United Nations Commission on Human Rights, chaired by American First Lady Eleanor Roosevelt.[127] The drafting committee and the Commission as a whole were broadly inclusive in membership. The main drafters included René Cassin (a Jewish jurist from France and later Nobel Peace Prize winner), Peng-chun Chang (a distinguished Confucian scholar from China), John Peters Humphrey (a leading Canadian jurist who was then part of the UN Secretariat and prepared much of the first draft), Charles Malik (a Maronite Christian from Lebanon), and Jacques Maritain (a prominent French Catholic philosopher and France's ambassador to the Vatican). The Commission itself had representation from countries with majoritarian Atheist, Buddhist, Christian, Confucian, Hindu, and Muslim populations, including India, China, the Philippines, the USSR, Iran, Egypt, Lebanon, Austria, France, the United States, Panama, and Chile. The Commission further drew on bills of rights from around the world and drew from the expert opinions of sundry scholars, advocates, and NGOs of all manner of professions and confessions.[128]

126 In Léon Duguit, *Les constitutions et les principales lois politiques de la France Depuis*, 4th ed. (Paris: R. Pichon et Durand-Auzias, 1925), 1.

127 This section is distilled and updated from John Witte, Jr. and M. Christian Green, eds., *Religion and Human Rights: An Introduction* (Oxford: Oxford University Press, 2012), 3–24.

128 See detailed documentation in William Schabas, *The Universal Declaration of Human Rights: The Travaux Préparatoires*, 3 vols. (Cambridge: Cambridge University Press, 2013) and analysis in Mary Ann Glendon, *A World Made New: Eleanor Roosevelt and the Universal Declaration of Human Rights* (New York: Random House, 2001).

Jacques Maritain, a member of the Declaration drafting committee, was asked how such a diverse group of participants holding such divergent viewpoints could agree to a definitive list of fundamental rights. He replied: "Yes, we agree about the rights *but on condition no one asks us why*." The goal, he elaborated, was to agree "not on the basis of common speculative ideas, but on common practical ideas, not on the affirmation of one and the same conception of the world, of man, and of knowledge, but upon the affirmation of a single body of beliefs for guidance in action."[129] That "single body of beliefs" was set out in the Preamble and Article 1 of the Universal Declaration, which affirmed that "the inherent dignity and the equal and inalienable rights of all members of the human family is the foundation of freedom, justice and peace in the world." Respect for human rights and human dignity is essential in all times and places, the Declaration insisted, and must be respected by and for all persons and peoples.

In thirty pithy articles, the Declaration set out the "universal rights" of all human beings: equality and freedom from discrimination; rights to life, liberty, privacy, and security of person; rights to national and cultural identity; freedom from slavery, servitude, and cruel and barbarous treatment; sundry criminal procedural protections; freedom of movement and asylum; rights to marriage and family life with special protections for mothers and children; rights to property; freedom of thought, conscience, religion, opinion, expression, and assembly; freedom to political representation and participation; rights to labor, employment, and social security; and rights to healthcare, education, and cultural participation. In the decades after the Declaration, many of these discrete rights became subjects of more elaborate covenants, conventions, and declarations on rights.[130] These international instruments, which fall largely under the vast auspices of the United Nations, were echoed and elaborated in both regional instruments like the 1950 European Convention on Human Rights and the 1969 American Convention on Human Rights. They were further elaborated in the numerous national constitutional provisions and cases issued during the political reconstruction of the world after World War II as well as in the many postcolonial democratic revolutions that followed in Africa, Latin America, and South Asia.[131]

The 1948 Universal Declaration and subsequent human rights instruments included both "freedom rights" (speech, press, religion, and the like) and "welfare rights" (education, labor, health care, and more). Later instruments also outlined rights to peace, orderly development, and environmental protection. One of the hallmarks of the modern international human rights movement is that human rights

[129] Ibid., 77–78 (emphasis added).

[130] See Ian Brownlie and Guy S. Goodwin-Gill, eds., *Basic Documents on Human Rights*, 6th ed. (Oxford: Oxford University Press, 2010).

[131] See a good overview in Jack Donnelly, *Universal Human Rights in Theory and Practice*, 3rd ed. (Ithaca, NY: Cornell University Press, 2013); Jack Donnelly and Daniel J. Whelan, *International Human Rights*, 6th ed. (London: Routledge, 2020).

are "interrelated," "indivisible," and "interdependent."[132] Freedom rights are useful only if a party's basic welfare rights to food, shelter, health care, education, and security are adequately protected. The rights to worship, speech, or association mean little to someone clubbed in their bed, starving in the street, or dying from a treatable disease. In turn, welfare rights to, say, education or work mean little if the state dictates what you learn, where you work, what you say, and with whom you associate. President Roosevelt already highlighted the interdependency of these rights in his famous "four freedoms" speech – freedom of religion and speech, and freedom from fear and want – that helped inaugurate the modern human rights revolution. The Universal Declaration and the international rights instruments that followed from it reflect this basic premise.

While religious persons and communities often find refuge in sundry rights claims shared with nonreligious claimants, a special category of religious rights and freedoms has also emerged to deal with some of the unique needs of religion. Articles 2 and 18 of the Universal Declaration called these the rights of "thought, conscience, and belief" and the freedom from religious discrimination. Four international instruments, elaborating the Declaration, contain the most critical protections of religious rights and liberties: (1) the International Covenant on Civil and Political Rights ("the 1966 Covenant"),[133] (2) the United Nations Declaration on the Elimination of All Forms of Intolerance and Discrimination Based on Religion or Belief ("the 1981 Declaration on Religion or Belief"),[134] (3) the Concluding Document of the Vienna Follow-up Meeting of Representatives of the Participating States of the Conference on Security and Cooperation in Europe (the "1989 Vienna Concluding Document"),[135] and (4) the Declaration on the Rights of Persons Belonging to National or Ethnic, Religious, and Linguistic Minorities ("the 1992 Minorities Declaration").[136]

The 1966 International Covenant on Civil and Political Rights, a binding treaty accepted by 165 countries today, largely repeats the capacious guarantee of religious rights and liberties first announced in the 1948 Universal Declaration. Article 18 of the 1966 Covenant reads:

> 1. Everyone shall have the right to freedom of thought, conscience and religion. This right shall include freedom to have or to adopt a religion or belief of his choice, and freedom, either individually or in community with others and in public or private, to manifest his religion or belief in worship, observance, practice and teaching.

[132] United Nations Office of the High Commission, "Vienna Declaration and Programme of Action" (June 14–25, 1993), para. 5.

[133] GA Res. 2200A (XXI), 21 UN GAOR Supp. (No. 16) at 52, UN Doc. A/6316, 999 UNTS (Dec. 16, 1966).

[134] GA Res. 36/55, UN GAOR Supp. (No. 151), UN Doc. A/RES/36/55 (Nov. 25, 1981).

[135] 28 ILM 527.

[136] GA Res. 47/135, Annex, UN Doc. A/Res/47/135/Annex (Dec. 18, 1992).

2. No one shall be subject to coercion which would impair his freedom to have or to adopt a religion or belief of his choice.
3. Freedom to manifest one's religion or beliefs may be subject only to such limitations as are prescribed by law and are necessary to protect public safety, order, health, or morals or the fundamental rights and freedoms of others.
4. The States Parties to the present Covenant undertake to have respect for the liberty of parents and, when applicable, legal guardians to ensure the religious and moral education of their children in conformity with their own convictions.

Article 18 distinguishes between the right to freedom of religion or belief and the freedom to manifest one's religion or belief – what American law labels as liberty of conscience and free exercise of religion respectively. The right to freedom of religion (the freedom to have, to alter, or to adopt a religion of one's choice) is an absolute right from which no derogation may be made and which may not be restricted or impaired in any manner. Freedom to manifest or exercise one's religion (individually or collectively, publicly or privately) may be subject only to such limitations as are prescribed by law and are necessary to protect public safety, order, health, or morals or the fundamental rights and freedoms of others. The latter provision is an exhaustive list of the grounds allowed to limit the manifestation of religion. The requirement of necessity implies that any such limitation on the manifestation of religion must be proportionate to its aim to protect any of the listed state interests. Such limitations must not be applied in a manner that would vitiate the rights guaranteed in Article 18.[137]

Article 20.2 of the 1966 Covenant calls for States Parties to prohibit "any advocacy of national, racial, or religious hatred that constitutes incitement to discrimination, hostility, or violence." Articles 2 and 26 further require equal treatment of all persons before the law and prohibit discrimination based, among other grounds, on religion.

The 1981 Declaration on Religion or Belief elaborates the religious liberty provisions that the 1966 Covenant adumbrated. Like the 1966 Covenant, the 1981 Declaration on its face applies to "everyone," whether "individually or in community," "in public or in private." Articles 1 and 6 of the 1981 Declaration set forth a lengthy illustrative catalogue of rights to "freedom of thought, conscience, and religion" – repeating but also illustrating more concretely the 1966 Covenant's guarantees of liberty of conscience and free exercise of religion. Article 6 enumerates these rights as follows:

(a) To worship or assemble in connection with a religion or belief and to establish and maintain places for these purposes;
(b) To establish and maintain appropriate charitable or humanitarian institutions;

137 See Symposium, "The Permissible Scope of Legal Limitations on the Freedom of Religion and Belief," *Emory International Law Review* 19 (2005), 465–1320.

(c) To make, to acquire and use to an adequate extent the necessary articles and materials related to the rites or customs of a religion or belief;
(d) To write, issue, and disseminate relevant publications in these areas;
(e) To teach a religion or belief in places suitable for these purposes;
(f) To solicit and receive voluntary financial and other contributions from individuals and institutions;
(g) To train, to appoint, to elect, or to designate by succession appropriate leaders called for by the requirements and standards of any religion or belief;
(h) To observe days of rest and to celebrate holy days and ceremonies in accordance with the precepts of one's religion or belief; and
(i) To establish and maintain communications with individuals and communities in matters of religion and belief at the national and international levels.

Further guidance for the protection of a person's freedom of conscience is provided in the 1990 Copenhagen Document which, glossing the 1981 Declaration, recognizes "the right of everyone to have conscientious objections to military service" and calls for "various forms of alternative service … of a non-combatant or civilian nature," which are "compatible with the reasons for conscientious objection."[138]

The 1981 Declaration also dwells specifically on the religious rights of children and their parents. It guarantees the rights of parents (or guardians) to organize life within their household and to educate their children "in accordance with their religion or beliefs." Such parental responsibility within and beyond the household, however, must be discharged in accordance with the "best interests of the child." At a minimum, the parents' religious upbringing or education of their child "must not be injurious to his physical or mental health or to his full development." Moreover, the Declaration provides more generically, "the child shall be protected from any form of discrimination on the ground of religion or belief. He shall be brought up in a spirit of understanding, tolerance, friendship among peoples, peace and universal brotherhood, respect for freedom of religion or belief of others, and in full conscience that his energy and talents should be devoted to the service of his fellow men." The Declaration leaves juxtaposed the parents' right to rear and educate their children in accordance with their own religion and beliefs and the state's power to protect the best interests of the child, including the lofty aspirations for the child's upbringing. Despite ample debate on point, the Declaration drafters offered no specific principles to resolve the disputes that would inevitably arise between the rights of parents and the powers of the state operating *in loco parentis*. Some further guidance on this subject is provided by the 1989 UN Convention on the Rights of the

138 Document of the Copenhagen Meeting of Representatives of the Participating States of the Conference on the Human Dimension of the Conference on Security and Co-operation in Europe (1990), Principle 18, reprinted in OSCE/ODIHR, *Guidelines for Review of Legislation Pertaining to Religion or Belief* (June 2004), 45. See discussion of conscientious objection cases in the European Court of Human Rights in Chapter 8, p. 237–38.

Child – though the issue of parental rights over their child's religious upbringing and welfare remains highly contested.[139]

As these children's rights provisions illustrate, the 1981 Declaration, like the 1966 Covenant, allows the "manifestation of religion" to be subjected to "appropriate" state regulation and adjudication. The 1981 Declaration permits states to enforce against religious individuals and institutions general regulations designed to protect public safety, order, health, or morals, or the fundamental rights and freedoms of others. It is assumed, however, that in all such instances, the grounds for such regulations are enumerated and explicit and that such regulations abide by the international legal principles of necessity and proportionality.

The 1981 Declaration includes more elaborate prohibitions than the 1966 Covenant on religious discrimination and intolerance. Article 2 bars religious "discrimination by any State, institution, group of persons, or person." And it defines such discrimination as "any distinction, exclusion, restriction or preference based on religion or belief, and having as its purpose or as its effect nullification or impairment of the recognition, enjoyment or exercise of human rights or fundamental freedoms on an equal basis." All such discrimination based on religion or belief, the Declaration insists, is "an affront to human dignity" and a "disavowal" of the "fundamental freedoms" that form the cornerstone of national and international peace and cooperation. Accordingly, the Declaration calls on all States Parties "to take effective measures to prevent and eliminate" such discrimination "in all fields of civil, economic, political, social, and cultural life," including rescinding laws that foster discrimination and enacting laws that forbid it.

The 1981 Declaration includes suggested principles of implementation and application of these guarantees. It urges states to take all "effective measures to prevent and eliminate discrimination on the grounds of religion or belief in the recognition, exercise and enjoyment of human rights and fundamental freedoms in all fields of civil, economic, political, social and cultural life." It urges states to remove local laws that perpetuate or allow religious discrimination and to enact local criminal and civil laws to combat religious discrimination and intolerance.

The 1989 Vienna Concluding Document extends the religious liberty norms of the 1981 Declaration, particularly for religious groups. Principle 16 rounds out the list of enumerated rights guarantees from the 1981 Declaration:

> 16. In order to ensure the freedom of the individual to profess and practice religion or belief the participating States will, inter alia,
>
> A. take effective measures to prevent and eliminate discrimination against individuals or communities, on the grounds of religion or belief in the recognition, exercise and enjoyment of human rights and fundamental

[139] See further John Witte, Jr., *Church, State, and Family: Reconciling Traditional Teachings and Modern Liberties* (Cambridge: Cambridge University Press, 2019), 234–73 and Symposium, "What's Wrong with Rights for Children?" *Emory International Law Review* 20 (2006), 1–239.

freedoms in all fields of civil, political, economic, social and cultural life, and ensure the effective equality between believers and non-believers;

B. foster a climate of mutual tolerance and respect between believers of different communities as well as between believers and non-believers;

C. grant upon their request to communities of believers, practicing or prepared to practice their faith within the constitutional framework of their states, recognition of the status provided for them in their respective countries;

D. respect the right of religious communities to establish and maintain freely accessible places of worship or assembly; organize themselves according to their own hierarchical and institutional structure; select, appoint and replace their personnel in accordance with their respective requirements and standards as well as with any freely accepted arrangement between them and their State; solicit and receive voluntary financial and other contributions;

E. engage in consultations with religious faiths, institutions and organizations in order to achieve a better understanding of the requirements of religious freedom;

F. respect the right of everyone to give and receive religious education in the language of his choice, individually or in association with others;

G. in this context respect, inter alia, the liberty of parents to ensure the religious and moral education of their children in conformity with their own convictions;

H. allow the training of religious personnel in appropriate institutions;

I. respect the right of individual believers and communities of believers to acquire, possess, and use sacred books, religious publications in the language of their choice and other articles and materials related to the practice of religion or belief;

J. allow religious faiths, institutions and organizations to produce and import and disseminate religious publications and materials;

K. favorably consider the interest of religious communities in participating in public dialogue, inter alia, through mass media.

A number of these religious group rights provisions in the Vienna Concluding Document reflect the international right to self-determination of peoples. This right has long been recognized as a basic norm of international law, and is included, among other places, in the 1966 Covenant, the 1989 Child Convention, and the 1990 Copenhagen Document. It has its fullest expression in the 1992 Minorities Declaration. The right to self-determination belongs to "peoples" within plural societies. It affords a religious community the right to practice its religion, an ethnic community the right to promote its culture, and a linguistic community the right to speak its language without undue state interference or legal restrictions. Governments are required to secure the interests of distinct sections of the population that constitute a people in this sense. The 1992 Minorities Declaration clearly spells out that obligation: protect and encourage conditions for the promotion of the concerned groups' identities as minorities; afford to minorities the special competence to participate effectively in decisions pertinent to the group to which they belong; do not discriminate in any way against any person on the basis of his or her group identity; take actions to secure their equal treatment at law. The Minorities Declaration further provides that: "States shall take measures to create favorable conditions to enable persons belonging to minorities to express their characteristics and to develop their culture, language, religion, traditions and customs, except where specific practices are in violation of national law and contrary to international standards."[140] So conceived, the right to religious self-determination provides religious groups some of the same strong protections afforded to religious individuals under the freedom of conscience guarantee.

The 2007 United Nations Declaration on the Rights of Indigenous Peoples gives specific elaboration of these rights of self-determination for Indigenous, aboriginal, or first peoples. Article 12 provides that "Indigenous peoples have the right to manifest, practise, develop and teach their spiritual and religious traditions, customs and ceremonies; the right to maintain, protect, and have access in privacy to their religious and cultural sites; the right to the use and control of their ceremonial objects; and the right to the repatriation of their human remains." Article 25 provides further that "Indigenous peoples have the right to maintain and strengthen their distinctive spiritual relationship with their traditionally owned or otherwise occupied and used lands, territories, waters and coastal seas and other resources and to uphold their responsibilities to future generations in this regard."[141]

These are the basic international provisions on religious rights and freedoms on the books. Various regional instruments, notably the European Charter on Human Rights (1950), the American Convention on Human Rights (1969), and the African Charter on Human and People's Rights (1981), elaborate some of these guarantees. Further amplification is provided in various religious declarations and treaties and concordats involving religious bodies.

These international instruments highlight the hottest religion and human issues that now regularly confront national and international tribunals: How to protect religious and cultural minorities within a majoritarian religious culture – particularly controversial groups like Muslims, Mormons, Bahias, Jehovah's Witnesses, Scientologists, Unification Church members, and Indigenous peoples who often bring charges of religious and cultural discrimination. How to define limits on religious and antireligious exercises and expressions that cause offense or harm to others or elicit charges of blasphemy, defamation, or sacrilege. How to adjudicate challenges that a state's proscriptions or prescriptions run directly counter to a party's core claims of conscience or cardinal commandments of the faith. How to balance private and public exercises of religion, including the liberty of conscience of one

140 1992 Minorities Declaration, art. 4.2.

141 United Nations Declaration on the Rights of Indigenous Peoples, UN GAOR, A/61/L.67/Annex (2007).

party to be left alone and the free exercise right of another to proselytize. How to balance conflicts between the rights of parents to bring up their children in the faith and the duties of the state to protect the best interest of the child. How to protect the distinct religious needs of prisoners, soldiers, refugees, and others who do not enjoy ready access to traditional forms and forums of religious worship and expression.

Many religion and human rights issues involve religious groups, for whom the right to organize as a legal entity with juridical personality is itself often a critical issue. How to negotiate the complex needs and norms of religious groups without according them too much sovereignty over their members or too little relief from secular courts in the event of fundamental rights violations by religious tribunals. How to balance the rights of religious groups to self-determination and self-governance and the guarantees of freedom from discrimination based on religion, gender, culture, and sexual orientation. How to balance competing religious groups who each claim access to a common holy site, or a single religious or cultural group whose sacred site is threatened with desecration, development, or disaster. How to protect the relations between local religious communities and their foreign coreligionists. How to adjudicate intra- or interreligious disputes that come before secular tribunals for resolution. How to determine the proper levels of state cooperation with and support of religious officials and institutions in the delivery of vital social services – child care, education, charity, medical services, disaster relief, among others.

Chapters 6 to 9 will analyze and illustrate how the US Supreme Court and the pan-European courts have dealt with some of these hard issues in concrete cases. But before getting to these, we will first analyze in more detail the development of other key human rights and religious freedom moments and movements in the Western legal tradition – beginning in the next chapter with Magna Carta, the anchor text of Anglo-American constitutionalism.

2

Magna Cartas Old and New

Rights and Liberties in the Anglo-American Common Law

Magna Carta was a critical early source of rights and liberties in the Anglo-American common law tradition. Charters and grants of rights, liberties, and privileges were quite common in the Middle Ages, both in England and on the Continent.[1] But unlike earlier charters, going back to eighth-century Anglo-Saxon days,[2] Magna Carta now "conveyed in general what the king had hitherto sold in particular" to a few elites, and it did so in much more sweeping terms.[3] Because of its new breadth, Magna Carta ultimately proved more inspirational for later English and American law than any other medieval charter.[4]

Stephen Langton, the archbishop of Canterbury, helped to guide the creation[5] of this famous document at Runnymede, England, in 1215 at the insistence of the barons, who were threatening civil war in retaliation for excessive taxes, forced loans, and other oppressive measures of King John and his royal predecessors. Although nullified ten weeks later, with consequent civil war, the charter was reissued with

1 R. H. Helmholz, "Magna Carta and the Law of Nations," in Robin Griffith-Jones and Mark Hill, eds., *Magna Carta, Religion, and the Rule of Law* (Cambridge: Cambridge University Press, 2015), 70–80; R. H. Helmholz, "Magna Carta and the *Ius Commune,*" *University of Chicago Law Review* 66, no. 2 (1999), 297–371.

2 See examples and sources in Chapter 1, p. 25–26.

3 J. C. Holt and George Garnett, *Magna Carta*, 3rd ed. (Cambridge: Cambridge University Press, 2015), 72–73. The text continues: "Magna Carta was not a sudden jump into the darkness of corporate liberties but rather the last strides on a long journey which had started far back in the history of the English kingdom, and which had been illuminated in the twelfth century by the increasing confidence with which men sought and granted such liberties." Ibid., 73. For illustrative antecedents, see A. J. Robertson, *Anglo-Saxon Charters*, repr. ed. (Cambridge: Cambridge University Press, 2009), esp. 69–71, 93–95, setting out earlier "chartered freedoms." See further Chapter 1, p. 25–26, of this book on various other "*rihta*" or "*ryhtae*" and *freoles* and *freo-doms* in Anglo-Saxon law.

4 More than 170 references to Magna Carta appear in US Supreme Court cases. Stephen J. Wermeil, "Magna Carta in Supreme Court Jurisprudence," in Daniel Barstow, Andrea Martinez, and Roy E. Brownell, eds., *Magna Carta and the Rule of Law* (Chicago: American Bar Association, 2014), 111–40.

5 How much direct influence Langton had on the document is disputed. See recently D. A. Carpenter, "Archbishop Langton and Magna Carta: His Doubts and His Hypocrisy," *English Historical Review* 126 (2011), 1041–65.

revisions several more times – most authoritatively in 1225 and 1297.[6] Although cast in the distinct feudal language of the day and still largely focused on the aristocracy, Magna Carta nevertheless made provision for early forms of fair taxation; rights related to marriage, property, and inheritance; various freedoms of trade, travel, and commerce; freedom of the church; and several procedural rights.[7]

Important for the later development of religious freedom was the opening guarantee of Article 1 of the original 1215 Magna Carta: "the English church is to be free, and is to have its rights in whole and its liberties unharmed."[8] Important for the rights of local government were the guarantees that London and "all other cities and boroughs, and villas and ports, have all their [ancient] liberties and free customs."[9] Particularly prescient for later Western procedural rights were Articles 39 and 40 (which became Article 29 in the better known 1225 version): "No freeman [or freewoman – *liber homo*[10]] shall be taken or imprisoned, or disseised, or outlawed, or banished, or in any ways destroyed, nor will we pass upon him, nor will we send upon him, unless by the lawful judgment of his peers, or by the law of the land. To no one will we sell, to none will we deny, or delay, right or justice."[11] Article 52 echoed this guarantee for pilgrims and crusaders who returned home to find their properties confiscated: "If any one has been dispossessed or deprived by us, without the judgment of his peers, of his lands, castles, liberties, or right, we will forthwith restore them to him."[12] The final Article 63 suggested even wider application of these guarantees: "Wherefore we will and firmly enjoin, that the Church of England be free, that all men in our kingdom have and hold all the aforesaid liberties, rights, and concessions, truly and peaceably, freely and quietly, fully and wholly to themselves and their heirs, in all things and places, for ever."[13]

6 For a careful tabular summary and review of the different editions of Magna Carta, see David Starkey, *Magna Carta: The Medieval Roots of Modern Politics* (New York: Quercus, 2015), 160–255.

7 Anne Pallister, *Magna Carta: The Heritage of Liberty* (Oxford: Clarendon Press, 1971).

8 Using translation in Randy J. Holland, ed., *Magna Carta: Muse and Mentor* (Eagan, MN: Thomson Reuters, 2014), 239. In the 9–0 Supreme Court case of *Hosanna-Tabor Evangelical Lutheran School v. EEOC*, 130 S. Ct. 694, 702–03 (2013), Chief Justice Roberts traced the modern concept of "church freedom" to Article 1 of Magna Carta: "By forbidding the 'establishment of religion' and guaranteeing the 'free exercise thereof,' the Religion Clauses ensured that the new Federal Government – unlike the English Crown – would have no rule in filling ecclesiastical roles." But see critical views in Steven K. Green, "The Mixed Legacy of Magna Carta for Religious Freedom," *Journal of Law and Religion* 32 (2017), 207–26.

9 Magna Carta, art. 13, in Holland, *Magna Carta*, 240.

10 See "Extracts from a Treatise on Magna Carta, Probably by William Fletewood (c. 1558)," in Sir John Baker, ed. *Selected Readings and Commentaries on Magna Carta 1400–1604* (London: Selden Society, 2015), 366–92. "In these statutes 'man' is understood both of male and female." Ibid., 384. Sir Edward Coke went further: "The words of this Act being *liber homo*, it extendeth as well to sole Corporations, as Bishops, &c. as to lay men, but not to Corporations aggregate of many, as Major and Commonalty." Sir Edward Coke, "Second Part of the Institutes," in Steve Sheppard, ed., *The Selected Writings of Sir Edward Coke* (Indianapolis, IN: Liberty Fund, 2003), 2:812.

11 Magna Carta, arts. 39–40, in Holland, *Magna Carta*, 243.

12 Magna Carta, art. 52. Ibid., 244.

13 Magna Carta, art. 63. Ibid., 247.

A 1354 statute designated Article 29 and related provisions a guarantee of "due process of law" and declared that "whoever broke this statute should be excommunicated."[14] A 1368 statute declared further that every act of Parliament that violated Magna Carta should be void.[15] In 1628, Sir Edward Coke referred to Magna Carta as the "sacred" and "fundamental law" of England by which all other laws should be judged.[16] In 1765, William Blackstone named Magna Carta "the foundation of the liberty of Englishmen,"[17] only to be rhetorically outdone a century later by William Stubbs who declared: "The whole of the Constitutional History of England is a commentary on this charter."[18]

Magna Carta and other medieval charters of rights, however, were not on the order of modern comprehensive statements of rights and liberties. The rights of speech, press, association, equality, and privacy, all so central to Western constitutional law today, were only very lightly touched upon, even in the most progressive of later medieval legal texts and commentaries. Many other civil, political, social, cultural, and economic rights set out in the 1948 Universal Declaration of Human Rights and later international human rights instruments were hardly prefigured at all in Magna Carta or other medieval charters. And these medieval texts said little about how rights were to be enforced, what standards of review courts were to apply in individual cases, or what remedies were at hand for violations.

Historians have been hard at work mapping how we got from there to here – how this early medieval seedbed of rights and liberties eventually grew into the thick forest of human rights norms in place today.[19] In this chapter, I focus on one small piece of this

14 28 Edw III, ch. 3 (1354). For late medieval echoes and elaborations in statutes, cases, and commentaries, see Faith Thompson, *Magna Carta: Its Role in the Making of the English Constitution* (Minneapolis: University of Minnesota Press, 1948), 90–94; John Baker, "The Legal Force and Effect of Magna Carta," in Holland, *Magna Carta*, 65–84, with primary sources in Baker, *Selected Readings and Commentaries*.

15 42 Edw. III, ch. 1. See further Charles H. McIlwain, "Due Process of Law in Magna Carta," *Columbia Law Review* 14 (1914), 27–51; Sir John Baker, *The Reinvention of Magna Carta, 1216–1616* (Cambridge: Cambridge University Press, 2017), 21–23, 32–42.

16 Edward Coke, *The Second Part of the Institutes of the Laws of England* (London: E & R Brooke, 1797), proem[ium], A 4–9, with modern edition in Coke, *Selected Writings*, 2:746–47. Hereafter Inst. 2.

17 William Blackstone, *Commentaries on the Laws of England*, vol. 1, repr. ed. (Buffalo, NY: Hein, 1992), ch. 1. See also Lord Denning, "Runnymede, Fount of English Liberty," *The Times* (June 9, 1965), 13, which calls Magna Carta "the greatest constitutional document of all times . . . the spirit of individual liberty which has influenced our people ever since."

18 William Stubbs, *Select Charters and Other Illustrations of English Constitutional History from the Earliest Times to the Reign of Edward the First*, 9th rev., ed. H. W. C. Davis (Oxford: Clarendon Press, 1921), 291. See further Charles Donahue, "The Whole of the Constitutional History of England Is a Commentary on This Charter," *North Carolina Law Review* 94 (2016), 1521.

19 See, e.g., Jones and Hill, *Magna Carta, Religion, and the Rule of Law*; Catharine MacMillan and Charlotte Smith, eds., *Challenges to Authority and the Recognition of Rights: From Magna Carta to Modernity* (Cambridge: Cambridge University Press, 2018); Nicholas Vincent, *Magna Carta: Origins and Legacy* (Oxford: Bodleian Library, 2015); Robert Hazell and James Melton, eds., *Magna Carta and Its Modern Legacy* (Cambridge: Cambridge University Press, 2015); Elizabeth Gibson-Morgan and Alexis Chommeloux, eds., *The Rights and Aspirations of the Magna Carta* (New York: Palgrave Macmillan, 2016).

emerging map, namely, the growth of rights in later sixteenth- and seventeenth-century England and in colonial America.[20] This was an era in English history, not unlike the early thirteenth century, when chronic royal abuses prompted various English groups, particularly Puritan Calvinist groups, to rise up to rebel against the Crown and demand greater rights and liberties. The mid-seventeenth century was also a time when a massive wave of revolutionary tracts pressed not just for the restoration and expansion of the old Magna Carta but also for the creation of new Magna Cartas with many more rights and far more sweeping protections than their medieval ancestor. While no such new Magna Carta was passed in England, the old Magna Carta gained vibrant new life in the turbulent seventeenth century. Moreover, many of the other provocative rights ideas advocated by Puritan dissenters and revolutionaries from 1580 to 1660 gradually made their way into such English documents as the Petition of Right (1628), the Habeas Corpus Act (1679), the Bill of Rights (1689), and the Toleration Act (1689).

Rights ideas came to more direct and dramatic expression across the Atlantic in colonial America, notably in Puritan New England, where leaders shared some of the Calvinist theological ideas of the English revolutionaries. While several early colonial laws invoked Magna Carta and enumerated the people's rights and liberties, none did so as fully as the Massachusetts Body of Liberties of 1641, drafted by Puritan jurist and theologian Nathaniel Ward. Known as the Magna Carta of New England, this was a twenty-five-page declaration of public, private, penal, and procedural rights. It distilled the long common law tradition of rights and liberties going back to Magna Carta and added several more protections, anticipating later American state and federal constitutional laws from 1776 to 1791, where, again, rights within and beyond Magna Carta found dramatic new expression and expansion.

PREREVOLUTIONARY PURITAN APPEALS TO MAGNA CARTA

From the mid-fourteenth to the mid-sixteenth century, Magna Carta was "practically a spent force," Sir John Baker reports after an exhaustive recent study.[21] It received only passing attention in cases and commentaries and had little constitutional authority. To be sure, occasional "readings" or lectures on Magna Carta and other medieval charters, statutes, and cases were still part of the education of young lawyers in the Inns of Court,[22] which included a score of readings on Article 1 of Magna Carta on the "rights and liberties of the English church."[23] These lectures

[20] For earlier treatments, especially around the 750th anniversary of the Magna Carta, see A. E. Dick Howard, *The Road from Runnymede: Magna Carta and Constitutionalism in America* (Charlottesville: University of Virginia Press, 1968); Herbert Butterfield, *Magna Carta in the Historiography of the Sixteenth and Seventeenth Centuries* (Reading: University of Reading, 1969).

[21] Baker, *Reinvention*, 449, echoing Thompson, *Magna Carta*, 139–232.

[22] See Samuel E. Thorne, *Readings and Moots in the Inns of Court*, 2 vols. (London: Selden Society, 1954, 1990).

[23] See Margaret McGlynn, ed., *The Rights and Liberties of the English Church: Readings from the Pre-Reformation Inns of Court* (London: Selden Society, 2015).

emphasized the church's grants of liberties from papal, royal, and feudal patrons; its claims to tithes, sanctuary, benefit of clergy, and exemption from secular taxes and duties; and the church courts' jurisdiction over priests and monks, church rates and properties, consecrated cemeteries and mortuaries, marriage, inheritance, trusts, defamation, and more. One reading argued that Magna Carta's guarantee of religious *liberties* meant that the church "should be free in itself from all secular charges" while religious *rights* meant "that the judges of the Holy Church shall have cognizance, punishment, and determination of all pleas ... [that] touch the correction of the soul."[24] Beyond this cluster of specialty instruction, however, Magna Carta made little appearance in the surviving late medieval legal records.

Magna Carta became a new force after 1570, however, when Elizabeth I and her retinue began to clamp down on the growing ranks of Calvinist clergy and laity in England. The Anglican establishment labeled these Calvinists pejoratively as "Puritan" dissenters, given their zeal for a "purer" reformation of the church than obtained in Elizabethan England. Puritan reformers sought to remove bishops, lay patronage, and strict forms of liturgical vestments and clerical living. They wanted more freedom to devise worship services, liturgies, lectionaries, and religious calendars beyond the prescribed rules of the Book of Common Prayer, and to use the Geneva Bible, not the authorized Great Bible of Thomas Cranmer.[25] Parliament parried such religious liberalism with a volley of new repressive acts.[26] Archbishops Grindal and Whitgift pushed Puritans out of their pulpits and professorships and prosecuted them for violating religious establishment rules. And royal courts, notably the High Commission, prosecuted Puritans and other religious "sectaries," imposing fines, imprisonment, defrockings, forced ex officio oaths, and other sanctions. In response, Puritan defenders appealed to their common law rights and liberties, including notably those set out in Magna Carta.[27]

In 1581, Roger Snagge, a Puritan lawyer and parliamentarian, presented Magna Carta as "God's blessing plentifully poured out" on England that served to "revive the ancient laws and restore the ancient liberty and liberties to the subjects." While "some kings have forgotten this charter," and some officers of church and state are ignorantly abridging it today, Snagge declared, with intended irony and hope,

24 Reprinted in ibid., 79; see similar views in ibid., 74.

25 See Peter Lake, *Moderate Puritans and the Elizabethan Church* (Cambridge: Cambridge University Press, 2004) and representative documents in Champlin Burrage, *The Early English Dissenters (1550–1641) in Light of Recent Research*, 2 vols., repr. ed. (Cambridge: Cambridge University Press, 2012); Baker, *Reinvention*, 133–43.

26 See, e.g., 1 Eliz., ch. 1; 13 Eliz., ch. 1; 35 Eliz., ch. 1.

27 See Christopher W. Brooks, "Magna Carta in Sixteenth-Century Legal Thought," in Ellis Sandoz, ed., *The Roots of Liberty: Magna Carta, Ancient Constitution, and the Anglo-American Tradition of Rule of Law* (Indianapolis, IN: Liberty Fund, 2008), 74–83; Elliot Rose, *Cases of Conscience: Alternatives Open to Recusants and Puritans Under Elizabeth I and James I* (Cambridge: Cambridge University Press, 2009); Baker, *Reinvention*, 133–43.

Magna Carta now "is in full use, to the great comfort of all good subjects and immortal fame of her most excellent majesty," Queen Elizabeth.[28]

In 1586, William Lambarde – parliamentarian, justice of the peace, and historian – declared similarly that Magna Carta had been "bought with blood" in earlier days but was now a staple of English law and needed to be maintained:

> The times hath been when the nobility and commons of this realm have (with all humility and heart's desire) begged at the hands of their princes the continuation of their country laws and customs; and not prevailing so, they have armed themselves and have sought by force and with the adventure of their honors, goods, and lives to extort it from them. But we (God's name be blessed for it) do live in such a time and under such a prince as we need not to make suit, much less to move war, for our country laws and liberties. We have no cause to strive so much and so long about Magna Charta, the Great Charter of England, as it was called. For our prince hath therein already prevented us, so that not only the parts of the Great Charter but also many other laws and statutes no less fit and profitable for us than they are freely yielded unto us.[29]

Writing in 1591, parliamentarian Robert Beale interpreted Magna Carta's due process guarantee against a person's being "disseised of his liberties" to include the "religious liberties" then being systematically and unilaterally stripped from Puritans and other nonconformists. "This manner of proceeding taketh away the benefit of the great charter, which is the franchise of the whole realm, in arresting and depriving men without sufficient cause, in depriving them of their freehold *absque et contra legem* [beyond and against the law], being not indicted and no suit of party offered against them, as the law speaketh."[30] Beale protested even more strongly that Puritans were forced to swear "ex officio" oaths, disavowing their Calvinism in favor of established Anglicanism on pain of forfeiting their property and profession, if not their life and limb: "The laws of England require an exterior fact or action contrary to law, as all human laws do or ought to do," Beale insisted. They "establisheth not an interior jurisdiction of men's hearts and thoughts." These coerced oaths "savoureth more of a Spanish inquisition than Christian charity."[31] Puritan lawyer and parliamentarian James Morice likewise denounced the High Commission's high-handed treatment of religious dissenters as an "ungodly and intolerable inquisition" by which "our secret deeds, words, and thoughts, no way offensive to the public peace, are abused as means and instruments to deprive us of our precious liberty, countenances, callings, freeholds and freedoms .... Where is now become the great

28 Snagge, *Antiquity of the Chancery*, 8–12, quoted and discussed in Baker, *Reinvention*, 251–55. See also Snagge's lectures on Magna Carta in Baker, *Readings*, 256–64.

29 Conyers Read, ed., *William Lambarde and Local Government: His "Ephemeris" and Twenty-Nine Charges to Juries and Commissions* (Ithaca, NY: Cornell University Press, 1962), 79–80. See context in Brooks, "Magna Carta," 80.

30 In Baker, *Reinvention*, 271.

31 Ibid., 259–60.

charter of England, obtained by many difficulties, confirmed by sundry Acts of Parliament, [and] fortified by public and solemn sentence of ex[communication]?"[32]

Appeals to Magna Carta grew more urgent and more frequent in the early seventeenth century, as James I and Charles I grew more repressive in their policies against religious dissenters and more insistent on their absolutist claims to "the divine right of kings."[33] Leading English jurists argued that Magna Carta's guarantees of rights and liberties were the birthright of all peaceable churches, not just the Church of England, and of all English subjects, not just aristocratic freemen. In 1616, for example, Sir Francis Ashley, a barrister and parliamentarian, called Magna Carta "the law of laws" of England. On account of Magna Carta, he declared with rhetorical flourish, all of us English subjects

> have property in our goods, title to our lands, liberty for our persons, and safety for our lives. . . . [B]y force of this statute every free subject may have remedy done to his persons, lands, or goods. And not only so, for that would but give recompense for a wrong done; but this statute also *prevents* wrongs, for by virtue thereof no man shall be punished before he be condemned, and no man shall be condemned before he be heard, and none shall be heard but his just defense shall be allowed.

Magna Carta protects other procedural rights, too, Ashley continued: "By this statute are condemned and prohibited all judgements without hearing the party and without trial, and all unlawful trials and all judgements by judges not lawfully authorized, and all manner of unlawful proceedings to judgment, and all unlawful executions." Everyone also has the privilege against self-incrimination: "No free subject may be compelled by any power to be his own accuser in judgement in causes criminal and penal." And parties must not be disseized of any liberty without due process of law: "for it is thralldom to all subjects that the liberty of the old common law should be taken from them."[34]

Sir Edward Coke. The strongest champion of Magna Carta in the early seventeenth century was Sir Edward Coke, the greatest jurist in his day, if not in the history of England altogether.[35] While serving as chief justice of the Court of Common Pleas from 1606 to 1613 and then as chief justice of the Court of King's Bench from 1613 to 1616, Coke repeatedly blocked the efforts of James I to impose taxes without the consent of Parliament; to make new laws by royal proclamation alone rather than by act of Parliament; and to remove church cases from the common law courts to the

32 Ibid., 272.

33 See esp. James I, *The True Lawe of Free Monarchies* (London: T.C., 1603) and *The Political Works of James I, Reprinted from the Edition of 1616* (Cambridge, MA: Harvard University Press, 1918).

34 BL MS. Harley, 4841, folio 3v, 41, 51–51v, with analysis and further texts in Baker, *Reinvention*, 427–35; Thompson, *Magna Carta*, 284–93.

35 See sources and discussion in Harold J. Berman, "The Origins of Historical Jurisprudence: Coke, Selden, Hale," *Yale Law Journal* 103 (1994), 1651, 1673–94; David Chan Smith, "Sir Edward Coke: Faith, Law, and the Search for Stability in Reformation England," in Mark Hill and R. H. Helmholz, eds., *Great Christian Jurists in English History* (Cambridge: Cambridge University Press, 2015), 93–114.

royal Court of High Commission. Coke cited these and other royal efforts as contrary to the laws of the land and the liberties of the people. When Coke refused to repent of his action, the king removed him from the bench in 1616 and ordered him to expunge from his writings any references to limits on royal prerogative, an order which Coke largely ignored. For the next dozen years, first as a member of the Privy Council and then as a member of Parliament, Coke continued to challenge what he saw as royal violations of the rights, liberties, and privileges of Parliament and the people.

When, in 1621, the king sought to close off parliamentary debate about his controversial royal policies concerning Spain and Catholicism, Coke confronted him in an epic speech in the House of Commons. Drawing on Magna Carta and other medieval authorities, Coke insisted that parliamentarians have an "ancient right" and "undoubted inheritance" to a "freedom to speak what we think good for government, either in church or commonwealth and what are the grievances" therein that need be redressed. Parliament must represent and speak for all people; "the freedom of the House is the freedom of the whole land." "We serve here for thousands and ten thousands."[36] This speech landed Coke in prison for seven months. But his views figured prominently in the formal Commons' Protestation of 1621 to the king, which argued "that the liberties, franchises, privileges, and jurisdictions of Parliament are the ancient and undoubted birthright and inheritance of the subjects of England."[37] In response, James dissolved Parliament, despite loud and ongoing protests.[38]

When Parliament reconvened under the new king, Charles I, these battles over controversial royal policies continued. Parliament issued a Petition of Right in 1628, authored primarily by Coke and the eminent legal historian John Selden. Parliament pressed this document on a very reluctant Charles in exchange for their consent to new taxes to support his unpopular wars. The petition urged the king, in Coke's words, to "maintain all his subjects in the just freedom both of their persons and estates" and to allow the people of England to "enjoy all our rights and liberties with as much freedom as ever any subjects have done in former times."[39] The petition echoed and added several provisions to Magna Carta in an effort to prevent any further royal abuses of power. It called for no taxation without "the good will" and "common consent" of the Parliament; no forced loans from the people; no taking of a person's life or liberty "but by the lawful judgment of his peers, or by the law of the land"; no taking of a man's land, no imprisonment, and no disinheritance without "due process of law"; no suspension of the writ of habeas corpus; no forced quartering of soldiers or

[36] Quotes in David Colclough, *Freedom of Speech in Early Stuart England* (Cambridge: Cambridge University Press, 2005), 172–81. See further Coke, *Selected Writings*, 3:1194–305.

[37] In Carl Stephenson and Frederick George Marcham, *Sources of English Constitutional History* (New York: Harper and Bros., 1937), 427, 429.

[38] See Stephen D. White, *Sir Edward Coke and "The Grievances of the Commonwealth" 1621–1628* (Chapel Hill: University of North Carolina Press, 1979).

[39] Sir Edward Coke, "Speech in House of Commons (May 9, 1628)," in Coke, *Selected Writings*, 3:1275–76.

mariners in private homes; no criminal prosecution or punishment save for actions that were expressly outlawed by parliamentary legislation; and no further use of martial law save in true emergencies. All of these "rights and liberties," the petition declared, were to be maintained and enforced "according to the laws and statutes of this realm," without "prejudice" to the people or to their Parliament.[40]

The Petition of Right would eventually become an important step in enumerating "the rights and liberties of Englishmen" based on natural law and common law, as well as in developing the doctrine of "judicial review."[41] But it got nowhere in its day, despite Coke and Selden's strenuous arguments in support of it. In response, Charles suspended Parliament and had Selden and seven others consigned to the Tower of London.[42] The king also suspended Parliament for the next eleven years, while strengthening his oppressive measures. The landed aristocracy and merchants chafed under oppressive taxation, forced loans, property confiscations, and strangulating regulations of trade. Clergy and laity suffered under harsh new establishment laws that drove religious nonconformists first out of their families, pulpits, and churches, and then out of England altogether. Much of the country came to resent the increasingly belligerent enforcement of oppressive royal measures by the prerogative courts, especially the Star Chamber, the Admiralty Court, the High Commission, and the Court of Requests.

While Coke retreated from the front lines of the parliamentary struggle for English rights and liberties after 1628, he took to his writing desk to defend his views. One result was a lengthy panegyric on Magna Carta to open the second volume of his famous *Institutes of the Laws of England* (1628–42). There, Coke insisted that Magna Carta was not just a dusty and dispensable agreement foisted onto King John by the restive barons, as the king's royalist opponents would have it.[43] The "Great Charter of the Liberties of England is the principal grounds of the fundamental laws of England," Coke insisted. Neither king, nor church, nor Parliament, nor any official, however lofty or petty, could breach its fundamental principles.[44] The highest judges of the land "are commanded to thunder out [*fulminare*] anathemas against all infringers of Magna Carta."[45] For "Magna Carta is such a fellow that he will have no sovereign."[46]

40 In Stephenson and Marcham, *Sources*, 450–53.

41 See R. H. Helmholz, "Bonham's Case, Judicial Review, and the Law of Nature," *Journal of Legal Analysis* 1 (2009), 325–54.

42 See Harold J. Berman and John Witte, Jr., "The Integrative Christian Jurisprudence of John Selden," in Hill and Helmholz, *Great Christian Jurists*, 139–62.

43 See especially Coke's colloquies with Francis Bacon, discussed in Maurice Ashley, *Magna Carta in the Seventeenth Century* (Charlottesville: University of Virginia Press, 1965), 8–17.

44 Coke, Inst. 2, proem[ium].

45 William Cobbett, ed., *Parliamentary History or England from the Earliest Period to the Year 1803* (London: T. C. Hansard, 1806), 2:323–28, and in Coke, *Selected* Writings, 3:1260.

46 Cobbett, *Parliamentary History*, 2:357; Coke, *Selected Writings*, 3:1285. But cf. Robert C. Johnson, et al., eds., *Commons Debates, 1628* (New Haven, CT: Yale University Press, 1977), 3:494–95, which renders Coke's quote as "Magna Carta is such a fellow that he will have no saving."

> If any judgment be given contrary to any points of the great charter, or *Charta de Foresta*, by the justices, or by any other of the king[']s ministers, etc., that shall be undone, and holden for nought .... If any statute be made contrary to the great charter, or the charter of the forest, that shall be holden for none: by which words all former statutes made against either of those charter[s] are now repealed.[47]

In 79 folio pages of his *Institutes* (168 pages in the modern critical edition), Coke commented on the first thirty-eight chapters of Magna Carta, adducing medieval statutes and precedents, and dwelling at length on those chapters that, in his view, guaranteed the most important rights and liberties of all English subjects.[48] He highlighted the foundational guarantee of religious freedom in Article 1 – which protected the church's extensive jurisdiction, its exemptions from tax and other civil duties, the benefit of clergy, and other religious rights "too numerous to mention," as he put it. "Ecclesiastical persons have more and greater liberties than other of the king's subjects," Coke recognized. But he also warned that expanding such religious liberties too far, or interpreting them too broadly, would jeopardize all other rights and liberties. "As the overflowing of waters doe many times make the river to lose his proper chanell, so in times past ecclesiasticall persons seeking to extend their liberties beyond their true bounds, either lost or enjoyed not that which of right belonged to them."[49]

Coke also zeroed in on the fundamental "due process" rights and liberties of Article 29.[50] Magna Carta's guarantees of due process, he wrote, included freedom from unlawful arrest or imprisonment and a guarantee that a person could not be indicted without an express statute nor convicted without the presentation of convincing evidence. Due process protected a person from "being destroyed, that is, fore-judged of life, or limbe, disinherited, or put to torture or death" without extensive criminal procedural protections – warranted searches and arrests, respect for the rights of habeas corpus, and the guarantee of a separate trial and judgment before one's peers or equals before the law. For "the liberty of a man's person is more precious to him than all the rest." Due process also included freedom of one's land and livelihood "as belong to him by his free birth right" as well as rights to "the franchise and privileges" that have been lawfully given or acquired. Due process included freedom from being outlawed, banished, or exiled from England, save by act of Parliament or on proper conviction for a felony. In sum, Coke declared, due process guarantees that

> every subject of this realme, for injury done to him, in *bonis, terries, vel persona* [in his goods, lands, or person], by any other subject, be he ecclesiastical, or temporal, freed, or bond, man, or woman, old, or young, or be he outlawed, excommunicated,

47 Coke, Inst. 2, proem[ium]; Coke, *Selected Writings*, 751–52.

48 Coke, *Selected Writings*, 2:745–914. A 1604 prototype memorandum of Coke's commentary on Chapter 29 is included in Baker, *Selected Readings*, 393–402.

49 Inst. 2, ch. 1 in Coke, *Selected Writings*, 2:756–63. See also Inst. 2, ch. 38 in ibid., 2:910–14.

50 Inst. 2, ch. 29, in ibid., 2:848–73.

or any other without exception, may take his remedy by the course of the law, and have justice, and right for the injury done to him, freely without sale, fully without denial, and speedily without delay . . . for the law is the surest sanctuary that a man can take, and the strongest fortresse to protect the weakest of all.[51]

Coke found compelling Magna Carta's further guarantee that the king "shall not sell, deny, or delay justice and right." The term "right" here is the English equivalent of the German *Recht* or Latin *ius*, Coke made clear, and it had a comparable range of meanings. "Right" could mean objective rightness, to be "in the right line," to distribute justice and to give each his due. It could mean the more technical "writ of right" to rights claims tied to and about property. And the term "right" in Magna Carta also had a subjective meaning, Coke argued. "It is called right, because it is the best birth-right the subject hath, for thereby his goods, lands, wife, children, his body, life, honor, and estimation are protected from injury and wrong."[52]

While a perennial champion of Magna Carta, Coke recognized the defects and limitations of this ancient instrument. But rather than discard, amend, or replace it, he thought it better for English law to build on its foundations, as Parliament had sought to do in the Petition of Right. "I would never yield to alter Magna Carta," Coke declared in 1628. "Never yet was any fundamental law shaken but infinite trouble ensued. . . . Shake Magna Carta, and we know what will come of it" – even more royal tyranny and abuse, and perhaps a worse fundamental law than the hard-fought instrument of 1215. "You have a rule in building, do not remove a misplaced stone." That should be the rule of the English common law, Coke concluded – to live by the ancient constitution of Magna Carta, to build on its strengths, and to build around its weaknesses.[53]

BEYOND MAGNA CARTA: RIGHTS AND LIBERTIES IN THE ENGLISH REVOLUTION

In 1640, the English "world was turned upside down."[54] For the first time in eleven years, Charles I called Parliament into session, and the members erupted in unprecedented fury against decades of royal abuses. A coalition of Puritan and Presbyterian leaders seized power by force of arms, and civil war erupted between the supporters of Parliament and the supporters of the king. The parliamentary party prevailed and passed an act "declaring and constituting the People of England to be a commonwealth and free state." The Commonwealth Parliament abolished the kingship, and the deposed King Charles was tried, convicted of treason, and executed in 1649. Parliament also abolished the aristocratic House of Lords and prerogative courts and declared that

51 Inst. 2, ch. 29, in ibid., 2:849–55; see further Inst. 2, ch. 17, in ibid., 2:818
52 Inst. 2, ch. 29, in ibid., 2:870–73.
53 Coke, "Speech in House of Commons (April 16, 1628)," in Coke, *Selected Writings*, 3:1268.
54 Christopher Hill, *The World Turned Upside Down: Radical Ideas during the English Revolution* (New York: Viking Press, 1972).

"supreme authority" resided in the people and their representatives. "Equal and proportional representation" was guaranteed in the election of local representatives. The Church of England, too, was formally disestablished.[55]

This radical commonwealth experiment lasted only until 1660, when the restoration of the traditional Crown, church, and commonwealth brought new rounds of restrictions and repression of religious dissenters, not least Puritan Calvinists. But in those brief twenty years after 1640, England was buried in an avalanche of new writings that would prove critical for the eventual expansion of rights and liberties in the common law tradition. More than twenty-two thousand pamphlets, sermons, and other tracts were published from 1640 to 1660 – some of them crafted in England and abroad well before 1640 but hitherto censored, and many more written in the heat of revolutionary battle. A great number of the pamphleteers denounced the tyranny of church and state and called for more robust protections of the "people's rights and liberties."[56]

A Proposed Puritan Constitution. Like their Puritan ancestors who had suffered under Elizabeth and James I, the English revolutionaries again invoked Magna Carta. The Puritan preacher and pamphleteer John Lilburne, for example, published a tract titled *By Law and Reason: Being a Collection of the Marrow and Soule of Magna Charta*, one of a number of such collections on Magna Carta in the 1640s and 1650s.[57] Here and in several other writings, Lilburne argued that the people's rights and liberties came not from the king or from Parliament, but from God, nature, and "the ancient constitution" of England, which vested sovereignty in the English people, and which grounded the enumerated rights and freedoms of earlier charters and the Great Charter of 1215.[58] Drawing on a "farrago of items"[59] from early

55 See Stephenson and Marcham, *Sources*, 503–33; Harold J. Berman, *Law and Revolution II: The Impact of the Protestant Reformations on the Western Legal Tradition* (Cambridge, MA: Harvard University Press, 2003), 199–230.

56 See *Catalogue of the Thomason Tracts in the British Museum* (London, 1906); Charles R. Gillett, ed., *Catalogue of the McAlpin Collection of British History and Theology*, vol. 5, Index (New York: Union Theological Seminary, 1930). See samples in William Haller, *Tracts in the Puritan Revolution, 1638–1647*, 3 vols. (New York: Columbia University Press, 1934); Don M. Wolfe, ed., *Leveller Manifestoes of the Puritan Revolution: 1638–1647* (New York: T. Nelson and Sons, 1944); Arthur S. P. Woodhouse, *Puritanism and Liberty: Being the Army Debates (1647–9)*, 2nd ed. (Chicago: University of Chicago Press, 1951). I have modernized the spelling of quotations from earlier English sources but have retained the original spelling of the titles. See discussion in William Haller, *Liberty and the Reformation in the Puritan Revolution* (New York: Columbia University Press, 1955); Henry N. Brailsford, *The Levellers and the English Revolution* (Stanford, CA: Stanford University Press, 1961); George P. Gooch, *English Democratic Ideas in the Seventeenth Century*, 2nd ed. (New York: Harper, 1959), and analysis of more recent scholarship in David Wootton, "Leveller Democracy and the Puritan Revolution," in James H. Burns and Mark Goldie, eds., *The Cambridge History of Political Thought, 1450–1700* (Cambridge: Cambridge University Press, 1991), 412–42.

57 Published in London, 1648. See also, e.g., J. C., *Magna Charta Containing That Which Is Very Much the Sence and Agreement of the Good People of These Nations, Notwithstanding Their Differences Relating to Worship* (London, 1659).

58 Vincent, *Magna Carta*, 94.

59 Corrine Weston, "England: Ancient Constitution and Common Law," in Burns and Goldie, *Cambridge History of Political Thought, 1450–1700*, 385.

Anglo-Saxon texts to Magna Carta to the 1628 Petition of Right, Lilburne insisted on the universality of the "Fundamental Lawes and Liberties, Franchises and Privileges" set out in these texts, on the "liberties, immunities, and privileges of all the commons of England."[60] He called them at once "our natural, rationall, nationall, and legall liberties, and freedoms."[61] Regardless of their origin or pedigree, he argued, these fundamental liberties are "the birth-right" of every Englishman, indeed every human being. While "I am no freeman ... I have as true a right to all the privileges that do belong to a freeman, as the greatest man in England."[62] "It is not only my undoubted naturall right; by the light and Law of nature; yea, and by the ancient common Law of England ... but it is also the naturall and undoubted right of every Englishmen [sic], yea and of every man, upon the face of the Earth, in what Countrey soever."[63]

Perhaps all this is true, declared fellow Puritan leader William Walwyn, but Magna Carta and other ancient instruments are "but a part of the people's rights and liberties," and they have "become a very blotted book" owing to the many decades of royal neglect and abuse.[64] We need "a new Magna Carta," said Walwyn, which provides sturdier safeguards of our liberties and surer remedies against the tyranny of Crown, church, and commonwealth.[65]

Walwyn and Lilburne thus joined forces with two other Puritans, Richard Overton and Thomas Prince, to draft such a new Magna Carta, which they called *An Agreement of the Free People of England*.[66] The Agreement, which circulated in various drafts in the 1640s until the final draft of 1649, was, in reality, a proposed new written constitution for England. The Agreement focused carefully on the forms and functions of government, calling for a representative parliament, with annual election of members and no member serving consecutive terms. All persons were to be eligible to run for office, save Catholics and foreigners. Interference in elections by anyone was a serious crime. Parliament was to stick to its clearly enumerated powers, including the power to impose taxes only at an "equal rate ...

60 John Lilburne, *An Anatomy of the Lord's Tyranny* (London, 1646), title page; John Lilburne, *London's Liberty in Chains* (London, 1646), 71–72. See careful analysis in Rachel Foxley, "John Lilburne and the Citizenship of 'Free-Born Englishmen,'" in John Rees, ed., *John Lilburne and the Levellers: Reappraising the Roots of English Radicalism 400 Years On* (London: Routledge, 2018), 6–31, esp. 10–14.

61 John Lilburne, *The Charters of London* (London, 1646), 1; John Lilburne, *The Juglers Discovered* (London, 1647), 5. See Foxley, "John Lilburne," 16–21.

62 John Lilburne, *Englands Birth-Right* (London, 1645). See Pauline Gregg, *Free-Born John: A Biography of John Lilburne*, repr. ed. (London: Phoenix Press, 2000 [1971]), 120–22, 129, 149.

63 John Lilburne, *The Lawes funeral* (London, 1648), 3.

64 Haller, *Tracts*, 3:313–15.

65 Ibid.

66 In Wolfe, *Leveller Manifestoes*, 400–10; see also with prototypes in ibid., 223–34, 291–303. See further Joseph Frank, *The Levellers: A History of the Writings of Three Seventeenth-Century Social Democrats, John Lilburne, Richard Overton, and William Walwyn* (Cambridge, MA: Harvard University Press, 1955); Jack R. McMichael and Barbara Taft, eds., *The Writings of William Walwyn* (Athens, GA: University of Georgia Press, 1989).

upon every real and personal estate."[67] Parliament could not interfere with the judiciary or executive or interfere in military matters, beyond appointment of generals and raising military revenues when needed. Enumerating and limiting the powers of government was considered essential to protecting the people's rights.[68]

Enumerating the people's rights in full was even more essential. The 1649 Agreement added to Magna Carta and the Petition of Right several rights that would become fundamental in the later common law tradition. A strong new religious freedom clause prohibited "any laws, oaths, or covenants, whereby to compel by penalties or otherwise any person to anything in or about matters of faith, religion or God's worship or to restrain any person from the profession of his faith, or to exercise of religion according to his conscience." Also included was a guarantee of freedom from compulsory tithes and appointed clergy and freedom for members of each parish or congregation to elect and contract their own ministers.[69]

In other pamphlets published around the same time, the authors of the Agreement called further for religious freedom from compulsory oath swearing and military service for the conscientiously opposed, freedom from "a single form of church government" enforced by excommunication, and a guarantee that no one could "be punished or persecuted as heretical" for preaching or publishing his opinion in religion "in a peaceable way."[70] They also called for a more general freedom of "speaking, writing, printing, and publishing" and freedom of the people for "contriving, promoting, or presenting any petitions" to Parliament concerning their "grievances or liberties."[71] Anyone who wanted to read more could turn to John Milton's brilliant defense of freedom of speech in his famous *Areopagitica* of 1644[72] and his series of tracts offering a spirited defense of several fundamental principles of religious freedom that would become axiomatic for the later Anglo-American legal tradition – freedom of conscience, free exercise of religion, equality of all peaceable faiths before the law, separation of church and state, and no establishment of religion.[73] These were far more sweeping protections of religion and speech than anything that appeared in Magna Carta.

In addition to freedoms of religion and speech, the 1649 Agreement set out several criminal procedural guarantees, echoing and elaborating Magna Carta and the

67 Wolfe, *Leveller Manifestoes*, 410.

68 Ibid., 139, 317.

69 Ibid., 300.

70 Ibid., 122–23, 139, 300–01.

71 Ibid., 195, 329. See further examples in Norah Carlin, "Lilburne, Toleration, and the Civil State," in Rees, *John Lilburne*, 32–48.

72 John Milton, *Areopagitica and Other Political Writings of John Milton*, ed. John Avis (Indianapolis, IN: Liberty Fund, 1999).

73 See detailed sources and discussion in John Witte, Jr., "Prophets, Priests, and Kings: John Milton and the Reformation of Rights and Liberties in England," *Emory Law Journal* 57 (2008), 1527–604.

Petition of Right: no prosecution or punishment for crimes in cases "where no law hath been before provided"; a guarantee of the privilege against self-incrimination; the right to call witnesses in one's own criminal defense; the right to jury trial; no capital punishment "except for murder" or other "like heinous offences," notably treason; punishments in noncapital cases that were "equal to the offence"; and no imprisonment for private debts. Elsewhere, the authors of the Agreement also called for "just, speedy, plain, and unburdensome" resolution of "controversies and suits in law," at least two witnesses "of honest conversation" for capital conviction, and no detention or imprisonment without a warrant.[74]

Finally, the Agreement protected commerce, business, and private property. It included guarantees of tax- and excise-free domestic and foreign trade as well as freedom from government-sponsored business monopolies, a subject of frequent complaint in earlier pamphlets. It forbade any government actions designed to "level men's estates, destroy property, or make all things common," and required officials to make provision for the poor and restore to the families the private estates of criminals, save those who had been executed for treason.[75]

Theological Foundations. The 1649 Agreement set out a quite typical list of the rights and liberties pressed by the Puritan pamphleteers in the mid-seventeenth century. Many pamphleteers presented them not merely as positive rights created by the state, but as "natural rights" created by God and confirmed by constitutional documents like Magna Carta and the Petition of Right.[76] As Richard Overton, one of the authors of the Agreement, put it in 1646:

> For by natural birth, all men are equally alike born to like property, liberty, and freedom, and as we are delivered of God by the hand of nature into this world, everyone with a natural, innate freedom and property (as it were writ in the table of every man's heart, never to be obliterated) even so we are to live, everyone equally and alike to enjoy his birthright and privilege; even all where God by nature hath made him free.[77]

Other pamphleteers cited Sir John Fortescue, who had written memorably:

> God almighty has declared himself the God of *liberty*: this being the gift of God to man in his creation ... whence it is, that every thing in nature is so desirous of liberty, as being a sort of restitution to its primitive state. So that to go about to lessen this, is esteemed both wicked and cruel: it is upon such considerations as these that the laws of England, in all cases, declare in favor of liberty.[78]

74 Wolfe, *Leveller Manifestoes*, 139–40, 406–08.

75 Ibid., 268–70, 288–89.

76 See, for example, R. Gleissner, "The Levellers and Natural Law," *Journal of British Studies* 20 (1980), 74–89; Brian Manning, "The Levellers and Religion," in J. F. McGregor and B. Reay, eds., *Radical Religion in the English Revolution* (Oxford: Oxford University Press, 1984), 65.

77 In Haller, *Tracts*, 1:113.

78 Sir John Fortescue, *De Laudibus Legum Angliae*, ed. and trans. S. B. Chrimes (Cambridge: Cambridge University Press, 1942), 105. See further Sandoz, *Roots of Liberty*, 5–13.

Putting theologically what later social contract theorists would put philosophically, some Puritan pamphleteers saw written constitutional protections of natural freedoms and rights as parts and products of covenant agreements between and among God, the rulers, and the people. By these covenants, each person agreed to limit the exercise of his or her natural rights for the sake of the common good. Each person further agreed to delegate control over a portion of their natural rights to life, liberty, and property to the authorities, in exchange for the authorities' protection and support. But every state official holds power on behalf of the people and in protection of their rights. "The rulers were made for the people, not the people for the rulers," Cambridge Calvinist don Christopher Goodman had written a century earlier.[79] State officials who abused the people's rights had to be resisted. Those who inflicted more persistent and pervasive abuses had to be removed, even if by organized revolutionary force and regicide.

John Milton laid out this argument in classic terms in *The Tenure of Kings and Magistrates* (1649), a tract that was used to justify the deposition and execution of King Charles for tyranny:

> [A]ll men naturally were born free, being in the image of and resemblance of God himself, and were by privilege above all the creatures, born to command and not to obey; and that they lived so. Till from the root of Adam's transgression, falling among themselves to do wrong and violence, and foreseeing that such courses must needs tend to the destruction of them all, they agreed by common league to bind each other from mutual injury, and jointly to defend themselves against any that gave disturbance or opposition to such agreement. Hence came cities, towns, and commonwealths. And because no faith in all was found sufficiently binding, they saw it needful to ordain some authority, that might restrain by force and punishment what was violated against peace and common right. This authority and power of self-defense and preservation being originally and naturally in every one of them, and unitedly in them all, for ease, for order, and lest each man should be his own partial judge, they communicated and derived either to one, whom for the eminence of his wisdom and integrity they chose above the rest, or to more than one who they thought of equal deserving . . . .
>
> The power of kings and magistrates is nothing else, but what is only derivative, transferred and committed to them in trust from the people, to the common good of them all, in whom the power yet remains fundamentally, and cannot be taken from them, without a violation of their natural birthright . . . . As the king or magistrate holds his authority of the people, both originally and naturally for their good in the first place, and not his own, then may the people as often as they shall judge it for the best, either choose him or reject him, retain him or depose him, though no tyrant, merely by the liberty and right of free born men, to be governed as seems to them best.[80]

79 See, e.g., Christopher Goodman, *How Superior Powers Ought to Be Obeyd*, ed. Charles H. McIlwain (New York: Columbia University Press, 1931). See also Chapter 3, p. 96–97 of this book.

80 In Milton, *Areopagitica and Other Political Writings*, 58–59, 63; see, more generally, ibid., 98–313.

Such revolutionary ideas of rights and liberties proved too radical for seventeenth-century England. Cromwell's interregnum government ultimately rejected the 1649 Agreement and similar constitutional proposals. With the Restoration of the Crown, the established church, and the commonwealth in 1660, many revolutionary writings were consigned to the flames, some of their authors and defenders were pilloried, punished, and banished, and a few were killed. Nonetheless, this short burst of expansive rights talk in the mid-seventeenth century set a normative totem for later generations of common lawyers to make ever more real. In 1679, Parliament passed a provisional Habeas Corpus Act.[81] In 1689, after the Glorious Revolution against the abuses of Charles II, Parliament passed a more expansive Bill of Rights and Toleration Act.[82] These provisions, too, attracted a long series of defenders, most notably John Locke in his *Two Treatises on Government* (1689) and *Letter Concerning Toleration* (1689). These early documents would prove critical for the gradual reform of English common law over the next centuries, albeit a very slow reform and without a written constitution.

MAGNA CARTAS OLD AND NEW IN EARLY AMERICA

The expansive ideas of rights and liberties born of the English Revolution came to more immediate legal application in colonial America. The English royal charters that first constituted many of the seventeenth-century American colonies gave the settlers broad latitude to conceive and create their ideal polities.[83] Even during the harsh reigns of James I and Charles I, in the early seventeenth century, the colonial charters imposed no royalist establishment on the young colonies. Most colonists were free to develop their own political and legal structures and to elect their own magistrates, provided that they did not act "contrary or repugnant to the laws" of England or trespass "the liberties, franchises, and immunities" or the "rights, liberties, and privileges" of "free and natural subjects."[84] Indeed, as the initial 1606 Virginia Company Charter, shaped by Sir Edward Coke, put it, both the new colonists and their children born there "shall have and enjoy all Liberties, Franchises, and Immunities ... as if they had been abiding and born, within this our Realm of England."[85]

81 In Stephenson and Marcham, *Sources*, 557–59.

82 Ibid., 599–608.

83 See detailed discussion in Howard, *Road from Runnymede*, 14–34; Anthony Pagden, "Law, Colonization, Legitimation, and the European Background," in Michael Grossberg and Christopher Tomlin, eds., *The Cambridge History of Law in America*, vol. 1, *Early America (1580–1815)* (Cambridge: Cambridge University Press, 2008), 1–31.

84 Charter of Massachusetts Bay (1629), in Francis Thorpe, ed., *The Federal and State Constitutions, Colonial Charters, and Other Organic Laws*, 7 vols. (Washington, DC: Government Printing Office, 1909), 3:1856–57; see additional examples in Howard, *Road from Runnymede*, 14–22. On the importance of these constitutional constraints in the American colonial charters, see Mary Sarah Bilder, *The Transatlantic Constitution: Colonial Legal Culture and the Empire* (Cambridge, MA: Harvard University Press, 2004).

85 Thorpe, *Constitutions*, 7:3788.

Several of the first colonial companies used this freedom to create something of a haven for European religious and political dissenters, offering them greater rights protection than they had at home. Both the Plymouth Colony of 1620 and the Massachusetts Bay Colony of 1629 were founded by Puritan dissenters from the Church of England and eventually became havens for Calvinist refugees from throughout Europe – though for few others before the eighteenth century.[86] In 1636, Plymouth set out its "General Fundamentals" of law, with the opening guarantee that no law was valid unless issued "by free consent according to the free liberties of the State and Kingdome of England."[87] Providence Plantation was established in 1636 as "a lively experiment [for] full liberty in religious concernments," in the words of its founder, Roger Williams, who had been banished from the Massachusetts Bay Colony because of his heretical views. Providence and later Rhode Island's progressive policies of protecting "liberty of conscience" and "the free exercise and enjoyment of all their civil and religious rights" eventually attracted diverse dissenters from both sides of the Atlantic.[88]

Maryland was founded by the Catholic Lord Baltimore in 1633 as an "experiment" in Catholic and Protestant coexistence. An Act of 1639, oft repeated in the colony, stated that the "Inhabitants of this Province shall have all their rights and privileges according to the Great Charter of England."[89] An Act of 1649 provided further that "no person … professing to believe in Jesus Christ, shall from henceforth be any way troubled … for his or her religion nor in the free exercise thereof … nor any way compelled to the belief or exercise of any other Religion against his or her consent."[90]

The Quaker William Penn instituted a "holy experiment of Christian liberty" in the Great Law of 1682, which he prepared for the new colony of Pennsylvania:

> [N]o person now or at any time hereafter living in this province, who shall confess and acknowledge one almighty God to be the creator, upholder, and ruler of the world, and who profess[es] himself or herself to be obliged in conscience to live peaceably and quietly under the civil government, shall in any case be molested or prejudiced for his or her conscientious persuasion or practice. Nor shall he or she at any time be compelled to frequent or maintain any religious worship, place, or ministry whatever contrary to his or her mind, but shall freely and fully enjoy his, or her, [C]hristian liberty in that respect, without any interruption or reflection.[91]

86 Ibid., 3:1827–60.

87 In George L. Haskins, "The Legal Heritage of Plymouth Colony," *University of Pennsylvania Law Review* 110 (1962), 847–59.

88 Ibid., 6:3205–206, 3211–213.

89 William H. Browne, ed., *Archives of Maryland*, vol. 1, *Proceedings and Acts of the General Assembly of Maryland, January 1637/8–September 1664*, repr. ed. (Baltimore, MD: Maryland Historical Society, 1965), 82–83; see discussion in Howard, *Road from Runnymede*, 53–65.

90 In Browne, *Archives*, 1:244, 246.

91 In James T. Mitchell and Henry Flanders, eds., *Statutes at Large of Pennsylvania* (1911), 1:107–09; see further Andrew R. Murphy, ed., *The Political Writings of William Penn* (Indianapolis, IN: Liberty Fund, 2002); J. William Frost, *A Perfect Freedom: Religious Liberty in Pennsylvania* (Cambridge: Cambridge University Press, 1990).

Penn also set out a series of fundamental public, penal, and procedural rights, which he deliberately anchored in Magna Carta. Indeed, Penn was the first to publish the text of Magna Carta in America, in a 1687 tract that included a commentary on the medieval charter, together with his own charter of liberties for the new colony.[92]

Similarly, in 1691, the colony of New York promulgated its Charter of Rights and Liberties, drawn in part from Magna Carta, the Petition of Right, and the 1649 Agreement. This New York charter also enumerated the powers of government and rights, liberties, and privileges of the people. Included was an echo of Article 29 of Magna Carta:

> THAT Noe freeman shall be taken and imprisoned or be disseized of his ffreehold or Libertye or ffree Customes or be outlawed or Exiled or any other wayes destroyed nor shall be passed upon adjudged or condemned But by the Lawfull Judgment of his peers and by the Law of this province. Justice nor Right shall be neither sold denyed or deferred to any man within this province.

Included as well were several other provisions on civil rights and constitutional due process guarantees:

> THAT Noe man of what Estate or Condition soever shall be putt out of his Lands or Tenements, nor taken, nor imprisoned, nor dishereited, nor banished nor any wayes distroyed without being brought to Answere by due Course of Law.
>
> ALL Tryalls shall be by the verdict of twelve men, and as neer as many be peers or Equalls And of the neighbourhood and in the County Shire or Division where the Fact Shall arise or grow Whether the Same be by Indictment Information Declaration or otherwise against the person Offender or Defendant.
>
> THAT In all Cases Capitall or Criminall there shall be a grand Inquest who shall first present the offence and then twelve men of the neighbourhood to try the Offender who after his plea to the Indictment shall be allowed his reasonable Challenges.
>
> THAT In all Cases whatsoever Bayle by sufficient Suretyes Shall be allowed and taken unlesse for treason or felony plainly and specially Expressed and menconed in the Warrant of Committment provided Alwayes that nothing herein contined shall Extend to discharge out of prison upon bayle any person taken in Execution for debts or otherwise legally sentenced by the Judgment of any of the Courts of Record within the province.
>
> THAT Noe person or persons which professe ffaith in God by Jesus Christ Shall at any time be any wayes molested punished disquieted or called in Question for Difference in opinion or Matter of Religious Concernment, who doe not actuall disturb the Civill peace of the province, But that all and Every such person or persons may from time to time and at all times freely have and fully enjoy his or their Judgments or Consciencyes in matters of Religion throughout all the

[92] William Penn and William Bradford, *The Excellent Priviledge of Liberty & Property, Being the Birth-Right of Free-Born Subjects of England*, repr. ed. (Philadelphia: The Philobiblon Club, 1897); also reprinted in part in Howard, *Road from Runnymede*, 412–25 and discussed in ibid., 78–95.

province, they behaveing themselves peaceably and quietly and not useing this Liberty to Lycentiousnesse nor to the civill Injury or outward disturbance of others.[93]

Massachusetts Body of Liberties. The most expansive colonial rights document was the 1641 Body of Liberties drafted for Massachusetts Bay "in resemblance of a Magna Charta," as Governor John Winthrop put it.[94] This colonial act incorporated not only the rights guarantees of Magna Carta and the Petition of Right but also many of the most daring rights proposals of the early modern pamphleteers in England, along with a number of surprising innovations. Although the 1691 Charter of Massachusetts, which strengthened England's control over the colony, eclipsed the 1641 Body of Liberties, many of these early rights and liberties were reconstructed anew by John Adams in his draft of the new state Constitution of Massachusetts in 1780.[95]

Nathaniel Ward, a distinguished Cambridge-trained lawyer and Heidelberg-trained Calvinist minister, drafted the 1641 document. Ward had come to New England in 1634 with ten years of legal experience as a barrister in England. He had also been a preacher in England but had been removed from his pulpit in 1631 because of his dissenting Puritan Calvinist views.[96] The document that Ward crafted fills twenty-five pages in modern edition and provides a detailed recitation of what he called the "first, basic, elemental, and essential" public, private, and procedural rights that were to obtain in the Massachusetts Bay Colony.[97]

The preamble to the 1641 Body of Liberties makes clear that the Massachusetts colonists regarded the protection of rights and liberties to be essential to the peace and stability of church, state, and society alike:

> The free fruition of such liberties, immunities and privileges as humanity, civility, and Christianity call for as due to every man in his place and proportion without impeachment and infringement hath ever been and ever will be the tranquility and stability of churches and commonwealths. And the denial or deprival thereof, the disturbance if not the ruin of both.
>
> We hold it therefore our duty and safety whilst we are about the further establishing of this government to collect and express all such freedoms as for present we

93 Charles Z. Lincoln, William H. Johnson, and Ansel J. Northrup, eds., *The Colonial Laws of New York From the Year 1664 to the Revolution*, 5 vols., repr. ed. (Clark, NJ: Lawbook Exchange, 2011), 1:111–16.

94 John Winthrop, *Winthrop's Journal: History of New England, 1630–1649*, ed. J. K. Hosmer (New York: C. Scribner's Sons, 1908), 1:151.

95 See further Chapter 4.

96 On Ward, see Jean Béranger, *Nathaniel Ward (ca. 1578–1652)* (Bordeaux: Société Bordelaise de Diffusion de Travaux des Lettres et Sciences Humaines, 1969); Samuel Eliot Morison, *Builders of the Bay Colony* (Boston: Houghton Mifflin, 1930), 217–43.

97 Nathaniel Ward [Theodore de la Guard], *The Simple Cobler of Aggawam in America*, ed. Paul M. Zall (Lincoln: University of Nebraska Press, 1969), 46. The Body of Liberties is reprinted in Edmund S. Morgan, ed., *Puritan Political Ideas: 1558–1794*, repr. ed. (Indianapolis, IN: Hackett, 2003), 177–202.

> foresee may concern us, and our posterity after us, and to ratify them with our solemn consent.
>
> We do therefore this day religiously and unanimously decree and confirm these following rights, liberties and privileges concerning our churches, and civil State to be respectively impartially and inviolably enjoyed and observed throughout our jurisdiction for ever.[98]

The document opens with strongly worded guarantees of the rights to life, liberty, property, family and, reputation, echoing in part the "due process" language of Magna Carta:

> No man's life shall be taken away, no man's honor or good name shall be stained, no man's person shall be arrested, restrained, banished, dismembered, nor any ways punished, no man shall be deprived of his wife or children, no man's goods or estate shall be taken away from him, nor any way damaged under color of law or countenance of authority, unless it be by virtue or equity of some express law of the country warranting the same, established by a general court and sufficiently published, or in case of the defect of a law in any particular case by the word of God.[99]

The Body of Liberties fleshed out these basic guarantees with a number of criminal procedural rights and protections. All persons, "whether inhabitant or foreigner," were to "enjoy the same justice" and "equal and impartial" execution of the law. Parties could be charged only for crimes that were explicitly prohibited by statute. Grand juries were to be used to make preliminary findings in cases of suspicious death. Defendants had a right to bail except in cases of capital crime (idolatry, witchcraft, blasphemy, homicide, homosexual sodomy, adultery, kidnapping, treason, or perjury leading to wrongful execution). They could not be punished for failure to appear in court because of unforeseen circumstances. They had a right to a hearing before an impartial judge, and the right to a speedy trial, whether a bench or jury trial. They were guaranteed the privilege against self-incrimination. They could not be subject to double jeopardy for the same offense, and official case records were to be kept by courts to ensure this protection. Conviction for crime required proof by "clear and sufficient evidence." Conviction in capital cases required "the testimony of two or three witnesses or that which is equivalent thereunto." A defendant could not be tortured to collect evidence against himself. Every defendant had the right to appeal to a higher court and ultimately to the General Council. If the defendant was sentenced to corporal punishment, the Body of Liberties provided that "we allow amongst us none that are inhumane, barbarous or cruel." In capital cases, "no man condemned to die shall be put to death within four days next after his condemnation, unless the court see special cause to the contrary, or in case of martial law."[100]

98 Ibid., 178–79.
99 Ibid., 179.
100 Ibid., 182–89

In civil suits, parties could select written or oral pleadings, and could elect a bench or jury trial. In a jury trial, jurors were selected from the electorate of the community, and both plaintiffs and defendants could challenge the selection of individual jurors. Jurors could deliberate together, and reach general, special, or partial verdicts, but only "clearly and safely" from the evidence presented. Parties could appear pro se or through (noncompensated) representatives. They could sue for legal damages or equitable relief. Defendants could counterclaim as apt. Parties could be compelled to testify in these civil cases at the judge's discretion. Plaintiffs could withdraw their suits any time before the verdict, after paying the defendant's fees in the first case. Cases could be dismissed and the plaintiff fined for "barratry," however, if the plaintiff was unduly litigious or sought simply to harass the defendant or harm his reputation. Defendants could plead contributory negligence by the plaintiff in cases of trespass or damage. Defendants were prohibited from feigning poverty to discourage lawsuits or collection of judgments against them. They could not be imprisoned for private debts, except in cases of extreme profligacy, and they could claim the equivalent of a modern homestead exemption from collections. In all cases, parties could appeal adverse orders or judgments.[101]

The Body of Liberties included strong guarantees of private property rights and private contracts based on the same. All competent males age twenty-one or older had the right to hold, alienate, devise, and inherit private properties without fees, taxes, or government interference. Married women, minors, and the mentally incompetent could do the same "if it be passed and ratified by the consent of a General Court." Forced or "fraudulent conveyances" and alienations of any sort, however, would be reversed and the perpetrators punished upon petition by the injured party. Private landowners had fishing and hunting rights on public lands. While everyone was expected to assist in the public work of the community, nobody could bear a disproportionate burden, and exemptions were to be granted to the aged and the disabled. While all persons were expected to pitch in what they could in cases of emergency, they could not be compelled to military service in offensive wars, and any of their private property taken for public use would need to be replaced or its costs reimbursed. The law banned monopolies in general but granted short-term exclusive patents for new inventions. The law also banned usury and price gouging but did allow interest charges on loans.[102]

The Body of Liberties included special liberties and protections for women, children, and servants, bracketing the traditional common law rules about the right of the paterfamilias to rule the home with little state interference. "Every married woman shall be free from bodily correction or stripes by her husband," and women had special procedural protections to bring complaints. A widow could also seek redress from her late husband's estate if her legacy proved inadequate.

101 Ibid., 183–86.
102 Ibid., 180–82.

Children were to be free from any "unnatural severity" from their parents and had special procedures to seek redress in such cases as well as in cases where parents "willfully and unreasonably" withheld their consent to their "timely or convenient marriage." Servants, too, were to be free from "the tyranny and cruelty of their masters" and were to be given sanctuary with other freemen if they escaped. While corporal discipline of servants was presupposed, they were to be freed if their masters injured them severely, and no indentured servitude could last more than seven years. Even domestic animals received some protection: "No man shall exercise any tyranny or cruelty towards any brute creature[s] which are usually kept for man's use."[103]

The Body of Liberties set forth a number of public or civil rights. All freemen (male church members twenty-one or older) had the right to vote in political election, to stand for political office, and to participate in popular referenda on fundamental issues of law and morality – and in all such contexts had the right to speak or to be silent and to vote or not to vote in accordance with their conscience. All competent adult males had the right and duty to serve on a jury when selected, though no more than twice a year. All adults, regardless of gender or status, had the right to appear and speak at regular town meetings, provided they were not disruptive or offensive. They had the further "liberty to come to any public court, council, or town meeting, and either by speech or writing to move any lawful, seasonable, and material question, or to present any necessary motion, complaint, petition, bill or information." They also had "free liberty to search" and make copies of public records. The Body of Liberties provided a right to sanctuary for anyone "professing the true Christian Religion" who fled to the colony to escape tyranny, oppression, war, famine, or shipwreck. It also included a general prohibition against "bond slavery," except for "lawful captives taken in just wars, and such strangers as willingly sell themselves or are sold to us. And these [lawful captives and strangers] shall have all the liberties and Christian usages which the law of God established in Israel concerning such persons doth morally require."[104]

This last admonition to the colonists to adhere to the law of God in their administration of state law underscored that the Body of Liberties was a self-consciously Christian recitation of rights and liberties. "No custom or prescription shall ever prevail amongst us in any moral cause," the law provided, "that can be proved to be morally sinful by the word of God." This overtly Christian commitment was further underscored by the detailed provisions on religious liberty for "true believers":

1. All the people of God within this jurisdiction who are not in a church way, and be orthodox in judgment, and not scandalous in life, shall have full liberty to gather themselves into a church estate. Provided they do it

[103] Ibid., 194–97.
[104] Ibid., 190–96.

in a Christian way, with due observation of the rules of Christ revealed in his word.

2. Every church hath full liberty to exercise all the ordinances of God, according to the rules of scripture.
3. Every church hath free liberty of election and ordination of all their officers from time to time, provided they be able, pious and orthodox.
4. Every church hath free liberty of admission, recommendation, dismissal, and expulsion, or disposal of their officers, and members, upon due cause, with free exercise of the discipline and censures of Christ according to the rules of his word.
5. No injunctions are to be put upon any church, church officers or member in point of doctrine, worship, or discipline, whether for substance or circumstance besides the institutions of the Lord.
6. Every church of Christ hath freedom to celebrate days of fasting and prayer, and of thanksgiving according to the word of God.
7. The elders of churches have free liberty to meet monthly, quarterly, or otherwise, in convenient numbers and places, for conferences, and consultations about Christian and church questions and occasions.
8. All churches have liberty to deal with any of their members in a church way that are in the hand of justice. So it be not to retard or hinder the course thereof.
9. Every church hath liberty to deal with any magistrate, deputy of court or other officer whatsoever that is a member in a church way in case of apparent and just offence given in their places, so it be done with due observance and respect.
10. We allow private meetings for edification in religion amongst Christians of all sorts of people. So it be without just offence for number, time, place, and other circumstances.[105]

Earlier the document had set out three provisions that ensured a basic separation of the offices and activities of church and state:

> Civil authority hath power and liberty to see the peace, ordinances and rules of Christ observed in every church according to his word so [long as] it be done in a civil and not in an ecclesiastical way.
>
> Civil authority hath power and liberty to deal with any church member in a way of civil justice, notwithstanding any church relation, office, or interest.
>
> No church censure shall degrade or depose any man from any civil dignity, office, or authority he shall have in the Commonwealth.[106]

The 1641 Body of Liberties was an impressively detailed list of public, private, penal, and procedural rights and liberties. It was all the more impressive in that it was drawn up for a scattered community of some fifteen thousand souls, founded only twelve years before, whose most pressing concern was mere survival for a second

105 Ibid., 199–201.
106 Ibid., 190.

decade of harsh winters, bad harvests, widespread disease, and bloody clashes with Native Americans. But enumerating and protecting rights and liberties was considered too essential a foundation for this new society to be put off for long.[107]

Nathaniel Ward later argued that this document was just a compilation of the rights and liberties of the English common law tradition in which he had been trained, many of them anchored in Magna Carta and in later medieval cases interpreting its provisions.[108] Ward was deprecating both the novelty and the sweep of his formulations – as Governor Winthrop and the General Council made clear a few years later in comparing the expansive Massachusetts protections with the more modest English formulations.[109] But Ward's argument underscored the reality that the New England Puritans, like their English counterparts, were drawing on a deep rights tradition in the common law.

What was new in New England was to have these widely scattered traditional common law rights (and many new rights besides) compiled in a single source, generally available to all subjects of the community regardless of the court in which they appeared, and generally binding on all officials and citizens at once. Nothing like that existed in the English common law of the day, with its byzantine complex of courts, writs, and procedures. The one recent attempt by Parliament to compile a few of the more important rights of the people, namely the Petition of Right of 1628, had been cavalierly ignored by the Crown.

What was also new in New England, compared to old England, was to have the Body of Liberties serve as something of a written constitutional text that gave preemptory instruction to government authorities on the limits of the law and that gave procedural rights to colonial citizens to press claims to vindicate the abuses of their rights and liberties. The Massachusetts colonists understood the novelty of this approach, and took pains to underscore it in the concluding paragraphs of the document:

> Howsoever these above specified rights, freedoms, immunities, authorities and privileges, both civil and ecclesiastical, are expressed only under the name and title of liberties, and not in the exact form of laws or statutes, yet we do with one

107 In Massachusetts, many provisions of the Body of Liberties were echoed – and some qualified – in Max Farrand, ed., *The Laws and Liberties of Massachusetts Bay: Reprinted from the Copy of the 1648 Edition in the Henry E. Huntington Library* (Cambridge, MA: Harvard University Press, 1929). For other documents and a discussion, see W. Keith Kavenagh, ed., *Foundations of Colonial America: A Documentary History*, 3 vols. (New York: Chelsea House, 1973); Donald S. Lutz, ed., *Colonial Origins of the American Constitution: A Documentary History* (Indianapolis, IN: Liberty Fund, 1998).

108 Ward, *Simple Cobler*, 40–61. In 1646, in fact, the Massachusetts Bay Authorities drew up a list of the "parallels" between English and colonial laws, arguing that the Body of Liberties "is framed according to the charter, and the fundamental and common laws of England ... beginning with Magna Carta." See appendix in Howard, *Road from Runnymede*, 401–11.

109 See John Winthrop, "Discourse on Arbitrary Government," *in Winthrop Papers*, vol. 4, 1638–1644 (Boston: Massachusetts Historical Society, 1944), 468–88; see also materials analyzed in Francis C. Gray, *Remarks on the Early Laws of Massachusetts Bay* (Boston: Charles C. Little and James Brown, 1843), 7, 11, 16.

consent fully authorize, and earnestly entreat all that are and shall be in authority to consider them as laws, and not to fail to inflict condign and proportional punishments upon every man impartially that shall infringe or violate any of them.

We likewise give full power and liberty to any person that shall at any time be denied or deprived of any of them, to commence and prosecute their suit, complaint or action against any man that shall so do in any court that hath proper cognizance or judicature thereof.

Lastly because our duty and desire is to do nothing suddenly which fundamentally concern us, we decree that these rights and liberties, shall be audibly read and deliberately weighed at every General Court that shall be held, within three years next ensuing, and such of them as shall not be altered or repealed they shall stand so ratified, that no man shall infringe them without due punishment.[110]

Constitutional Adoptions of the Rights of Magna Carta. As many scholars have noted, these colonial charters of rights, together with William Blackstone's 1765 *Commentaries on English Law,* elevated Magna Carta to new prominence in the American founding era.[111] The founding generation drew directly on this tradition both in the revolutionary struggles against royal tyranny and in their construction of new constitutions.

The colonial protests against the Sugar Act, Stamp Act, and other royal exactions in the 1760s drew on the "no taxation without representation" principle of Article 14 of Magna Carta. Their protests against forced quartering of English soldiers and military confiscation of private property built on Magna Carta's ample protections of private property rights in Articles 28–31 and 52 and their echoes in the Petition of Right. Protests against the heavy new English intrusions on colonial commerce, navigation, and trade were based in part on Article 42 of Magna Carta and the free trade provisions of seventeenth-century English and colonial laws. The new Massachusetts colonial seal of 1775 captured this allegiance to Magna Carta and its legacy rather nicely in depicting a revolutionary soldier holding a sword in one hand and Magna Carta in the other.[112] The American Declaration of Independence of 1776 further echoed Magna Carta in reciting its violations of familiar Magna Carta rights in its list of grievances against the Crown. "For imposing taxes on us without our consent; for depriving us in many cases, of the benefits of trial by jury, [and] . . . for transporting large armies of foreign mercenaries to complete the works of death, desolation, and tyranny" the English king has proved himself a "tyrant . . . unfit to be the ruler of a free people."[113]

110 Body of Liberties, in Morgan, *Puritan Political Ideas,* 202.

111 See an early classic article by H. D. Hazeltine, "Magna Carta and the U.S. Constitution," *in Magna Carta: Commemoration Essays,* ed. Henry E. Malden (London: Royal Society, 1917). See illustrations of recent scholarship in Holland, *Magna Carta* and sources in n. 18.

112 See picture in Vincent, *Magna Carta,* 107. Cf. Chapter 3, p. 85, where Protestant jurist Philip Melanchthon depicted the magistrate "holding a sword in one hand and the Decalogue in the other."

113 See Dan Jones, *Magna Carta: The Birth of Liberty* (New York: Penguin, 2015), 194–95.

The new state constitutions that emerged during and after the American Revolution worked hard not only to limit the powers of government but especially to enumerate the rights and liberties of the people. Here, too, Magna Carta and its seventeenth-century echoes and elaborations proved inspirational. Echoing Article 1 of Magna Carta, every state included provisions for religious freedom, with or without religious establishments.[114] The rights to due process and remedy in Article 29 appear in nine of the new state constitutions and were soon part of constitutional processes in every state. The influential 1776 Pennsylvania Constitution, based in no small part on William Penn's original Great Law of 1682 and his commentary on Magna Carta, included ample protections of private property, immigration, jury trial, and more. The 1777 New York Constitution laid out almost every right from the Petition of Right and 1689 Bill of Rights of England and echoed the 1691 colonial charter. The equally influential 1780 Massachusetts Constitution drew directly on Magna Carta and the 1641 Body of Liberties to set out all manner of detailed rights guarantees, not least the strong protection of procedural rights and the right to remedy in public and private cases.[115] Several early state constitutions and cases provided protections for free trade, travel, and commerce, private property, inheritance, and family life that were central concerns for the barons who shaped Magna Carta.[116]

The US Constitution likewise drew directly on the provisions and traditions of Magna Carta. Article 1, which protects habeas corpus rights and prohibits *ex post facto* laws and impairment of contracts, has roots in Magna Carta and the 1628 English Petition of Right and 1679 Habeas Corpus Act as well as in sundry colonial bills of rights. The First Amendment guarantee of religious freedom draws on Article 1 of Magna Carta and the Toleration Act of 1689 as well as early colonial American guarantees of religious freedom. The First Amendment guarantees of free speech, press, and petition and grievances echoes the Petition of Right as well as the 1689 English Bill of Rights. The Fifth Amendment due process clause echoes Article 29 of Magna Carta, which guarantees that "no person should be deprived of life, liberty, or property, without due process of law; nor shall private property be taken for public use, without unjust compensation." The Sixth Amendment echoes Article 40 of Magna Carta by guaranteeing that "in all criminal prosecutions, the accused shall enjoy the right to a speedy and public trial, by an impartial jury." And the ample Fourth through Eighth Amendments reflect the letter and spirit of Magna Carta and the Petition of Right in their protections of criminal and civil procedure, not least

114 See examples in Chapter 5, p. 146–49.

115 See further in Chapter 4.

116 See sources and discussion in G. Alan Tarr, "American State Constitutions and the Three Faces of Magna Carta," in Holland, *Magna Carta*, 122–30; and A. E. Dick Howard, "Magna Carta's American Journey," in ibid., 103–21; Howard, *Road From Runnymede*; David Little, "Differences over the Foundation of Law in Seventeenth- and Eighteenth-Century America," in Jones and Hill, *Magna Carta*, 157–76.

the right to jury trial, the privilege against self-incrimination, and the freedom from cruel and unusual punishment.

Like the English revolutionaries and the American colonists of the seventeenth-century, the eighteenth-century American founders rooted these written constitutional rights not only in Magna Carta but also in other "ancient constitutions" and customs, which they sometimes traced back to the earliest Greek, Roman, and Anglo-Saxon sources of the West.[117] The founders also rooted these rights in the "laws of nature and nature's God," who had created human beings with reason, will, and memory, and vested them with "natural and unalienable" rights of life, liberty, property, family, labor, and more.[118] The eighteenth-century American founders saw themselves as new embodiments of the same restive spirit that had driven the medieval barons of Runnymede and the early modern revolutionaries of England to stand up anew for their God-given rights against tyrannical usurpers and to create even stronger constitutional bulwarks of liberty.

SUMMARY AND CONCLUSIONS

A central thesis of the first two chapters of this volume is that subjective rights were commonplace in Western law. For Western jurists and judges, rights talk was a common way to define and defend the law's protection, support, limitations, and entitlements of persons and groups in society as well as the proper relationships between political and other authorities and their respective subjects. For Western lawyers, subjective rights were not a modern invention, a seductive new form of liberal exotica crafted by Enlightenment philosophers in manifestation of their new secular theories of individualism, rationalism, and contractarianism. Lawyers since classical Roman and medieval times used rights ideas and terms as a plain and uncontroversial way of talking about the claims one legal subject could legitimately make against another, the charges that an authority could legitimately impose upon its subjects, and the procedures that were to be followed in these legal interactions.

117 See, e.g., Richard Bland, *Inquiry into the Rights of the British Colonies*, repr. ed. (Richmond, VA: Appeals Press, 1922); John Adams, A *Defense of the Constitutions of the United States of America*, 3 vols., vol. 1, chaps. 3–9 in *The Works of John Adams*, ed. C. F. Adams, 10 vols. (Boston: Little and Brown, 1851), vol. 4. See generally, H. Trevor Colbourn, *The Lamp of Experience: Whig History and the Intellectual Origins of the American Revolution* (Chapel Hill: University of North Carolina Press, 1965), 158–84; Stanley R. Hauer, "Thomas Jefferson and the Anglo-Saxon Language," *PMLA* 98 (1983), 880–81; James Muldoon, *John Adams and the Constitutional History of the Medieval British Empire* (New York: Palgrave MacMillan, 2018); John Philip Reid, *The Ancient Constitution and the Origins of Anglo-American Liberty* (Dekalb: Northern Illinois University Press, 2005); David J. Bederman, *The Classical Foundations of the American Constitution: Prevailing Wisdom* (Cambridge: Cambridge University Press, 2008); and the discussion of John Adams in Chapters 4 and 5 of this book.

118 Antislavery critics used these natural law and rights teachings to castigate the American constitutional acceptance of slavery. See, e.g., Justin B. Dyer, "Slavery and the Magna Carta in the Development of Anglo-American Constitutionalism," *Political Science & Politics* 43, no. 3 (2010), 479–82.

This chapter illustrates how one important Western legal system – the Anglo-American common law tradition – articulated these rights in medieval and early modern times, and how common law jurists came to ever more refined and elaborate statements of public, private, penal, and procedural rights guarantees in their political advocacy and legal documents.

Another central thesis is that Christianity, in various forms, played an important role in uncovering, enumerating, and enforcing rights, building on both classical and biblical foundations, and eventually working alongside Enlightenment liberals, some of whom largely rejected Christianity. This chapter illustrates that proposition, too. "Magna Carta can be read as an historical, constitutional, or legal document," writes Robin Griffith-Jones, Master of the Temple at the Inns of Court. "But it was first and foremost a *religious* document."[119] It not only provided a guarantee of religious freedom for the church in England. It was not only sealed by King John "in the presence of God, and for the salvation of our soul, and the souls of our ancestors and heirs, and unto the honour of God and the advancement of [the] Holy Church."[120] But the document was filled with rights provisions that were part and product of the medieval Christian culture in which it was forged. This was a Christian society that had already drawn from the Bible, from Roman law, and from many centuries of legal experience a whole series of substantive and procedural rights and liberties – *iura* and *libertates* as they were called in Latin, *ryhtes* and *rihta(e)*, *freoles* and *fred-oms* as they came to be called in Anglo-Saxon texts. This was a Christian society whose canon law systems of the church had already developed a rich latticework of subjective rights, liberties, privileges, and immunities that were defined in ecclesiastical legislation, defended in litigation in church courts, and refined by sophisticated deliberation among jurists, philosophers, and theologians in the new universities. This was, further, a Christian society whose secular systems of imperial, royal, ducal, manorial, feudal, and urban law also operated in part with rights, norms, and procedures, as those were set out in sundry charters, constitutions, concordats, statutes, cases, and codes.

Some of these grander principles had Christian inspiration as well.[121] Take Magna Carta's early statements of "due process of law." This famous guarantee was designed not only to protect subjects from unjust loss of life, liberty, property, and more without the procedural protections of the law of the land. It also served to protect the judge from divine condemnation for failing to render a just judgment in accordance with proper procedures. This concern was of central importance in thirteenth-century Christian thought. "Judge not, that you not be judged," the Bible stated baldly, but then gave several examples of just judgements. For a medieval canonist

119 Robin Griffith-Jones, "Magna Carta and Religion: For the Honor of God and the Reform of Our Realm," in Holland, *Magna Carta*, 48. See detailed discussion in ibid., 47–64.

120 Magna Carta, preamble, in Holland, *Magna Carta*, 239.

121 Thomas Andrew, *Christianity and the Charter: Christianity and the Forgotten Roots of the Magna Carta* (London: Theos, 2015), 31–44.

like Raymond of Penyafort, the key was "keeping to the order [the procedures] of the law (*iuris ordine servato*)." "If it is done out of love and justice, the judge does not sin in condemning [the accused] to death and ordering his minister to kill him, nor is the minister condemned if he kills having been ordered to do so. Still, either of them will commit mortal sin if he does it without observing the procedures of the law (*iuris ordine non servato*)."[122] "The judge 'must observe the procedures of the law' when killing," writes leading criminal law historian James Whitman in elaboration. Due process of law "marked out a path of safety for the judge that would be followed both in England and on the Continent: the salvation of the judge was to be found in the law of procedure."[123]

To be sure, some of Magna Carta's rights provisions were far less lofty in inspiration and were peculiar local creatures of their time and place – such as the right to fishing weirs on the Thames, offensive restrictions on loans from the Jews, the arcane talk (to the modern ear) of "assizes of novel disseisin," "mort d'ancestor," "darrien presentment," or "fee-farm, socage, or burgage," and the like.[124] But other provisions set out grand principles that would grow into central commands of the common law tradition, eventually on both sides of the Atlantic. And in hard individual cases and in dire times of revolution and crisis, these more enduring principles were given new life and expanded into ever more elaborate and specific constitutional precepts.

The long seventeenth century was one such crisis moment in the common law tradition. The crisis in England was the mounting religious repression of the Puritans, beginning in Queen Elizabeth's later reign, which escalated into the tyranny of the Stuart kings. This repression forced parliamentarians, pamphleteers, and lawyers alike to articulate those fundamental rights whose pervasive and persistent violation by a tyrant justified armed revolution. The crisis in colonial America was the daunting challenge of creating a legal and political system for the new colonial societies that sprung up all along the Atlantic seaboard and needed to define and maintain ordered liberty. On both sides of the Atlantic, Anglo-American common lawyers went back to the core rights principles of Magna Carta and drew them out into ever more elaborate rights precepts. They also went back to biblical ideas of justice and mercy, covenant and community, liberty and equality to work out an ever more refined Christian theory of constitutional rights, social and political order, and rule of law.

Seventeenth-century rights formulations anticipated many of the rights guarantees of the eighteenth-century American constitutions. Taken together, the seventeenth-century

122 Ibid., 34, citing James Whitman, *The Origins of Reasonable Doubt: Theological Roots on the Criminal Trial* (New Haven, CT: Yale University Press, 2016), 48.

123 X. Ochoa and A. Diez, eds., S. *Raimundus de Pennaforte Summa de Paenitentia in Universa Bibliotheca Iuris* (Rome: Commentarium pro Religionis, 1976), 1:443, using translation in Whitman, *The Origins of Reasonable Doubt*, 48. On Penyafort, see José Miguel Viejo-Ximénez, "Raymond of Penyafort," in Rafael Domingo and Javier Martínez Torrón, eds., *Great Christian Jurists in Spanish History* (Cambridge: Cambridge University Press, 2018), 50–68.

124 Magna Carta, arts. 12, 18, 33, and 37 in Holland, *Magna Carta*, 241–44.

texts offered citizens robust protections of freedoms of religion, speech, press, assembly, association, and petition. Citizens had rights to hold and bear arms in their own defense and in defense of their community. They had rights to be free from forced quartering of soldiers, sailors, and other military men. They had rights to property and freedom from government takings of property without just compensation. They had rights to the privacy of their homes, businesses, and papers. They had rights to jury trial in civil and criminal cases. They had rights to fair and speedy trials, rights to confront and cross examine witnesses, rights to appeal, and freedom from cruel and unusual punishment. Even the rights to vote and to pursue political office were adumbrated in these early texts. The American constitutional founders, like the liberal Enlightenment philosophers, inherited many more rights than they contributed. What they contributed more than anything was a philosophical defense of these rights that transcended particular religious premises and a constitutional system of governance that allowed for a much broader, if not universal, application.

3

Natural Law and Natural Rights in the Early Protestant Tradition

Ever since Karl Barth issued his famous "Nein!" to natural theology in 1934,[1] many Protestants have viewed natural law and natural rights with suspicion, if not derision. Some view natural law and natural rights as inextricably tied to Catholic moral theories that Protestants have always purportedly rejected because of their deprecation of cruciform ethics. Some view human rights as a dangerous invention of the Enlightenment, predicated on a celebration of reason over revelation, of greed over charity, of nature over scripture, of the individual over the community, and of the pretended sovereignty of humanity over the absolute sovereignty of God. A number of critics view the occasional references to natural law and natural rights among some early Protestant reformers as a scholastic hangover that later Protestants happily expunged from the tradition by a clearer reading of scripture. Others see the devolution of modern human rights into endless lists of personal whims and special interests as ample proof of the dangers of separating law from religion, reason from revelation, rights from duties.[2]

While such skepticism might make for good theology in some Protestant circles today, it is not good history. The reality is that early modern Protestant theologians and jurists on both sides of the Atlantic expounded complex theories of natural law and natural rights with considerable alacrity, and these proved to be important to the development of human rights and religious freedom in the Western legal tradition, especially in Protestant majority lands on both sides of the Atlantic. Some early Protestants did echo conventional classical and medieval teachings with only modest reforms. But a number of their followers made striking innovations to the tradition of natural law and rights, reflecting in part the new Protestant teachings on *sola scriptura*, total depravity, divine sovereignty, and the Decalogue. This theological and jurisprudential work soon led to political platforms, constitutional

[1] Emil Brunner and Karl Barth, *Natural Theology: Comprising "Nature and Grace" by Emil Brunner and the Reply "No" by Karl Barth*, trans. Peter Fränkel, repr. ed. (Eugene, OR: Wipf and Stock Publishers, 2002).

[2] See 291–94 and a good sampling in Stephen J. Grabill, *Rediscovering the Natural Law in Reformed Theological Ethics* (Grand Rapids, MI: Eerdmans, 2006), 1–53.

reforms, and revolutionary manifestoes that helped catalyze the early modern democratic revolutions in France, the Netherlands, Scotland, England, and America.

This chapter samples these early Protestant teachings on natural law and natural rights and their influence on the development of human rights and religion freedom. After an overview of the Protestant Reformation of the law and religion of medieval Catholicism, the chapter offers brief case studies of Lutheran, Anabaptist, and Calvinist contributions respectively.

SETTING THE CONTEXT: THE PROTESTANT REFORMATION OF RELIGION AND LAW

The Protestant Reformation erupted in 1517 with Martin Luther's posting of the Ninety-Five Theses on the church door in Wittenberg and his burning of the medieval canon law books at the city gates three years later. The Reformation soon split into four main branches – Lutheranism, Anabaptism, Anglicanism, and Calvinism – with ample regional and denominational variation within each branch. Lutheranism spread throughout the northern territories of the Holy Roman Empire, Prussia, and Scandinavia and their later colonies around the Atlantic, consolidated by Luther's catechisms and the Augsburg Confession (1530) and by local liturgical books and Bible translations. Anabaptists fanned out in small communities throughout Western and Eastern Europe, Russia, and eventually North America, most of them devoted to the founding religious principles of the Schleitheim Confession (1527). Anglicanism was established in England by King Henry VIII and Parliament in the 1530s, and, once standardized by the Great Bible (1539) and the Book of Common Prayer (1559), spread throughout the vast British Empire in North America, Africa, the Middle East, and south Asia. Calvinist or Reformed communities, modeled on John Calvin's Geneva and anchored by the Geneva Bible and Genevan Academy, spread into portions of the Swiss Confederation, France, the Palatinate, Hungary, Poland, the Lowlands, Scotland, England, and North America. This checkerboard of Protestant communities, living tenuously alongside each other and their Catholic neighbors, was protected for a time by the Peace of Augsburg (1555), the Union of Utrecht (1579), the Edict of Nantes (1598), the Peace of Westphalia (1648), and other treaties, though religious persecution and religious warfare were tragically regular events in early modern Europe.[3]

While new confessions, creeds, and catechisms helped to inspire and integrate these Protestant movements, it was new laws that usually set them in motion and

[3] See Thomas Albert Howard and Mark A. Noll, eds., *Protestantism After 500 Years* (Oxford: Oxford University Press, 2016); Udo Di Fabio and Johannes Schilling, eds., *Die Weltwirkung der Reformation: Wie der Protestantismus unsere Welt verändert hat* (Munich: C.H. Beck, 2017); John Witte, Jr. and Amy S. Wheeler, eds., *The Protestant Reformation of the Church and the World* (Louisville, KY: Westminster John Knox Press, 2018).

consolidated them. Hundreds of local "church ordinances" *(Kirchenordnungen)*, or "legal reformations" *(Rechtsreformationen)* were issued by Lutheran German cities, duchies, and principalities after 1520, and were echoed in national church ordinances in Sweden, Denmark, Norway, Finland, and Iceland over the next century. Local Anabaptist elders issued short "church orders" to establish and govern their small, self-sufficient Anabaptist communities, many of their rules drawn directly from biblical and early apostolic teachings. Parliament's Supremacy Act (1534) declared the English monarch to be "supreme head" and "defender of the faith" in the freestanding Church of England, and that triggered a long series of reformation measures. Geneva's Reformation Edict (1536), modeled on similar edicts passed the decade before in Zurich and other Swiss cities, was echoed in scores of European towns and provinces and later North American colonies that accepted Reformed Protestantism.

All of these early Protestant legal declarations of reformation were, in part, firm rejections of the law and theology of medieval Catholicism. The Catholic Church had been the universal legal authority of the West since the twelfth century. Medieval church authorities claimed exclusive jurisdiction over doctrine, liturgy, clergy, polity, marriage, family, inheritance, trusts, education, charity, contracts, moral crimes, and more. They also claimed concurrent jurisdiction over many other legal subjects, sometimes filling gaps in local civil rules and procedures, but often rivaling local civil authorities in governing the local population. And the church had huge property holdings – more than a quarter of the land in some regions of Europe – which remained under church control and free from secular taxes and regulation.

To exercise this power, the medieval church developed an intricate system of canon laws promulgated by the pope, bishops, and church councils, and enforced by a hierarchy of church courts and clerical officials under the final papal authority of Rome. A vast network of church officials, immune from secular legal control, presided over the medieval church's executive and administrative functions. The church registered its citizens through baptism, educated them in church schools, taxed them through tithes, and conscripted them through crusades. It nurtured them in cloisters, monasteries, chantries, hospitals, and guilds. It cared for them and their families even after death through perpetual obits, indulgences, and foundations.[4] The medieval church was, in F. W. Maitland's apt phrase, "the first true state in the West."[5] Its canon law was the first international law in place since the fall of Rome in the fifth century.

Already in the fourteenth and fifteenth centuries, strong political rulers started to rebel against the power, prerogatives, and privileges of the medieval church and put

4 Harold J. Berman, *Law and Revolution: The Formation of the Western Legal Tradition* (Cambridge, MA: Harvard University Press, 1983); R. H. Helmholz, *The Spirit of the Classical Canon Law*, repr. ed. (Athens: University of Georgia Press, 2010).

5 Quoted by Berman, *Law and Revolution*, 276.

in place legal reforms. In fourteenth-century England, several statutes of "provisors" and "praemunire" limited papal control over local clerical appointments, church taxes, and local property disputes. Beginning in 1414, the Holy Roman emperors called a series of great church councils that put limits on the operation of canon law and church courts in the empire and aimed to regularize papal succession and the appointments of bishops, abbots, and abbesses. In the Pragmatic Sanction of Bourges (1438) and again in the Concordat of Bologna (1516), French kings banned various papal taxes, limited appeals to Rome, required election of French bishops by local church councils called by the king, and subjected French clergy and church property to royal controls. Fifteenth-century Spanish monarchs subordinated church courts to civil courts on many legal subjects and assumed political and legal control over the Inquisition. Fifteenth-century German and Scandinavian princes and city councils passed numerous legal reformations that placed limits on church property and religious taxation, disciplined wayward clergy and monastics, and curtailed the jurisdiction of church courts over crime, family, inheritance, and contracts. Medieval reformers like Marsilius of Padua (ca. 1280–ca. 1343), John Wycliffe (ca. 1330–84), John Hus (ca. 1370–1415), and many others pressed for attendant theological reforms, some at the cost of their lives.[6]

The sixteenth-century Protestant reformers built on these late medieval reforms but went beyond them. The reformers now called for full freedom from the medieval Catholic legal regime – freedom of the individual conscience from intrusive canon laws, freedom of political officials from clerical power and privilege, freedom of local clergy from centralized papal and conciliar rule. "Freedom of the Christian" was the rallying cry of the early Protestant Reformation.[7] It led the reformers to denounce canon law and clerical authority altogether and to urge radical legal and political reforms on the strength of the new Protestant theology. The church's canon law books were burned. Church courts and episcopal offices were forcibly closed. Clerical privileges and immunities were stripped. Mendicant begging was banned. Mandatory celibacy was suspended. Indulgence trafficking was condemned. Annates and tithe payments to Rome or to distant bishops were outlawed. Diplomatic and appellate ties to the pope and his curia were severed. Catholic bishops, priests, and monastics were banished from their homes, sometimes maimed or killed. The church's vast properties and institutions were seized, often with violence and bloodshed. Priceless church art, literature, statuary, and icons were looted, sometimes destroyed.

The Protestant reformers defended this revolutionary purging of the medieval Catholic Church as a theological necessity. All of the early Protestant leaders – Martin Luther (1483–1546), John Calvin (1509–64), Thomas Cranmer (1489–1556),

[6] See sources and discussion in John Witte, Jr., *Law and Protestantism: The Legal Teachings of the Lutheran Reformation* (Cambridge: Cambridge University Press, 2002), 33–52.

[7] Martin Luther, *Freedom of a Christian* (1520) in Jaroslav Pelikan et al., eds., *Luther's Works* (Philadelphia, PA: Muhlenberg Press, 1955–68), 31:327–77.

Menno Simons (1496–1561), and others – taught that salvation comes through faith in the Gospel, not by works of the law written on the heart and rewritten in the Old Testament. Each individual was to stand directly before God, to seek God's gracious forgiveness of sin and to conduct life in accordance with the Bible and Christian conscience. To the reformers, the Catholic canon law administered by the clergy obstructed the individual's direct relationship with God and obscured simple biblical norms for right living. Most of the early Protestant reformers further taught that the church was at heart a community of saints, not a corporation of law. Its cardinal signs and callings were to preach the Word, to administer the sacraments, to catechize the young, and to care for the needy. The Catholic clergy's legal rule in Christendom obstructed the church's divine mission and usurped the state's role as God's vice-regent called to appropriate and apply divine and natural law in the earthly kingdom. Protestants did recognize that the church needed internal rules of order to govern its own polity, teaching, and discipline. Church officials and councils needed to oppose legal injustice and combat political tyranny. For most early Protestants, however, law was primarily the province of the state not of the church, of the magistrate not of the pastor.

These new Protestant teachings helped to transform Western law in the sixteenth and seventeenth centuries. The Protestant Reformation broke the international rule of the Catholic Church and canon law, permanently splintering Western Christendom into competing nations and regions, each with its own religious and political rulers. The Protestant Reformation triggered a massive shift of power and property from the church to the state. State rulers now assumed jurisdiction over numerous subjects and persons previously governed by the church and its canon law.

The wide variety of early modern Protestant confessions yielded a wide array of legal and political arrangements in Protestant lands. Absolute monarchists in France, Denmark, England, and Prussia were as fervently Protestant as democratic revolutionaries in Scotland, the Netherlands, England, and America. Strict Anglican or Lutheran religious establishments were as deeply rooted in Reformation teachings as novel Anabaptist or Calvinist theories of religious freedom. Some early modern Protestant groups were intense religious pietists and political quietists, while others worked relentlessly to develop written constitutions, enumerated bills of rights, clear separations of powers, and federalist structures of government. Some Protestants turned cheeks in expression of Christian love and martyrdom; others swung swords in pursuit of just wars and democratic revolutions.

Moreover, these diverse Protestant communities had varying attitudes toward traditional legal sources, despite their opening call to return to the Bible alone for authority (*sola Scriptura*). Anabaptist communities remained the most steadfast in adopting literal biblical norms and early apostolic canons as the backbone of their internal community rules. Anglican and Lutheran Protestant leaders, despite their shrill rejection of canon law and papal jurisdiction, eventually transplanted many

Catholic canon law rules and procedures directly into the new Protestant state laws – some trimmed of theologically offensive provisions, others reformed in light of new teachings, but many retained largely in their medieval forms, though now administered by the state instead of the church. Many Protestant authorities also drew afresh on Christianized Roman law and medieval civilian jurisprudence, Christian republican political thought, and biblical and Talmudic law, all of which were staples in the new Protestant law faculties. And Protestant leaders worked hard to convert some of their own distinct new theological teachings, especially concerning family, charity, education, and crime, into new legal forms. Emerging from the Protestant Reformation were impressive new legal syntheses that skillfully blended classical and biblical, Catholic and Protestant, civilian and canonical teachings.

Included in these new Protestant theological and legal syntheses were fresh insights into natural law and natural rights, religious freedom and human rights, church–state relations and the respective roles of each in the governance of a (Christian) republic. The most original insights came from the Lutheran, Anabaptist, and Calvinist traditions, which the next three sections take up briefly.

THE LUTHERAN TRADITION

Martin Luther. Luther grounded his teachings on natural law in his complex two-kingdoms framework. God has ordained two kingdoms or realms in which humanity is destined to live, Luther argued – the earthly kingdom and the heavenly kingdom. The earthly kingdom is the realm of creation, of natural and civil life, where a person operates primarily by reason and law. The heavenly kingdom is the realm of redemption, of spiritual and eternal life, where a person operates primarily by faith and love. These two kingdoms embrace parallel heavenly and earthly, spiritual and temporal forms of righteousness and justice, government and order, truth and knowledge. They interact and depend upon each other in a variety of ways, not least through biblical revelation and the faithful exercise of Christian vocations in the earthly kingdom. But the two kingdoms ultimately remain distinct – the earthly kingdom distorted by sin and governed by the law, the heavenly kingdom renewed by grace and guided by the Gospel. A Christian is a citizen of both kingdoms at once and invariably comes under the distinct government of each. As a heavenly citizen, the Christian remains free in conscience, called to live fully by the light of the Word of God. But as an earthly citizen, the Christian is bound by law and called to obey the natural orders and offices that God has ordained and maintained for the governance of the earthly kingdom.[8]

Earthly authorities, Luther argued, operate first and foremost by the law of nature – the set of norms ordained by God in the creation, written on each

[8] Witte, *Law and Protestantism*, 87–118. See also Philip Melanchthon, *Melanchthon on Christian Doctrine: Loci Communes* 1555, trans. and ed. Clyde L. Manschrek (Oxford: Oxford University Press, 1965), 39–44, 274–79, 323–44.

human heart, and rewritten in the Bible. Luther called this variously the "law of nature," "natural law," "divine law," "godly law," "the law of the heart," "the teachings of conscience," "the inner law," and other terms.[9] His main point was that the natural law continued to operate in the earthly kingdom after the fall into sin, and it provides a foundation for positive law and public morality in earthly life.

The natural law, said Luther, defined the basic duties owed to God, neighbor, and self. The clearest expression of these duties was the Ten Commandments, which God gave to Moses on two tables. The First Table set out basic duties to honor the Creator God, respect God's name, observe the Sabbath, and avoid idolatry and blasphemy. The second set out basic duties to one's neighbor – to honor authorities, and not to kill, commit adultery, steal, bear false witness, or covet. Luther believed this to be a universal statement of natural law, binding on everyone. "The Decalogue is not the law of Moses ... but the Decalogue of the whole world, inscribed and engraved in the minds of all men from the foundation of the world." "[W]hoever knows the Ten Commandments perfectly must know all the scriptures, so that, in all affairs and cases, he can advise, help, comfort, judge, and decide both spiritual and temporal matters, and is qualified to sit in judgment upon all doctrines, estates, spirits, laws, and whatever else is in the world."[10]

Knowledge of this natural law comes not only through the Bible but also through natural reason, Luther continued. Since the law is written on every human heart, every rational person "feels" and "knows" the law of God, even if only obliquely. The basic teaching of the natural law "lives and shines in all human reason, and if people would only pay attention to it, what need would they have of books, teachers, or of law? For they carry with them in the recesses of the heart a living book which would tell them more than enough about what they ought to do, judge, accept, and reject."[11]

Sinful persons, however, do not always, of their own accord, abide by the natural law. Thus, God has called on the natural authorities of the earthly kingdom to elaborate its basic requirements. Parents must teach the natural law to their children and dependents, preachers preach it to their congregants and catechumens, and magistrates elaborate and enforce it through positive laws. "Natural law is a practical first principle in the realm of public morality," Luther wrote in elaborating his political theory; "it forbids evil and commands good. Positive law is a decision that

9 See sample quotes in Hermann W. Beyer, *Luther und das Recht*, repr. ed. (Paderborn: Salzwasser-Verlag Gmbh, 2013), with analysis in Johannes Heckel, *Lex Charitatis: A Juristic Disquisition on Law in the Theology of Martin Luther*, trans. and ed. Gottfried G. Krodel (Grand Rapids, MI: Wm. B. Eerdmans, 2010); Antii Raunio, "Divine and Natural Law in Luther and Melanchthon," in Virpi Mäkinen, ed., *The Lutheran Reformation and the Law* (Leiden: Brill, 2006), 21–62.

10 See, especially, Pelikan et al., *Luther's Works*, 44:15–114; *D. Martin Luthers Werke: Kritische Gesamtausgabe*, repr. ed., 78 vols. (Weimar: H. Böhlaus Nachfolger, 1883–1987), 39/1:478; *Triglott Concordia: The Symbolic Books of the Ev. Lutheran Church German-Latin-English* (St. Louis, MO: Concordia Press, 1921), 573, 581–67.

11 *Luthers Werke: Kritische Gesamtausgabe*, 17/2:102.

takes local conditions into account" and "credibly" elaborates the general principles of the natural law into specific precepts to fit these local conditions. "The basis of natural law is God, who has created this light, but the basis of positive law is the earthly authority," the magistrate, who represents God in this earthly kingdom.[12] The magistrate must promulgate and enforce positive laws by combining faith, reason, and tradition. He must pray to God earnestly for wisdom and instruction and must maintain "an untrammeled reason" in judging the needs of his people and the advice of his counsellors. The magistrate must consider the wisdom of the legal tradition – particularly that of Roman law, which Luther called a form of "heathen wisdom."[13]

Philip Melanchthon. Luther's fellow reformer in Wittenberg, the theologian and moralist Philip Melanchthon (1497–1560), repeated and endorsed many of Luther's teachings. But already in his early writings, Melanchthon was more explicit than Luther in expounding the content of natural law and directing it to an understanding of natural rights. Drawing on the Bible and various classical and postbiblical sources, Melanchthon ultimately identified ten common principles of natural law:

1. To worship God and honor God's law
2. To protect life
3. To testify truthfully
4. To marry and raise children
5. To care for one's relatives
6. To harm no one's person, property, or reputation
7. To obey all those in authority
8. To distribute and exchange property on fair terms
9. To honor one's contracts and promises
10. To oppose injustice[14]

Melanchthon also went well beyond Luther in grounding natural law philosophically. Starting with the two-kingdoms theory, he taught that God has implanted in all persons certain "inborn elements of knowledge" *(notitiae nobiscum nascentes)*. These *notitiae*, or elements, were forms of "natural light," "rays of divine wisdom poured into us," without which we could not find our way in the earthly kingdom. They included various "theoretical principles" of logic, dialectics, geometry, arithmetic, physics, and other sciences – that two plus two equals four, that an object thrown into the air will come down, that the whole is bigger than any one of its parts, and the like. They also included "practical principles" *(principia practica)* of ethics,

[12] Ibid., 51:211; *D. Martin Luthers Werke: Tischreden*, 6 vols. (Weimar: H. Böhlaus Nachfolger, 1912–), 3:3911.

[13] Pelikan et al., *Luther's Works*, 45:120–26; *Luthers Werke: Kritische Gesamtausgabe*, 51:242. See also ibid., 12:243; ibid., 14:591, 714; ibid., 16:537; ibid., 30/2:557; ibid., 51:241.

[14] G. Bretschneider, ed., *Melanchthons Werke*, 28 vols., in *Corpus Reformatorum* (Brunswick: Brunsvigae Schwetschke, 1864), 21:25–27; 119–20 [hereafter CR].

politics, and law – that "men were born for civil society," that offenses which harm society should be punished, that "promises should be kept," and many others. "All these natural elements of knowledge," Melanchthon believed, "are congruent with the eternal and unchanging norm of the divine mind that God has planted in us." They provide the starting point for earthly life and learning.[15]

Melanchthon sometimes cast this understanding of natural instincts and inclinations into natural rights terms. For example, in discussing the natural foundation of marriage in the created order, he argued that marriage was not only a natural duty and remedy from sin but also a natural faculty and right that no human ordinance should discourage or impede:

> Genesis 1:28 teaches that persons were created to be fruitful, and that one sex in a proper way should desire another. For we are speaking not of concupiscence, which is sin, but of the appetite which would have existed in nature even if it had remained uncorrupted, which they call physical love. And this love of one sex for the other is truly a divine ordinance . . . .
>
> Because this creation or divine ordinance is a natural right (*ius naturale*), jurists have accordingly said wisely and correctly that the union of male and female belongs to the [order of] natural laws (*iuris naturalis*). But since natural law is immutable, the right to contract marriage (*ius contrahendi conjugi*) must always remain. For where nature does not change, that ordinance with which God has endowed nature does not change, and cannot be removed . . . . Moreover a natural right is truly a divine right (*ius divinum*), because it is an ordinance divinely impressed upon nature. But inasmuch as this right cannot be changed without an extraordinary work of God, it is necessary that the right to contract marriage remains, because the natural desire of [one] sex for [the other] sex is an ordinance of God (*ordinatio Dei*) in nature, and for this reason is a right.[16]

Melanchthon eventually included his list of ten principles of natural law among these "natural elements of knowledge concerning morals." Human reason cannot prove the existence of natural law principles, he insisted.[17] They are facets of human nature, forms of innate knowledge that exist in the mind of God, who placed them in our mind when God created us in his image. Moreover, natural law principles cannot be fully understood using reason alone. "Our nature is corrupted by original sin," Melanchthon wrote, sounding the familiar Protestant doctrine of total depravity. "Thus, the law of nature is greatly obscured." The best way for a Christian to understand the natural law, therefore, was to turn to the Bible, including the Torah, the Beatitudes, the moral codes of Jesus and Saint Paul. The best single summary, however, was the Ten Commandments, which Luther had also extolled. In

15 CR 11:918–19; CR 13:150, 647–54; 16:228; 20:695–99; 21:117, 398–400, 711–13.
16 *Triglott Concordia*, 366–67.
17 CR 21:399–400.

a Christian society, parents, pastors, and political officials alike would do well to start with this formulation of natural law.[18]

Melanchthon took this image directly into his account of state positive laws. "When you think about *Obrigkeit* [authorities], about princes or lords," he wrote, "picture in your mind a man holding in one hand the tables of the Ten Commandments and holding in the other a sword. Those Ten Commandments are above all the works which he must protect and maintain," using the sword if necessary. Those Ten Commandments are "also the source from which all teaching and well-written laws flow and by which all statutes should be guided."[19]

As custodians of the First Table of the Ten Commandments, or Decalogue, Melanchthon wrote, magistrates must pass laws against idolatry, blasphemy, and violations of the Sabbath – offenses that the First Table prohibits on its face. Magistrates must also pass laws to "establish pure doctrine" and right liturgy, "to prohibit all wrong doctrine," "to punish the obstinate," and to root out the heathen and the heterodox. "[W]orldly princes and rulers who have abolished idolatry and false doctrine in their territories and have established the pure doctrine of the Gospel and the right worship of God have acted rightly," Melanchthon argued. "All rulers are obliged to do this."[20]

Melanchthon's endorsement of state establishments of Christianity by positive law was a marked departure from Luther's original teaching. In 1523, for example, Luther had written:

> Earthly government has laws that extend no further than to life, property, and other external things on earth. For God cannot and will not allow anyone but himself alone to rule over the soul. Thus, when the earthly power presumes to prescribe laws to souls, it encroaches upon God and his government and only seduces and corrupts souls.[21]

Luther eventually softened this stance, particularly in his late-life railings against Jews, antinomians, and Anabaptists.[22] But he remained firmly opposed to the magistrate defining by positive law which Christian doctrines and liturgies were orthodox and which heterodox.

Melanchthon had held similar views in the 1520s and 1530s. But he eventually retreated from this position, despite Luther's objections, in response to two decades of intense religious rivalries among Catholics and Protestants in Germany. He had become increasingly dismayed at the fracturing of German society and the perennial outbreaks of violent antinomianism and spiritual radicalism. He had become especially incensed at the "great many frantic and bewildered souls" who were

18 Robert Stupperich, ed., *Melanchthons Werke in Auswahl*, 6 vols. (Gütersloh, 1951), 3:208, 4:146; CR 13:547–55; 21:116–17; 21:392–402; 22:201–02, 256–57.

19 CR 22:615.

20 CR 16:87–88; 22:615–617.

21 *Luthers Werke: Kritische Gesamtausgabe*, 11:262.

22 Pelikan et al., eds., *Luther's Works*, 47:99–119, 121–306.

blaspheming God and God's law with their "monstrous absurdities" and "diabolical rages." To allow such blasphemy and chaos to continue without rejoinder, Melanchthon believed, was ultimately to betray God and to belie the essence of the political office. After all, he reasoned,

> earthly authority is obliged to maintain external discipline according to *all* the commandments. External idolatry, blasphemy, false oaths, untrue doctrine, and heresy are contrary to the First Table [of the Decalogue]. For this reason, earthly authority is obliged to prohibit, abolish, and punish these depravities [and] to accept the Holy Gospel, to believe, confess, and direct others to true divine service.

The political office "before all else should serve God, and should regulate and direct everything to the glory of God."[23]

With this teaching, Melanchthon helped to lay the theoretical basis for the welter of new religious-establishment laws promulgated in Lutheran cities and territories in the sixteenth and seventeenth centuries. These church ordinances both reflected and directed the resystematization of dogma; the truncation of the sacraments; the reforms of liturgy, devotional life, and the religious calendar; the vernacularization of the Bible, liturgy, and sermon; the expansion of catechesis and religious instruction in schools and universities; the revamping of corporate worship, congregational music, religious symbolism, and church art and architecture; the radical reforms of ecclesiastical discipline and local church administration; the new practices of tithing, baptism, confirmation, weddings, and burial; diaconal care, sanctuary, and much more.[24] All of these aspects of church and spiritual life had been governed in detail by the medieval Catholic Church's canon laws and sacramental rules. They were now subject to the Protestant state's religious establishment laws. Vestiges of these laws still remain in Lutheran lands, though strong new policies of religious disestablishment are now afoot in Scandinavia and several German states.[25]

While the First Table of the Decalogue supported state positive laws governing relations between God and persons, the Second Table supported positive laws governing the relations between persons. Melanchthon and Lutheran jurists whom he inspired like Johann Oldendorp (ca. 1486–1567) and Nicolaus Hemming (1513–1600) set out a whole series of positive laws under each commandment of the Second Table. On the basis of the Fourth Commandment ("Honor thy father and mother"), magistrates are obligated to prohibit and punish disobedience, disrespect, or disdain of authorities – not only parents but also political rulers, teachers, employers, masters,

[23] Melancthon, *Loci Communes* 1555, 324, 335–36 (rendering "*weltliche*" as "earthly" not "worldly"); CR 11:918.

[24] See Emil Sehling, et al., eds., *Die evangelischen Kirchenordnungen des 16. Jahrhunderts*, 24 vols. (Tübingen: Mohr Siebeck, 2017–).

[25] See Kjell Å. Modéer and Helle Vogt, *Law and the Christian Tradition in Scandinavia: The Writings of Great Nordic Jurists* (London: Routledge, 2020); Lisbet Christoffersen, Kjell Å Modeer, and Svend Andersen, eds., *Law and Religion in the 21st Century: Nordic Perspectives* (Copenhagen: Djøf Publishers, 2010).

and others. On the basis of the Fifth Commandment ("Thou shalt not kill"), they are to punish unlawful killing, violence, assault, battery, and other offenses against neighbors. On the basis of the Sixth Commandment ("Thou shalt not commit adultery"), they are to prohibit adultery, fornication, unchastity, prostitution, obscenity, and other sexual offenses. On the basis of the Seventh Commandment ("Thou shalt not steal"), they are to outlaw theft, burglary, embezzlement, and similar offenses against another's property, as well as waste or noxious use or sumptuous use of one's own property. On the basis of the Eighth Commandment ("Thou shalt not bear false witness"), they are to punish all forms of perjury, fraud, defamation, and other violations of a person's reputation or status. Finally, on the basis of the Ninth and Tenth Commandments ("Thou shalt not covet"), they are to punish all attempts to perform these or other offensive acts against another's person, property, reputation, or relationships.[26]

Magdeburg Confession. Early modern Lutherans did not develop an elaborate theory of natural rights based on the Decalogue or other foundations, but they did make some notable contributions that became important anchors for other Protestants, particularly Calvinists. In defending his Reformation, Luther had called for "freedom of a Christian" from oppressive papal rule, and this famous early statement fueled later arguments for religious freedom from abusive church or state authorities. Lutheran jurists and moralists also repeated traditional canon law and civil law teachings on the rights *(iura)* and liberties *(libertates)* that were part of the public, private, procedural, and penal laws of the day.

The strongest early Lutheran statements on natural rights came in the Magdeburg Confession (1550).[27] The leaders of the small Saxon city of Magdeburg had drafted this Confession in response to the order of the Holy Roman emperor to impose uniform Catholic doctrines and liturgies in the empire, and to stamp out the "raging Lutheran heresy" that was causing such "discord," "dissension," "calamity and destruction."[28] The emperor aimed to end this once and for all. Lutheran polities that persisted in their heresy would face military conquest and destruction. Several had already capitulated. Magdeburg would not. Imperial forces laid siege to the city. The Magdeburgers stood firm and issued the Confession in defense of their actions. Its opening lines read:

> If the high authority does not refrain from unjustly and forcibly persecuting not only the lives of their subjects but even more their rights under divine and natural law, and if the high authority does not desist from eradicating true doctrine and true

[26] Melancthon, *Loci Communes* 1555, 97 ff.; CR 21:294 ff., 387 ff.; 22:256 ff.; 16:70 ff.

[27] *Confessio et apologia pastorum & reliquorum ministrorum Ecclesiae Magdeburgensis* (Magdeburg, 1550). See further analysis in David M. Whitford, *Tyranny and Resistance: The Magdeburg Confession and the Lutheran Tradition* (St. Louis, MO: Concordia Publishing, 2001).

[28] Preamble to "The Interim, or Declaration of Religion of His Imperial Majesty Charles V," in *Tracts and Treaties in Defense of the Reformed Faith*, trans. Henry Beveridge, ed. T. F. Torrance, 3 vols. (Grand Rapids, MI: Eerdmans, 1958), 3:190–94.

worship of God, then the lower magistracy is required by God's divine command to attempt, together with their subjects, to stand up to such superiors as far as possible [and] to protect themselves and their people against this.[29]

The right to resist tyranny lies first with lower magistrates, the Confession argued. If a higher magistrate commits only a minor or personal offense, lower magistrates should admonish him quietly and gently, following biblical examples. But if he unjustly endangers "life and limb," "wife and child," and the "local liberties of the people," then lower magistrates "may make use of their rights to defend themselves" and their subjects. Even worse, if the higher magistrate commits a premeditated attack on "the highest and most essential rights of the people" – indeed, if he attacks "our Lord himself, the author of these rights" – then even the most "insignificant and weakest regents" must rise up against him. For we must "obey God rather than men" (Acts 5:29).[30]

The Confession did not define the "local liberties of the people," or "the highest and most essential rights of the people" that could trigger escalating resistance and revolt. The authors hinted broadly that the threatened establishment of "unnatural" and "unbiblical" Catholic family laws might be such an example. They stated more plainly that their "procedural rights" had been abridged: "Divine, natural, and secular laws" alike recognize that criminals have a right to a public hearing and their day in court. But we have been "accused only on hearsay evidence," and have not had a chance to "face our accusers." Just because other Lutheran towns have capitulated does not mean that we should lose "our rights by default." "Our case must be judged in accordance with proper justice."[31]

The Confession's main concern, however, was that the emperor was violating the people's "essential rights" of religion, and those violations merited a more forceful response. We "seek nothing else but the freedom to remain and be left in the true recognized religion of the holy and only redeeming Gospel." We act peaceably. We educate our children to be good and useful citizens. We pray daily for our rulers. We pay our taxes and tributes. We register our properties. We "desire no one's land and people and covet no one's worth and goods." "Your Imperial Majesty allows both Jews and heathens to follow their religion, and do not force them from their religions to the papacy"; but "we are not even allowed to have the same freedom of religion that is granted to non-Christians." Instead, the emperor seeks "to reintroduce the pope's idolatry, to suppress or exterminate the pure doctrine of the Holy Gospel ... in violation not only of divine law but also of written civil law." Against such oppression, the people must exercise their "universal" and "natural" "law of legitimate self-defense."[32]

29 *Confessio et apologia*, A1v.
30 Ibid., J4r–k1r, K2R–L1r, M1r–M2r, P2r–P3r.
31 Ibid., H2r, K4r.
32 Ibid., H4r–J2r, K1r, N.

The Magdeburg Confession was the strongest Lutheran statement of the day on resistance to political tyranny based on systematic violations of the people's natural rights. This document helped turn popular opinion against the emperor and led to the gradual collapse of other imperial military campaigns against the Lutherans. Ultimately, the emperor was forced to accept the Peace of Augsburg, which allowed each polity to establish either Catholicism or Lutheranism, giving dissenters to the right to emigrate peaceably.

ANABAPTIST TEACHINGS

Early modern Anabaptists expounded a two-kingdoms theory that more fully separated the redeemed realm of religion and the church from the fallen realm of politics and the state, and introduced new forms of church–state separation and religious freedom.[33] Emerging as a new form of Protestantism in the early 1520s, Anabaptists were scattered into various groups of Amish, Brethren, Hutterites, Mennonites, Baptists, and others. Some of the early splinter groups, like the followers of Thomas Müntzer (1489–1525) and Caspar Schwenckfeld (d. 1561) were politically radical or utopian spiritualists. Others, like the Anabaptist sect in Münster under John of Leiden (d. 1536), practiced polygamy for a short time, which they enforced ruthlessly against detractors. But most Anabaptist communities by the mid-sixteenth century were quiet Christian separatists, monogamists, and pacifists, taking their lead from such theologians as Menno Simons, Pilgrim Marpeck (d. 1556), Dirk Philips (1504–68), and Peter Riedemann (1506–56), who urged their followers to return to the simple teachings of the New Testament and apostolic church.

Separation of Church and State. Adducing the first-century apostolic churches as their model, Anabaptist communities ascetically withdrew from civil and political life into small, self-sufficient, intensely democratic communities. These communities were governed internally by biblical principles of discipleship, simplicity, charity, and nonresistance. They set their own standards of worship, liturgy, diet, discipline, dress, and education. They handled their own affairs of property, contracts, commerce, marriage, and inheritance – so far as possible by appeal to biblical laws and practices, not those of the state. They enforced these internal religious laws not by coercion but by persuasion, and not for the sake of retribution but for the redemption of the sinner and restoration of that person to community. Recalcitrant sinners and community members who grew violent or destructive or persistently betrayed the community's ideals were shunned and, if necessary, banned from the

[33] For illustrative writings, see Michael G. Baylor, *The Radical Reformation* (Cambridge: Cambridge University Press, 1991); Walter Klaassen, *Anabaptism in Outline* (Scottdale, PA: Herald Press, 1981). For overviews, see William R. Estep, *The Anabaptist Story: An Introduction to Sixteenth-Century Anabaptism* (Grand Rapids, MI: Eerdmans, 1996); Robert Friedmann, *The Theology of Anabaptism*, repr. ed. (Scottdale, PA: Herald Press, 1998); Guy F. Hershberger, ed., *The Recovery of the Anabaptist Vision*, repr. ed. (Scottdale, PA: Herald Press, 2001); George Huntston Williams, *The Radical Reformation*, 3rd rev. ed. (Kirksville, MO: Truman State University Press, 2000).

community. Moreover, when Anabaptist communities grew too large or too internally divided, they deliberately colonized themselves, eventually spreading Anabaptists from Russia to Ireland to the farthest frontiers of North America.

The state and its law, most Anabaptists believed, were part of the fallen world, which was to be avoided so far as possible in accordance with biblical injunctions that Christians should not be "of the world" or "conformed" to it. Once the perfect creation of God, the world was now a fallen, sinful regime that lay beyond "the perfection of Christ" and beyond the daily concern of the Christian believer. God had built a "wall of separation" (*paries maceriae*) between the redeemed church and the fallen world, Menno Simons wrote, quoting Ephesians 2:14. God had allowed the world to survive by ordaining and empowering magistrates to use positive laws and, if necessary, coercion and violence to maintain a modicum of order and peace. Christians should obey the laws of political authorities, so far as the Bible commanded – paying taxes, registering properties, avoiding theft and homicide, keeping promises, and testifying truthfully. But Christians should avoid active participation in and unnecessary interaction with the world and the state – avoiding litigation, oath-swearing, state education, banking, large-scale commerce, trade fairs, public festivals, drinking houses, theaters, games, political office, policing, or military service. Most early modern Anabaptists were pacifists, preferring derision, exile, or death to participation in war or violence.[34] This aversion to common political and civic activities often earned Anabaptists scorn, reprisal, and repression by Catholics and Protestants alike – violent martyrdom in many instances.[35]

Religious Liberty. While unpopular in its genesis, Anabaptism ultimately proved to be a vital source of Western constitutional arguments for religious freedom.[36] Baptists and other Free Church groups in England and early America advocated "a wall of separation between the garden of the Church and the wilderness of the world," as Rhode Island founder Roger Williams put it famously in 1643.[37] They also advocated the liberty of conscience of every individual and the freedom of association of every peaceable religious group without state establishments of religion.

"The notion of an [established] Christian commonwealth should be exploded forever," declared John Leland (1754–1841), the fiery American Baptist preacher in later summary of two centuries of Anabaptist teachings. All religious establishments are "evil," because when "uninspired, fallible men make their own opinions tests of

34 Klaasen, *Anabaptism in Outline*, 245–57.

35 See J. Thieleman Van Braght, *Martyr's Mirror*, repr. ed. (Scottdale, PA: Herald Press, 1981).

36 Harold S. Bender, *The Anabaptists and Religious Liberty in the Sixteenth Century* (Philadelphia: Fortress Press, 1970); Chris Beneke and Christopher S. Grenda, *The Lively Experiment: Religious Toleration in America from Roger Williams to the Present* (Lanham, MD: Rowman and Littlefield, 2015).

37 *The Complete Writings of Roger Williams*, 7 vols. (New York: Russell and Russell, 1963), 1:392. For other early statements on the "wall of separation," and comparable metaphors, see John Witte, Jr. and Joel A. Nichols, *Religion and the American Constitutional Experiment*, 4th ed. (New York: Oxford University Press, 2016), 52–57; John Witte, Jr., *God's Joust, God's Justice: Law and Religion in the Western Tradition* (Grand Rapids, MI: Eerdmans, 2006), 207–42.

orthodoxy," then religion is stunted and stilted, "ignorance and superstition prevail, or persecution rages." Establishments inspire hypocrisy because people embrace the religion favored and pampered by law. "Establishments not only wean and alienate the affections of one from another" but also drive nonconformists to leave the state and take their loyalty, work, and taxes with them, leaving behind dull, anemic religions to propagate themselves or convert others by coercion or bribery. Establishments reduce religion and the church into an agent and "trick of the state." And establishments merely cover for the insecurity and doubt not of only church leaders who lack faith in the cogency of their views but also of political rulers, who "often fear that if they leave every man to think, speak, and worship as he pleases, that the whole cause [of statecraft] will be wrecked in diversity."[38]

In place of state establishments of religion and Christian commonwealths, Anabaptists advocated religious voluntarism – the freedom of each person to choose, change, or reject religion. God called the adult individual to make a conscientious choice to accept the faith and to signal that acceptance through adult baptism – metaphorically, to scale the wall of separation between the fallen world and the garden of religion to come "within the perfection of Christ." State coercion or control of this choice – either directly through persecution and repression or indirectly through withholding civil rights and benefits from those who made the choice – was an offense both against the individual and against God. A plurality of religions should coexist in the community. It was for God, not the state, to decide which religion should flourish and which should fade.[39]

In place of state patronage of religion, Anabaptists demanded autonomy of church governance. Every religious body, they argued, should be free from state control of its assembly and worship, from state regulations of its property and polity, from state incorporation of its society and clergy, from state interference in its discipline and government, and from state collection of religious tithes and taxes. Some free-church advocates went further to oppose such traditional state supports of religion as tax exemptions, civil immunities, and property donations. They feared that religious bodies receiving any state benefits would invariably become beholden to the state, dependent on its largess, and distracted from their divine mandates. "[I]f civil Rulers go so far out of their Sphere as to take the Care and Management of religious affairs upon them," reads a 1776 Baptist declaration, "Farwel[l] to 'the free exercise of Religion.'"[40]

38 L. F. Greene, ed., *The Writings of John Leland* (New York: Arno Press, 1969), 118, 179–92.

39 See the early statement in the Schleitheim Confession (1527), in *The Mennonite Quarterly Review* 19 (October 1945), 247–53, Article VI and early exposition in *The Complete Writings of Menno Simons, c. 1496–1561*, trans. L. Verduin, ed. J. C. Wenger (Scottsdale, PA: Herald Press, 1984), 29, 117–20, 158–59, 190–206; *Biblical Concordance of the Swiss Brethren, 1540*, ed. C. A. Synder, trans. G. Fast and G. A. Peters (Ontario: Pandora Press, 2001), 56–60. For later Baptist views, see sources and discussion in Witte and Nichols, *Religion and the American Constitutional Experiment*, 29–32, particularly the classic study William C. McLoughlin, *New England Dissent, 1630–1833: The Baptists and the Separation of Church and State*, 2 vols. (Cambridge, MA: Harvard University Press, 1971).

40 "Declaration of the Virginia Association of Baptists (December 25, 1776)," in Julian P. Boyd, ed., *The Papers of Thomas Jefferson* (Princeton: Princeton University Press, 1950), 1:660–61.

CALVINIST TEACHINGS

The Calvinist or Reformed tradition was comprised of large but widely scattered religious groups in cities and provinces of Switzerland, France, Germany, Hungary, Poland, Scotland, the Netherlands, and England, and eventually their many colonies overseas. In the sixteenth and seventeenth centuries, they were variously called Reformed, Huguenots, Pietists, Puritans, Presbyterians, Congregationalists, and other terms. Although these denominational and regional labels sometimes signaled serious differences among these groups, they were largely united in their teachings on natural law, natural rights, and religious freedom.

Most Calvinists charted a course between Lutherans, who subordinated the church to the state, and Anabaptists, who withdrew the church from the state and society.[41] Like Anabaptists, Calvinists insisted on a basic separation of the offices and operations of church and state, leaving the church to govern its own doctrine and liturgy, polity and property, without interference from the state. John Calvin set the foundation for this church–state division in the Ecclesiastical Ordinances of Geneva (1541/1561), which were echoed in many later Calvinist polities. "There is a great difference and unlikeness between the ecclesiastical and civil power" of the church and state, Calvin explained. "A distinction should always be observed between these two clearly distinct areas of responsibility, the civil and the ecclesiastical." The church has no authority to punish crime, remedy civil wrongs, collect taxes, make war, or meddle in the affairs of the state. The state, in turn, has no authority to preach the Word, administer the sacraments, enforce spiritual discipline, collect tithes, interfere with church property, appoint or remove clergy, obstruct bans or excommunications, or meddle in the internal affairs of a congregation. To permit any such interference between church and state, said Calvin, would "unwisely mingle these two which have a completely different nature."[42]

Like Lutherans, Calvinists insisted that each local polity must be an overtly Christian commonwealth adhering to the general principles of natural and biblical law, which they translated into detailed new positive laws of religious worship, Sabbath observance, public morality, marriage and family, crime and tort, contract

[41] For sources, see Emile Rivoire and Victor van Berchem, eds., *Les sources du droit du canton de Genève*, 4 vols. (Arau: Sauerländer, 1930). For overviews, see Philip Benedict, *Christ's Church Purely Reformed: A Social History of Calvinism* (New Haven, CT: Yale University Press, 2002); Matthew J. Tuininga, *Calvin's Political Theology and the Public Engagement of the Church* (Cambridge: Cambridge University Press, 2017); Harro Höpfl, *The Christian Polity of John Calvin* (Cambridge: Cambridge University Press, 1982); Robert M. Kingdon, *Church and State in Reformation Europe* (London: Variorum Reprints, 1985); Christoph Strohm, *Calvinismus und Recht* (Tübingen: Mohr Siebeck, 2008); John Witte, Jr., *The Reformation of Rights: Law, Religion, and Human Rights in Early Modern Calvinism* (Cambridge: Cambridge University Press, 2007).

[42] John Calvin, *Institutes of the Christian Religion*, ed. John T. McNeill, trans. Ford Lewis Battles (Philadelphia, PA: Westminster Press, 1960), 3.19.15; 4.11.3–16; 4.20.1–4; *Ioannis Calvini opera quae supersunt omnia*, ed. G. Baum, et al., 59 vols. (Brunswick: Böhlau, 1863–1900), 10/1:15–30, 215–17, 223–24.

and business, charity and education. Calvin drafted many of these new laws for Geneva during his tenure there from 1541 to 1564, and these Genevan laws were also duplicated and expanded in hundreds of Calvinist polities over the next two centuries.

Unlike both Lutherans and Anabaptists, however, Calvinists stressed that both church and state officials were to play complementary roles in creating the local Christian commonwealth and cultivating the Christian citizen. Calvinists regarded each community as a unitary Christian society, a miniature *corpus Christianum* under God's sovereignty and law. Within this unitary society, the church and the state stood as coordinate powers. Both were ordained by God to help achieve a godly order and discipline in the community and to aid and accommodate each other on a variety of levels.

John Calvin. Natural rights and liberties were a part of the Calvinist tradition from the beginning, particularly as Calvinists responded to waves of religious persecution.[43] As a young man, Calvin was exiled from his Catholic French homeland on account of his Protestant beliefs. He thus opened his first major work, the *Institutes of the Christian Religion* (1536), with a dedication to the French king, Francis, that was, in fact, a brief, "boldly groan[ing] for freedom" from "overbearing tyranny" and abuses that defied widely recognized rights and freedoms of the day. In his dedication, Calvin protested the widespread and unchecked instances of "perjury," "lying slanders," "wicked accusations," and the "fury of evil men" that conspired to incite "public hatred" and "open violence" against believers. He protested that "the case" of the Protestants "has been handled with no order of law and with violent heat rather than judicial gravity." He protested various forms of false imprisonment and abuses of prisoners. "Some of us are shackled with irons, some beaten with rods, some led about as laughingstocks, some proscribed, some most savagely tortured, some forced to flee." He protested the many procedural inequities. Protestants are "fraudulently and undeservedly charged with treason and villainy" and convicted for capital offenses "without confession or sure testimony." "[B]loody sentences are meted out against this doctrine without a hearing." He protested the bias of judges and the partiality of judicial proceedings. "Those who sit in judgment ... pronounce as sentences the prejudices which they have brought from home." He protested the intrusions on the church's freedoms of assembly and speech. "The poor little church has either been wasted with cruel slaughter or banished into exile, or so overwhelmed by threats and fears that it dare not even open its mouth." All these offenses stood diametrically opposed to basic political rights and freedoms recognized at the time both in the Holy Roman Empire and in France.[44]

43 See detailed references in Witte, *The Reformation of Rights*.

44 John Calvin, *Institution of the Christian Religion*, trans. Ford Lewis Battles (Atlanta: Westminster Press, 1975), dedication.

In this same edition of the *Institutes*, Calvin called for the freedom not just of Protestants but of all peaceable believers, including Catholics, Jews, and Muslims. He denounced forced baptisms, inquisitions, crusades, and other forms of religious persecution practiced by the medieval church and state:

> We ought to strive by whatever means we can, whether by exhortation and teaching or by mercy and gentleness, or by our own prayers to God, that they may turn to a more virtuous life and may return to the society and unity of the church. And not only are excommunicants to be so treated, but also Turks and Saracens, and other enemies of religion. Far be it from us to approve those methods by which many until now have tried to force them to our faith, when they forbid them the use of fire and water and the common elements, when they deny them to all offices of humanity, when they pursue them with sword and arms.[45]

While Calvin later hardened in his opposition to Christian heretics – just ask Michael Servetus, whose trial and execution for heresy Calvin supported – he continued to press his general case for freedom over the next quarter century. "There is nothing more desirable than liberty," he wrote. Liberty is "an inestimable good," "a singular benefit and treasure that cannot be prized enough," something worth "more than half of life." "How great a benefit liberty is, when God has bestowed it on someone." Calvin emphasized the importance of political suffrage and the franchise in the political community. The "right to vote," he once said, is the "best way to preserve liberty." "Let those whom God has given liberty and the franchise use it." "The reason why tyrannies have come into the world, why people everywhere have lost their liberty ... is that people who had elections abused the privilege." "There is no kind of government more salutary than one in which liberty is properly exercised with becoming moderation and properly constituted on a durable basis."[46]

Drawing on his legal training, Calvin also discussed the subjective rights *(iura, droits)* of individuals alongside their liberties *(libertates, libertés)*. Sometimes he used general phrases like "the common rights of humankind" *(iura commune hominum)*, the "natural rights" *(iura naturali)* of persons, the "rights of a common nature" *(communis naturae iura)*, and "the equal rights and liberties" *(pari iura et libertates)* of all.[47] Usually he referenced more specific subjective rights. He spoke, for example, about the "rights of Christian liberty," the "rights of citizenship" in the kingdom of God, the "right of adoption" that Christians enjoy as new sons and daughters of God and brothers and sisters in Christ. He referenced the right "to inhabit," "to dwell in," and "to claim the territory" that Yahweh gave to the chosen

45 Ibid., 2.28.

46 Calvin, *Institutes*, 3.19.1–8, 14; Serm., Gen. 39:11; Serm., 1 Sam. 8, 17; Comm., Harm. Law Deut. 15:1–11; 17:14–18; 24:7; Serm., Deut. 16:18–19; 18:14–18 collected in *Ioannis Calvini opera quae supersunt omnia*, ed. G. Baum et al., 59 vols. (Brunswick: Schwetzke, 1863–1900).

47 Comm., Gen. 4:13; Comm., Harm. Law Num. 3:5–10, 18–22; Deut. 5:19; Comm., Ps. 7:6–8; Lect., Jer. 22:1–3; 22:13–14; Lect., Ezek. 8:17; Comm., 1 Cor. 7:37.

people of Israel. He mentioned "Paul's rights of Roman citizenship." He spoke frequently, as a student of Roman law would, about property rights: the right to land and other property; "the right to enjoy and use what one possesses;" the right "to recover" and "to have restored" lost or stolen property; the right to compensation for work; the right to sell, bequeath, and inherit property, particularly in accordance with the "natural rights of primogeniture." He spoke of the right to bury one's parents and other relatives. He also spoke frequently of the marital rights of husband and wife, and the "sacred," "natural," and "common" rights of parents over their children – in particular, the right and authority of a father to name and raise his child and to set the child up in marriage. He spoke in passing about the "sacred right of hospitality" of the sojourner, the "right of asylum" or of sanctuary for those in flight, the "right of redemption" for slaves, and the natural rights and "just rights" of the poor, needy, orphans, and widows.[48]

But Calvin's talk about rights was always coupled with talk about duties. The whole point of having rights and liberties, Calvin insisted, was to enable a person to discharge the duties and responsibilities of the faith. "We obtain liberty in order that we may more promptly and more readily obey God in all things" spiritual and temporal, he wrote.[49] Freedoms and commandments, rights and duties remained together in Calvin's formulation, balancing and bolstering each other. Subjective claims about rights were grounded in an objective right order.

Calvin spent a great deal of time defining this right order. Sometimes he described it as a "natural order," an "order of nature," or an "order of creation." Sometimes he used more anthropological language: our "human conscience," "natural conscience," "inner voice," "natural inclination" or "sense of right and wrong." More often, he described this order as a divine, spiritual, moral, or natural law. What this untidy gaggle of terms basically described was the set of norms that undergird and legitimize the positive laws of human authorities. God has written this natural law on the hearts and consciences of all persons, rewritten it in the pages of scripture, and summarized it in the Decalogue.[50]

Like Luther and Melanchthon, Calvin often used the Decalogue as a crisp summary of the natural law, as well as a template of the natural rights and duties of each person toward God. The First Table's "religious rights" to worship, keep the Sabbath, honor God, and avoid false swearing are "inherent human rights," said Calvin, "part of our human nature," which church, state, and neighbor alike must respect. Such religious rights and duties are also extensions of God's divine rights: the "eternal right of God himself, to be properly worshipped and glorified," as Calvin

48 See detailed sources in Witte, *Reformation of Rights*, 57–58.

49 Comm. 1 Peter 2:16; Calvin, *Institutes*, 3.17.1–2; 3.19.14–16; 4.10.5.

50 Calvin, *Institutes*, 2.7.1; 2.8.1; 4.20.15; *Ioannis calvini*, 24:262–724; ibid., 26:236–432. See I. John Hesselink, *Calvin's Concept of the Law* (Allison Park, PA: Pickwick Publications, 1992), 18–24, 51–85; John T. McNeill, "Natural Law and the Teaching of the Reformers," *Journal of Religion* 26 (1946), 168.

put it.[51] Similarly, Calvin hinted, each person's natural duties toward a neighbor in the Second Table can be cast as a neighbor's natural rights to have those duties discharged.[52] Calvin's followers, beginning with his Genevan successor Theodore Beza (1519–1605) and the exiled Cambridge don Christopher Goodman (1520–1603), elaborated these teachings into a theory of "inherent" or "inalienable" natural rights, which German-born jurist Johannes Althusius (1563–1638) greatly expanded.

Christopher Goodman. Goodman's 1558 tract, *How Superior Powers Ought to Be Obey[e]d*, argued that magistrates must strike a mean between granting their subjects too much liberty and too little liberty. Granting too much, he argued, will lead the people to contempt, sedition, "dissoluteness," "carnal liberty," rioting, tumult, and "contempt" for law and order, "whether divine or human." But giving them too little liberty will do exactly the same. "[T]he people ought not suffer all power and liberty to be taken from them, and thereby to become brute beasts without judgment and reason, thinking all things lawful, which their rulers do without exception, command them, be they never so far from reason or godliness." God will "not suffer" that the liberties that he has given to all his people "be taken from them."[53]

What are these God-given rights and liberties that cannot be taken from the people – that literally cannot be "alienated"? They are the unalienable rights and liberties set out in the Bible, particularly in the Ten Commandments, Goodman answered:

> [I]t is an easy matter for all manner of subjects to know what liberty belongs unto them by the word of God, which they may lawfully claim as their own possession, are likewise bound at all times to practice: wherein also appears what things are prohibited unto them, which they may in no case exercise. ... [T]here may be nothing lawful for you by any commandment of man, which your Lord God in any case forbids: and nothing unlawful or forbidden to you which he commands, whether it appertains to the first table or the second [table of the Decalogue]. Which rule if ye observe, you may be assured to please God: like as by doing the contrary you shall purchase his heavy wrath and indignation.[54]

This was Goodman's rights formula. The rights and liberties that God gives to each person as an inalienable possession are set out in the Decalogue. Nothing that God requires there may the magistrate forbid. Nothing that God forbids there may the magistrate require. Persons thus have the inalienable right to keep the Sabbath, to honor their parents, to worship properly and to speak appropriately – and the correlative freedom from laws commanding them to worship false gods, maintain graven images, swear false oaths, or otherwise take the name of God in vain. People have the inalienable right (and correlative freedom) to life (freedom from killing),

[51] Lect. Dan. 6:22; Serm. 2 Sam. 1:1–4.

[52] Sources in Witte, *Reformation of Rights*, 121–41.

[53] Christopher Goodman, *How Superior Powers Ought to Be Obeyd*, facs. ed., ed. Charles H. McIlwain (New York: Columbia University Press, 1931), 147–54 (spelling modernized).

[54] Ibid., 160–61.

property (freedom from stealing), marital integrity (freedom from adultery), and reputation and fair process (freedom from false testimony). They have the right to their privacy, and freedom from having their family, household, and possessions subject to the covetous privations of neighbors. If the magistrate requires or condones conduct contrary to this formula, the magistrate is violating each subject's rights and liberties. To do so is to practice tyranny and to invite resistance for God's sake.

Johannes Althusius. Goodman's Decalogue-based method for outlining natural rights and duties became a commonplace for later Calvinists and was gradually expanded in a full blown theological jurisprudence. German-born Calvinist jurist Johannes Althusius (1557–1638), for example, developed an elaborate system of natural rights and liberties for the war-torn Netherlands where he lived and the Holy Roman Empire from which he hailed. Natural rights, he said, were either affirmative or negative claims that a party could make on the basis of natural law – "the right, freedom, or power to act by and for oneself" and to be free from or to forgo acting, or more simply the "rights to freedoms" of various sorts. Again, using the natural law distillation in the Decalogue, Althusius distinguished two main classes of natural rights: (1) "religious rights and liberties" and (2) "social rights and liberties." Althusius called both classes of rights "fundamental rights" – indispensable to the survival of a person and polity and foundational to any more specific rights formulations by positive laws, whether set out in statutes or in written constitutions.[55]

Like Goodman, Althusius enumerated the natural religious rights anchored in the First Table. "[E]ach and everyone in the whole realm should worship freely and fully without any fear or peril," he wrote expansively.[56] Generalizing from these First Table duties, Althusius defended the absolute liberty of conscience *(libertas conscientiae)* and a qualified right of religious exercise *(ius religionis exercitium)*.[57] He saw absolute liberty of conscience as the natural corollary to the absolute sovereignty of God, a doctrinal staple of Calvinism. Sovereignty is a legal term, said Althusius, a power to command and control. Through the opening words of the Decalogue, "I am the Lord, thy God," the Bible makes clear that "God alone can command the conscience." God alone can bring a person "out of the house of sinful bondage" and into the "promised land" – whether in this life or in the next. God alone can change the hearts and charge the souls of men and women. No person or authority may thus require a person "to believe against his will. Faith must be persuaded, not commanded; it must be taught, not ordered." To invade the sanctuary of conscience is to impugn the sovereignty of God; "to impose a penalty on the thoughts of men" is to

55 Johannes Althusius, *Dicaeologicae libri tres, totum et universum Jus, quo utimur, methodice complectentes* (Frankfurt, 1618), I.25.1–8; Johannes Althusius, *Politica Methodice Digesta*, ed. Carl J. Friedrich (Cambridge, MA: Harvard University Press, 1932), with abridged English translation, *Politica Johannes Althusius*, ed. and trans. F. S. Carney (Indianapolis: Liberty Fund, 1995), XXI.22–24

56 Ibid., 20.12–13, 20–22; ibid., 37.21–22, 33–34, 36; ibid., 28.14, 53–66; ibid., 38.10–14, 77–78; Althusius, *Dicaeologicae*, 1.101.32–33, 42–43; ibid., 1.113.8–9, 12; ibid., 1.115.10–36.

57 Ibid., 1.25.8; Althusius, *Politica*, 28.62.

obstruct the work of the Holy Spirit. "The natural law imparts to all men a freedom of the soul or mind [*libertas animi*]," Althusius wrote. "The exercise of this right cannot be hindered by a command or order, by fear or compulsion."[58]

While everyone must enjoy absolute freedom of conscience, lest the sovereignty of God be invaded, Althusius continued, no one can enjoy absolute "freedom of religious exercise," lest the integrity of society be imperiled. The ideal is that all will see the same divine light and come to the "one true orthodox Christian religion" – by which Althusius meant Calvinism. But no such religious uniformity has ever existed in history, and it cannot be obtained in our day. Yes, individual households and congregations, sometimes even small villages and towns, might be able to practice a uniform faith, but at the provincial, national, and imperial levels, religious pluralism is inevitable. These magistrates must tolerate all forms of faiths whose presence does not offend God, threaten the integrity of the true church, or endanger the common good of society as whole.[59] In practice, for Althusius this meant toleration for Jews and Catholics but only so far as they stayed to themselves, had no public sanctuaries for worship, and received no state support. He also called for toleration of peaceable heretics and nonbelievers in the community, but only so long as they remained unorganized and unpublished.

Althusius' call for a limited religious toleration falls far short of modern constitutional ideals. But Althusius's theory was generous for the time. His was a day when most states gave little place to religious dissenters and had little pause about slaughtering or banishing the religiously wayward or impure. Spain was establishing the Catholic decrees of the Council of Trent on all parties by the point of the sword and the terrors of the Inquisition. The Peace of Augsburg empowered magistrates to establish either Catholicism or Lutheranism in the Holy Roman Empire, with religious dissenters granted only the right to leave – and quickly at that. The Edict of Nantes (1598) reestablished Catholicism in France and granted toleration only to Calvinists, but these restricted rights were melting away by the time Althusius was writing, on their way to being violently rejected by the Edict of Fontainebleau (1685). England's Parliament issued a whole series of severely repressive acts against "papists," "sectaries," and others who dissented from the Church of England, and these laws triggered bitter persecutions of non-Anglicans from the 1580s to the 1630s. The Netherlands, by comparison, was something of a haven for religious dissenters, and Althusius defended its policies more progressively than did many others. John Locke's *Letter on Toleration*, for example, published three generations later, in 1689, granted no toleration to Catholics, Muslims, and other believers "who deliver themselves up to the service and protection of another prince," and no toleration to those "who deny the being of a God" for "promises, covenants, and oaths which are the bonds of human society, can have no hold upon an atheist."[60]

58 Ibid., 7.4–7; ibid., 11.33–45; ibid., 28.14, 37–73, 62–66; Althusius, *Dicaeologicae*, 1.25.8–10.

59 Althusius, *Politica*, 11.33–45; ibid., 28.60–66.

60 John Locke, *The Works of John Locke*, 12th ed., 9 vols. (London: T. Tegg, 1824), 5:47.

Using the commandments of the Second Table of the Decalogue, Althusius set out five clusters of natural social rights and five corresponding duties that other persons and groups, including the church and state, owed to the rights holder. First, everyone has the right to "natural life" and "bodily liberty and protection." This Althusius called "the most important" and basic right of the person. He included within it the freedom to nourish, protect, and care for one's own life and limb, the right to carry arms for protection, the right to proportionate defense of oneself and one's possessions that are needed for life, freedom from murder, assault, and personal injury, and freedom from unjust punishment, imprisonment, repression, or detainment. The commandment not to kill imposes the corresponding duties on everyone not to "hurt, strike, or treat his body in any inhumane way," or to "diminish or take away the use of his body." Among family members, this commandment imposes on each the duty to protect and care for parents, siblings, and children, as well as kin, if possible. Second, everyone has the "right to purity and chastity" *(ius castitus et pudicitia)* – the right to keep oneself holy, chaste, and pure in mind and body, and to restrict and resist the actions of others who threaten or violate this right. The commandments against adultery and coveting one's neighbor's possessions impose the corresponding duties on all to desist from fornication and lust, and to deal with the neighbor "free from the passion of our concupiscence and perverse desire." Third, everyone has the "right to property," to the "fruit of his labors," and "to goods that he uses and enjoys." The commandment against stealing requires others to respect and conserve a neighbor's "title, possession, and use" of his or her property and not to injure, diminish, or remove these property interests. Fourth, everyone has the right to a good reputation – the right to enjoy the honor, good name, "standing, excellence, dignity, fame, authority, esteem, and prominence" that become his or her status and station in society as accorded by nature, custom, law, and circumstance. The commandment not to bear false witness imposes the corresponding duty on everyone to protect the reputation and good name of their neighbors and desist from insults, lies, defamation, and slander. Fifth, everyone has the "right to a family" *(ius familiae)* – the right to marry, procreate, nurture, and educate their children, and to have their marriage, family, and household respected and protected. The commandments about honoring parents, not committing adultery, and not coveting a neighbor's wife or maidservant, in turn, impose on everyone else the duty to respect the "honor, authority, dignity, and preeminence, and indeed the right of the family."[61] These five basic natural rights of social life undergirded a whole series of public, private, penal, and procedural rights that were to be constituted and supported by the positive law of the state, which Althusius spelled out in numbing detail.

Written Constitutions. Althusius was but one of many early modern Calvinists who called for integrating these political covenants and statements of fundamental

[61] Althusius, *Dicaeologicae*, 1.25–26; ibid., 1.117–22; Althusius, *Politica*, 10.5–7.

rights into written constitutions.[62] (We saw the parallel views of John Lilburne (1614–57) and John Milton (1608–74) in the previous chapter.) A written constitution, Althusius said, provided the commonwealth with "a guiding light of civil life, a scale of justice, a preserver of liberty, a bulwark of public peace and discipline, a refuge for the weak, a bridle for the powerful, a norm and straightener of rulership." For Althusius, a properly governed nation or state needed more than a mythical or ancient founding political covenant or contract. It needed more than just a collection of dusty old charters, like Magna Carta (1215) and its Continental analogues that once protected the rights of the aristocracy. Rule-of-law commonwealths needed clear and comprehensive written constitutions that bound all rulers and all subjects. Such constitutions should specify in detail the mutual rights and duties, powers and prerogatives of the rulers and the people, and the principles and procedures for the creation and enforcement of positive laws. "Written constitutions," Althusius wrote, provide the best "fences, walls, guards, or boundaries of our life, guiding us along the appointed way for achieving wisdom, happiness, and peace in human society."[63]

Puritan Calvinists in seventeenth- and eighteenth-century England and New England emphasized strongly that written constitutions needed adequate checks and balances on church and state authorities, as both constraints on power and bulwarks of liberty. While the offices of church and state were ordained by God and represented God's authority on earth, their individual officers were sinful human beings. Without built-in restraints, even the best officers would slowly convert their offices into instruments of self-gain and self-promotion at the cost of their subjects. Drawing eclectically on traditional constitutional lore, Puritans thus advocated a number of constitutional safeguards: popular election of ministers and magistrates; limited tenures and rotations of ecclesiastical and political office; separation of church and state; separation of preaching, disciplinary, and diaconal powers within the church and separation of executive, legislative, and judicial powers within the state; various checks and balances between and among each of these powers; federalist layers of authority with shared and severable sovereignty; open meetings in congregations and towns with rights of petition for the people; clearly enumerated and codified canons and laws for churches and states; and transparent proceedings and records within consistories, courts, and councils.[64]

Rights, Resistance, and Revolution. A final important contribution of Calvinists to the development of rights and liberties came in their responses to the bitter persecution, repression, and genocide that killed tens of thousands of them from the 1550s onward. In response, they developed a robust theory of rights, resistance, and revolution against tyranny, drawing on a lengthy Western tradition going to back

62 For Liburne's efforts, see Chapter 2, p. 56–59.

63 Althusius, *Politica*, X.4; XIX.6, 15, 23, 29, 49; XX.18; XXVIII.30–32. For the views of Lilburne, Milton, and other English constitutionalists, see Witte, *Reformation of Rights*, 209–26.

64 See sources in ibid., 294–320.

to Roman law, building on the Lutheran Magdeburg Confession and other early statements, and anticipating the later insights of English, American, and French Revolutions.

Several key biblical texts seemed to stand in the way. "Let every person be subject to the governing authorities," reads Romans 13:1–5. "For there is no authority except from God, and those that exist have been instituted by God. Therefore, he who resists the authorities resists what God has appointed, and those who resist will come into judgment. For rulers are not a terror to good conduct, but bad. Therefore one must be subject, not only to avoid God's wrath, but for the sake of conscience." 1 Peter 2:13–17 is even more pointed: "Be subject for the Lord's sake to every human institution, whether it be to the emperors as supreme, or to governors as sent by him to punish those who do wrong and to praise those who do right. . . . Live as free men, yet without using your freedom as a pretext for evil." Biblical laws commanded honoring father and mother and other divinely appointed authorities, "so that your days may be long in the land which the Lord your God has given you" (Exodus 20:13). All of this seemed rather firm and clear biblical injunction that a conscientious Christian must respect and obey the authorities and suffer patiently and prayerfully if they become tyrants.

In defending the Christian right to resist and revolt against tyranny, Calvinists like Theodore Beza (1519–1605), John Knox (ca. 1513–72), Philip de Mornay (1549–1623), and many of their followers first flipped these biblical passages onto their heads. Yes, we must honor the authorities "so that our days may be long," they argued. But if our days are being cut short, then we should not honor those authorities who shorten them. Yes, the authorities were "appointed by God to do good." But if they are not doing good, then they could not have been appointed by God. Yes, magistrates are not "a terror to good conduct but to bad." But if they become a terror to good conduct, then they must no longer be legitimate magistrates. Yes, we must "render to Caesar the things that are Caesar's, and to God the things that are God's." But if Caesar wants or takes what is God's, then we must withhold or retrieve it for God's sake. Yes, "he who resists the authorities resists God." But if the authorities themselves resist God, then surely we must avenge God's honor. Yes, "vengeance is mine," God says (Romans 12:19). But we believers, as God's sovereign image bearers and ambassadors, are also God's "instruments of righteousness" (Romans 6:13), and we must execute God's judgment of wrath on earth when needed.[65]

Calvinists also built on the familiar legal doctrine of legitimate self-defense. Defense of oneself and of third parties against attack, using proportionate, even deadly force and violence when necessary, was an ancient legal teaching. The law of resistance to tyranny was simply the law of self-defense writ large, Calvinists argued. When magistrates exceed their authority, they forfeit their offices and become like

[65] See sources in ibid., 102–33, 181–202, 219–25.

any other private person, indeed like any other criminal, whom their victims and third parties may resist passively or actively.

Calvinists also drew on the biblical idea of covenant. The political government of each community, they argued, was formed by a three-way covenant among God, the rulers, and the people, modeled in part on ancient biblical covenants. By this covenant, God agreed to protect and bless the rulers and the people in return for their obedience to the laws of God and nature. The rulers agreed to honor these higher laws and protect the people's essential rights, particularly those rights rooted in the Bible. The people agreed to exercise God's political will for the community by electing and petitioning their rulers and by honoring and obeying them so long as the rulers honored God's law and protected the people's rights. If any of the people violated the terms of this political covenant and became criminals, the magistrate could properly prosecute and punish them – and sentence them to death in extreme cases. In turn, however, if any of the magistrates violated the terms of the political covenant and became tyrants, they could be properly resisted and removed from office – and sentenced to death in extreme cases, if convicted.[66]

The power to resist and remove such tyrants lay not directly with the people, however, for that would produce anarchy. The exercise of this power involved "constitutional judgments" by the lower magistrates, wrote Calvin's protégé, Theodore Beza. In cases of seeming tyranny, these lower magistrates were called to judge the tyrant's behavior against the terms of the political covenant – an early statement of the idea of judicial review. The remarkable trial and execution of King Charles I of England, in 1649, was a textbook example of this stern Calvinist logic of resistance in action. But if the tyrant refused to leave or persisted in tyranny, the lower magistrates were to organize and direct the people in revolt – in all-out revolution, if needed, to unseat this tyrant.[67] This logic animated Calvinist revolutionary movements in France, the Netherlands, Scotland, England, and eventually America from the later sixteenth to the later eighteenth centuries.[68]

Calvinists also built on the idea of fundamental rights, whose chronic and pervasive breach by a tyrant triggered the most basic right to resist and revolt. Early modern Protestants accepted the enumerated lists of rights and liberties set out in classical Roman law and expanded in medieval and early modern laws. But they rearranged, prioritized, and expanded this roll of rights on the basis of the Bible,

[66] See ibid., 130–39.

[67] Théodore de Bèze, *Du Droit des Magistrats*, ed. Robert M. Kingdon (Geneva: Droz, 1970), translated as Theodore Beza, *Concerning the Rights of Rulers over Their Subjects and the Duties of Subjects Toward Their Rulers*, trans. Henri-Louis Gonin (Cape Town: Juta, 1956), 27, 36–38, 72–74.

[68] See Michael Walzer, *The Revolution of the Saints: A Study in the Origins of Radical Politics* (Cambridge, MA: Harvard University Press, 1965); R. R. Palmer, *The Age of the Democratic Revolution*, 2 vols. (Princeton: Princeton University Press, 1959–64); John W. Sap, *Paving the Way for Revolution: Calvinism and the Struggle for a Democratic Constitutional State* (Amsterdam: VU Press, 2001); David T. Ball, *The Historical Origins of Judicial Review, 1536–1803: The Duty to Resist Tyranny* (Lewiston, NY: Edwin Mellen Press, 2005).

in part. The most important rights, they reasoned, had to be the religious rights of liberty of conscience and free exercise of religion. After all, persons are created first and foremost as subjects and ambassadors of the Creator God and called to honor God above all else. The Ten Commandments enjoined them to worship God, to observe the Sabbath, and to avoid blasphemy and idolatry. The New Testament ordered the faithful to "obey God rather than men."[69] If the political magistrate – created by God and representing God's authority on earth – breaches a person's rights to discharge these religious duties, then nothing can be sacred and secure any longer.

Moreover, protecting religious rights and duties required protecting several other correlative rights that early modern Calvinists came to deem essential when they faced persecution as minorities. The rights of individuals to religious conscience and exercise required attendant rights to assemble, speak, worship, evangelize, educate, parent, travel, and more. The rights of the religious group to worship and govern itself as an ecclesiastical polity required attendant rights to legal personality, corporate property, freedom of association, organized charity, parochial education, freedom of press, freedom of contract, and more. Both individuals and groups had to live by many other biblical commandments that set out the rights and duties of life, liberty, property, marriage, family, household, sanctuary, poor relief, charity, education, and more.[70] By the 1560s, Calvinist writers like Beza and Knox were calling these rights "unalienable" and "fundamental."[71]

Early modern Protestants enumerated these fundamental rights not only in learned tracts but also in lofty texts forged in the aftermath of revolution against tyranny. In their 1581 Declaration of Independence, for example, Dutch Protestant revolutionaries declared independence from Spain and its tyrannical rules "in accordance with the law of nature and in order to preserve and defend ourselves and our fellow countrymen, our rights, the privileges and ancient customs and the freedoms of our fatherland," which they then enumerated and expanded at length in national and provincial constitutions.[72] In the 1628 Petition of Right directed against the tyranny of Charles I, the English Parliament called for protection of such fundamental rights as no taking of "any man's life, liberty," or "property" "but by due process of law"; no taxation without "common consent"; no forced quartering of soldiers or mariners in private homes; no suspension of the writ of habeas corpus; and no criminal prosecution or punishment without a clear statute, among others.[73] Across the Atlantic in 1641, Calvinist jurist and theologian Nathaniel Ward, steeped in Protestant opposition to the tyranny of the English monarchy, set out a twenty-five-page "Body of

69 Acts 5:29

70 This is the central thesis of Witte, *Reformation of Rights*.

71 Christopher Goodman, *How Superior Powers Ought to Be Obeyd*, facs. ed., ed. Charles H. McIlwain (New York: Columbia University Press, 1931), 160–61. See further ibid., 52–53, 74–76, 97–99, 142.

72 Formally known as the Act of Abjuration (1581), in Herbert H. Rowen, ed., *The Low Countries in Early Modern Times: A Documentary History* (New York: Harper & Row, 1972), 102.

73 In Stephenson and Marcham, *Sources*, 450–53.

Liberties" for the new colony in Massachusetts Bay, detailing sundry public, private, procedural, and penal rights.[74] The Toleration Act and Bill of Rights, both passed by Parliament in 1689 in the aftermath of the Glorious Revolution against the tyranny of King James II, added further protections for the freedoms of speech, press, and assembly, an act that governed both the English mother country and her many colonies, including in America.[75]

SUMMARY AND CONCLUSIONS

Natural law and natural rights, then, were common topics for early modern Protestant theologians, jurists, and moralists. These early reformers did echo classical and scholastic teachings, and their lists of natural law principles and natural rights precepts overlapped with Catholic, humanist, and early liberal formulations in their day. But the reformers also grounded their teachings in distinct accounts of the created order, human nature, the Ten Commandments, law and Gospel, divine sovereignty and natural order in the two kingdoms, which gave their views unique accents.

The teachings of Luther, Melanchthon, Magdeburg, Simons, Schleitheim, Calvin, Goodman, Althusius, and others touched on here had parallels in hundreds of other Protestant sources. These sources accentuated the range of Protestant contributions to the Western legal tradition of human rights, and religious freedom. Some Protestants like Lutherans and Anglicans were staunch supporters of religious establishment and active agents of crushing religious dissenters. Other Protestants, notably Anabaptists, were ardent advocates of religious freedom for all, with no religious establishments. Some like the Calvinist Althusius fell in between allowing for local religious establishments and gradual religious toleration. Even when they differed on matters of religious freedom and church–state relations, most Protestants championed basic rights to life, property, family, reputation, and procedural justice, and most called for written constitutions that enumerated the people's fundamental rights and delimited the powers of government. And while a number of pious Protestants preferred to turn the other cheek to popular and political tyranny even at the risk of martyrdom, the Lutherans of Magdeburg, and various Calvinists groups in Europe and America rose up in fierce righteous revolution against tyrants who pervasively and systematically abridged the people's fundamental rights and liberties.

74 In Edmund S. Morgan, *Puritan Political Ideas, 1558–1794*, repr. ed. (Indianapolis, IN: Liberty Fund, 2003), 177–203.

75 In Stephenson and Marcham, *Sources*, 599–608.

4

"A Most Mild and Equitable Establishment of Religion"

Religious Freedom in Massachusetts, 1780–1833

The 1780 Constitution of Massachusetts is the oldest continuously operating written constitution in the world.[1] The principal drafter was John Adams (1735–1826) – the "Atlas" and "colossus" of the Revolution, America's future second president, and already a formidable lawyer and constitutional historian.[2] In drafting the 1780 Massachusetts Constitution, Adams sought to balance generous protection of religious freedom for all peaceable faiths with the gentle establishment of Christianity. His draft reflected his belief that the law "should begin by setting conscience free"[3] and ensuring that "all men of all religions consistent with morals and property ... enjoy equal liberty [and] security of property ... and an equal chance for honors and power."[4] At the same time, he said, the law should support a "most mild and

[1] Robert J. Taylor, *Construction of the Massachusetts Constitution* (Worcester, MA: American Antiquarian Society, 1980), 317. Among countless overviews, see esp. the classic by Samuel Eliot Morison, *A History of the Constitution of Massachusetts* (Boston: Wright & Potter, 1917). For principal primary texts, see Oscar Handlin and Mary Handlin, eds., *The Popular Sources of Political Authority: Documents on the Massachusetts Constitution of 1780* (Cambridge, MA: Harvard University Press, 1966); Robert J. Taylor, ed., *Massachusetts, Colony to Commonwealth: Documents on the Formation of Its Constitution* (Chapel Hill: University of North Carolina Press, 1961); Ronald M. Peters, Jr., *The Massachusetts Constitution of 1780: A Social Compact* (Amherst: University of Massachusetts Press, 1978).

[2] See John Adams, *A Defense of the Constitutions of Government in the United States of America* in C. F. Adams, ed., *The Works of John Adams*, 10 vols. (Boston: Little & Brown, 1850–56), vols. 4–6. See recent biographies: David McCullough, *John Adams* (New York: Simon and Schuster, 2008); Gordon S. Wood, *Friends Divided: John Adams and Thomas Jefferson* (New York: Penguin Books, 2017).

[3] "Adams to Dr. Price, April 8, 1785," in Adams, *Works*, 8:232, and quotations in Frank Donavon, ed., *The John Adams Papers* (New York: Dodd, Mead, 1965), 181. Also see Adams, *Works*, 4:290–97; John Adams, *A Dissertation on the Canon and Feudal Law* (1765), in Adams, *Works*, 3:451.

[4] "Adams to Dr. Price." In a letter to Adrian van der Kemp (Oct. 2, 1818), Adams again praised "freedom of religion" so long as it was "consistent with morals and property." Quoted by John R. Howe, *The Changing Political Thought of John Adams* (Princeton, NJ: Princeton University Press, 1966), 227. But see his earlier harsh treatment of Quakers and Baptists documented in Arthur Scherr, "John Adams Confronts Quakers and Baptists During the Revolution: A Paradox of the Quest for Liberty," *Journal of Church and State* 59 (2017), 256–79.

equitable establishment of religion,"[5] featuring covenant ceremonies, religious test oaths for political office, and special protections, privileges, and funding for Christian worship, education, morality, and charity.

Adams's formulation sought to balance the demands of the once-dominant Puritan Congregationalists of Massachusetts, who favored a traditional religious establishment, with the demands of swelling groups of Baptists, Methodists, Quakers, Catholics, and freethinkers, who wanted freedom for all faiths and establishment of none. Adams's formulation mustered just enough support to win ratification in 1780, but the balance fell apart in subsequent decades, as Congregationalists fractured into Unitarian and Trinitarian factions, and religious pluralism in the state grew. While the Constitution retained the ceremonial and moral forms of religious establishment built into the 1780 text, amendments in 1821 and 1833 outlawed religious test oaths and religious taxes, the two most controversial features of the traditional institutional establishment.[6]

This chapter surveys the arguments for and against religious establishment and religious freedom in early Massachusetts. The coalitions of politicians, preachers, and citizens making these arguments changed between 1778, when the first constitutional draft failed, and 1833, when religious taxes were repealed by the Eleventh Amendment. The logic of their arguments, however, remained relatively stable. Virtually everyone agreed that religion was an essential source of public and private morality, and that the Constitution should encourage diverse religious beliefs and practices, at least among Protestants. Nearly everyone also agreed that the laws should equally respect and reflect the religious sentiments of all citizens. What was controversial was how to achieve these goals. Did the integrity of governmental institutions require public officials to swear religious test oaths of office? Did religious liberty extend equally to all churches and creeds – including Catholics, Unitarians, Quakers, and non-Christians, who remained deeply suspect in the day? Did the moral functions and vitality of religion require tax-funded churches and clergy, or would religion flourish better if left on its own? Such questions divided Massachusetts lawmakers along political, regional, and religious lines, and ultimately led to a new consensus about how best to order church–state relations.

5 Adams, *Works*, 2:399 (referring to the Congregational establishment of colonial Massachusetts, largely preserved in the 1780 Constitution). For further discussion of Adams' theory of (religious) liberty from various perspectives, see, e.g., C. Bradley Thompson, *John Adams and the Spirit of Liberty* (Lawrence: University Press of Kansas, 1988); Richard Alan Ryerson, *John Adams's Republic: The One, the Few, and the Many* (Baltimore, MD: Johns Hopkins University Press, 2016).

6 See overviews in Jacob C. Meyer, *Church and State in Massachusetts from 1740 to 1833: A Chapter in the History of the Development of Individual Freedom*, repr. ed. (New York: Russell & Russell, 1968); William C. McLoughlin, *New England Dissent, 1630–1833: The Baptists and the Separation of Church and State*, 2 vols. (Cambridge, MA: Harvard University Press, 1971); Johann N. Neem, "The Elusive Common Good: Religion and Civil Society in Massachusetts, 1780–1833," *Journal of the Early Republic* 24, no.3 (Fall 2004), 381–417; John D. Cushing, "Notes on Disestablishment in Massachusetts, 1780–1833," *William and Mary Quarterly* 26, no.2 (April 1969), 169–90.

THE CONSTITUTIONAL *VIA MEDIA*: RELIGIOUS FREEDOM AND RELIGIOUS ESTABLISHMENT

The Failed 1778 Constitution. The 1780 Constitution replaced the 1691 provincial charter that the British Crown had issued as the organic law of the colony of Massachusetts Bay. The charter had ruled continuously in the colony until June 17, 1774, when the last General Court called by the royal governor adjourned. During the rumblings of the American Revolution in 1774 and 1775, the colonists formed three successive Provincial Congresses. In July 1775, they elected their own representative General Court – for the first time without royal permission and without compliance with the procedures of the provincial charter. The General Court, in turn, elected a council and vested it with legislative and executive powers as well as appellate jurisdiction over the lower courts. The council was transformed into a constitutional convention in June 1777. John Adams, who was serving at the time first in the Continental Congress and then in Europe, did not participate in these convention or ratification debates.

On February 28, 1778, the council submitted a draft constitution for popular ratification. The draft was largely a bare-bones blueprint of government. It seemed calculated more to respond to immediate concerns of representation of the townships than to the enduring needs of the commonwealth. Most of its thirty-six articles concerned the rights and restrictions of popular suffrage and regional representation, and the powers and procedures of the executive, legislative, and judicial offices of the commonwealth. Article XXXII simply confirmed as presumptively constitutional all colonial laws, including the laws on religion – "such parts only excepted as are repugnant to the rights and privileges contained in this Constitution." But few such rights and privileges were set forth. Article XXXII guaranteed for all "the inestimable right of trial by jury." Two other articles confirmed the traditional privileges and protections of Protestants: Article XXIX stated: "No person unless of the Protestant religion shall be Governor, Lieutenant Governor, a member of the Senate or of the House of Representatives, or hold any judiciary employment within this State." Article XXXIV provided: "The free exercise and enjoyment of religious profession and worship shall forever be allowed to every denomination of Protestants within this State."[7] For the rest, the document was silent on religious and civil rights.

The 1778 draft constitution was roundly rejected by the people of Massachusetts. A leading opponent of ratification was Theophilus Parsons (1750–1813), a young lawyer from Newburyport, who would later figure prominently in the formation and enforcement of the religion clauses of the 1780 Massachusetts Constitution. In his *Essex Result*, a pamphlet that both galvanized and systematized popular objections to the draft constitution, Parsons singled out for special criticism the absence of a declaration of civil rights and the deliberate abridgment of religious rights and

[7] Reprinted in Handlin and Handlin, *Popular Sources*, 190–201.

freedoms for all. "[T]he rights of conscience are not therein clearly defined and ascertained," he wrote.

> We have duties, for the discharge of which we are accountable to our Creator and benefactor, which no human power can cancel. What those duties are, is determinable by right reason, which may be, and is called, a well-informed conscience. What this dictates as our duty, is so; and that power which assumes a controul over it, is an usurper; for no consent can be pleaded to justify the controul, as any consent in this case is void.

Moreover, "the free exercise and enjoyment of religious worship is there said to be allowed to all protestants of the State, when in fact, that free exercise and enjoyment is the natural and uncontrollable right of every member of the State."[8]

Platforms for and against Religious Establishment. On February 20, 1779, the Massachusetts House of Representatives called for a new constitutional convention, and "lawfully warned" the "Selectmen of the several Towns" to deliberate their concerns and to instruct their delegates.[9] The constitutional protection of religious liberty figured prominently in these deliberations and instructions, with the townships revealing wide-ranging concerns. The township of Stoughton, for example, instructed its delegate "to use and employ your assiduous Endeavours as Soon as the Convention meets that a Bill of Rights be in the first place compiled, wherein the inherent and unalienable Rights of Conscience . . . . shall be clearly, fully and unequivocally defined and explained."[10] The delegate of Pittsfield came armed with a recommended provision:

> [E]very man has an unalienable right to enjoy his own opinion in matters of religion, and to worship God in that manner that is agreeable to his own sentiments without any control whatsoever, and that no particular mode or sect of religion ought to be established but that every one be protected in the peaceable enjoyment of his religious persuasion and way of worship.[11]

The township of Sandisfield instructed its delegate to seek protection of both local control over the establishment of Protestantism and guarantees of toleration for other faiths:

> [Y]ou will Endeavour in the forming of the Constitution that the Free Exercise of religious principles or Profession, worship and Liberty of Conscience shall be for ever Secured to all Denominations of Protestants – and Protestant Dis[s]enters of all Denominations within the State, without any Compulsion whatever. Always allowing the Legislative Body of this State the Power of Toleration to other Denominations of Christians from time to time as they Shall see Cause, at the

8 *The Essex Result* (Apr. 29, 1778), reprinted in Handlin and Handlin, *Popular Sources*, 326, 330.

9 Resolve on the Question of a Constitution, Feb. 20, 1779, reprinted in Handlin and Handlin, *Popular Sources*, 383–84.

10 Reprinted in Handlin and Handlin, *Popular Sources*, 423.

11 Reprinted in Taylor, *Massachusetts, Colony to Commonwealth*, 118.

> same time, Reserving to our Selves, the Right of Instructions to our Representatives Respecting Said Toleration as well as in other Cases.[12]

Delegates who were not furnished with explicit directives from the townships could draw inspiration and instruction from the scores of sermons and pamphlets on the constitutional protection of religious liberty that circulated in Massachusetts in the later 1770s.[13] The intense volume and volatility of these writings led Adams later to quip: "A whole company of earthly hosts hath debated these heavenly things with an hellish intensity."[14]

The oft-printed pamphlet *Worcestriensis Number IV* of 1776 offered a typical moderate position, defending both the generous toleration of all religions and the gentle establishment of the Protestant religion. The pamphlet began with a defense of liberty of conscience and religious pluralism.

> In a well regulated state, it will be the business of the Legislature to prevent sectaries of different denominations from molesting and disturbing each other, to ordain that no part of the community shall be permitted to perplex and harass the other for any supposed heresy, but that each individual shall be allowed to have and enjoy, profess and maintain his own system of religion, provided it does not issue in overt acts of treason undermining the peace and good order of society. To allow one part of a society to lord it over the faith and consciences of the other, in religious matters, is the ready way to set the whole community together by the ears.[15]

State officials thus had an important role to keep the peace among the plural faiths of the community.

State officials were also empowered, however, "to give preference to that profession of religion which they take to be true," the author of *Worcestriensis* insisted. State officials could not command citizens to conform to this preferred religion, nor could they subject nonconformists "to pains, penalties, and disabilities." But they could "exert themselves in favor of one religion over the other."

> The establishment contended for in this disquisition . . . must proceed only from the benign principles of the legislature from an encouragement of the General Principles of religion and morality, recommending free inquiry and examination of the doctrine said to be divine; using all possible and lawful means to enable its citizens to discover the truth, and to entertain good and rational sentiments, and taking mild and parental measures to bring about the design; these are the most probable means of bringing about the establishment of religion.[16]

State officials could thus "exert themselves in favor of one religion over the other." They could extract religious oaths from their officials, "for there is no stronger

[12] Reprinted in Handlin and Handlin, *Popular Sources*, 419.
[13] See Peters, *The Massachusetts Constitution*, 24–30.
[14] Adams, *Works*, 8:55.
[15] *Worcestriensis, Number IV* (1776), in Charles S. Hyneman and Donald S. Lutz, eds., *American Political Writing* (Indianapolis, IN: Liberty Press, 1983), 450 (emphases omitted).
[16] Ibid., 452 (emphases and capitalization omitted).

cement of society." They could punish profanity, blasphemy, and debauchery, all of which "strike a fatal blow at the root of good regulation, and well-being of the state." They could provide "able and learned teachers [that is, ministers] to instruct the people in the knowledge of what they deem the truth, maintaining them by the public money, though at the same time they have no right in the least degree to endeavor the depression of professions of religious denomination."[17]

Phillips Payson (1736–1801), an influential Congregationalist minister, laid greater stress on the need for a public religious establishment, warning against "dangerous innovations" and deviations from inherited colonial patterns. To be sure, Payson wrote, "religious or spiritual liberty must be accounted the greatest happiness of man, considered in a private capacity."[18] But, he insisted:

> [R]eligion, both in rulers and people [is] . . . of the highest importance to . . . civil society and government, . . . as it keeps alive the best sense of moral obligation, a matter of such extensive utility, especially in respect to an oath [of office], which is one of the principal instruments of government. The fear and reverence of God, and the terrors of eternity, are the most powerful restraints upon the minds of mind; and hence it is of special importance in a free government, the spirit of which being always friendly to the sacred rights of conscience, it will hold up the Gospel as the great rule of faith and practice. Established modes and usages in religion, more especially the public worship of God, so generally form the principles and manners of a people that changes or alterations in these, especially when nearly conformed to the spirit and simplicity of the Gospel, may well be deemed very dangerous experiments in government. . . . Let the restraints of religion once broken down, as they infallibly would be, by leaving the subject of public worship to the humours of the multitude, and we might well defy all human wisdom and power, to support and preserve order and government in the State.[19]

By marked contrast, Isaac Backus (1724–1806), the most learned Baptist voice of the day, laid greater stress on the protection of private religious liberty, warning against the "hypocrisy" and "futility" of public religious establishments. In a series of pamphlets in the 1770s, he charged that the Massachusetts authorities were "assuming a power to govern religion, rather than being governed by it."[20] "I am as sensible of the importance of religion and of the utility of it to human society, as Mr. Payson

[17] Ibid., 452–53 (emphases omitted). Samuel West, an influential Congregationalist preacher in Dartmouth, argued similarly. Samuel West, *A Sermon Preached Before the Honorable Council . . . of the Massachusetts-Bay in New England* (Boston: John Gill, 1776), reprinted in J. W. Thornton, *The Pulpit of the American Revolution* (Boston: Gould and Lincoln, 1860), 297–99.

[18] Phillips Payson, "Election Sermon of 1778," in Hyneman and Lutz, *American Political Writing*, 523–38.

[19] Ibid., 528–30. A bit later, Payson declared grandly: "The eyes of the whole world are upon us in these critical times, and, what is yet more, the eyes of Almighty God. . . . With diligence let us cultivate the spirit of liberty, of public virtue, of union and religion, and thus strengthen the hands of government and the great pillars of the state. Our own consciences will reproach us and the world condemn us if we do not properly obey, respect, and reverence the government of our choosing." Ibid, 538.

[20] Isaac Backus, *Government and Liberty Described* (1778), in William G. McLoughlin, ed., *Isaac Backus on Church, State, and Calvinism: Pamphlets, 1754–1789* (Cambridge, MA: Harvard University Press, 1968), 351.

is," Backus wrote. "And I concur with him that the fear and reverence of God and the terrors of eternity are the most powerful restraints upon the minds of men. But I am so far from thinking with him that these restraints would be broken down if equal religious liberty was established."[21] Look at the long history of Christian establishment, Backus wrote. It has led not to pure religion; instead "tyranny, simony, and robbery came to be introduced and to be practiced under the Christian name."[22] Look at the city of Boston, which has had no religious establishment of late; there religion, state, and society all flourish without fail.[23] Look at the principles of the American Revolution; "all America is up in arms against taxation without representation." But just as certainly as we Americans were not represented in the British Parliament, so we religious dissenters are not represented among the established civil authorities. Yet we are still subject to their religious taxes and regulations.[24] Look at the principles of the Bible; God has given the sword to magistrates but not to the church:

> [I]t is impossible to blend church and state without violating our Lord's commands to both. His command to the church is, Put away from among yourselves that wicked person. His command to the state is, Let both grow together until the harvest. But it has appeared for these thousand years that pure Gospel discipline in the church is very little if at all known in state establishments of religion and that instead of letting conformists thereto, and dissenters therefrom, grow together to enjoy equal worldly privileges, [and] pervert all equity.[25]

Striking a Constitutional *Via Media*. Such were some of the discordant sentiments on religious establishment and religious freedom on the eve of the second constitutional convention in Massachusetts. It was clear that the Congregationalists would insist on some form of religious establishment. As John Adams put it: "We might as soon expect a change in the solar system as to expect they would give up their establishment."[26] It was equally clear that religious dissenters would insist on disestablishment and free exercise of religion – particularly since other states had

21 Ibid., 358. See also Isaac Backus, *Policy as Well as Honesty, Forbids the Use of Secular Force in Religious Affairs* (1779), in McLoughlin, *Backus*, 367–83: "The necessity of a well-regulated government in civil states is acknowledged by all, and the importance and benefit of true Christianity in order thereto is no less certain."

22 Ibid., 373–74.

23 Ibid., 357.

24 Ibid. See further ibid., 361: "Many of the Baptists of this State have long been convinced, that a giving in the annual certificates required by the ruling party as the condition of our exemption from TAXES to their ministers contains an explicit acknowledgment of a power assumed by man which in reality belongs only to God. And in our Appeal to the Public, printed in Boston five years ago, we have given the particular reasons why we cannot in conscience perform that condition. Yet only because we have refused to wrong our consciences in that respect our people in various places have been taxed from year to year to [support] pedobaptist ministers."

25 Ibid., 375.

26 As reported by Isaac Backus in McLoughlin, *Backus*, 12. See also Adams, *Works*, 2:399.

granted such liberties. Some *via media* between these competing perspectives was needed.

On September 1, 1779, 293 delegates gathered in Boston.[27] In the convention were many of the leading lights of Massachusetts – thirty-nine merchants, thirty-one lawyers, twenty-two farmers, twenty-one clergy, eighteen physicians, and eighteen magistrates.[28] Most delegates were Congregationalists; five were Baptists, and a few were suspected to be Quaker, Anglican, or Catholic.[29] On September 4, the convention elected a committee of twenty-seven members – later augmented by four – to prepare a declaration of rights and frame of government. This committee, in turn, delegated the drafting to a three-member subcommittee of James Bowdoin (1726–90), Samuel Adams (1722–1803), and John Adams, with John Adams selected to push the pen for the subcommittee. He completed a draft by mid-October. First the three-member subcommittee, then the full drafting committee made modest alterations to Adams's draft. The committee submitted its draft to the convention on October 28, 1779.[30] The convention debated the draft until November 12. Adams participated to this point but then set sail for France. The convention completed its deliberations between January 27 and March 1, 1780, now without Adams. After ample deliberation, the people of Massachusetts ratified the Constitution, and it went into effect on October 25, 1780.

FREEDOM OF RELIGION, BUT WITH LIMITS

The original text of the 1780 Constitution, without amendments, is a hefty document of nearly twelve thousand words. It has a preamble and two main parts. Part One is a Declaration of Rights in thirty articles. Part Two is a Frame of Government in six chapters. Issues of religion, church–state relations, and religious freedom figured in ten of these provisions – the preamble, Articles I, II, III, VII, and XVIII of the Declaration of Rights, and Chapters I, II, V and VI of the Frame of Government.

The Constitution included several provisions on religious freedom. Article I of the Declaration of Rights stated: "All men are born free and equal, and have certain natural, essential, and unalienable rights" of life, liberty, property, and pursuit of happiness.[31] Article II tendered more specific protections:

> It is the right as well as the duty of all men in society, publickly, and at stated seasons to worship the SUPREME BEING, the great Creator and preserver of the Universe.

27 The delegates did not attend all sessions; the highest recorded vote on any issue was 247. Samuel Eliot Morison, "The Struggle over the Adoption of the Constitution of Massachusetts, 1780," *Proceedings of the Massachusetts Historical Society* 50 (1916–17), 356.

28 Peters, *Massachusetts Constitution of* 1780, 24.

29 Ibid., 23–31; McLoughlin, *Backus*, 386.

30 The draft is in Adams, *Works*, 4:213–67.

31 In 1976, Article I was amended by Mass. Const. art. CVI, which rendered "all men" as "all people" and added: "Equality under the law shall not be denied or abridged because of . . . creed."

> No subject shall be hurt, molested, or restrained, in his person, Liberty, or Estate, for worshipping GOD in the manner and season most agreeable to the Dictates of his own conscience, or for his religious profession or sentiments; provided he doth not Disturb the public peace, or obstruct others in their religious Worship.

Article III tacitly acknowledged the right to form religious associations, to select one's own minister, and to pay tithes directly to one's own church. And Chapter VI of the Frame of Government exempted Quakers from the swearing of oaths because of scruples of conscience.

Yet the 1780 Constitution imposed several limits on religion as well. Religious worship was not just a right but also a duty in Article II. Indeed, Adams's original draft spoke only of the duty to worship. Only after other delegates objected was it amended to guarantee both the right and the duty of all to worship. Moreover, while a person could worship in the manner and time that conscience dictated, such worship was to be directed to the Supreme Being and Creator, leaving nontheists without religious freedom protection. Moreover, worship, per Article III, was to include "conscientious and convenient . . . attendance upon the instructions of ministers . . . at stated times and seasons," as well as payment of tithes.

Religious freedom was more restricted for those in political office. In Chapter I of the Frame of Government, Adams stipulated that no person was eligible to serve in the House of Representatives "unless he be of the Christian religion." The convention struck this provision, but it left untouched Chapter II, where Adams imposed the same religious conditions upon the offices of governor and lieutenant governor.[32] In the same spirit, Adams proposed in Chapter VI that all state officials and appointees swear the same religious test oath "that I believe and profess the Christian religion and have a firm persuasion of its truth." The convention insisted on a slightly reworded oath for elected executive and legislative officers, requiring all other officers to declare their "true faith and allegiance to this Commonwealth." After several delegates argued for a specifically Protestant test oath, the convention added to both oaths a rather obvious anti-Catholic and anti-Anglican provision, which Adams and others later protested without success: "I do renounce and abjure all allegiance, subjection and obedience to . . . every . . . foreign Power whatsoever: And that no foreign . . . Prelate . . . hath, or ought to have, any jurisdiction, superiority, pre-eminence, authority, dispensing, or other power, in any matter, civil, ecclesiastical or spiritual within this Commonwealth."[33] Adams's draft oath had concluded, "so help me God," but then made a specific provision "that any person who has

32 Chap. I, sec. III. See chap. II, sec. II (requiring that the governor "shall be of the Christian religion"); sec. III (requiring that the lieutenant governor "shall be qualified, in point of religion"). Adams, *Works*, 4:241, 242, 245, 251.

33 See chap. VI, art. I. Also see *Journal of the Convention for Framing a Constitution of Government for the State of Massachusetts Bay, from the Commencement of Their First Session, September 1, 1779, to the Close of Their Last Session, June 16, 1780* (Boston: Dutton and Wentworth, 1832), 97, 109–10 (summarizing debates on Feb. 10, 14, and 15, 1780).

conscientious scruples relative to taking oaths, may be admitted to make solemn affirmation" by other means. After delegates protested that so generic an exemption might be abused, the convention restricted the exemption to Quakers.[34]

By comparison with other state constitutions of the day, the Massachusetts Constitution was rather restrained in its protection of private religious freedom. Other states defined liberty of conscience expansively to include the right to choose and change religion, to be free from all discrimination on the basis of religion, and to be exempt from a number of general laws that prohibited or mandated conduct about which a religious party or group had scruples of conscience. Many states also defined free exercise rights expansively to include freedom to engage in religious assembly, worship, speech, publication, press, education, travel, parentage, and the like, without political or ecclesiastical conditions or controls.[35] Few such protections appear in the 1780 Massachusetts Constitution.

Adams was convinced that such a "tempered" form of religious freedom would bring the best "improvements to the character of each citizen."[36] On the one hand, following conservative conventions of the day, he believed that to grant too much freedom of religion would only encourage depravity in citizens.[37] "Man is not to be trusted with his unbounded love of liberty," one preacher put it, "unless it is under some other restraint which arises from his own reason or the law of God – these in many instances would make a feeble resistance to his lust or avarice; and he would pursue his liberty to the destruction of his fellow-creature, if he was not restrained by human laws and punishment."[38] The state was thus required to "take mild and parental measures" to educate, encourage, and emulate right belief and conduct.[39] On the other hand, following more liberal conventions of the day, Adams believed that "[c]ompulsion, instead of making men religious, generally has a contrary tendency, it works not conviction, but most naturally leads them into hypocrisy. If they are honest enquirers after truth; if their articles of belief differ from the creed of their civil superiors, compulsion will bring them into a sad dilemma" of choosing either a feigned or a firmly held faith.[40] The state was thus required to refrain from

[34] Chap. VI, art. I, in Adams, *Works*, 4:260–66.

[35] See sources and discussion in John Witte, Jr. and Joel A. Nichols, *Religion and the American Constitutional Experiment*, 4th ed. (New York: Oxford University Press, 2016), 24–63.

[36] Adams, *Works*, 8:232.

[37] This emphasis on human depravity, and the need for its restraint, is especially pronounced in Adams's earlier writings, notably his 1788 *Defense*, bk. 1. Later in his life, Adams tempered this view. See, e.g., "Letter to Thomas Jefferson, April 19, 1817," in Adams, *Works*, 10:253–55: "So far from believing in the total and universal depravity of human nature, I believe there is no individual totally depraved. The most abandoned scoundrel that ever existe[d], never yet wholly extinguished his conscience, and while conscience remains, there is some religion." Ibid., 254.

[38] Simeon Howard, *A Sermon Preached Before the Honorable Council . . . of Massachusetts-Bay* (Boston: John Bill, 1780), reprinted in Thornton, *The American Pulpit*, 362–63.

[39] *Worcestriensis*, in Hyneman and Lutz, *American Political Writing*, 452.

[40] Ibid., 450.

dictating the exact doctrines, liturgies, and texts of a right religion. This was the balance of religious freedom that Adams struck in crafting the Constitution.

THE CEREMONIAL, MORAL, AND INSTITUTIONAL ESTABLISHMENT OF RELIGION

Not only was religious liberty rather narrowly drawn in the 1780 Constitution, compared to some other state constitutions in the day; it was further limited by religious establishment norms. The establishment set out by the Massachusetts Constitution had ceremonial, moral, and institutional features. The ceremonial and moral features reflected a general consensus about the role of religion in both government and society, and these provisions passed with little controversy. The institutional features of establishment, especially the compulsory payment of religious taxes, were contested in the convention and ratification debates.

Ceremonial Establishment. The ceremonial elements of establishment were most evident in the Preamble's declaration that "the whole people covenants with each Citizen, and each Citizen with the whole people, that all shall be governed by certain Laws for the Common good."

> [T]he people of Massachusetts, acknowledging, with grateful hearts, the goodness of the Great Legislator of the Universe, in affording us, in the course of his Providence, an opportunity, deliberately and peaceably, without fraud, violence, or surprize, o[f] entering into an Original, explicit, and Solemn Compact with each other; and of forming a New Constitution of Civil Government for ourselves and Posterity; and devoutly imploring His direction in so interesting a Design, DO agree upon, ordain and establish the following Declaration of Rights and Frame of Government.

This was classic liturgical language rooted in a New England tradition going back to the Mayflower Compact of 1620.[41] The nature of the Constitution was clear; it was a solemn covenant or compact that invoked God as witness, judge, and participant. The purposes of the covenant were clear: to create and confirm the identity of the "citizens of Massachusetts," their devotion to the "common good," and the rights of the people and the powers of the government. The ethic of the covenant was also defined – featuring gratitude, peacefulness, integrity ("without fraud, violence, or surprize"), and prayerful devotion ("devoutly imploring His direction in so interesting a Design").

Covenant rituals also informed the religious test oaths for public servants to be sworn before the people and their representatives in full assembly: "I, A. B., do declare, that I believe the christian religion, and have a firm persuasion of its truth … and I do swear, that I will bear true faith and allegiance to the said

[41] See esp. Donald S. Lutz, *The Origins of American Constitutionalism* (Baton Rouge: Louisiana State University Press, 1988). See also John Witte, Jr., *The Reformation of Rights: Law, Religion, and Human Rights in Early Modern Calvinism* (Cambridge: Cambridge University Press, 2007), 277–320.

Commonwealth … so help me God." This language reflected the conventional view that oaths functioned as "a cement of society" and as "one of the principal instruments of government." Oaths were not merely symbolic but a tangible confirmation of the covenant among God, the people, and the rulers, with solemn duties undergirded by "the fear and reverence of God, and the terrors of eternity."[42]

These preambular and oath-swearing provisions were not merely a bit of hortatory throat-clearing that preceded the real business of constitutional government. They established the favorite ceremonies of the Puritan Congregationalists. In the minds of more conservative Puritan sermonizers and citizens of the day, they raised the traditional image of Massachusetts being "under a solemn divine Probation,"[43] and the image of the magistrate as God's vice-regent, called to exemplify and enforce a godly life. Traditionally, New England Puritans stressed ambition, austerity, frugality, and other virtues because the covenant rendered them agents of God, instruments of God's providential plan. For them to be lax in zeal, loose in discipline, or sumptuous in living would be a disservice to God, a breach of their covenant with God. Such a breach, particularly if committed or condoned by God's magistrate, would bring divine condemnation on the community in the form of war, pestilence, poverty, and other forms of force majeure.[44] It was this tradition, albeit in a less denominationally and doctrinally rigorous form, that was established in the 1780 Constitution.

Beyond the preamble and test oaths, the Constitution had other ceremonial elements of a religious establishment. God is invoked, by name or pseudonym ("the Great Legislator of the Universe" and "Supreme Being") a dozen times. References to the common good or public good appear four more times, as do two further references to divine blessings and privileges. With the exception of the oath requirement, these provisions were passed without comment and still remain in place.

Moral Establishment. The 1780 Constitution established not only Puritan covenant ceremonies but also general Christian morality for the people and their rulers. Article II of the Declaration of Rights, we saw, rendered religious worship both a right and a duty for all. Article III followed with the reason for this duty: "the happiness of a people, and good order and preservation of civil government, essentially depend upon piety, religion, and morality; and … these cannot be generally diffused

42 See Payson, "Election Sermon," 529. This was also one reason why Adams wrote into his draft of chaps. I and II that every official must be "of the Christian religion." Adams later wrote in his diary: "One great advantage of the Christian religion is it brings the great principle of the law of nature and nations – Love your neighbor as ourself, and to do to others that others should do to you – to the knowledge, belief, and veneration of the whole people." Diary of John Adams (Aug. 14, 1796), in Adams, *Works*, 3:423.

43 W. Stoughton, *New Englands True Interest: Not to Lie (1670), in The Puritans: A Sourcebook of Their Writings*, ed. Perry Miller and Thomas H. Johnson (New York: Harper & Row, 1963), 243.

44 See detailed sources in John Witte, Jr., "Blest Be the Ties that Bind Us: Covenant and Community in Puritan Thought," *Emory Law Journal* 36 (1987), 579–601.

through a Community, but by the institution of publick Worship of God, and of public instructions in piety, religion, and morality."

Article XVIII further rendered adherence to these moral duties integral to the character of public offices and public officials:

> A frequent recurrence to the fundamental principles of the constitution, and a constant adherence to those of piety, justice, moderation, temperance, industry, and frugality, are absolutely necessary to preserve the advantages of liberty, and to maintain a free government. The people ought, consequently, to have a particular attention to all those principles, in the choice of their Officers and Representatives, and they have a right to require of their lawgivers and magistrates, an exact and constant observance of them, in the formation and execution of the laws necessary for the good administration of the Commonwealth.

For, as Article VII of the Declaration put it: "Government is instituted for the Common good; for the protection, safety, prosperity, and happiness of the people."

Moral considerations also animated the constitutional provisions on education. Chapter V of the Frame of Government provided: "Wisdom, and knowledge, as well as virtue, diffused generally among the body of the people, [are] necessary for the preservation of their rights and liberties." Officials were thus called

> to cherish the interests of literature and sciences, and all seminaries of them; . . . to encourage private societies and public institutions, rewards and immunities, for the promotion of [education] . . . to countenance and inculcate the principles of humanity and general benevolence, public and private charity, industry and frugality, honesty and punctuality in their dealings, sincerity, good humour, and all social affections, and generous sentiments among the people.

Chapter V also confirmed and commended the incorporation of Harvard College, since "the encouragement of arts and sciences, and all good literature, tends to the honor of God, the advantage of the [C]hristian religion, and the great benefit of this and other United States of America."[45]

None of these provisions establishing a public religious morality triggered much debate during the constitutional convention, and most were not amended, even if they have become dead letters in our day. Indeed, the famous Eleventh Amendment of 1833 – famous because it was the last constitutional text in America purportedly to "disestablish" religion – simply repeated the mantra of this moral establishment: that "the public worship of GOD and instructions in piety, religion and morality,

[45] For an overview of the subsequent controversies concerning the leadership and religious affiliation of Harvard College, see Meyer, *Church and State*, 87–91; Yan Li, "The Transformation of the Constitution of Massachusetts, 1780–1860" (PhD diss., University of Connecticut, 1991), 82–84. Also see debates in Nathan Hale and Charles Hale, eds., *Journal of Debates and Proceedings in the Convention of Delegates, Chosen to Revise the Constitution of Massachusetts, Begun and Holden at Boston, November 15, 1820, and Continued by Adjournment to January 9, 1821, Reported for the Boston Daily Advertis.*, rev. and cor. ed. [*Making of Modern Law: Primary Sources, 1620–1926*] (Boston: Boston Daily Advertiser, 1853), 15–16, 491–93, 527–32, 556–57, 619, 630–31.

promote the happiness and prosperity of a people and the security of a Republican Government."

Institutional Establishment. It was the third dimension of the established public religion – Article III's provision for support of specific religious institutions by state taxes – that drew fire in the convention and ratification debates, and eventually was outlawed by the Eleventh Amendment to the Massachusetts Constitution in 1833. Here, critics charged, the balance between private religious freedom and a public religious establishment tilted too much toward the latter.

It was one thing for the Constitution to establish general public religious ceremonies and to define basic public morals and mores – to encourage "piety, religion, and morality," to endorse public worship of God, to list the "moral virtues" necessary in a good ruler, to commend schools and colleges that offered religious and moral education, to limit breaches of the peace and interferences in another's religious right, all on the assumption, as Adams put it, that "the happiness of a people, and the good order and preservation of civil government" depended upon these things.[46] Such provisions at least left a good deal of religious expression and participation open to voluntary choice and individual accent. It was quite another thing, however, for the Constitution to institute religious practices by law – to require persons to attend a preferred form of public worship, to compel them to pay tithes in support of ministers and teachers, to force them to incorporate themselves into state-registered religious societies, and to require them to attend worship faithfully lest their tithes be diverted or their societies dissolved. For many, such an establishment crossed the line from gentle patronage to odious persecution.

The most controversial aspect of the institutional establishment was Article III's imposition of religious taxes "for the support and maintenance of public protestant teachers of piety, religion and morality." This provision continued colonial patterns. A Massachusetts colonial law of 1692 had effectively blended church and state for purposes of taxation.[47] The law designated each of the approximately 290 territories within the colony as both a parish and a township under the authority of one city council. In townships with more than one church, the multiple parishes were called precincts, and each of these likewise was subject to the same council's authority. Each town/parish was required to have at least one Congregationalist "teacher of religion and morality," who would lead the local community in worship and often in

[46] Adams put it: "Happiness, whether in despotism or democracy, whether in slavery or liberty, can never be found without virtue. The best republics will be virtuous, and have been so; but we may hazard a conjecture, that the virtues have been the effect of the well-ordered constitution, rather than the cause. And, perhaps, it would be impossible to prove that a republic cannot exist even among highwaymen, by setting one rogue to watch another; and the knaves themselves may in time be made honest men by the struggle." Adams, *Works*, 6:219.

[47] *The Acts and Resolves, Public and Private, of the Province of the Massachusetts Bay: To Which Are Prefixed the Charters of the Province: With Historical and Explanatory Notes, and an Appendix*, 21 vols. [*Making of Modern Law: Primary Sources, 1620–1926*] (Boston: Wright and Potter, 1869–1922), 1:62–63.

education and charity as well. The community was required to provide the minister with a salary, sanctuary, and parsonage, paid for from religious taxes usually called tithes or church, parish, or religious rates. These were collected from all persons in the township, who were by definition also members of the parish, regardless of which church they attended.[48]

This system worked well enough when all persons within a township or parish were also active members of the established Congregational church. It did not work for persons who were religiously inactive or were members of a non-Congregationalist church, whether Baptist, Quaker, Anglican, Catholic, or free church. As the number of dissenting churches and unchurched citizens grew, so did the protests against taxes to support Congregationalist ministers and churches. During the eighteenth century, colonial courts eventually carved out exceptions for some religious dissenters, allowing them to direct their tithes to support their own ministers and churches. Such dissenters, however, were required to register each church as a separate religious society and to prove their faithful attendance there. Not all dissenting churches were able or willing to meet the registration requirements, and not all townships cooperated in granting the registrations or tithe exemptions.[49] If the dissenting church was too small to have its own full-time minister, the township denied it registration. If the dissenting church was conscientiously opposed to incorporation or registration, as were Baptists after 1773, their members were not exempt from taxation. Members of a registered dissenting church who were lax in attending worship were denied exemption from tithe payments. And if a town treasurer was pressed for revenue, or prejudiced against a certain group, he could refuse to give dissenting ministers their share of the tithes. In many cases, the Massachusetts courts proved churlish in granting standing, let alone relief, to individuals who protested such inequities.[50]

Article III on Religious Taxes. It was this century-long system of religious taxes that the 1780 Massachusetts Constitution aimed to perpetuate in Article III. The article proved so controversial that it took up more than a third of the Convention's debates.[51] The initial draft of Article III, submitted to the Convention on October 28, 1779, stated:

> Good morals, being necessary for the preservation of civil society; and the knowledge and belief of the being of GOD, His providential government of the world, and of a future state of rewards and punishment, being the only true foundation of morality, the legislature hath, therefore, a right, and ought to provide, at the expense

48 See sources and discussion in John Witte, Jr., "Tax Exemption of Church Property: Historical Anomaly or Valid Constitutional Practice?," *Southern California Law Review* 64 (1991), 368–80. See further Chapter 7 of this book, p. 203–05.

49 Morison, "The Struggle," 353–412, esp. 370.

50 See details in Cushing, "Notes on Disestablishment," 169–90; McLoughlin, *New England Dissent*, 547–65; Meyer, *Church and State*, 32–89.

51 Taylor, *Construction of Massachusetts Constitution*, 331.

of the subject, if necessary, a suitable support for the public worship of GOD, and of the teachers of religion and morals; and to enjoin upon all the subjects an attendance upon these instructions, at stated times and seasons; provided there be any such teacher, on whose ministry they can conscientiously attend.

All monies, paid by the subject of the public worship, and of the instructors in religion and morals, shall, if he requires it, be uniformly applied to the support of the teacher or teachers of his own religious denomination, provided there be any on whose instructions he attends; otherwise it may be paid towards the support of the teacher or teachers of the parish or precinct in which the said moneys are raised.[52]

The first paragraph of this draft, stipulating the necessity and utility of public worship and religious instruction, was not particularly controversial. The second paragraph, however, mandating the collection of religious tithes to support these activities, was a matter of great controversy. The initial reaction to the draft was so heated, that delegates voted to put off further debate for a three-day period, starting November 1. They also voted to suspend the rule that no delegate could speak twice to the same issue without special privilege from the chair. Rancorous debate over the draft article broke out immediately when the floor was opened on November 1 – some condemning the provision as too pale an approximation of a proper establishment, others calling for abolition of the article altogether, and still others decrying the insufficient recognition of the concessions that religious dissenters had arduously won over the years in litigating their claims before colonial courts.

With the convention deadlocked on November 3, the delegates appointed a seven-member ad hoc committee, chaired by a Baptist delegate, the Reverend Noah Alden of Bellingham, to redraft Article III.[53] On November 6, this committee offered the convention a new draft that spelled out the religious tax system in more detail. This draft was debated intermittently for the next four days, and modest changes were approved.[54] On November 10, a motion to abolish Article III altogether was defeated. A slightly amended committee draft was passed the following day. It stated in full:

As the happiness of a people, and good order and preservation of civil government, essentially depend upon piety, religion, and morality; and as these cannot be generally diffused through a Community, but by the institution of publick Worship of God, and of public instructions in piety, religion, and morality: Therefore, to promote the happiness and to secure the good order and preservation of their government, the people of this Commonwealth have a right to invest their legislature with power to authorize and require, and their Legislature shall, from time to time, authorize and require, the several Towns, Parishes[,] precincts[,] and other bodies politic, or religious societies, to make suitable provision, at their own

52 In Adams, *Works*, 4:221–22; a slightly reworded version appears in the *Journal of the Convention*, Appendix 2, 193.

53 *Journal of the Convention*, 38–40.

54 Ibid., 43.

> Expence, for the institution of the Public worship of GOD, and for the support and maintenance of public protestant teachers of piety, religion and morality, in all causes which provision shall not be made Voluntarily. – And the people of this Commonwealth have also a right to, and do, invest their legislature with authority to enjoin upon all the Subjects an attendance upon the instructions of the public teachers aforesaid, at stated times and seasons, if there be any on whose instructions they can Conscientiously and conveniently attend. – PROVIDED, notwithstanding, that the several towns, parishes, precincts, and other bodies politic, or religious societies, shall, at times, have the exclusive right of electing their public Teachers, and of contracting with them for their support and maintenance. – And all monies, paid by the Subject of the support of the public teacher or teachers of his own religious sect or denomination, provided there be any on whose institution he attends; otherwise it may be paid towards the support of the teacher or teachers of the parish or precinct in which the said monies are raised. – And every denomina[t]ion of christians demeaning themselves peaceably, and as good Subjects of the Commonwealth, shall be equally under the protection of the Law: And no subordination of any one sect or denomination to another shall ever be established by law.[55]

This final text made some concessions to dissenters.[56] The system for collecting tithes was now to be voluntary and local rather than statewide – allowing Boston and, later, other townships to forgo mandatory tithing, with churches securing their own support from their members through voluntary tithes, tuition, or pew rents. Religious societies could contract individually with their own minister – allowing them to pay their tithes directly to their chosen minister rather than to a potentially capricious town treasurer. Local townships and religious societies could now participate in the selection of their parish minister, rather than be automatically saddled with a Congregationalist minister. In later years, this provision "had some unexpected results. Several of the towns and parishes, which thereby were given the exclusive right to elect their ministers . . . were converted to Unitarianism and settled Unitarian pastors over old Calvinist churches."[57]

Although Article III notably acknowledged the equality of diverse religious groups before the law, the final draft of the article largely retained the traditional tithing system and jettisoned some of the hard-fought concessions that Baptists, Anglicans, and other dissenters had secured through litigation. As Samuel Eliot Morison wrote in his definitive study:

> Article III was even less liberal than [the colonial] system, for instead of exempting members of dissenting sects from religious taxation, it merely gave them the privilege of paying their taxes to their own pastors. Unbelievers, non–church

55 Ibid., 46–47.

56 See Yan Li, "Transformation of the Constitution," 68, arguing that members of dissenting churches were not uniformly opposed to Article III.

57 Morison, "The Struggle," 375.

> goers, and dissenting minorities too small to maintain a minister had to contribute to Congregational worship. The whole Article was so loosely worded as to defeat the purpose of the fifth paragraph [guaranteeing the equality of all sects and denominations]. Every new denomination that entered the Commonwealth after 1780, notably the Universalists and Methodists, had to wage a long and expensive lawsuit to obtain recognition as a religious sect. … [A] subordination of sects existed in fact.[58]

RATIFICATION DEBATES ABOUT RELIGIOUS FREEDOM

On March 2, 1780, the convention put the draft constitution before the people for ratification. Eighteen hundred copies of the constitution were printed, sent out, and read from pulpits and lecterns and posted in town halls throughout the state. Surprisingly, no (surviving) newspaper of the day ran copies of the draft constitution, a familiar technique used by others states to ensure wide dissemination. The convention also sent out a committee report that explained the rationale of the constitution and encouraged the people to ratify it. The committee report dealt directly with the provisions juxtaposing religious freedom and religious establishment:

> [W]e have, with as much Precision as we were capable of, provided for the free exercise of the Rights of Conscience: We are very sensible that our Constituents hold those Rights infinitely more valuable than all others; and we flatter ourselves, that while we have considered Morality and Public Worship of GOD, as important to the happiness of Society, we have sufficiently guarded the rights of Conscience from every possible infringement. This Article underwent long debates, and took Time in proportion to its importance; and we feel ourselves peculiarly happy in being able to inform you, that the debates were managed by persons of various denominations, it was finally agreed upon with much more unanimity than usually takes place in disquisitions of this Nature. We wish you to consider the Subject with Candor, and Attention. Surely it would be an affront to the People of Massachusetts-Bay to labour to convince them, that the Honor and Happiness of a People depend upon Morality; and that the Public Worship of GOD has a tendency to inculcate the Principles thereof, as well as to preserve a people from forsaking Civilization, and falling into a state of Savage barbarity.[59]

Critics of Institutional Establishment. As the committee requested, the people did give the draft constitution their full candor and attention. Of the 290 eligible townships, 188 sent in returns that have survived, a number of them criticizing the religion provisions, others defending them, each with a range of arguments.[60]

58 Ibid., 371.
59 *Journal of the Convention*, Appendix 3, 218.
60 Morison, "The Struggle," 364–65.

A large group charged that Article III's establishment of religion contradicted the religious liberties set out in Article II.[61] The return of the Town of Dartmouth put it thus:

> It appears doubtful in said Articles whether the Rights of Conscience are sufficiently secured or not to those who are really desirous to, and do attend publick Worship, and who are not limited to any particular outward Teacher. ... [W]e humbly conceive it intirely out of the power of the legislature to establish a way of Worship that shall be agreable to the Conceptions and Convictions of the minds of the individuals, as it is a matter that solely relates to and stands between God and the Soul before whose Tribunal all must account each one for himself.[62]

A second group of critics retorted that the happiness of a people and the good order and preservation of civil government did not, as a matter of historical fact, depend upon piety, religion, and morality.[63] The return of the Town of Natick put it well:

> When both antient History and modern authentik information concur to evince that flourishing civil Governments have existed and do still exist without the Civil Legislature's instituting the publick Christian worship of God, and publick Instruction in piety and the Christian, – but that rather wherever such institutions are fully [executed] by the civil authority have taken place among a people instead of essentially promoting their happiness and the good order and preservation of Civil Government, it has We believe invariably promoted impiety, irreligion, hypocrisy, and many other sore and oppressive evils.[64]

A third group of critics acknowledged the public utility of piety, morality, and religion but thought that an establishment would jeopardize both religion and the state. The return of the Town of Petersham put it thus:

> We grant that the Happiness of a People and the good Order and preservation of Civil Government Greatly Depends upon Piety, Religion, and Morality. But we Can by no Means Suppose that to Invest the Legislature or any Body of men on Earth with a power absolutely to Determine For others What are the proper Institutions of Divine Worship and To appoint Days and seasons for such Worship With a power to impose and Indow Religious Teachers and by penalties and punishments to be able to Enforce an Attendance on such Publick Worship or to Extort Property from any one for the Support of what they may Judge to be publick Worship Can have a Tendency to promote true piety Religion or Morality But the Reverse and that such a Power when and where Ever Exercised has more or

61 See, e.g., "The Returns of New Salem," in Handlin and Handlin, *Popular Sources*, 482; "Town of Shutesbury," 597; "Town of Ashby," 633; "Town of Sherborn," 674; "Town of Westford," 682–83; "Return of Buxton," 731; "Town of Petersham," 855; see also "Return of Ashby," in Taylor, *Documents*, 151–52.

62 "Return of Dartmouth," in Handlin and Handlin, *Popular Sources*, 509–10.

63 Peters, *Massachusetts Constitution of 1780*, 33–35.

64 "Return of Westford," in Handlin and Handlin, *Popular Sources*, 681, 682.

> Less Been an Engine in the Hands of Tyrants for the Destruction of the Lives Liberties and Properties of the People and that Experience has abundantly Taught Mankind that these are Natural Rights which ought Never to be Delegated and Can with the greatest propriety be Exercised by Individuals and by every Religious Society of men.[65]

A fourth group of critics believed that to institute even a mild establishment of religion would lead to more odious forms. A pamphleteer named "Philanthropos" puts this argument well:

> Perhaps it will be said that the civil magistrate has a right to oblige the people to support the ministers of the gospel, because the gospel ministry is beneficial to society. [But if so] it will follow, by the same law, that he may adopt any of the maxims of the religion of Christ into the civil constitution, which he may judge will be beneficial to civil society ... if magistrates may adopt any the least part of the religion of Christ into their systems of civil government, that supposes magistrates to be judges what parts shall be taken, and what left; power, then which nothing can be more dangerous, to be lodged in the hands of weak and fallible men.[66]

A fifth group of critics repeated Isaac Backus's earlier charge that Article III constituted a species of taxation without representation. As the return of Ashby put it:

> Religeous Societys as such have no voice in Chusing the Legeslature, the Legeslature therefore have no right to make law binding on them as such; every religeous Society, as such, is intirely independent on any body politick, the Legeslature having therefor no more right to make laws Binding on them, as such, then the Court of Great Britton have to make Laws binding on the Independent states of America."

Indeed, the Ashby return commented later, "to invest their Legeslature with power [to] make Laws that are binding on Religious Society ... is as much to say we will not have Christ to reign over us[,] that the Laws of this Kingdom are not sufficient to govern us, that the prosperity of this Kingdom is not equally important with the Kingdoms of this world."[67]

A sixth group of critics argued that Article III's guarantee of equality for all denominations contradicted the provisions on tax support for some denominations. If "all religious sects or denominations peaceably demeaning themselves" are equal before the law, why are some supported by taxes and others not? Why must religions be incorporated by the state in order to receive taxes, when some religions do not accept religious incorporation by the state? True religious liberty would leave the "several religious societies of the Commonwealth, whether corporate or incorporate" to their own peaceable devices. It would grant them "the right to elect their

65 "Return of Petersham," in Handlin and Handlin, *Popular Sources*, 855.

66 *Continental Journal*, Apr. 6, 1780, quoted in Peters, *Massachusetts Constitution of* 1780, 82. See also "Return of the Town of Westford" in Handlin and Handlin, *Popular Sources*, 682–83.

67 Quoted in Taylor, *Documents*, 151–52.

pastors or religious teachers, to contract with them for their support, to raise money for erecting and repairing houses for public worship, for the maintenance of religious instruction, and for the payment of necessary expenses."[68]

Defenders of Institutional Establishment. Proponents of Article III responded harshly, accusing critics of religious bigotry and chastising them for inviting moral decay under the guise of religious liberty. The "ancient atrocities of the German Anabaptists were raked up" to discredit Backus and his fellow Baptists, who were portrayed as "Disguised tories, British emissaries, profane and licentious deists, avaricious worldlings, disaffected sectaries, and furious blind bigots."[69]

A second group of proponents, comprising Congregationalist ministers, invoked traditional theocratic arguments in favor of Article III. One writer argued that since civil government is God's creation, it would "counter the divine command to provide for worship and the spiritual edification of the people but refuse to support religious institutions."[70] Others argued that outlawing the state collection of tithes would "deprive a respectable part of the people of the state of the privilege of discharging their duty to God in a way that they judge to be most agreeable to his will."[71] Others thundered jeremiads predicated on the covenantal language of the preamble, warning that "if the people and their representatives withhold their support of God's church, God will withhold His support of them, and raine down his woeful vengeance."[72]

A third group of proponents thought such an institutional establishment was merely an inevitable and innocuous act of a political majority seeking to promote the common good and the personal happiness of all subjects. Boston, which itself did not establish religious institutions, nonetheless supported Article III, arguing in its return:

> Though we are not supporting the Kingdom of Christ, may we not be permitted to Assist civil society by an adoption, and by the teaching of the best act of Morals that were ever offered to the World? To object to these Morals, or even to the Piety and Religion we aim to inculcate, because they are drawn from the Gospel, must appear very singular to an Assembly generally professing themselves Christians. Suspend all provision for the inculcation of morality, religion, and Piety, and confusion and every evil work may be justly dreaded.[73]

68 Ibid.

69 Meyer, *Church and State*, 111. Also see original quote in Morison, "The Struggle," at 368: "Baptist Advocates of religious liberty . . . retorted by comparing religious taxation to a certain practice of the sons of Eli." (Likely referring to 1 Samuel 2:12–36.) Even John Adams allegedly tried to inflame the convention against Backus in order to secure passage of the controversial Article III. See Taylor, *Construction*, at 333, as cited in Wood, *Friends Divided*, 175.

70 *Boston Independent Chronicle* (Feb. 10, 1780), quoted by Charles H. Lippy, "The 1780 Massachusetts Constitution: Religious Establishment or Civil Religion?" *Journal of Church and State* 20 (1978), 539–40. See also Howard, *Election Sermon*, 13–15.

71 Irenaeus, *Independent Ledger* (Apr. 11, 1780), quoted in Morison, "The Struggle," 380.

72 Abel Holmes, *A Sermon Preached at Brattle Street Church in Boston* (Boston: Young & Minns, 1799), 17–18.

73 Full quote in Taylor, *Documents*, 148–50.

A fourth group of proponents argued that tithing and other forms of state support for religious institutions would ultimately serve to keep the political government and state smaller and more efficient, since churches effectively communicate values and discharge functions that would otherwise depend on the state. Congregationalist preacher Joseph McKeen (1757–1807) put this well:

> But in proportion as the principles, inculcated by the religion of Jesus Christ, prevail in the minds of a people, the number of crimes will be diminished, truth and justice will be maintained, kind and friendly offices will be multiplied, and happiness will be diffused through society. Were the benevolence of the gospel imbibed by all the members of the community, no human laws, nor officers of justice, would be necessary to compel them to do their duty, nor to restrain one from injuring another; and were their temper and conduct generally formed and regulated by it, civil rulers would need to exercise but little power to preserve tranquility in the state. The more, therefore, that the principles of piety, benevolence, and virtues are diffused among a people, the milder may their government and laws be, and the more liberty are they capable of enjoying, because they govern themselves. But if there be little or no regard to religion or virtue among a people, they will not govern themselves, nor willingly submit to any laws, which lay restraint upon their passions; and consequently they must be wretched or be governed by force: they cannot bear freedom; they must be slaves.

For McKeen, therefore, the benefits of a mild institutional establishment of religion outweighed its risks – at least for the time being.

> The wise institutions of our forefathers, the schools which they established for the education of youth, the provision which they made for the public worship of God, and a religious observance of the Christian Sabbath, have doubtless contributed very much to the tranquil state in which our country is at this day. Let us not discard these institutions, before we are certain that we have got something better to substitute in their room.[74]

RATIFICATION

These and similar arguments in favor of Article III proved just cogent enough to win ratification for the 1780 Massachusetts Constitution, perhaps aided by a bit of sleight of hand. The clerks kept close tallies on the votes for Article III, and historians now believe that in fact they "fell some 600 votes short of the necessary two-thirds majority for ratification" – with the popular vote in favor standing at 8,865 to 6,225 or a little over 58 per cent.[75] Though the individual township tallies were less closely

74 Joseph McKeen, *A Sermon Preached on the Public Fast in the Commonwealth of Massachusetts* (Salem: Thomas C. Cushing, 1793), 17–21.

75 Meyer, *Church and State*, 113. The township returns are included in Handlin and Handlin, *Popular Sources*, 475–932.

kept for other provisions, it also appears that Chapter II and Chapter VI, requiring the governor to be a Christian and to profess adherence to Christianity in an oath, did not garner two-thirds support.[76] Nevertheless, delegates to the convention – out of ignorance of or indifference to the exact vote tally, given the political pressure to succeed – treated the Constitution as fully ratified.

On June 16, 1780, James Bowdoin, president of the convention, announced that the entire Constitution had garnered the requisite two-thirds vote. On October 25, 1780, the Constitution went into effect, the first day that the General Court sat after ratification. Among the first acts of the General Court was a politically expedient pledge of support for religious liberty: "Deeply impressed with a sense of the importance of religion to the happiness of men in civil society to maintain its purity and promote this efficacy, we shall protect professors of all denominations, demeaning themselves peaceably and as good subjects of the Commonwealth, in the free exercise of the rights of conscience."[77] In a 1780 case, William Cushing (1732–1810), chief justice of the Massachusetts Supreme Juridical Court and later associate justice of the US Supreme Court, repeated the balance of religious freedom and religious establishment set out by the Constitution:

> As to the rights of conscience, which ought ever to be held sacred, they stand as well secured as may be, all sects and persuasions being left unrestricted to associate for the worship of God, in such manner and season as they think best; and under this restriction it cannot be thought an infringement to the right that the Legislature, if need be, should compel the support of public worship, and of the teachers of religion and morals; as the public social veneration of the Supreme Governor of the world is a duty essential to all religion and morality.[78]

GRADUAL INSTITUTIONAL DISESTABLISHMENT

The Massachusetts experiment in balancing religious liberty and religious establishment encountered numerous challenges over the next half century. On the one hand, the 1780 Constitution – softened by a pair of acts of religious freedom in 1811 and 1824 – was "mild and equitable" enough for dissenting churches to grow in number, membership, and influence. On the other hand, as established Congregational churches splintered into Trinitarian and Unitarian factions, public support for the state establishment of religion eroded.[79] New political coalitions took

76 Taylor, *Documents*, 113.

77 In Taylor, *Documents*, 164. Also see Meyer, *Church and State*, 110–11, noting that the Convention "seems to have counted as in favor of an article all those who did not definitely and specifically vote in the negative on it, if the votes were needed to pass the article. This is the procedure which Professor Samuel Eliot Morison has called 'political jugglery.'"

78 Quoted from handwritten notes in the Massachusetts History Society, vol. 11, in F. William O'Brien, "Has Government an Interest in Religion," *Villanova Law Review* 5 (1960), 339.

79 Also see Jonathan J. Den Hartog, *Patriotism and Piety: Federalist Politics and Religious Struggle in the New American Nation* (Charlottesville, VA: University of Virginia Press, 2015).

up old arguments to challenge the 1780 Constitution.[80] The provisions of Article III for religious taxation and the provisions for a religious test of office in Chapters II and VI in the Frame of Government were the main targets. But dissenters also challenged other aspects of the law – the laws and policies supporting traditional religious instruction at Harvard College; the hiring practices for clergy in parish churches; the tests used by courts and legislatures for dividing church property between schismatic factions; the compulsory church attendance laws; and more.

Court Battles. Almost as soon as the Constitution was ratified, Article III proved to be "fruitful in lawsuits, bad feeling, and petty prosecution."[81] Many of these cases were technical disputes over the details of religious taxation, religious incorporation, clerical appointments, intrachurch property disputes, and more.[82] Particularly nettlesome were ongoing disputes about whether Unitarian Universalists and other minority religious groups could be incorporated as religious societies; whether their ministers could be licensed as "public teachers of piety, religion, and morality"; and whether new or unincorporated religious societies or churches were eligible for state-collected religious taxes.[83]

One of the earliest of such cases in the 1780s involved a Universalist minister, the Reverend John Murray, who served as minister in a loosely associated Independent Church of Christ in the town of Gloucester. Murray's theology of universal salvation without necessary baptism, and the church's appointment of him without the traditional ordination rite of laying on of hands, made him and his church suspect in the eyes of the local establishment. Article III allowed local taxpayers to direct their church taxes to the church of their choice, and Murray's church thus requested the share of taxes paid by their congregants. The town authorities refused to deliver the tax revenues. Moreover, in an effort to drive him out, the local police arrested Murray for consecrating marriages without being properly licensed as a religious minister or justice of the peace. Murray filed suit in Massachusetts Superior Court. The town officials were represented by Congregationalist Theophilus Parsons, author of the 1778 *Essex Result*[84] and, after 1806, the state's chief justice. Parsons argued that Murray was not a properly ordained minister; that his theology of universal salvation was a teaching contrary to "piety, religion, and morality," indeed

80 See the careful sifting of this case law in McLoughlin, *New England Dissent*, 636–59, 1084–106, 1189–284, with summaries in William G. McLoughlin, "The Balkcom Case (1782) and the Pietistic Theory of Separation of Church and State," *William and Mary Quarterly* 24, no.2 (April 1967), 267–83; Cushing, "Notes on Disestablishment."

81 Morison, *History of the Constitution*, 24–25. See further *The Register of the Lynn Historical Society* (Lynn, MA: Nichols Press, 1899), 40–52.

82 See Cushing, "Notes on the Disestablishment"; O'Brien, "Has Government an Interest in Religion," 338–53; William E. Nelson, *The Americanization of the Common Law: The Impact of Legal Change on Massachusetts Society*, 1760–1820 (Athens: University of Georgia Press, (1994), 89–144, esp. 103–05; Philip A. Hamburger, *Law and Judicial Duty* (Cambridge, MA: Harvard University Press, 2008), 643–54.

83 See sources in n. 82 and report on the earliest such local case in McLoughlin, "The Balkcom Case."

84 See p. 107–08.

altogether "immoral"; and that the Independent Church of Gloucester was (thus) not a proper "religious sect or denomination . . . of the christian religion," as Article III defined it. Murray was represented by Episcopalian Rufus King (1755–1827), signer of both the Massachusetts and US Constitutions and soon to be US senator and vice presidential candidate. King argued for a more generous interpretation of Article III. After all, he argued, this article on its face allowed each person to direct their church taxes "to the support of the public teacher or teachers of his own religious sect or denomination" and required the authorities to treat "every denomina[t]ion of christians . . . equally under the protection of the Law." By any interpretation of Article III, King argued, Murray was a religious minister or teacher involved in the usual activities of religious ministry; his congregation was a religious society that called itself Christian (the Independent Church of Christ); and this religious sect or denomination was in the same legal position as the established Congregationalist churches and the dissenting Baptist and Episcopalian churches that now received state-collected tax revenues when directed by local taxpayers who were members of those churches. To treat Murray and his church otherwise was to violate the constitutional mandate of equal protection of all peaceable churches. Parsons's argument prevailed in the lower court; King's prevailed in the Supreme Judicial Court in 1786. Several subsequent cases upheld the rights of Unitarians and other peaceable religious dissenters to direct their church taxes to their own religious church or denomination, however unorthodox their beliefs or practices.[85]

Once elevated to the Massachusetts Supreme Judicial Court, however, Parsons succeeded for a time in limiting the distribution of Article III church taxes and defending the Congregationalist establishment. In the 1810 case of *Barnes v. Falmouth*,[86] Thomas Barnes, a Universalist minister, sought to reclaim the funds collected from the estates of two Universalist parishioners which had been paid over to the locally established Congregationalist church rather than to the Universalist church that they had attended. The Supreme Judicial Court denied Barnes's claim. Parsons's opinion for the Barnes case used the same argument he had pressed twenty-four years earlier in the Murray case.

The *Barnes* case was more significant, however, for its lengthy dicta offering Parsons's "diligent examination" of "the motives which induced the people to introduce into the Constitution a religious establishment, the nature of the establishment introduced, and the rights and privileges it secured to the people, and to their teachers."[87] "The object of a free civil government is the promotion and

85 The case is not officially reported, but recounted in William Cushing, "Notes of Cases Decided in the Superiour and Supreme Judicial Courts of Massachusetts from 1772–1789 – Taken by the Honorable William Cushing," Harvard Law School Manuscript 4083, 54–56; see discussion and quotations in Cushing, "Notes on Disestablishment," 173–81. See further Hamburger, *Law and Judicial Duty*, 652–54.

86 6 Mass. 401 (1810). Reprinted with revisions as Theophilus Parsons, *Defence of the Third Article of the Massachusetts Declaration of Rights* (Worcester, MA: Manning and Trumbull, 1820).

87 *Barnes* v. *Falmouth*, 6 Mass. 401, 404 (1810) (Barnes, C. J.).

security of the happiness of the citizens," Parsons wrote. In a nutshell, he argued that the happiness of citizens is the goal of government, which, however, cannot legislate "the temper and disposition of the heart"; rather, morality and virtue are essential ingredients to the achievement of happiness because they attune people to the enjoyment of family life, patriotism, and civil society; religion and faith are essential wellsprings of this morality and virtue; and thus government must support religion and faith.[88]

Having demonstrated the necessity and utility of religion generally for civil society and government, Parsons then turned to the reasons for state support of Christian institutions in particular – in effect, combining the arguments of Joseph McKeen and the return of Boston sampled earlier.

> [T]he people of Massachusetts, in the frame of their government, adopted and patronized a religion, which, by its benign and energetic influences, might cooperate with human institutions, to promote and secure the happiness of the citizens, so far as it might be consistent with the imperfections of man. In selecting a religion, the people were not exposed to the hazard of choosing a false and defective religious system. Christianity had long been promulgated, its pretensions and excellences well known, and its divine authority admitted. . . . And this religion, as understood by Protestants, tending, by its effects, to make every man submitting to its influence, a better husband, parent, child, neighbor, citizen, and magistrate, was by the people established as a fundamental and essential part of their constitution.[89]

Parsons then moved to answer criticisms that the institutionalization of religion mandated by Article III was "inconsistent, intolerant, and impious."[90] First, he argued, the establishment recognized the rights of conscience and religious practice while protecting these rights from "the interference of the civil magistrate . . . for every man, whether Protestant or Catholic, Jew, Mahometan, or Pagan."[91] It is perfectly consistent, Parsons said, for the state to guarantee liberty of conscience while providing for "the public teaching of the precepts of Protestant Christians to all the people" by collecting tithes to support their ministers and churches. To object that this is a violation of conscience, Parsons wrote, is "to mistake a man's conscience for his money," and to deny the state the right of collecting taxes from those whom it represents. Every citizen benefits from the protection of the state and therefore owes the state "the price of this protection," which is paid to the state through taxes. But if every citizen sought to veto the uses to which the state appropriated those taxes, "the authority of the state to levy taxes would be annihilated; and without money it would soon cease to have any authority. . . . The great error lies in not distinguishing between liberty of conscience in religious opinions and worship, and the right of appropriating money by the state."[92]

88 Ibid., 404–05.
89 Ibid., 405.
90 Ibid., 405, 408.
91 Ibid., 405–06.
92 Ibid., 407–08.

Second, Parsons argued, the notion that support for religious institutions was intolerant of the nonreligious fails to recognize the great public benefits that all receive through support of religious institutions. "Public religious instruction" teaches and enforces "a system of correct morals" and cultivates "reasonable and just habits and manners" that are every bit as effective as courts of law in ensuring persons' property, social well-being, and personal happiness. Objecting to public support of religion is akin to objecting to public education and being equally blind to the public benefits of both.[93]

Abolishing Religious Test Oaths in 1821. While these kinds of arguments proved cogent enough in the 1810s, by the 1820s support for the Congregationalist establishment was rapidly waning around the state. A popular referendum in 1820 called for a new constitutional convention to reconsider several provisions in the 1780 Constitution, including those on religious test oaths for public office,[94] the leadership and religious affiliation of Harvard College,[95] and the provision of public funds for religious worship under Article III.[96]

The convention debates in 1820 centered on religious test oaths for political officers, and the arguments on both sides echoed familiar themes from 1780. Virtually everyone continued to affirm the value of religion as a foundation for personal morality and the political common good. But critics challenged religious test oaths on practical, theological, and political grounds. James Prince of Boston (1784–1849), for example, emphasized that the rights of conscience were unalienable, and that religion was solely "a matter between God and the individual." The coercive imposition of religious test oaths for political office, he argued, violated an individual's rights of conscience and jeopardized the common good of society. "An inquiry into opinions for which man is only accountable to his God" would constitute, in Prince's view, an injustice that "is neither politic nor expedient":

> first, because . . . it may deprive society of talent and moral excellence, which should always be secured and cherished as one of the best means of preserving the prosperity of the Commonwealth; and secondly, while it may thus exclude men possessing such useful and amiable qualification, yet it is no effectual safeguard whereby to keep out ambitious, unprincipled men from office, or a seat in the public councils.

Not only that, Prince argued, but Christianity does not need this kind of defense. Its "divine origin, and its own intrinsic merit, ever have been, and ever will be, its firmest support."[97]

93 Ibid., 408–09. See also the conclusion of Lippy, "The Massachusetts Constitution," 534–35: Article III did not establish Puritan Congregationalism but "providing public support for religious institutions was seen as a way to promote political stability and social cohesion by guaranteeing that individuals would receive instruction in moral principles, rooted in the common religious sensibilities of the people, which would make them good citizens."

94 See McLoughlin, *New England Dissent*, 1145–85.

95 Ibid., 1156.

96 See *Journal of Debates and Proceedings*, 612–39.

97 Ibid., 163–65.

Defenders of traditional religious test oaths argued that the Massachusetts Constitution confirmed the people's fundamental religious beliefs in the Creator God, and that political leaders who represent the people must pledge under oath to exhibit and maintain these Christian beliefs and practices. The Reverend Joseph Tuckerman of Chelsea (1778–1840), for example, argued that "if our religion be from God," there followed a duty "to promote its progress," while we should pause to ask whether opening the door to "high and responsible office" for "enemies of Christianity" would bring in its train regrettable consequences.[98]

Others were more ambivalent about religious tests and oaths for political office. The famous orator and statesman Daniel Webster (1782–1852) saw no reason why the people could not impose religious qualifications – or any other qualifications, for that matter – on public offices. "All bestowment of office remaining in the discretion of the people, they have, of course, a right to regulate it, by any rules which they may deem expedient."[99] But Webster concluded that religious test oaths were not necessary, insofar "as there is another part of the constitution which recognizes in the fullest manner the benefits which civil society derives from those Christian institutions which cherish piety, morality, and religion." "I am desirous," he continued, "in so solemn a transaction as the establishment of a constitution, that we should keep in it an expression of our respect and attachment to christianity; – not, indeed, to any of its peculiar forms, but to its general principles."[100] Webster believed, in effect, that the general ceremonial and moral establishment provisions of the Constitution were enough to ensure adherence to Christian values.

Ultimately, the convention proposed to abolish the religious test requirement and to modify the oath to read, "I, A. B., do solemnly swear that I will bear true faith and allegiance to the Commonwealth of Massachusetts and will support the constitution thereof. *So help me God.*"[101] The proposed amendment further allowed Quakers to affirm rather than swear the oath, and to replace the words "so help me God" with "this I do, under the pains and penalties of perjury." Chief Justice Isaac Parker (1768–1830), who served as president of the 1820 Convention, reported these changes matter-of-factly in his official "Address to the People":

> We have agreed that the declaration of belief in the Christian religion ought not to be required in the future; because we do not think the assuming of civil office a suitable occasion for so declaring; and because it is implied, that every man who is selected for office, in this community, must have such sentiments of religious duty as relate to his fitness for the place to which he is called.[102]

98 Ibid., 170.
99 Ibid., 161.
100 Ibid.
101 Ibid., 620.
102 Ibid., 630.

The fight over religious test oaths was finished. Massachusetts voters ratified the Sixth Amendment to their Constitution in 1821 with the new oath applied to "every person chosen or appointed to any office, civil or military under the government of this commonwealth." And while initially only Quakers could substitute "so help me God" with an affirmation "under the pains and penalties of perjury," Massachusetts law gradually extended this guarantee to all who had conscientious scruples to oaths.

Abolishing Religious Taxation in 1833. The 1820 convention proposed other amendments to Article III[103] that aimed to reform and clarify the patchwork of court rulings and political measures from 1780 forward, but all these efforts were defeated.[104] One proposed amendment sought to raise to constitutional status the Religious Freedom Act of 1811, which had standardized the application process for any group claiming exemption from tithes – a statute passed in response to *Barnes* v. *Falmouth*.[105] Another proposed amendment sought to regularize state procedures for the incorporation of religious groups,[106] while still another aimed to abolish mandatory church attendance. Another would have entitled citizens to transfer their religious taxes to any Christian church, rather than to Protestant churches alone.[107] The voters, however, rejected these amendments, leaving Article III in its original 1780 form.

Subsequent lawsuits and controversies continued to erode popular and political support for it. The 1820 *Dedham* case, for example, pitted liberal Unitarians against traditional Trinitarian Congregationalists in an intrachurch dispute over property and clerical appointment. The Unitarian members of the local parish or township (who were required to pay religious taxes to support the local churches) sought to appoint a liberal minister for that local church. The Trinitarian members of the local church objected, claiming to be the true owners of the church and entitled to elect their own like-minded clergy. As the controversy unfolded, the Trinitarian deacons and congregants left the church, taking the communion silver and other valuable church property with them. The remaining Unitarian faction filed suit, claiming title and possession in the church property. The Massachusetts courts held for the Unitarians – arguing that the parish or religious society, not the local church and clergy, controlled the church property, and this society had authority to decide on the clerical appointments. Those church members and leaders who left were no longer the church and had no control or say in its future use or leadership.[108] The same Chief Justice Parker who had presided over the 1820 Constitution offered

103 Ibid., 613–14, 623–24, 634.

104 See, e.g., the "exemption laws" of 1790–91, in McLoughlin, *New England Dissent*, 925–28, 935–38.

105 Ibid., 1084–106.

106 Debates about the legal status of church corporations played a notable role in the emergence of nonprofit corporations in the United States. See Johann N. Neem, "Politics and the Origins of the Nonprofit Corporation in Massachusetts and New Hampshire, 1780–1820," *Nonprofit and Voluntary Sector Quarterly* 32, no. 3 (September 2003), 344–65.

107 McLoughlin, *New England Dissent*, 1183.

108 *Baker* v. *Fales*, 16 Mass. 488 (1820).

a lengthy opinion showing how the 1780 Massachusetts Constitution had changed traditional colonial rules to mandate this result:

> A church may exist, in an ecclesiastical sense, without any officers . . . [but what] gives a church any legal character, is its connection with some regularly-constituted society; and those who withdraw from the society cease to be members of that particular church, and remaining members continue to be the identical church. This is analogous to the separation of towns and parishes – the effect of which, by law, is to leave the original body politic entire, with its powers and privileges undiminished, however large may be the proportion which secedes. And so it is of all voluntary societies. . . .
>
> [T]he property sued for belongs to the first church in *Dedham, sub modo*; that is, to be managed by its deacons under the superintendence of the church for the general good of the inhabitants of the first parish, in the support of the public worship of God – that the members of the church now associated and worshipping with the first parish constitute the first church, – and that the plaintiffs are duly appointed deacons of that church.[109]

Unitarians won legal victories in several other intrachurch disputes in the 1820s and 1830s, and gradually consolidated their control of other parishes, as well as of Harvard Divinity School.

In response, Trinitarians formed political alliances with opponents of the traditional establishment, making legislative concessions that ultimately undermined the religious tax system created by Article III. For example, the Religious Liberties Act of 1824 made it even easier for non–church members and religious dissenters to claim exemptions from religious taxes, weakening the ability of parishes to collect tithes from dissenters and to support traditional Congregationalist ministries.[110] By 1831, Samuel Lathrop (1772–1846), a leading member of the Senate, observed that Article III had grown decrepit, and the law on the books bore little resemblance to the law in practice:

> Whenever any provision of the Constitution ceases to have any obligatory effect – when public opinion clearly and unequivocally demands of the legislature a disregard of its injunctions – when we are obliged to frame our laws in such a manner as to evade it, or directly to contravene it, and when our judicial tribunals give the sanction of constitutionality to such enactments, the continuance of the article remains not merely useless – it also tends to diminish our veneration for the whole instrument, and necessarily leads to a practice of immoral tendency. Will not these observations apply to the third article in our Bill of Rights?[111]

One year later, a widely circulated set of petitions decried the Constitution's religious tax provisions as anachronistic, un-American, and even tyrannical – and

109 Ibid., 504–05, 522.
110 McLoughlin, *New England Dissent*, 1205.
111 "Domestic Intelligence: Massachusetts Legislature," *Christian Register* (March 19, 1831), 47.

quite in contrast to other New England states that had recently rejected religious taxes and other supports for religion.

> Massachusetts stands alone among the States in the Union in making *legal* provision for the support of Religion; and notwithstanding the reverence which has by some been paid to the Third Article, it has become settled that it is a subject of vexation to many, a means of petty tyranny in the hands of a few, and altogether injurious to the cause of pure and undefiled religion.[112]

In 1833, those who sought to foster such "pure and undefiled religion" by way of stronger separation of church and state finally prevailed by passing the Eleventh Amendment to the Massachusetts Constitution. This amendment replaced Article III with a system of religious voluntarism:

> As the public worship of God and instructions in piety, religion and morality, promote the happiness and prosperity of a people and the security of a republican government; – therefore, the several religious societies of this commonwealth, whether corporate or unincorporate, at any meeting legally warned and holden for that purpose, shall ever have the right to elect their pastors or religious teachers, to contract with them for their support, to raise money for erecting and repairing houses for public worship, for the maintenance of religious instruction, and for the payment of necessary expenses: and all persons belonging to any religious society shall be taken and held to be members, until they shall file with the clerk of such society, a written notice, declaring the dissolution of their membership, and thenceforth shall not be liable for any grant or contract which may be thereafter made, or entered into by such society: – and all religious sects and denominations, demeaning themselves peaceably, and as good citizens of the commonwealth, shall be equally under the protection of the law; and no subordination of any one sect or denomination to another shall ever be established by law.[113]

The Eleventh Amendment of 1833 thus made church membership and funding entirely voluntary. It granted all religious societies – Christian or not, incorporated or not – the right to hire their own clergy, to build their own churches, and to manage their own membership rolls. It promised equal protection of the law to believers of all sects and nonbelievers alike, and it ensured that individual members of those sects could exit without incurring liability for contracts subsequently made by the other members of that sect. Additional amendments to the Constitution in 1855, 1917, and 1974 closed the door tightly against any form of state fiscal and material aid to religious institutions and endeavors – provisions that the Massachusetts courts have enforced with alacrity.[114]

112 McLoughlin, *New England Dissent*, 1246.

113 Mass. Const. amend., art. XI (1833).

114 Mass. Const. amend., art. XVI (1855) provides that tax "moneys shall never be appropriated to any religious sect for the maintenance exclusively of its own schools." This was superseded by art. XLVI (1917), which provides, in pertinent part, that "no law shall be passed prohibiting the free exercise of religion" and that no tax money was to be paid to religious groups or activities. Art. XLVI, in turn, was further amended by art. CIII (1974): "No grant, appropriation, use of public money or property or loan

SUMMARY AND CONCLUSIONS

John Adams placed private religious freedom and public religious establishment in soft dialectical tension. Too little religious freedom, he insisted, is a recipe for immorality and impiety. But too much religious freedom is an invitation to abuse and license. Too firm a religious establishment by law breeds coercion and hypocrisy. But too little religious establishment in law allows secular prejudices to become constitutional prerogatives. Somewhere between these extremes, Adams believed, a society must find its balance.

The balance that John Adams struck between a "mild and equitable establishment" of Protestantism and the generous protection of religious freedom for all peaceable faiths was just enough to convince a majority of Massachusetts citizens to ratify the 1780 Constitution. While the amendments expunging religious test oaths and religious taxes made the institutional establishment of religion even milder and more equitable, much of the establishment continued uninterrupted. Yes, the 1821 amendment removed religious test oaths for political office. But political officials were still to swear oaths or make affirmations "to bear true faith and allegiance" to a constitution that still established covenant ceremonies and rituals in its preamble and demanded from its leaders "constant adherence to ... piety, justice, moderation, temperance, industry, and frugality, [which] are absolutely necessary to preserve the advantages of liberty, and to maintain a free government." Yes, the 1833 amendment ended state collection and management of religious taxes in support of religious worship. But state support of voluntary religious worship continued apace through laws allowing for incorporation of religious societies, exemption of religious properties from taxation, criminal prohibition against desecrations of sanctuaries and cemeteries, and guarantees of religious freedom for all peaceable individuals and groups. Moreover, Article II still protected the "right as well as the duty of all men in society, publicly, and at stated seasons to worship the Supreme Being, the great Creator and Preserver of the universe." The Eleventh Amendment still justified the principle of religious voluntarism on the ground that, "the public worship of God and instructions in piety, religion and morality, promote the happiness and prosperity of a people and the security of a republican government." The Preamble still acknowledged, "with grateful hearts, the goodness of the great Legislator of the universe, in affording us, in the course of His providence, an opportunity, deliberately and peaceably, without fraud, violence or surprise, of entering into an original, explicit, and solemn compact with each other; ... [while] devoutly imploring His direction" in this constitutional covenant.

of credit shall be made by the Commonwealth or any political subdivision thereof for the purpose of founding, maintaining, or aiding any ... charitable or religious undertaking which is not publicly owned and under the exclusive control of [the Commonwealth]." For summary of the cases, see Herbert P. Wilkins, "Judicial Treatment of the Massachusetts Declaration of Rights in Relation to Cognate Provisions of the United States Constitution," *Suffolk University Law Review* 14, no. 4 (Summer 1980), 892–94.

Massachusetts is often described as "the last American establishment state," which finally, in 1833, came in line with the unique American system of "no establishment of religion."[115] But this later disestablishment in Massachusetts was much more mild and equitable than some of the contemporaneous and current calls for "a high and impregnable wall of separation between church and state" and an absolute separation between conscience and commandment, religion and law, faith and politics.[116] In some ways, the chastened remnants of religious establishment in Massachusetts, combined with stronger protections for religious freedom, more fully reflect John Adams's original vision of a truly gentle and fair establishment along with a guarantee that "all men of all religions consistent with morals and property . . . enjoy equal liberty [and] security of property . . . and an equal chance for honors and power."[117]

To be sure, the balance that Adams struck for Massachusetts at the end of the eighteenth century can no longer serve that state, let alone the whole of the United States today, in view of the country's intense religious and postreligious pluralism and its First Amendment commitment that "Congress shall make no law respecting an establishment of religion or prohibiting the free exercise thereof." But the nation has not been well served by the balance that the twentieth-century US Supreme Court has tried to strike in insisting that state laws must serve "a secular purpose" while accommodating religions that are burdened by those laws. Too often, as Adams predicted, the disestablishment of traditional religion has led to the establishment of new secular beliefs and values that are sometimes enforced with as much as dogmatism, hardness, and cruelty as any established religious regime of the past. Too often, as Massachusetts had already discovered after 1780, even constitutionally grounded claims to religious exemption from laws that violate the dictates of conscience or the commands of the faith often meet with resistance, rejoinder, and recrimination by those in the majority. In Adams's day, it was Quakers, Baptists, Catholics, Unitarians, and Universalists who struggled constantly with the majoritarian Congregationalist establishment to gain their exemptions and accommodations. In our day, Christians, Muslims, and other faith communities are struggling to maintain their religious freedom against a growing and increasingly harsh secularist establishment. What this case study thus exposes is the limitation of a simple dialectic method of juxtaposing religious establishment and religious freedom. Further principles and precepts are needed to ensure ordered religious liberty for all peaceable faiths. The next chapters take up this story – first in the United States, and then in Europe.

115 See the variety of views in T. Jeremy Gunn and John Witte, Jr., eds., *No Establishment of Religion: America's Original Contribution to Religious Liberty* (New York: Oxford University Press, 2012); Carl H. Esbeck and Jonathan Den Hartog, eds., *Religious Dissent and Disestablishment: Church-State Relations in the New American States, 1776–1833* (Columbia: University of Missouri Press, 2019).

116 See cases and other sources in Witte and Nichols, *Religion and the American Constitutional Experiment*, 52–57, 103–07, 173–80.

117 Adams, *Works*, 8:232.

5

Historical Foundations and Enduring Fundamentals of American Religious Freedom

"A page of history is worth a volume of logic," Oliver Wendell Holmes, Jr. (1841–1935), once wrote.[1] In that spirit, this chapter sketches the historical context for the development of modern American religious freedom. I focus on the American founding era of 1760 to 1820, and the teachings of leading founders like John Adams (1735–1826), Thomas Jefferson (1743–1826), and James Madison (1751–1836). Like their English counterparts, the American founders drew deeply on the Western legal tradition. They, too, were inspired by biblical, classical, and republican theories of liberty.[2] They, too, drew on Magna Carta and the common law tradition of rights and liberties that it inspired.[3] Especially important for the American founders were seventeenth-century constitutional developments in England from the 1628 Petition of Right to the 1689 Bill of Rights, and the defenses of religious and civil rights and liberties by great English minds like Edward Coke (1552–1634), John Milton (1608–74), and John Locke (1632–1704), and their colonial allies in the New World like Nathaniel Ward (1578–1652), Roger Williams (1603–83), and William Penn (1644–1718).[4]

But the later eighteenth century in America was also an era of violent revolution against England's political, military, and economic policies – and notably against the Anglican religious establishment, too. After fighting the revolutionary war and issuing the Declaration of Independence in 1776, the American founders unleashed what Thomas Jefferson called a "fair" and "novel experiment" of guaranteeing religious freedom to all and granting religious establishments to none.[5] These religious freedom guarantees were set out in the new state constitutions forged

1 *New York Trust Co.* v. *Eisner*, 256 US 345, 349 (1921).

2 See the collection of sentiments in in Philip B. Kurland and Ralph S. Lerner, eds., *The Founders' Constitution*, 5 vols., repr. ed. (Indianapolis, IN: Liberty Fund, 2000).

3 See Robin Griffith-Jones and Mark Hill, eds., *Magna Carta, Religion, and the Rule of Law* (Cambridge: Cambridge University Press, 2015), 81–156.

4 See Chapters 1–2 and further John Witte, Jr., *The Reformation of Rights: Law, Religion, and Human Rights in Early Modern Calvinism* (Cambridge: Cambridge University Press, 2007), 209–320.

5 Julian Boyd, ed., *The Papers of Thomas Jefferson*, 16 vols. (Princeton, NJ: Princeton University Press, 1950–1990), 1:537–39.

between 1776 and 1784 and in the 1791 First Amendment to the US Constitution. These constitutional texts defied the millennium-old assumptions inherited from Western Europe – that one form of Christianity must be established in a community and that the state must protect and support it against all other forms of faith. America would no longer suffer such governmental prescriptions and proscriptions of religion. All forms of Christianity had to stand on their own feet and on an equal footing with all other religions. Their survival and growth had to turn on the cogency of their word, not the coercion of the sword, on the faith of their members, not the force of the law. This was a new experiment in religious freedom, something the West had not seen on this scale since Roman Emperor Constantine issued the "Edict of Milan" in 313.[6]

FOUNDING PRINCIPLES OF RELIGIOUS FREEDOM

The eighteenth-century American founders adopted and advocated six major principles of religious freedom: (1) liberty of conscience; (2) free exercise of religion; (3) religious pluralism; (4) religious equality; (5) separation of church and state; and (6) no establishment of a national religion. These six principles – some ancient, some new – appeared regularly in the debates over religious liberty and religion–state relations in the eighteenth century, although with varying definitions and priorities. They were also commonly incorporated into the original state constitutions, and they helped to shape the First Amendment to the US Constitution. They remain at the heart of the American experiment today – as central commandments of the American constitutional order and as cardinal axioms of a distinct American logic of religious liberty.[7]

First, the founders embraced the ancient Western principle of liberty of conscience. For them, liberty of conscience protected religious voluntarism – "the unalienable right of private judgment in matters of religion," the freedom to choose, change, or discard one's religious beliefs, practices, or associations.[8] Faith was not something inherited, predestined, or predetermined by birth, status, or caste, the founders insisted. It was something to be chosen and fashioned by each person using their reason, will, and experience. "The Religion . . . of every man must be left to the conviction and conscience of every man," James Madison wrote; "and it is the right of every man to exercise it as these may dictate."[9]

6 See Chapter 1, p. 22–23.

7 This section is distilled and updated from John Witte, Jr. and Joel A. Nichols, *Religion and the American Constitutional Experiment*, 4th ed. (Oxford: Oxford University Press, 2016), chaps. 2–4, which have detailed sources.

8 Elisha Williams, *The Essential Rights and Liberties of Protestants* (Boston: S. Kneeland and T. Green, 1744), 42; Hugh Fisher, *The Divine Right of Private Judgment, Set in a True Light*, repr. ed. (Boston: n. p., 1790).

9 James Madison, "Memorial and Remonstrance Against Religious Assessments," *in The Papers of James Madison*, ed. W. T. Hutchinson, et al. (Chicago: University of Chicago Press, 1962), 8:298.

For the founders the constitutional guarantee of freedom of conscience protected believers not only from traditional forms of torture, inquisitions, pogroms, imprisonment, heresy trials, and other such forms of "soule rape," in Roger Williams' pungent phrase.[10] It also protected them from official or popular coercion, pressure, or inducements to accept certain religious beliefs or practices or face penalties and deprivations for choosing another. In addition, this guarantee permitted persons to claim exemptions and accommodations from military conscription orders, oath-swearing requirements, state-collected church taxes, or comparable general laws that conflicted with their core claims of conscience.[11] As George Washington (1732–99) put it: "[T]he conscientious scruples of all men should be treated with great delicacy and tenderness" and "as extensively accommodated" as "the protection and essential interests of the nation may justify and permit."[12]

Second, the principle of free exercise of religion was the right to act publicly and peaceably on one's conscientious beliefs. Quaker founder William Penn had already linked these two guarantees, arguing that religious liberty requires "not only a mere Liberty of the Mind, in believing or disbelieving" but equally "the free and uninterrupted exercise of our consciences, in that way of worship, we are most clearly persuaded, God requires us to serve Him."[13] Most founders included alongside freedom of worship and religious assembly protections for the freedoms of religious

[10] Roger Williams, *The Complete Writings of Roger Williams*, 7 vols. (New York: Russell & Russell, 1963), 3:220.

[11] Isaac Backus, *Appeal to the Public for Religious Liberty Against the Oppressions of the Present Day* (Boston: John Boyle, 1773); Jonathan Parsons, *Freedom from Civil and Ecclesiastical Slavery* (Newburyport, MA: Thomas & Tinges, 1774); Thomas Jefferson, "Draft of Bill Exempting Dissenters from Contributing to the Support of the Church, 30 Nov. 1776," in Kurland and Lerner, *The Founders' Constitution*, 5:74.

[12] George Washington, "Letter to the Religious Society Called Quakers, October, 1789," in John C. Fitzpatrick, ed. *The Writings of George Washington* (Washington, DC: Government Printing Office, 1931), 30:416. See also Edward F. Humphrey, ed., *George Washington on Religious Liberty and Mutual Understanding: Selections from Washington's Letters* (New York: National Conference of Jews and Christians, 1932).

[13] William Penn, *The Political Writings of William Penn*, ed. Andrew R. Murphy (Indianapolis: Liberty Fund, 2002), 79, 81–82. Presciently, a Dutch pamphleteer in 1584 had argued that true religious freedom requires freedom of conscience as well as freedom of worship, speech, association, and education: "I know that they promise freedom of conscience provided there is no public worship and no offence is given, but this is only to trap and ensnare us. For it is well known that conscience, which resides in people's minds, is always free and cannot be examined by other men and still less be put under their control or command. And in fact, no one has ever been executed or harassed merely on grounds of conscience, but always for having committed some public act or demonstration, either in words, which are said to be an offence, or in acts which are described as exercise of religion. There is no difference between so-called freedom of conscience without public worship, and the old rigour of the edicts and inquisition of Spain .... How is it possible to grant freedom of conscience without exercise of religion? For what are the consequences for people who wish to enjoy the benefit of this freedom? If they have no ceremonies at all and do not invoke God to testify to the piety and reverence they bear Him, they are in fact left without any religion and without fear of God .... And I have not even mentioned that one will not of course be allowed to state what one thinks; any one who says any word detrimental to the dignity of the ecclesiastical state or the Roman religion will be accused of acting scandalously or of desecrating human and divine majesty. But this is only the start. The

speech, publication, education, charity, mission work, pilgrimage, and more. They also called for religious groups "to have the full enjoyment and free exercise of those purely spiritual powers . . . as may be consistent with the civil rights of society," and to enjoy rights to religious property, polity, incorporation, ecclesiastical discipline, and property tax exemption (and sometimes state-collected tithes, too).[14]

Third, the founders regarded religious pluralism as an important and independent principle of religious liberty, and not just a sociological reality. Rather than having one established faith per territory with separate classes of establishment conformists and dissenting nonconformists, the founders called for a plurality of forms of religious belief and worship, each equal before the law. They also called for a plurality of religious forums that deserved free exercise protection – sanctuaries, schools, charities, publishing houses, Bible societies, missionary groups, and other such "little platoons" of religion.[15] Part of their argument for religious pluralism was theological. As Baptist preacher Isaac Backus (1724–1806) argued, it was God's "sole prerogative" to decide which forms and forums of religion should flourish and which should fade, without influence or interference by state, church, or anyone else. "God's truth is great, and in the end He will allow it to prevail."[16] Part of their argument was political. Madison put it crisply in Federalist Paper No. 51: "In a free government, the security for civil rights must be the same as that for religious rights; it consists in the one case in the multiplicity of interests, and in the other in the multiplicity of sects."[17] "Checks and balances" are as important in religion as in politics, John Adams concurred. They "are our only Security, for the progress of Mind, as well as the Security of Body. Every Species of these Christians would persecute Deists, as [much] as either Sect would persecute another, if it had unchecked and unbalanced Power . . . . Know thyself, Human Nature!"[18]

authorities will go further and search books and cabinets and coffers, they will eavesdrop on private conversation, a father will not be allowed to teach his children how to call on God, nor will we be allowed to use our mother-tongue in our prayers. Soon, as I have said before, it will be necessary to restore the edicts and the inquisition in their full severity everywhere." *Discourse of a Nobleman* (1584), in E. H. Kossman and A. Mellink, eds., *Texts Concerning the Revolt of the Netherlands* (Cambridge: Cambridge University Press, 1974), 264–66.

14 Levi Hart, *Liberty Described and Recommended* (Hartford, CT: E. Watson, 1775), 14; William G. McLoughlin, ed., *Backus on Church, State, and Calvinism, Pamphlets, 1754–1789* (Cambridge, MA: Harvard University Press, 1968), 348–49; "A Declaration of Certain Fundamental Rights and Liberties of the Protestant Episcopal Church in Maryland," quoted by Anson P. Stokes, *Church and State in the United States* (New York: Harper & Bros., 1950), 1:741.

15 Benjamin Rush, "Letter to John Armstrong (March 19, 1793)," in Kurland and Lerner, eds., *The Founders' Constitution*, 5:78. The phrase "little platoon" was made popular in Edmund Burke, *Reflections on the Revolution in France* (London: J. Dodsley, 1790), 68.

16 McLoughlin, *Backus on Church, State, and Calvinism*, 317; Humphrey, *George Washington on Religious Liberty*, 12; *The Freeman's Remonstrance Against an Ecclesiastical Establishment* (Williamsburg, VA: John Dickson and William Hunter, 1777), 13.

17 Alexander Hamilton, James Madison, and John Jay, *The Federalist Papers*, ed. Clinton Rossiter (New York: New American Library, 1961), 324.

18 John Adams, "Letter to Thomas Jefferson, June 25, 1813," in Lester J. Cappon, ed., *The Adams-Jefferson Letters: The Complete Correspondence Between Thomas Jefferson and John and Abigail Adams* (Chapel Hill, NC: University of North Carolina Press, 1988), 333, 334.

Fourth, these principles of liberty of conscience, free exercise of religion, and religious pluralism depended on a guarantee of equality of all peaceable religions before the law. For the state to single out specific persons, groups, or religious practices for preferential benefits or discriminatory burdens would skew the choices of conscience, encumber the free exercise of religion, and upset the natural plurality of forms and forums of faith. Many of the founders therefore called for equality of all peaceable religions before the law. Madison captured the prevailing sentiment: "A just Government ... will be best supported by protecting every Citizen in the enjoyment of his religion, with the same equal hand which protects his person and property; by neither invading the equal rights of any sect, nor suffering any sect to invade those of another."[19] The founders invoked this principle especially to fight against religious test oaths and loyalty oaths that were traditionally imposed as a condition for political office or benefits and contributed to the religious divisions of society and politics.[20] They also pressed this principle of equality to challenge traditional state practices of discriminating in decisions about tax exemption, religious incorporation, licenses for teachers, schools, charities, and missionary societies, and similar state-based benefits.

Most founders called for religious equality of all peaceable theistic religions, usually mentioning Christians, Jews, Muslims, and Hindus, although they paid little heed to the many Native American and African American religions of the day. A few founders pressed for the legal equality of the religious and nonreligious, too. Jefferson put it memorably: "The legitimate powers of government extend to such acts only as are injurious to others. But it does me no injury for my neighbor to say there are twenty gods, or no god. It neither picks my pocket nor breaks my leg."[21] Such passages were unusual. Most of the founders were concerned about the equality of peaceable theistic religions before the law, not equality between religion and nonreligion, which has become the norm in our day.

Fifth, the founders invoked the ancient Western principle of separation of church and state, or what Saint Paul had already called "a wall of separation" (*paries maceriae*).[22] This institutional separation served to keep church and state officials and their operations free and focused on their core missions of soulcraft and statecraft, undistracted and well protected from the encroachments or privations of the other. "Religion and government are equally necessary, but their interests should be kept separate and distinct," wrote Jeffersonian pamphleteer Tunis Wortman. "Upon no plan, no system can they become united, without endangering the purity and usefulness of both – the church will corrupt the state, and the state pollute the

19 Madison, "Memorial and Remonstrance," paras. 4, 8.

20 See the example of Massachusetts in Chapter 4, p. 113–14, 131–33.

21 Thomas Jefferson, "Notes on the State of Virginia, Query 17," in Padover, ed., *The Complete Jefferson*, 673–76.

22 Ephesians 2:14. On the history of this concept, see John Witte, Jr., *God's Joust, God's Justice: Law and Religion in the Western Tradition* (Grand Rapids, MI: Eerdmans, 2007), 207–42.

church."[23] John Dickinson of Pennsylvania (1732–1808) argued similarly that when church and state "are kept distinct and apart, the peace and welfare of society is [sic] preserved, and the ends of both answered. But mixing them together fuels animosities, and persecutions have been raised, which have deluged the world in blood and disgraced human nature."[24] This understanding of separation of church and state helped to inform the movement in some states to exclude clergy and other religious officials from holding political office or exercising political power.

Some founders also called for separation of church and state in order to protect the individual's liberty of conscience. Madison warned that church and state officials must "not be suffered to overleap the great barrier [between them] which defends the rights of the people" to hold the religious beliefs and practices they choose.[25] Jefferson tied the "wall of separation" metaphor directly to protection of liberty of conscience:

> Believing with you that *religion is a matter which lies solely between a man and his God,* that he owes account to none other for his faith or his worship, that the [legitimate] powers of government reach actions only, and not opinions, I contemplate with sovereign reverence that the act of the whole American people which declared that their legislature should "make no law respecting an establishment of religion, or prohibiting the free exercise thereof," *thus building a wall of separation between church and State.* Adhering to this expression of the supreme will of the nation *in behalf of the rights of conscience,* I shall see with sincere satisfaction the progress of those sentiments which tend to *restore to man all his natural rights,* convinced he has no natural right in opposition to his social duties.[26]

In Jefferson's formulation, which was often quoted by courts and commentators, separation of church and state assured individuals of their natural, inalienable right of conscience, which could be exercised freely and fully to the point of breaching the peace or shirking their social duties. Jefferson was not speaking here of separating politics and religion altogether. Indeed, in the next paragraph of his letter, President Jefferson performed an avowedly religious act of offering prayers on behalf of his Baptist correspondents: "I reciprocate your kind prayers for the protection and blessing of the common Father and Creator of man."[27]

[23] Tunis Wortman, *A Solemn Address to Christians and Patriots* (1800), in Ellis Sandoz, ed., *Political Sermons of the American Founding Era, 1730–1805* (Indianapolis: Liberty Fund, 2000), 1477, 1482, 1487–88.

[24] John Dickinson, "Centinel Number VIII," in Elizabeth I. Nybakken, ed., *The Centinel: Warnings of a Revolution* (Newark: University of Delaware Press, 1980), 128.

[25] Madison, "Memorial and Remonstrance," para. 2.

[26] Thomas Jefferson, *The Writings of Thomas Jefferson*, ed. H. Washington, 9 vols. (Washington, DC: Taylor & Maury, 1853–1854), 8:113 (emphasis added). This Washington edition of the letter inaccurately transcribes "legitimate" as "legislative." See a more accurate transcription in Daniel L. Dreisbach, *Thomas Jefferson and the Wall of Separation Between Church and State* (New York: NYU Press, 2003), 148.

[27] Ibid.

Sixth, some founders also called for the disestablishment of religion. This was the most novel and controversial principle in the day. Seven of the original states – including Massachusetts as we saw in our detailed case study in Chapter 4 – insisted on retaining their own state religious establishment even while calling for no national establishment of religion by the emerging federal government. Though local establishment practices varied, these states still exercised some control over religious doctrine, governance, clergy, and other personnel. They still required church attendance of all citizens, albeit at a church of their choice. They still collected tithes for support of the church that the tithe-payer attended, and often gave state money, tax exemptions, and other privileges preferentially to one favored religion. They still imposed burdensome restrictions on education, voting, and political involvement of religious dissenters. They still obstructed the organization, education, and worship activities of dissenting churches, particularly Catholics and Quakers. They still conscripted established church institutions and their clergy for weddings, education, poor relief, political rallies, and distribution of state literature. They still often administered religious test oaths for political officials, and sometimes even for lower state bureaucrats and employees, too.[28]

But disestablishment movements were gaining rapid support throughout the young American republic, with Massachusetts the final holdout until 1833. Disestablishment of religion, the founders argued, was the best way to integrate and protect all the other principles of religious liberty. Disestablishment protected the principles of liberty of conscience and free exercise by foreclosing government from coercively mandating or symbolically favoring certain forms of religious belief, doctrine, and practice and skewing each person's choices and changes of faith and religious affiliation. As the Delaware Constitution stated: "[N]o authority can or ought to be vested in, or assumed by any power whatever, that shall in any case interfere with, or in any manner controul, the right of conscience in the free exercise of religious worship."[29] Disestablishment further protected the principles of religious equality and pluralism by preventing government from singling out certain religious beliefs and bodies for preferential treatment, or favoring or privileging certain clerics, sanctuaries, or forms of worship to the inevitable deprecation of all others. Virginia's conventioneers called for government to "prevent the establishment of any one sect in prejudice to the rest, and will forever oppose all attempts to infringe religious liberty."[30] Several early state constitutions provided "there shall be no establishment of any one religious sect … in preference

[28] Michael W. McConnell, "Establishment at the Founding," in T. Jeremy Gunn and John Witte, Jr., eds., *No Establishment of Religion: America's Original Contribution to Religious Liberty* (Oxford: Oxford University Press, 2014), 45–69.

[29] Delaware Declaration of Rights (1776), sec. 2; see also Pennsylvania Declaration of Rights (1776), art. II. See https://avalon.law.yale.edu/subject_menus/18th.asp for the original state constitutions quoted here and later. See also the collection in Francis Thorpe, ed., *The Federal and State Constitutions: Colonial Charters, and Other Organic Laws of the State, Territories, and Colonies Now or Hertofore Forming the United States of America*, 7 vols. (Washington, DC: Government Printing Office, 1909).

[30] For Edmund Randolph, see Jonathan Elliot, ed., *The Debates in the Several State Conventions on the Adoption of the Federal Constitution* (Washington, DC: Government Printing Office, 1836), 3:208; see also ibid., 3:431. See also ibid., 3:330; 3:645–46.

to another."[31] And disestablishment of religion served to protect the principle of separation of church and state. As Jefferson wrote, it prohibited government "from intermeddling with religious institutions, their doctrines, discipline, or exercises" and from "the power of effecting any uniformity of time or matter among them. Fasting & prayer are religious exercises. The enjoining them is an act of discipline. Every religious society has a right to determine for itself the times for these exercises, & the objects proper for them, according to their own peculiar tenets."[32] To allow government to establish or even meddle in the internal affairs of religious bodies would inflate the competence of government, Madison added. It "implies either that the Civil Magistrate is a competent judge of religious truth; or that he may employ religion as an engine of civil policy. The first is an arrogant pretension falsified by the contradictory opinions of rulers in all ages, and throughout the world, the second an unhallowed perversion of the means of salvation."[33]

The question that remained controversial in the founding era as much as in our own was whether more gentle and generic forms of governmental support for religion could be countenanced. Did disestablishment of religion prohibit all such support – mandating "a high and impregnable wall of separation between church and state," as the Supreme Court later put it, quoting Jefferson[34] – or did it simply require that such governmental support be distributed non-preferentially among all religions? Some founders viewed the principle of no establishment as a firm ban on all state financial and other support for religious beliefs, believers, and bodies, including traditional indirect forms of support like religious tax exemptions and religious corporations. Others viewed this principle more narrowly as a prohibition against direct financial support of one preferred religion, but regarded non-preferential forms of state funding and land grants for all religious schools, charities, publishers, missionaries, military chaplains, and the like as not only permissible under a no-establishment policy, but necessary for good governance.[35]

THE FIRST STATE CONSTITUTIONS

Liberty of conscience, free exercise of religion, religious pluralism, religious equality, separation of church and state, and disestablishment of religion: These six religious freedom principles circulated in the young early American republic, and they helped to shape the first state constitutions as well as the First Amendment to the US Constitution.

31 See, e.g., New Jersey Constitution (1776), art. XIX.

32 Thomas Jefferson, "Letter to Rev. Samuel Miller (1808)," in Kurland and Lerner, eds., *The Founders' Constitution*, 5:98–99.

33 Madison, "Memorial and Remonstrance," para. 5.

34 *Everson* v. *Board of Education*, 330 US 1, 17 (1947).

35 See the collection of quotations from the founders in James H. Hutson, *Forgotten Features of the Founding: The Recovery of Religious Themes in the Early American Republic* (Lexington, MD: Lexington Books, 2003), 1–44.

Original State Constitutions. Eleven of the thirteen original states issued new constitutions between 1776 and 1784; Connecticut and Rhode Island retained their truncated colonial charters until 1819 and 1843 respectively.[36] The earliest state constitutions of 1776 and 1777 set the tone for the southern and mid-Atlantic colonies, just as the Massachusetts Constitution of 1780 shaped the constitutionalism of New England states, as we saw in Chapter 4.[37] These original state constitutions incorporated these founding principles of religious freedom in various forms.

Virginia's influential Bill of Rights of 1776 set its religious freedom provisions in a basic natural rights and social contract framework, but also grounded its guarantees of religious rights and liberties on correlative moral duties and social virtues of "Christian forbearance, love, and charity":

> I. That all men are by nature equally free and independent, and have certain inherent rights, of which, when they enter into a state of society, they cannot, by any compact, deprive or divest their posterity; namely, the enjoyment of life and liberty, with the means of acquiring and possessing property, and pursuing and obtaining happiness and safety . . . .
>
> XV. That no free government, or the blessings of liberty, can be preserved to any people but by a firm adherence to justice, moderation, temperance, frugality, and virtue and by frequent recurrence to fundamental principles.
>
> XVI. That religion, or the duty which we owe to our Creator and the manner of discharging it, can be directed by reason and conviction, not by force or violence; and therefore, all men are equally entitled to the free exercise of religion, according to the dictates of conscience; and that it is the mutual duty of all to practice Christian forbearance, love, and charity towards each other.[38]

Pennsylvania opened its 1776 Constitution with the same social contract and natural rights language, but focused more singly on freedom of conscience and free exercise of all theistic religions:

> II. That all men have a natural and unalienable right to worship Almighty God according to the dictates of their own consciences and understanding: And that no man ought or of right can be compelled to attend any religious worship, or erect or support any place of worship, or maintain any ministry, contrary to, or against, his own free will and consent: Nor can any man, who acknowledges the being of a God, be justly deprived or abridged of any civil right as a citizen, on account of his religious sentiments or peculiar mode of religious worship: And that no authority can or ought to be vested in, or assumed by any power whatever, that shall in any

[36] See https://avalon.law.yale.edu/subject_menus/18th.asp with excerpts and analysis in Chester J. Antieau, et al., *Religion Under the State Constitutions* (Brooklyn, NY: Central Book Company, 1965); Vincent Philip Muñoz, "Church and State in the Founding-Era Constitutions," *American Political Thought* 4 (2015), 1–38.

[37] G. Alan Tarr, *Understanding State Constitutions* (Princeton: Princeton University Press, 1998), 29–93.

[38] https://avalon.law.yale.edu/subject_menus/18th.asp.

case interfere with, or in any manner control, the right of conscience in the free exercise of religious worship.[39]

The 1776 Constitution of New Jersey provided comparable protections for freedom of conscience and free exercise of religion and against religious coercion and discrimination, and then spoke against traditional Protestant religious establishments:

XIX. That there shall be no establishment of any one religious sect in this Province, in preference to another; and that no Protestant inhabitant of this Colony shall be denied the enjoyment of any civil right, merely on account of his religious principles; but that all persons, professing a belief in the faith of any Protestant sect, who shall demean themselves peaceably under the government, as hereby established, shall be capable of being elected into any office of profit or trust, or being a member of either branch of the Legislature, and shall fully and freely enjoy every privilege and immunity, enjoyed by others their fellow subjects.[40]

The Maryland Constitution of 1776 was expansive in its protection of religious conscience, free exercise of religion, and equality of peaceable Christian believers, including explicit protections for Quakers, Baptists ("Dunkers"), and Mennonites who were conscientiously opposed to oath-swearing and military service. Maryland also banned religious test oaths for political office. Nonetheless, the new constitution allowed for state collection of religious taxes to be directed to the taxpayer's preferred congregation. It vested the historically established Anglican church in its expansive property holdings – quite unlike neighboring Virginia that was calling for the dissolution of such Anglican church property. At the same time, the Maryland Constitution put severe limits on new private donations of property to all other religious groups:

XXXIII. That, as it is the duty of every man to worship God in such manner as he thinks most acceptable to him; all persons, professing the Christian religion, are equally entitled to protection in their religious liberty; wherefore no person ought by any law to be molested in his person or estate on account of his religious persuasion or profession, or for his religious practice; unless, under colour of religion, any man shall disturb the good order, peace or safety of the State, or shall infringe the laws of morality, or injure others, in their natural, civil, or religious rights; nor ought any person to be compelled to frequent or maintain, or contribute, unless on contract, to maintain any particular place of worship, or any particular ministry; yet the Legislature may, in their discretion, lay a general and equal tax for the support of the Christian religion; leaving to each individual the power of appointing the payment over of the money, collected from him, to the support of any particular place of worship or minister, or for the benefit of the poor of his own denomination, or the poor in general of any particular county: but the churches, chapels, glebes, and all other property now belonging to the church of England,

39 Ibid.
40 Ibid.

> ought to remain to the church of England forever. And all acts of Assembly, lately passed, for collecting monies for building or repairing particular churches or chapels of ease, shall continue in force, and be executed, unless the Legislature shall, by act, supersede or repeal the same ....
>
> XXXIV. That every gift, sale, or devise of lands, to any minister, public teacher, or preacher of the gospel, as such, or to any religious sect, order or denomination, or to or for the support, use or benefit of, or in trust for, any minister, public teacher, or preacher of the gospel, as such, or any religious sect, order or denomination—and every gift or sale of goods, or chattels, to go in succession, or to take place after the death of the seller or donor, or to or for such support, use or benefit—and also every devise of goods or chattels to or for the support, use or benefit of any minister, public teacher, or preacher of the gospel, as such, or any religious sect, order, or denomination, without the leave of the Legislature, shall be void; except always any sale, gift, lease or devise of any quantity of land, not exceeding two acres, for a church, meeting, or other house of worship, and for a burying-ground, which shall be improved, enjoyed or used only for such purpose-or such sale, gift, lease, or devise, shall be void.
>
> XXXV. That no other test or qualification ought to be required, on admission to any office of trust or profit, than such oath of support and fidelity to this State, and such oath of office, as shall be directed by this Convention or the Legislature of this State, and a declaration of a belief in the Christian religion.
>
> XXXVI. That the manner of administering an oath to any person, ought to be such, as those of the religious persuasion, profession, or denomination, of which such person is one, generally esteem the most effectual confirmation, by the attestation of the Divine Being. And that the people called Quakers, those called Dunkers, and those called Menonists, holding it unlawful to take an oath on any occasion, ought to be allowed to make their solemn affirmation, in the manner that Quakers have been heretofore allowed to affirm; and to be of the same avail as an oath, in all such cases, as the affirmation of Quakers hath been allowed and accepted within this State, instead of an oath. And further, on such affirmation, warrants to search for stolen goods, or for the apprehension or commitment of offenders, ought to be granted, or security for the peace awarded, and Quakers, Dunkers or Menonists ought also, on their solemn affirmation as aforesaid, to be admitted as witnesses, in all criminal cases not capital.

The New York State Constitution of 1777 set out its religious freedom provisions in loftier language that was deeply critical of traditional religious persecution brought on by the conflation of religious and political authorities, and accordingly called for the separation of church and state officials:

> XXXVIII. And whereas we are required, by the benevolent principles of rational liberty, not only to expel civil tyranny, but also to guard against that spiritual oppression and intolerance wherewith the bigotry and ambition of weak and wicked priests and princes have scourged mankind, this convention doth ... declare, that the free exercise and enjoyment of religious profession and worship, without discrimination or preference, shall forever hereafter be allowed, within this State,

to all mankind: *Provided*, That the liberty of conscience, hereby granted, shall not be so construed as to excuse acts of licentiousness, or justify practices inconsistent with the peace or safety of this State.

XXXIX. And whereas the ministers of the gospel are, by their profession, dedicated to the service of God and the care of souls, and ought not to be diverted from the great duties of their function; therefore, no minister of the gospel, or priest of any denomination whatsoever, shall, at any time hereafter, under any presence or description whatever, be eligible to, or capable of holding, any civil or military office or place within this State.

XL. And whereas it is of the utmost importance to the safety of every State that it should always be in a condition of defence; and it is the duty of every man who enjoys the protection of society to be prepared and willing to defend it . . . . [But] all such of the inhabitants of this State being of the people called Quakers as, from scruples of conscience, may be averse to the bearing of arms, be therefrom excused by the legislature; and do pay to the State such sums of money, in lieu of their personal service, as the same; may, in the judgment of the legislature, be worth.[41]

These early state constitutions formed the backbone of religious freedom in the United States for the first 150 years of the republic. State constitution-making and enforcement remained a complex and shifting legal business throughout this period. Only Massachusetts and New Hampshire retained their original constitutions of 1780 and 1784 respectively, albeit with many amendments. Each of the other original states created at least one new constitution after 1787 – Georgia leading the way with eight new constitutions, the last ratified in 1945. Thirty-seven new states joined the union, each adding its own new constitution, half of them adopting at least one replacement constitution before 1947 – Louisiana leading the way with ten, the last ratified in 1921.[42] Religious freedom figured prominently in almost all of these state constitutions, with all six founding principles of religious freedom coming to varying forms of expression.[43] The state constitutions empowered state courts to hear constitutional cases from its own citizens or subjects, notably including religious freedom claims. These state cases, together with state legislative acts, helped translate the founding principles of religious freedom into a rich latticework of specific precepts, practices, and policies concerning religion.

THE FIRST AMENDMENT TO THE US CONSTITUTION

The US Constitution, drafted in the summer of 1787 and ratified by the original states in 1789, is largely silent on questions of religion and religious freedom. The

41 Ibid.

42 See Cynthia E. Browne, *State Constitutional Conventions* (Westport, CT: Greenwood Press, 1973), xxviii–xxix, for convenient tables and Thorpe, *The Federal and State Constitutions* for the multiple version of each state constitution.

43 See examples of each principle in state constitutions from 1791–1947 in Witte and Nichols, *Religion and the American Constitutional Experiment*, 98–108, 299–302.

preamble to the Constitution speaks generically of the "Blessings of Liberty." Article I recognizes the Christian Sabbath: "If any Bill should not be returned by the President within ten days (Sundays excepted) after it shall have been presented to him, the Same shall be a Law." Article VI provides "no religious Test shall ever be required as a Qualification to any Office or public Trust under the United States." A reference to "the Year of our Lord" sneaks into the dating of the instrument. But nothing more. The "Godless Constitution" has been both celebrated and lamented ever since.[44]

The federal constitutional drafters commonly assumed that questions of religious freedom and other rights and liberties were for the states and their people to resolve in accordance with their own state constitutions – and not for the budding federal government. As Madison put it: "There is not a shadow of right in the general government to intermeddle with religion. Its least interference with it, would be a most flagrant usurpation."[45] James Wilson (1742–98) thought the idea of a national bill of rights was "impracticable – for who will be bold enough to undertake to enumerate all the rights of the people? – and when the attempt to enumerate them is made, it must be remembered that if the enumeration is not complete, everything not expressly mentioned will be presumed to be purposely omitted."[46] Alexander Hamilton (d. 1804) thought any such attempt would also be "dangerous." For this national bill of rights "would contain various exceptions to powers not granted; and, on this very account, would afford a colorable pretext to claim more than was granted. For why declare that things shall not be done which there is no power to do?"[47]

The states, however, demanded explicit federal protections for religious freedom and other basic rights and liberties of the people, and they conditioned their ratification of the constitution on the creation and ratification of a separate bill of rights. The First Congress created the Bill of Rights in the summer of 1789, and the states ratified it in 1791. The Bill of Rights opened with the four freedoms guaranteed in the First Amendment: "Congress shall make no law respecting an establishment of religion, or prohibiting the free exercise thereof; or abridging the freedom of speech, or of the press; or the right of the people peaceably to assemble, and to petition the Government for a redress of grievances." The next eight amendments guaranteed the right to bear arms, freedom from forced quartering of soldiers, freedom from property takings without just compensation, sundry important criminal and civil procedural protections, and a general guarantee in the Fifth

44 See Isaac Kramnick and R. Laurence Moore, *The Godless Constitution: The Case Against Religious Correctness* (New York: Norton, 1996). See rejoinder in Hutson, *Forgotten Features*, 111–32; Martin E. Marty, "Getting Beyond the Myth of Christian America," in Gunn and Witte, *No Establishment of Religion*, 364–78.

45 Elliot, *Debates*, 3:313.

46 Max Farrand, ed., *Records of the Federal Convention* (New Haven, CT: Yale University Press, 1911), 3:143–44.

47 Catherine Drinker Bowen, *Miracle at Philadelphia: The Story of the Constitutional Convention, May to September, 1787* (Boston: Little, Brown, and Co., 1966), 243–53.

Amendment that no person shall be "deprived of life, liberty, or property without due process of law." Heeding Wilson's warning about the dangers of trying to list all fundamental rights, the Ninth Amendment provided: "The enumeration in the Constitution, of certain rights, shall not be construed to deny or disparage others retained by the people." Yielding to the strong political pressure to guarantee a federalist system of government, the Tenth Amendment guaranteed that all the powers not explicitly enumerated for the federal government were "reserved" for the individual states.

Here, in brief, was what Benjamin Franklin (1706–90) once called a "triple layer cake of sovereignty . . . delicately balanced."[48] The foundational layer of this constitutional cake was the sovereignty of the people with a guarantee of the rights and liberties protected by both the state and federal constitutions. The middle layer consisted of the sovereignty of the individual states to exercise all powers not exclusively enumerated for the federal government in accordance with their own state constitutions, including the power to protect the sovereignty and rights of their own state citizens. The top layer was the sovereignty of the new federal government, with its specifically enumerated powers set out in the United States Constitution, but specifically limited by the few rights provisions of Articles I and IV of the Constitution and the more elaborate rights and liberties in the Bill of Rights.

The First Amendment uniquely targeted "Congress." This differed from all the other provisions in the Bill of Rights that were generically phrased or in the passive voice: "the right of the people to bear and keep arms shall not be infringed"; "excessive bail shall not be required" and the like. This specific choice of language – "*Congress* shall make no law" – meant that the First Amendment guarantees of no establishment of religion and no prohibition on its free exercise were binding only on the federal government, and not on state or local governments. It further meant that the federal courts could not hear cases where citizens sought religious freedom protection against state or local encroachments on them. "The Constitution makes no provision for protecting the citizens of the respective states in their religious liberties," the Supreme Court declared early on; "this is left to the state constitutions and laws."[49] In the nineteenth century, Congress tried repeatedly but failed to pass constitutional amendments and national laws on religious liberty that would apply to the states and would be enforceable in the federal courts. The most notable attempt was the Blaine Amendment to the US Constitution that was only narrowly defeated in 1876.[50] But until 1940, the First Amendment applied only to Congress,

48 Nathan G. Goodman, ed., *A Benjamin Franklin Reader* (New York: Thomas Y. Cromwell, 1945), 421–22.

49 *Permoli* v. *Municipality No. 1 of New Orleans*, 44 US (3 How.) 589, 609 (1845). See also *Barron* v. *Baltimore*, 32 US (7 Pet.) 243 (1833) (holding that the Bill of Rights in general, and the Fifth Amendment in particular, applied only to the national government).

50 The proposed Blaine Amendment reads: "No state shall make any law respecting an establishment of religion, or prohibiting the free exercise thereof; no money raised by taxation in any state for the support of public schools, or derived from any public fund therefor nor any public lands devoted

and it was a weak restriction at that. Not a single US Supreme Court case before 1940 found a violation of the First Amendment religious freedom guarantees.

Not only was the First Amendment narrowly focused on Congress, but, unlike many of the earlier state constitutions on religious freedom, this federal constitutional text was rather cryptic. Of the six principles of religious freedom incorporated into the new state constitutions of 1776 to 1784, the First Amendment explicitly embraced only two; the free exercise of religion and no establishment of religion. The First Congress that crafted the First Amendment did have much more expansive religious freedom language available in the twenty-five drafts of the First Amendment proposed and debated in 1788 and 1789.[51] Ten of these drafts were proposed by the ratifying states in 1788 and 1789. North Carolina, for example, packed a whole series of principles in its proposed amendment:

> That any person *religiously scrupulous* of bearing arms ought to be exempted, upon payment of an equivalent to employ another to bear arms in his stead. That *religion*, or the duty which we owe to our Creator, and the manner of discharging it, can be directed only *by reason and conviction, not by force or violence*; and therefore all men have an *equal, natural, and unalienable right to the free exercise of religion according to the dictates of conscience*, and that no particular religious sect or society ought to be favored or *established by law in preference* to others."[52]

Ten more draft provisions on religious freedom came in for discussion during the First House debates in the summer of 1789. The House finally distilled these wide-ranging proposals into a proposed draft of August 25, 1789, embracing three principles:

> Congress shall make no law *establishing* religion, or prohibiting the *free exercise* thereof, nor shall the *rights of conscience* be infringed.[53]

Five more drafts circulated in the First Senate thereafter; the final proposed draft sent back to the House on September 9, 1789, now had only two principles:

> Congress shall make no law *establishing* articles of faith or a mode of worship or prohibiting the *free exercise* of religion.[54]

thereto, shall ever be under control of any religious sect or denomination; nor shall any money so raised or lands so devoted be divided between religious sects or denominations." The Amendment proposed by Rep. Blaine in 1875 passed the House but was narrowly defeated in the Senate. 4 Congressional Record 5190 (1876). A furious lobbying effort in the 1880s and 1890s sought to resurrect this amendment, but in vain. See Alfred W. Meyer, "The Blaine Amendment and the Bill of Rights," *Harvard Law Review* 64 (1951), 939; F. William O'Brien, "The States and 'No Establishment': Proposed Amendments to the Constitution Since 1789," *Washburn Law Journal* 4 (1965), 183–210 (listing 21 failed attempts to introduce such amendments to the US Constitution).

51 All these drafts are reprinted in Witte and Nichols, *Religion and the American Constitutional Experiment*, Appendix 1, 295–98.

52 North Carolina Proposal, Aug. 1, 1788; Repeated by Rhode Island, June 16, 1790, in ibid.

53 Final Draft Proposed by the Style Committee, Passed by the House, and Sent to the Senate, Aug. 25, 1789, in ibid.

54 Draft Proposed and Passed by the Senate, and Sent to the House, Sept. 9, 1789, in ibid.

A joint House and Senate style committee stuck with these two principles, but it made the no-establishment guarantee more generic and ambiguous in the final formulation of the First Amendment: "Congress shall make no law *respecting an establishment of religion*, or prohibiting the free exercise thereof." The states ratified the Bill of Rights on December 15, 1791, and the sixteen final words of the First Amendment have been the law of the land to this day governing religious freedom.

The First Amendment on its face sets clear outer limits to Congress's actions toward religion. Congress may not establish or prescribe religion; nor may Congress prohibit or proscribe religion. While that sounds minimalist to modern ears, this was already a marked departure from the common practice of most European national governments in 1789. England, for example, still made communicant status in the Anglican Church a condition for national citizenship and for many positions and privileges in state and society. Protestants were only tolerated by the state, and with ample limits on their freedom. Catholics and Jews remained formally banned from the land until the Emancipation Acts of 1829 and 1833. Similarly, just as the First Amendment was being crafted and ratified, French authorities were ransacking the Catholic Church and its vast properties, literature, and artwork, and murdering hundreds of its clergy, monks, and congregants with reckless abandon, having done the same to French Calvinists a century earlier. The First Amendment clearly commanded the new American Congress to do nothing of the sort.

Less clear was whether the First Amendment prohibited federal laws and governmental actions short of outright prescribing or proscribing religion. Earlier drafts of the First Amendment no-establishment guarantee had included much more sweeping and exact language: Congress was not to "touch" or "favor" religion; not to give "preference" to any religion or any religious "sect," "society," or "denomination"; not to "establish articles of faith or mode of worship."[55] Such provisions were left aside for the more ambiguous provision that Congress could not make laws "respecting an establishment of religion." Adding the word "respecting" to this guarantee could mean that Congress could make no laws "concerning" or "regarding" the various state establishments of religion that still prevailed. Or it could mean that Congress could make no laws that "reflected" or showed "respect for" old establishments of religion like the established Anglican Church in England, or various Lutheran, Reformed, Orthodox, and Catholic establishments on the Continent. Or it could mean that Congress could make no law that "pointed to" or "moved toward" a new establishment of religion even in piecemeal fashion, lest they become the "nose of the camel under the tent."[56] All these understandings fit within eighteenth-century dictionary definitions of "respecting."[57]

55 Draft nos. 6, 8–10, 16, 21–23, 25, in ibid.

56 *Walz* v. *Tax Comm'n*, 397 US 664, 678 (1970).

57 See Samuel Johnson, *A Dictionary of the English Language*, 4th ed. (1773); William Perry, *The Royal Standard English Dictionary*, 1st Am. ed. (1788) and early modern sources quoted in *Oxford English Dictionary* (1971), s.v. "respect."

What also remained an open question was whether the no-establishment provision allowed Congress to favor or support religion "generally" or "non-preferentially" as several earlier drafts had put it. No founder publicly supported the idea of Congress "establishing" a single national religion that "fixed," "defined," and "settled" by law the doctrine, liturgy, worship, religious canon, and other traditional features of established Christianity. For them, the most notorious example to be avoided at all costs was the established Church of England. The new American nation wanted no royal or presidential Supreme Head of a national Church; no bench of bishops sitting in Congress; no prescribed *Book of Common Prayer* that set the nation's liturgy, lectionary, and religious calendars; no mandated King James Version of the Bible; no church courts with jurisdiction over family, charity, education, inheritance, defamation, and the like. Those prevailing English establishment patterns were all well beyond the pale for the young American republic.

The issue was whether the new First Amendment outlawed or permitted more "mild and equitable" forms of support for religion. It is instructive that the same First Congress that drafted the First Amendment did pass laws that funded and supported various forms and forums of religious education, missionaries on the frontier, legislative and military chaplains, presidential Thanksgiving Day proclamations and other government-led religious ceremonies, and comparable measures – all of which later Congresses continued to support and fund.[58] And the First Congress also included overt religious language and strong religious freedom guarantees in its first treaties, land grants, and territorial ordinances, like the Northwest Ordinance, which read: "No person, demeaning himself in a peaceable and orderly manner, shall ever be molested on account of his mode of worship, or religious sentiments"; and "Religion, morality and knowledge, being necessary to good government and the happiness of mankind, schools and the means of education shall forever be encouraged."[59] The lesson taken by some later courts and commentators was that non-preferential support for religion was not necessarily an establishment of religion contrary to the First Amendment.

Likewise, the various drafts of the free exercise of religion guarantee had included much more sweeping language: Congress was not to "infringe," "abridge," "violate," "compel," or "prevent" the exercise of religion or the rights and freedom of

58 See, e.g., Nathan S. Chapman, "Forgotten Federal-Missionary Partnerships: New Light on the Establishment Clause," *Notre Dame Law Review* 96 (2020), 677–748; Mark Storslee, "Church Taxes and the Original Understanding of the Establishment Clause," *University of Pennsylvania Law Review* 169 (2020), 111–92.

59 *Journals of the Continental Congress* (Washington, DC: Government Printing Office, 1904–37), 32:340. On various earlier drafts of the Northwest Ordinance, with more expansive language on religious liberty, see Edwin S. Gaustad, *Faith of the Founders: Religion and the New Nation, 1776–1826*, 2nd ed. (Waco, TX: Baylor University Press, 2004), 115–17, 151–56. See further Matthew J. Hegreness, "An Organic Law Theory of the Fourteenth Amendment: The Northwest Ordinance as the Source of Rights, Privileges, and Immunities," *Yale Law Journal* 120 (2011), 1820–84.

conscience, or indeed even "touch" religion in a way that might obstruct, impede, or hinder its free exercise.[60] Again, such provisions were left aside for the blunter provision: Congress could simply not "prohibit" the free exercise of religion. This left little textual guidance on what short of outright prohibition on the freedom to exercise religion was allowed or outlawed. Importantly, too, the First Amendment dropped the guarantee of freedom of conscience in general as well as in the specific protections of conscientious objection to military service which earlier drafts of the First Amendment and every state constitution protected. (Article V of the Constitution did ban federal religious test oaths, in part because they violated freedom of conscience.) It was left an open question what government laws and actions that fell short of outright prohibition of religious exercise are outlawed by the First Amendment, and whether the guarantee of the free exercise of religion allows or requires accommodations and exemptions from general laws that offend conscience. All these remained contested issues in the eighteenth century, and they remain so still today.

The historical sources do allow for a more nuanced reading of the final sixteen words of the First Amendment religious freedom guarantee; elsewhere I have done a molecule-by-molecule parsing of these words to extract richer lessons of the original understanding of this text.[61] But even without such linguistic hairsplitting, it's worth remembering that the founders saw the principle of no establishment of religion as integral to the protection of the principles of religious equality, liberty of conscience, and separation of church and state. And they saw the protection of free exercise of religion – or the "freedom to exercise religion"[62] – as essentially tied to the principles of liberty of conscience, religious equality, religious pluralism, and separation of church and state. But rather than spelling this out in detail as some state constitutions had done, the First Amendment, like other provisions in the Bill of Rights, simply set out the most basic limits of no prescription or proscription of religion, leaving it to Congress and the federal courts to develop a fuller religious freedom jurisprudence, drawing as apt on the founders' fuller views of religious freedom and on the expanding state experiments with religious freedom.

ENDURING LESSONS FROM THE CONSTITUTION-MAKING PROCESS

In his three-volume masterwork, *A Defence of the Constitutions of Government of the United States of America,* John Adams offered a robust appraisal of this new

[60] Draft nos. 2, 6, 11–13, 15–18, 20–23 in Witte and Nichols, *Religion and the American Constitutional Experiment*, 295–98.

[61] Ibid., 81–94.

[62] This was the language of the proposal from New York, tendered on July 26, 1788: "That the people have an equal, natural, and unalienable right freely and peaceably to exercise their religion, according to the dictates of conscience." Draft no. 9, in ibid., 296.

American constitutional experiment in rights and liberties, showing both its broad continuity with the long history of Western constitutionalism and its bold innovations, especially in the area of religious freedom:

> The people in America have now the best opportunity and the greatest trust in their hands, that Providence ever committed to so small a number, since the transgression of the first pair [Adam and Eve]; if they betray their trust, their guilt will merit even greater punishment than other nations have suffered, and the indignation of Heaven. . . .
>
> The United States of America have exhibited, perhaps, the first example of governments erected on the simple principles of nature; and if men are now sufficiently enlightened to disabuse themselves of artifice, imposture, hypocrisy, and superstition, they will consider this event as [a new] era in their history. Although the detail of the formation of the American governments is at present little known or regarded either in Europe or in America, it [is] destined to spread over the northern part of . . . the globe. . . . The institutions now made in America will not wholly wear out for thousands of years. It is of the last importance, then, that they should begin right. If they set out wrong, they will never be able to return, unless it be by accident, to the right path. . . . . [T]he eyes of the world are upon [us].[63]

For all of their failures and shortcomings, the eighteenth-century Americans founders did indeed begin on the "right path" toward a free society. Today, Americans enjoy a good deal of religious, civil, and political freedom as a consequence. American principles of religious freedom, in particular, have had a profound influence around the globe, and they now figure prominently in a number of national constitutions and international human rights instruments issued by political and religious bodies.[64]

One key to the enduring success of this American experiment in religious freedom lies in the eighteenth-century founders' most elementary insight – that religion is special and needs special constitutional protection. "[W]e cannot repudiate that decision without rejecting an essential feature of constitutionalism, rendering all constitutional rights vulnerable to repudiation if they go out of favor," writes leading religious liberty advocate Douglas Laycock.[65] Although America's religious landscape has changed, religion remains today a unique source of individual and personal identity for many, involving "the duty which we owe to our Creator, and the manner of discharging it," in Madison's words.[66] The founders' vision was that

63 Charles F. Adams, ed., *The Works of John Adams, Second President of the United States*, 9 vols. (Boston, MA: Little and Brown, 1850–1857), 4:290–98; 8:487.

64 See John T. Noonan, Jr., *The Lustre of Our Country: The American Experience of Religious Freedom* (Berkeley, CA: University of California Press, 2000); W. Cole Durham, Jr. and Brent W. Scharffs, *Law and Religion: National, International, and Comparative Perspectives*, 2nd ed. (New York: Wolters Kluwer, 2019).

65 Douglas Laycock, "Religious Liberty as Liberty," *Journal of Contemporary Legal Issues* 7 (1996), 313, 314.

66 James Madison, "Article on Religion Adopted by Convention (June 12, 1776)," in *The Papers of James Madison*, 1:175.

religion is more than simply another form of speech and assembly, privacy and autonomy; it deserves separate constitutional treatment. The founders thus placed freedom of religion *alongside* freedoms of speech, press, and assembly, giving religious claimants special protection and restricting government in its interaction with religion. Religion is also a unique form of public and social identity, involving a vast plurality of sanctuaries, schools, charities, missions, and other forms and forums of faith. All peaceable exercises of religion, whether individual or corporate, private or public, properly deserve the protection of the First Amendment. And such protection sometimes requires special exemptions and accommodations that cannot be afforded by general statutes. "The tyranny of the legislative majority," Madison reminds us, is particularly dangerous to religious minorities.[67]

A second key to the success of this experiment lies in the eighteenth-century founders' insight that, in order to be enduring and effective, the constitutional process must seek to involve all voices and values in the community – religious, nonreligious, and anti-religious alike. Healthy constitutionalism ultimately demands "confident pluralism," in John Inazu's apt phrase.[68] Thus in creating the new American constitutions, the founders drew upon all manner of representatives and voters to create and ratify these new organic laws. Believers and skeptics, churchmen and statesmen, Protestants and Catholics, Quakers and Jews, Civic Republicans and Enlightenment Liberals – many of whom had slandered, if not slaughtered each other with a vengeance in years past – now came together in a rare moment of constitutional solidarity. The founders understood that a proper law of religious liberty required that all peaceable religions and believers participate in both its creation and its unfolding. To be sure, both in the founders' day and in subsequent generations, some Americans showed little concern in action for the religious or civil rights of Jews, Catholics, Mormons, Native Americans, Asian Americans, or African Americans, and too often inflicted horrible abuses upon them. And today, some of these old prejudices are returning anew in bitter clashes over race, immigration, and refugees, and in fresh outbreaks of nativism, anti-Semitism, Islamophobia, and anti-clericalism. But a generous willingness to embrace all peaceable religions in the great project of religious freedom is one of the most original and compelling insights of the American experiment. John Adams put it generously: religious freedom "resides in Hindoos and Mahometans, as well as in Christians; in Cappadocian monarchists, as well as in Athenian democrats; in Shaking Quakers, as well as in . . . Presbyterian clergy; in Tartars and Arabs, Negroes and Indians" – indeed in all "the people of the United States."[69]

67 James Madison, "Letter from James Madison to Thomas Jefferson (Oct. 17, 1788)," in *The Writings of James Madison*, 5:272.

68 John D. Inazu, *Confident Pluralism: Surviving and Thriving Through Deep Difference* (Chicago, IL: University of Chicago Press, 2016).

69 John Adams, "Letter from John Adams to John Taylor (Apr. 15, 1814)," in Adams, *Works*, 6:474; see also John Adams, "Letter from John Adams to Thomas Jefferson (June 28, 1813)," in *Adams-Jefferson Letters*, 2:339–40.

A third key to enduring success lies in balancing the multiple principles of religious liberty that the founders set forth in the frugal, sixteen-word phrase of the First Amendment: "Congress shall make no law respecting an establishment of religion, or prohibiting the free exercise thereof." While limited in their initial reach, these twin guarantees helped to chart the pathway of a robust American religious freedom jurisprudence that is still being developed today. On one side, the no-establishment guarantee outlaws government *prescriptions* of religion – actions that unduly coerce the conscience, mandate forms of religious expression and activity, discriminate in favor of one religion, or improperly ally the state with churches or other religious bodies. On the other side, the free exercise guarantee outlaws government *proscriptions* of religion – actions that unduly burden the conscience, restrict religious expression and activity, discriminate against religion, or invade the autonomy of churches and other religious bodies. These twin First Amendment guarantees of no establishment of any religion and free exercise of all religions thereby provided complementary protections to the other constitutive principles of the American experiment – liberty of conscience, religious equality, religious pluralism, and separation of church and state.[70]

These three founding insights were not only part of the original vision of the eighteenth-century founders; they were also part of the original vision of the Supreme Court as it created the modern constitutional law of religious freedom in the 1940s and thereafter. All three insights recur in *Cantwell* v. *Connecticut* (1940)[71] and in *Everson* v. *Board of Education* (1947),[72] the two landmark US Supreme Court cases that first applied the First Amendment religion clauses to state and local governments and inaugurated the modern era of universal religious liberty in America.

Cantwell and *Everson* declared anew that religion had a special place in the Constitution and deserved special protection in the nation. In a remarkable counter-textual reading, the Supreme Court took it upon itself and the lower federal courts to enforce the First Amendment religion clauses against all levels and branches of government in the nation – federal, state, and local alike. The Court did so by "incorporating" the First Amendment religion clauses into the Fourteenth Amendment Due Process Clause that provided that: "No State shall ... deprive any person of life, liberty, or property, without due process of law." Part of the "body" or "corpus" of liberties in this Fourteenth Amendment guarantee, the Court argued, were the religious liberties set out in the First Amendment. Thus while the First Amendment was still binding only on Congress and the federal government, its religious liberty guarantees of no-establishment and free exercise of religion were binding on state and local governments as well, but now through the Fourteenth Amendment. Through this act of "incorporation" (as this method of constitutional

70 Witte and Nichols, *Religion and the American Constitutional Experiment*, 92–94.

71 310 US 296, 303–04, 310 (1940).

72 330 US 1, 16 (1947).

interpretation is called) "*Congress* shall make no law" now became, in effect, "*Government* shall make no law respecting an establishment of religion, or prohibiting the free exercise thereof."

More than 170 religious freedom cases have reached the Supreme Court since 1940 (compared to only 48 cases in the prior 150 years). Fully 80 percent of these post-1940 cases dealt with state and local government issues, and roughly half of the cases have found religious freedom violations (while no case before 1940 had found constitutional violations).[73] And for each of these Supreme Court cases, there have been hundreds of cases in the lower courts. While this universalization of First Amendment religious liberty after 1940 did – and still sometimes does – anger federalist states' rights activists, it was the growing local bigotry at home and abroad that compelled the Court to act decisively. Local bigotry was also the reason that America and the world embraced religious freedom in the 1940s as a universal and nonderogable human right of all persons – one of the famous "four freedoms" that Roosevelt championed to rebuke the horrific abuses inflicted on Jews and other religious and cultural minorities during World War II and the Holocaust. Religious freedom for all was considered too important and universal a right to be left to the political calculus of state governments or to local religious and cultural prejudices and preferences.

Cantwell and *Everson* also declared anew that all religious voices were welcome in the modern constitutional process of protecting religious liberty. These two cases welcomed hitherto marginal voices: *Cantwell* welcomed a devout Jehovah's Witness who sought protections for his very unpopular missionary work. *Everson* welcomed a skeptical citizen who sought protection from paying taxes in support of religious education. Subsequent cases have drawn into the American constitutional dialogue a host of other religious and anti-religious groups – Catholics, Protestants, and Orthodox Christians; Jews, Muslims, and Hindus; Mormons, Quakers, and Hare Krishnas; Wiccans, Santerians, and Summumites; Skeptics, Atheists, and Secularists; Religionists, A-Religionists, and Anti-Religionists alike. While critics have charged the Court with favoring Christian theologies and practices, and with clumsily applying Christian religious terms and categories to measure the faith claims of others, the Court has been quite solicitous of a number of new and minority religions, including Atheists early on and Muslims since 9/11.[74] Glaring blind spots remain, notably in its churlish dealing with Native American Indian claims, but the Court has sought to heed the command to protect the religious freedom of all.

73 A table of all Supreme Court cases on religious freedom from 1815 to 2016 is in Witte and Nichols, *Religion and the American Constitutional Experiment*, 303–37.

74 See, e.g., *Torcaso* v. *Watkins*, 367 US 488 (1961) (upholding an atheist's claim that a mandatory oath proclaiming a belief in God is unconstitutional); *Holt* v. *Hobbs*, 135 S. Ct. 2218 (2015) (upholding a Muslim prisoner's statutory right to maintain a longer beard contrary to state prison regulations).

And *Cantwell* and *Everson* declared anew the efficacy of the founding principles of the American experiment in religious freedom. The Free Exercise Clause, the *Cantwell* Court proclaimed, protects "[f]reedom of conscience and freedom to adhere to such religious organization or form of worship as the individual may choose." It "safeguards the free exercise of the chosen form of religion," the "freedom to act" on one's beliefs. It protects a plurality of forms and expressions of faith, each of which deserves equal protection under the law. "The essential characteristic of these liberties is, that under their shield many types of life, character, opinion and belief can develop unmolested and unobstructed."[75] The Establishment Clause, the *Everson* Court echoed, means that no government "can set up a church"; "can force nor influence a person to go to or to remain away from church against his will or force him to profess a belief or disbelief in any religion"; can "punish [a person] for entertaining or professing religious beliefs or disbeliefs, for church attendance or non-attendance"; "can, openly or secretly, participate in the affairs of any religious organizations or groups and *vice versa*." Government may not "exclude individual Catholics, Lutherans, Mohammedans, Baptists, Jews, Methodists, Non-believers, Presbyterians, or the members of any other faith, *because of their faith, or lack of it*, from receiving the benefits of public welfare legislation" or participating in the American public arena or political process.[76] "The Constitution has erected a wall of separation between church and state," the Court said in summary.[77]

RESPONDING TO MODERN ATTACKS ON RELIGIOUS FREEDOM

The next chapters in this volume will sample a few topics of religion, human rights, and religious freedom that have applied these founding principles both in American courts and in European courts. What deserves notice here is that religious freedom has come under increasing attack in America in recent years – and in Europe, too, as we will see in a later chapter.

In America, some of these attacks the US Supreme Court has brought on itself. From 1980 to 2010, the Court's opinions both weakened the First Amendment religion clauses and introduced all manner of conflicting logics and contradictory tests to deal with religious freedom claims. That left lower courts and legislatures without clear enough direction, and produced sometimes widely variant approaches to many basic religious freedom questions, including how courts should resolve intrachurch disputes over property; or government disputes over religious school support; or local contests over religious symbols and ceremonies in public life, and other issues. In response, leading scholars began to write openly that America's

75 *Cantwell*, 310 US at 303, 310.

76 *Everson*, 330 US at 15–16.

77 Ibid. 17.

experiment in religious freedom is a "foreordained failure," an "impossibility" to achieve, and was sliding into its "twilight."[78]

Religions also brought some of these attacks on themselves. The horrors of 9/11 and scores of later attacks as well as the bloody and costly wars against Islamist terrorism worldwide have renewed traditional warnings that religion is a danger to modern liberty. *The New York Times* ran a sensational six-part exposé describing the "hundreds" of special statutory protections, entitlements, and exemptions that religious individuals and groups quietly enjoy, prizes extracted by a whole phalanx of religious lobbyists in federal and state legislatures.[79] The Catholic Church was rocked by an avalanche of news reports and lawsuits about the pedophilia of delinquent priests and cover-ups by complicit bishops – all committed under the thick veil of religious autonomy and corporate religious freedom. Evangelical megachurches faced withering attacks in Congress and the media for their massive embezzlement of funds, and the lush and luxurious lifestyles of their pastors – all the while enjoying tax exemptions for their incomes, properties, and parsonages. Various Protestant denominations faced their own new public reports of massive sex abuses by their clergy and other church leaders against wives, children, parishioners, clients, and students. And, most recently, some Christian churches and other religious groups have drawn public scorn and political rebuke for holding large worship services, weddings, baptisms, funerals, and the like during the pandemic, becoming COVID-19 super-spreaders in so doing and blatantly ignoring not only the biblical commands to love their neighbors but state laws to limit public gatherings to protect public health. All these developments have fueled a two-decade-long media and academic narrative about the underside and dangers of religion and have eroded popular and political support for religion and religious freedom.

Even bigger challenges of late have come with the culture wars between religious freedom and sexual freedom, which dominated the public airwaves until the COVID-19 crisis began and will likely resume after that crisis is over. The legal questions for religious freedom keep mounting. Must a religious official with conscientious scruples marry a same-sex or interreligious couple? How about a justice of the peace or a military chaplain asked to solemnize their wedding? Or a county clerk asked to give them a marriage license? Must a devout medical doctor or a religiously chartered hospital perform an elective abortion or assisted-

78 Steven D. Smith, *Foreordained Failure: The Quest for a Constitutional Principle of Religious Freedom* (Oxford: Oxford University Press, 1995); Winnifred Sullivan, *The Impossibility of Religious Freedom* (Princeton, NJ: Princeton University Press, 2005); David Sehat, *The Myth of American Religious Freedom* (New York: Oxford University Press, 2011); Symposium, "Rethinking Religious Freedom," *Journal of Law and Religion* 29 (2014), 355–547; Symposium, "Is Religion Outdated (as a Constitutional Category)," *San Diego Law Review* 51 (2014), 971–1133; Steven K. Green, *Inventing a Christian America: The Myth of the Religious Founding* (Oxford: Oxford University Press, 2015).

79 Diana B. Henriques, "In God's Name," *New York Times* (Oct. 8–11, 20, Nov. 23, and Dec. 19, 2006). See further Diana B. Henriques and Andfrew W. Lehren, "Religious Groups Reap Federal Aid for Pet Projects," *New York Times* (May 13, 2007); Diana B. Henriques and Andrew W. Lehren, "Federal Grant for a Medical Mission Goes Awry," *New York Times* (June 13, 2007).

reproduction procedure to a single mother directly contrary to their religious beliefs about marriage and family life? How about if they are receiving government funding? Or if they are the only medical service available to the patient for miles around? Must a conscientiously opposed pharmacist fill a prescription for a contraceptive, abortifacient, or morning-after pill? Or a private employer carry medical insurance for the same prescriptions? What if these are franchises of bigger pharmacies or employers that insist on these services? May a religious organization dismiss or discipline its officials or members because of their sexual orientation or sexual practices, or because they had a divorce, abortion, or IVF treatment? May private religious citizens refuse to photograph or cater a wedding, to rent an apartment, or offer a general service to a same-sex couple whose lifestyle they find religiously or morally wanting – especially when the state's new laws of civil rights and nondiscrimination command otherwise?[80]

These are only a few of the headline issues today, which officials and citizens are now struggling to address under heavy pressure from litigation, lobbying, and social media campaigns on all sides. Recent sharply divided Supreme Court cases on point have only exacerbated these tensions. In *Christian Legal Society* v. *Martinez* (2010) and *Obergefell* v. *Hodges* (2015), same-sex rights trumped religious freedom concerns.[81] In *Burwell* v. *Hobby Lobby* (2014) and *Masterpiece Cakeshop* v. *Colorado Civil Rights Commission* (2018), religious freedom concerns trumped reproductive and sexual freedom claims. The culture wars have only escalated as a consequence.[82] "Each side is intolerant of the other; each side wants a total win," Douglas Laycock wrote after a thorough study of these new culture wars. "This mutual insistence on total wins is very bad for religious liberty."[83] For the first time in American history, the nation's commitment to religious liberty has moved from the status of "being taken for granted" to "being up for grabs."[84] And with easy political talk afoot about repealing unpopular statutes – not just the Affordable Care Act – legislative protections for religious freedom appear vulnerable, particularly at the state level. Add the fact that both the free exercise and establishment clauses have weakened, it is hard to resist the judgment of Mary Ann Glendon that American religious freedom is in danger of becoming "a second-class right."[85]

That's exactly how it should be, say a number of legal scholars who have challenged the idea that religion is special or deserving of special constitutional or

80 See analysis in John Witte, Jr., *Church, State, and Family: Reconciling Traditional Teachings and Modern Liberties* (Cambridge: Cambridge University Press, 2019), 315–35.

81 561 US 661 (2010) and 135 S. Ct. 2584 (2015).

82 134 S. Ct. 2751 (2014) and 138 S. Ct. 1719 (2018).

83 Douglas Laycock, "Religious Liberty and the Culture Wars," *University of Illinois Law Review* (2014), 839, 879.

84 Paul Horwitz, "The *Hobby Lobby* Moment," *Harvard Law Review* 128 (2014), 154, 156.

85 Mary Ann Glendon, "Religious Freedom – A Second-Class Right?" *Emory Law Journal* 61 (2012), 971–90.

legislative protection.[86] Even if this idea existed in the eighteenth-century founding era – and that is now sharply contested by revisionist historians, too – it has become obsolete in our post-establishment, postmodern, and post-religious age, these critics argue. Religion, they say, is too dangerous, divisive, and diverse in its demands to be accorded special constitutional protection. Freedom of conscience claimants unfairly demand the right to be a law unto themselves, to the detriment of general laws and to the endangerment of other people's fundamental rights and legitimate interests. Church or religious autonomy norms are too often just a special cover for abuses of power and forms of prejudice that should not be countenanced in any organization – religious or not. Religious liberty claims are too often proxies for political or social agendas that deserve no more protection than any other agenda. Religion, these critics thus conclude, should be viewed as just another category of liberty or association, with no more preference or privilege than its secular counterparts. Religion should be treated as just another form of expression, subject to the same rules of rational democratic deliberation that govern other ideas and values. To accord religion any special protection or exemption discriminates against the nonreligious. To afford religion a special seat at the table of public deliberation or a special role in the implementation of government programs invites religious self-dealing contrary to the First Amendment Establishment Clause. We cannot afford these traditional constitutional luxuries. "The perils of extreme religious liberty" are now upon us.[87]

Too many of these critical arguments, however, trade in revisionist history that pretends that the American founders cared rather little about religious freedom, that the First Amendment was only an "afterthought" and "foreordained" to fail,[88] or that principles like separation of church and state were really designed to protect Protestant hegemonies against surging Catholicism.[89] The historical reality is that the founding generation spent a great deal of time debating and defending religious freedom for all peaceable faiths, and wove multiple principles of religious freedom into the new state and federal constitutions of 1776 to 1791. Yes, sadly, some later Protestant majorities did abuse Catholics, Jews, Mormons, Native Americans, and many others. But these were violations of constitutional freedom norms, not

[86] For a good, recent sample of arguments pro and con, see Austin Sarat ed., *Legal Responses to Religious Practices in the United States: Accommodation and Its Limits* (Cambridge: Cambridge University Press, 2014); Douglas Laycock, *Religious Liberty: Religious Freedom Restoration Acts, Same-Sex Marriage Legislation, and the Culture Wars* (Grand Rapids, MI: Eerdmans, 2018); David Little, *Essays on Religion and Human Rights: Ground to Stand On* (Cambridge: Cambridge University Press, 2015), 57–82, 170–76.

[87] Marci A. Hamilton, *God vs. the Gavel: The Perils of Extreme Religious Liberty*, 2nd rev. ed. (Cambridge: Cambridge University Press, 2014).

[88] See, e.g., Steven D. Smith, *The Rise and Decline of American Religious Freedom* (Cambridge, MA: Harvard University Press, 2014), 48–75; Smith, *Foreordained Failure*.

[89] See, e.g., Philip Hamburger, *Separation of Church and State* (Cambridge, MA: Harvard University Press, 2004), 191–284. See my review, John Witte, Jr., "That Serpentine Wall of Separation," *Michigan Law Review* 101 (2003), 1869–1905.

manifestations of their prejudicial designs – as some nineteenth-century cases and many more twentieth-century constitutional cases made abundantly clear.

Too many of these critical arguments trade in outmoded philosophical assumptions that serious public and political arguments about the fundamentals of life and the law can take place under the "factitious or fictitious scrim of value neutrality."[90] The reality, the last generation of political philosophy has taught us, is that every serious position on the fundamental values governing public and private life – on warfare, marriage reform, bioethics, environmental protection, and much more – rests on a set of founding metaphors and starting beliefs that have comparable faith-like qualities.[91] Liberalism and secularism are just two belief systems among many, and their public policies and prescriptions are enlightened, improved, and strengthened by full public engagement with other serious forms of faith, belief, and values. Today, easy claims of rational neutrality and objectivity in public and political arguments face very strong epistemological headwinds. Even the leading architects of religion-free public reason a generation or two ago have abandoned these views. John Rawls and Jürgen Habermas, for example, have affirmed in their later writings that religion can play valuable and legitimate roles in the lawmaking processes of liberal democracies.[92] A growing number of serious political thinkers now acknowledge that deeply held beliefs and values, whether they issue from secular or religious sources, are not easily bracketed in public discourse; that efforts to exclude an entire class of moral and metaphysical knowledge are more likely to yield mutual distrust and hostility than social accord; that free speech norms do not allow the prohibition of religion from the public square; and that avowedly secular values are not inherently more objective than their religious counterparts. Secular norms and idioms can serve as useful discursive resources in religiously pluralistic societies. But purging religion altogether from public life and political deliberation, as some aggressive interpreters of secularization and the Establishment Clause demand, is impractical, shortsighted, and unjust.

Too many of these critical arguments against religious liberty trade in caricatures of religion that bear little resemblance to reality. For example, Professor Brian Leiter's leading text on point, *Why Tolerate Religion?*, treats religion as an irrational opiate of the masses. Religion, he writes, by definition consists of categorical beliefs that "are insulated from ordinary standards of evidence and rational justification, the ones we employ in both common sense and in science." Religions place "*categorical* demands on action . . . that must be satisfied no matter what an individual's antecedent desires

90 Lenn E. Goodman, *Religious Pluralism and Values in the Public Sphere* (Oxford: Oxford University Press, 2014), 101.

91 John Perry, *The Pretenses of Loyalty: Locke, Liberal Theory, and American Political Theology* (Oxford: Oxford University Press, 2011); Steven L. Winter, *A Clearing in the Forest: Law, Life, and Mind* (Chicago: University of Chicago Press, 2001).

92 See, e.g., Jürgen Habermas, et al., *An Awareness of What Is Missing: Faith and Reason in a Post-Secular Age*, trans. Ciaran Cronin (Cambridge: Polity Press, 2010), 15; John Rawls, "The Idea of Public Reason Revisited," *University of Chicago Law Review* 64 (1997), 765–807.

and no matter what incentives or disincentives the world offers up." And religion provides mainly "existential consolation" about "the basic existential facts about human life, such as suffering and death." Why should a claim or claimant that is so irrational, unscientific, categorical, abstract, and impervious to empirical evidence or common sense get special constitutional treatment, Professor Leiter asks? Just because religion provides existential consolation? Many other nonreligious things do, too. Just because religion leads some people to do good to others? People do good for all kinds of nonreligious reasons, too, and plenty of religious folks also do very bad things. There's nothing to religion that makes it more special or more deserving of constitutional protection than other types of thought or action, Professor Leiter concludes. If anything, because religion is irrational and categorical, it should be subject to special supervision, not special accommodation.[93]

Few people of faith, and even fewer scholars of religion, would recognize this caricature of religion. For many adherents, religion consists of complex and comprehensive "life-worlds" (as anthropologists call them). Religion involves daily rites and practices, patterns of social life and culture, and institutional structures and activities that collectively involve almost every dimension of an individual's public and private life. Professor Leiter and many other critics of religious freedom posit a flat and anachronistic concept of "religion" as mere irrational belief and self-interested truth claim. And even then, they pay little attention to the immense literature on philosophy of religion and religious epistemology, hermeneutics, theological ethics, and more, which has placed religious ideas and beliefs, metaphors and norms, and canons and commandments into complex and edifying conversations with nonreligious premises and worldviews. It is this diverse and often sophisticated world of religious ideas and institutions, norms and practices, and cultures and communities whose freedom is at stake, not the imagined religious abstractions that haunt the law review world.[94]

Too many of these critical arguments trade in one-sided sociologies that dwell on the negatives rather than the positives of religion. It is undeniable that religion has been, and still is, a formidable force for both political good and political evil, that it has fostered both benevolence and belligerence, and both peace and pathos of untold dimensions. But when religious officials or religious group members do commit crimes – embezzling funds, perpetrating fraud, evading regulations, withholding medical care, betraying trust, raping children, abusing spouses, fomenting violence, harming the life and limb of anyone, including their own members – they are and should be prosecuted just like everyone else. Religious freedom does not and should not provide protections or pretexts for crime. But the grim reality is that these crimes occur in every organization, and are perpetrated by all manner of people,

93 Brian Leiter, *Why Tolerate Religion* (Princeton, NJ: Princeton University Press, 2017), 59–64, 73–85.

94 For further discussion, see Christopher J. Eberle, "Religion and Insularity: Brian Leiter on Accommodating Religion," *San Diego Law Review* 51 (2014), 977; Michael W. McConnell, "Why Protect Religious Freedom?" *Yale Law Journal* 123 (2013), 770–810.

religious and nonreligious alike. That these abuses must be rooted out, however, does not mean that the perpetrator's individual or corporate rights must end as a consequence. Governments do not close down schools, libraries, clubs, charities, or corporations when a few of their members commit these crimes. They prosecute the criminals, following the norms of due process. The same should take place in our churches, synagogues, temples, and mosques that harbor criminal suspects.

Moreover, we would do well to remember the immensely valuable goods that religion offers to a community. America's leading religious historian, Martin E. Marty, has documented the private and public goods of religion over a sixty-year career. Religions, he shows, deal uniquely with the deepest elements of individual and social life. Religions catalyze social, intellectual, and material exchanges among citizens. Religions trigger economic, charitable, and educational impulses in citizens. Religions provide valuable checks and counterpoints to social and individual excess. Religions help diffuse social and political crises and absolutisms by relativizing everyday life and its institutions. Religions provide prophecy, criticism, and exemplars for society. Religions force others to examine their presuppositions. Religions are distinct repositories of tradition, wisdom, and perspective. Religions counsel against apathy. Religions often represent practiced and durable sources and forms of community. Religions provide leadership and hope, especially in times of individual and social crisis. Religions contribute to the theory and practice of the common good. Religions represent the unrepresented, teach stewardship and preservation, provide fresh starts for the desperate, and exalt the dignity and freedom of the individual.[95] No religion lives up to all these claims all the time; some religions never do. But these common qualities and contributions have long been among the reasons to support the special place of religion in the American constitutional and cultural order.[96]

Finally, too many of these critical arguments fail to appreciate how dearly fought religious freedom has been in the history of humankind, how imperiled religious freedom has become in many parts of the world today, and how indispensable religious freedom has proved to be for the protection of other fundamental human rights in modern democracies.[97] Even in postmodern liberal societies, religions help to define the meanings and measures of shame and regret, restraint and respect, and responsibility and restitution that a human rights regime presupposes. Religions help

95 See, e.g., Martin E. Marty and Jonathan Moore, *Politics, Religion, and the Common Good: Advancing a Distinctly American Conversation About Religion's Role in Our Shared Life* (San Francisco: Jossey-Bass, 2000).

96 Thomas C. Berg, "Secular Purpose, Accommodations, and Why Religion Is Special (Enough)," *University of Chicago Law Review Dialogue* 80 (2013), 24–42; Andrew Koppelman, "Religion's Specialized Specialness," *University of Chicago Law Review Dialogue* 80 (2013), 71–83.

97 See Brian J. Grim and Roger Finke, *The Price of Freedom Denied: Religious Persecution and Conflict in the Twenty-First Century* (Cambridge: Cambridge University Press, 2011); Daniel Philpott and Timothy Samuel Shah, "In Defense of Religious Freedom: New Critics of a Beleaguered Human Right," *Journal of Law and Religion* 31 (2016), 380–95; Daniel Philpott and Timothy Samuel Shah, *Under Caesar's Sword: How Christians Respond to Persecution* (Cambridge: Cambridge University Press, 2018).

to lay out the fundamentals of human dignity and human community, and the essentials of human nature and human needs upon which human rights norms and instruments are built. Moreover, religions stand alongside the state and other institutions in helping to implement and protect the rights of a person and community – especially at times when the state becomes weak, distracted, divided, cash-strapped, corrupt, or is in transition. Religious communities can create the conditions (sometimes the prototypes) for the realization of civil and political rights of speech, press, assembly, and more. They can provide a critical (sometimes the principal) means of education, healthcare, childcare, labor organizations, employment, and artistic opportunities, among other things. And they can offer some of the deepest insights into the duties of stewardship and service that lie at the heart of environmental rights and protection.[98]

Because of the vital role of religion in the cultivation and implementation of other human rights, many social scientists and human rights scholars have come to see that providing strong protections for religious beliefs, practices, and institutions enhances, rather than diminishes, human rights for all. Many scholars now repeat the American founders' insight that religious freedom is "the first freedom" from which other rights and freedoms evolve. For the religious individual, the right to believe often correlates with freedoms to assemble, speak, worship, evangelize, educate, parent, travel, or to abstain from the same on the basis of one's beliefs. For the religious association, the right to practice religion collectively implicates rights to corporate property, collective worship, organized charity, religious education, freedom of press, and autonomy of governance.[99]

Several detailed studies have shown that the protection of "religious freedom in a country is strongly associated with other freedoms, including civil and political liberty, press freedom, and economic freedom, as well as with multiple measures of well-being" – less warfare and violence, better healthcare, higher levels of income, and better educational and social opportunities, especially for women, children, the disabled, and the poor.[100] By contrast, where religious freedom is low, communities tend to suffer and struggle, with arrests and detentions; desecration of holy sites, books, and objects; denial of visas, corporate charters, and entity status; discrimination in employment, education, and housing; closures of worship centers, schools, charities, cemeteries, and religious services; and worse: rape, torture, kidnappings, beheadings, and the genocidal slaughter of religious believers in alarming numbers in war-torn areas of the Middle East and Africa.[101] In light of these grim global

98 See John Witte, Jr. and M. Christian Green, eds., *Religion and Human Rights: An Introduction* (Oxford: Oxford University Press, 2012).

99 Ibid.; Michael W. McConnell, "Why Is Religious Liberty the 'First Freedom'?" *Cardozo Law Review* 21 (2000), 1243–61.

100 Brian J. Grim, "Restrictions on Religion in the World: Measures and Implications," in Allen D. Hertzke, ed., *The Future of Religious Freedom: Global Challenges* (Oxford: Oxford University Press, 2013), 86, 101.

101 See p. 7–8, 295–96 and Allen Hertzke, *Freeing God's Children: The Unlikely Alliance for Global Human Rights* (Lanham, MD: Rowman & Littlefield, 2006).

realities, it is important to affirm that religious freedom is an essential cornerstone of ordered liberty and constitutional law, not an academic plaything or dispensable cultural luxury.

Constitutions work like "clock[s]," John Adams reminds us. Certain parts of them are "essentials and fundamentals," and, to operate properly, "their pendulums must swing back and forth" and their operators must get "wound up" from time to time.[102] We have certainly seen plenty of constitutional operators get wound up of late about religious freedom, and seen wide pendular swings in First Amendment jurisprudence over the past century. But despite the loud criticisms from the academy and media, and the anguished lamentations about the sorry state of religious liberty in America, we may well have come to the end of a long constitutional swing of cases away from religious freedom protection from 1980 to 2010, and are now witnessing the start of a pendular swing back in favor of stronger religious freedom protection by the federal courts. Since 2011, ten of the last twelve Supreme Court cases on religious freedom yielded wins for religion,[103] and the Supreme Court seems ready to usher in stronger protections still in current cases on its docket.[104] While cases like *Hobby Lobby* and *Masterpiece Cakeshop* attracted massive popular attention and criticism, these other recent cases have been quietly but steadily shifting First Amendment jurisprudence back in favor of stronger religious freedom.

Moreover, and more gravely, the blood of the many thousands of religious martyrs, especially in the genocidal attacks on communities of faith in the Middle East, Central Africa, and Central Eurasia, is now crying out so loudly that the world community will have to move toward concerted action in protection of religious freedom. As in Adams's day, so in our own, the United States remains well positioned to provide global leadership in this effort. Most of the core principles of American religious freedom – liberty of conscience, freedom of exercise, and religious equality and pluralism – forged in the crucible of the revolution against religious establishments and oppression are now at the heart of the international

[102] John Adams, "Letter from the Earl of Clarendon to William Pym (Jan. 27, 1766)," in George W. Carey, ed., *The Political Writings of John Adams* (Washington, DC: Regnery Publishers, 2000), 644, 647 (originally printed in the *Boston Gazette*, with John Adams using the pseudonym of the Earl of Clarendon).

[103] *Arizona Christian School Tuition Organization* v. *Winn*, 563 US 125 (2011); *Hosanna-Tabor Evangelical Lutheran Church and School* v. *EEOC*, 132 S. Ct. 694 (2012); *Town of Greece* v. *Galloway*, 134 S. Ct. 1811 (2014); *Burwell* v. *Hobby Lobby Stores, Inc.*, 134 S. Ct. 2751 (2014); *Holt* v. *Hobbs*, 135 S. Ct. 853 (2015); *Reed* v. *Town of Gilbert*, 135 S. Ct. 2218 (2015); *Zubik* v. *Burwell*, 136 S. Ct. 1557 (2016); *Masterpiece Cakeshop* v. *Colorado Civil Rights Commission*, 138 S. Ct. 1719 (2018); *American Legion* v. *American Humanist Association*, 139 S. Ct. 2067 (2019); *Espinoza* v. *Montana Department of Revenue*, 140 S. Ct. 2246 (2020); *Our Lady of Guadalupe School* v. *Morrissey-Berru*, 140 S. Ct. 2049 (2020); *Little Sisters of the Poor* v. *Pennsylvania*, 140 S. Ct. 2367 (2020); *Roman Catholic Diocese of Brooklyn* v. *Cuomo*, 590 US ___ (2020); but cf. *Calvary Chapel Dayton Valley* v. *Sisolak*, 591 US ___ (2020) (upholding an order that limited in-person worship services to 50 people); *South Bay United Pentecostal Church* v. *Newsom*, 590 US ___ (2020) (upholding an executive order limiting in-person worship to 25 percent capacity or 100 people, whichever was lower).

[104] *Fulton* v. *City of Pennsylvania* (to be argued 2021).

human rights protections. And the work of our constitutional courts remains the envy of the world, even if individual cases are sometimes denounced.

It is essential, in my view, that these core principles of religious freedom remain vital parts of our American constitutional life and are not diluted into neutrality or equality norms alone, and not weakened by too low a standard of review or too high a law of standing. It is essential that we address the glaring blind spots in our religious freedom jurisprudence – particularly the long and shameful treatment of Native American Indian claims[105] and the growing repression of Muslims and other minorities at the local level, which are not being addressed very well.[106] It is essential that we show our traditional hospitality and charity to the "sojourners within our gates"[107] – migrants, refugees, asylum seekers, and others – and desist from some of the outrageous nativism and xenophobia that have marked too much of our popular and political speech of late.[108] It is essential that we balance religious freedom with other fundamental freedoms, including sexual and same-sex freedoms, and find responsible ways of living together with all our neighbors, and desisting from mutually destructive strategies of defaming, demonizing, and destroying those who hold other viewpoints.[109] And it is essential that we make our landmark International Religious Freedom Act[110] a strong focus of our international diplomacy and policy again, not something to be ignored when economic, military, or geopolitical interests get in the way, or deprecated and underfunded when other special administration interests gain political favor. Now is the time for American governments, academics, NGOs, religious and political groups, and citizens alike to stand for strong religious freedom at home and abroad, for all peaceable people of faith.

Religion is too vital a root and resource for democratic order and rule of law to be passed over or pushed out. Religious freedom is too central a pillar of liberty and

105 See, e.g., *Lyng* v. *Northwest Indian Cemetery Protective Association*, 485 US 439, 451 (1988) (rejecting a challenge to the federal government's logging and road construction activities on lands sacred to several Native American tribes, even though it was undisputed that these activities "could have devastating effects on traditional Indian religious practices"); *Employment Division* v. *Smith*, 494 US 872 (1990) (holding that the state may prohibit the sacramental use of peyote in Native American Church); *Bowen* v. *Roy*, 476 US 693 (1986) (holding that an agency's use of a social security number does not violate the free exercise rights of a Native American, who believed such use would impair his child's spirit). See also Kathleen Sands, "Territory, Wilderness, Property, and Reservation: Land and Religion in Native American Supreme Court Cases," *American Indian Law Review* 36 (2012), 253.

106 But see the recent case of *Herrara* v. *Wyoming* (slip op. May 20, 2019) (upholding Crow Indian treaty claims to hunting rights). On the harsh treatment of Muslims in lower federal courts, see, e.g., Gregory C. Sisk and Michael Heise, "Muslims and Religious Liberty in the Era of Post 9/11: Empirical Evidence from the Federal Courts," *Iowa Law Review* 98 (2012), 291.

107 Exodus 20:10.

108 See, e.g., Robert Heimburger, *God and the Illegal Alien: Federal United States Immigration Law and a Theology of Politics* (Cambridge: Cambridge University Press, 2018).

109 See overview in John Witte, Jr., *Church, State and Family: Reconciling Traditional Teachings and Modern Liberties* (Cambridge: Cambridge University Press, 2019).

110 22 USC § 6401 (2012).

human rights to be chiseled away or pulled down. In centuries past – and in many regions of the world still today – disputes over religion and religious freedom have often led to violence, sometimes to all-out warfare. We have the extraordinary luxury in America of settling our religious disputes and vindicating our religious rights and liberties with patience, deliberation, due process, and full ventilation of the issues on all sides. We would do well to continue to embrace this precious constitutional heritage and process, and help others to achieve the same. As John Adams reminds us: "[T]he eyes of the world are upon [us]."[111]

111 Adams, *Works*, 8:487.

6

Balancing the Guarantees of No Establishment and Free Exercise of Religion in American Education*

American education is a massive social undertaking today. The United States has more than 130,000 lower schools (from kindergarten through twelfth grade), and more than 6,000 postsecondary schools. Nearly 100,000 lower schools are public or state-run institutions, with fifty-six million American children enrolled. Alongside these are 33,000 private lower schools (two-thirds of them religious) with six million students. About 1.7 million American children are regularly homeschooled at least until high school – although that number temporarily approached forty million nationwide because of restrictions during the COVID-19 pandemic. The country is also home to some 1,650 state and 4,300 private colleges, universities, and academies enrolling nearly twenty million students. More than ten million employees work in these schools, and last year education comprised 7.1 percent of America's GDP.[1]

American education is not only a massive industry but also a major battleground for religious freedom. While a complex scaffolding of federal, state, and local laws and regulations supports and governs education,[2] all schools are subject to the same First Amendment guarantee that "Congress shall make no law respecting an establishment of religion or prohibiting the free exercise thereof." This constitutional guarantee of religious freedom has produced a substantial and shifting body of case law. Nearly one-third of the US Supreme Court's cases on religious freedom – 74 out of its 240 cases issued through 2020[3] – have addressed issues of religion and education. All but six of these cases were decided after 1940, the year the Court first began

* This chapter draws on and updates John Witte, Jr. and Joel A. Nichols, *Religion and the American Constitutional Experiment*, 4th ed. (Oxford: Oxford University Press, 2016), 154–203.

1 National Center for Education Statistics, 2019 Tables and Figures, Table 105.20, 105.50, https://nces.ed.gov/programs/digest/2019menu_tables.asp; and ibid., "Private Schools and Enrollment," https://nces.ed.gov/programs/schoolchoice/ind_03.asp. In addition, there are some 7,200 lower charter schools, which are public/private partnerships featuring state charters and funding but active private administration, including sometimes religious leadership. See https://nces.ed.gov/fastfacts/display.asp?id=30.

2 See Michael I. Levin, *United States School Laws and Rules*, 3 vols. (St. Paul, MN: Thomson Reuter, 2020).

3 See tabular summary of all these Supreme Court cases in Witte and Nichols, *Religion and the American Constitutional Experiment*, Appendix 3, 303–38.

to apply these guarantees to state and local governments alongside Congress.[4] For each Supreme Court case, there are scores, sometimes hundreds of lower federal court cases and sometimes many state court cases, too, that add further nuance and amplification.

The US Supreme Court's cases on religious freedom and education are the main focus in this chapter. These cases address three main questions: (1) What role may religion play in public education? (2) What role may government play in private religious education? (3) What religious rights do parents and students have in public and private schools? The Court has worked out a set of rough answers to these questions, albeit with ample vacillation over the past century. While government has the power to mandate basic education for all children, parents have the right to choose public, private, or homeschool education for their minor children, and government may now facilitate that choice through vouchers and tax relief for private-school students. While the First Amendment forbids most forms of religion in public schools, it protects most forms of religion in private schools. While the First Amendment forbids government from funding the core religious activities of private schools, it permits delivery of general governmental services, subsidies, scholarships, and tax breaks to public and private schools, teachers, and students alike. While the First Amendment forbids public-school teachers and outsiders from offering religious instruction and expression in public-school classes and at formal school functions, it permits public-school students to engage in private religious expression and protects these students from coerced religious activities. The amendment further requires that religious parties have equal access to public facilities, forums, and funds that are open to their nonreligious peers.

The Supreme Court has developed these holdings in distinct lines of First Amendment cases on the place of religion in public schools and on the role of government in private religious schools. These cases, however, have left blurrier distinctions between religious freedom questions in lower education and higher education. Colleges and universities have thus often absorbed the Court's directives to primary and secondary schools, and vice versa. For example, many state universities adopted the Court's repeated principle in early cases mandating strict separation of church and state in lower public schools, even though no Supreme Court case explicitly ordered the universities' application of the principle. In turn, the Court's more recent rulings about equal access and equal treatment were created for state universities but trickled down into public high schools and then public grade schools, and are now firmly rooted in the Free Speech and Free Exercise Clauses.

4 See *Cantwell* v. *Connecticut*, 310 US 296 (1940) and *Everson* v. *Board of Education*, 330 US 1 (1947), which incorporated the Free Exercise and Establishment Clauses of the First Amendment into the Due Process Clause of the Fourteenth Amendment, and applied these guarantees for the first time against state and local governments. See Chapter 5 of this book, p. 158–59.

RELIGION AND PUBLIC EDUCATION

Separation of Church and State. The Supreme Court's most famous First Amendment teaching is that the Constitution has "erected a wall of separation between church and state."[5] This teaching emerged in a series of cases from 1948 to 1987 that limited the place of religious teachers, prayers, texts, symbols, and teachings in public grade schools and high schools.

A common logic governed this forty-year run of cases. The public school is a government entity, often one of the most visible and well-known arms of the government in any community. The public school is furthermore a model of constitutional democracy and designed to communicate and facilitate core democratic norms and constitutional practices to students. The state mandates that all able students attend schools, at least until the age of sixteen. These students are young and impressionable. Given all these factors, the Court maintained, the public school must cling closely to core constitutional and democratic values, including the core value of separation of church and state. Some relaxation of constitutional values is possible in other public contexts, where adults can make informed assessments of the values being transmitted. But no such relaxation can occur in public schools, which youths are compelled to attend. In public schools, if nowhere else in public life, strict separation of church and state must be the norm.

The case that opened this series was *McCollum* v. *Board of Education* (1948). At issue was a release-time program adopted by a local public-school board for fourth- through ninth-grade students. Once a week, students were released from their regular classes to be able to participate in a religious class taught on the school campus. Three religious classes were on offer – Protestant, Catholic, and Jewish – reflecting the religious makeup of the local community. These classes were voluntarily taught by qualified outside teachers approved by the principal. Students whose parents did not consent continued their "secular studies" during this release time. The *McCollum* Court held that this program violated the First Amendment Establishment Clause, for it constituted the use of "tax-supported property for religious instruction and the close cooperation between school authorities and the religious council in promoting religious education."[6]

In *Engel* v. *Vitale* (1962), the Court outlawed a nondenominational prayer recited by public-school teachers and their students at the commencement of each school day: "Almighty God, we acknowledge our dependence upon Thee, and we beg Thy blessings upon us, our parents, our teachers, and our Country." Students who did not wish to pray could remain silent or be excused from the room during this recitation. The *Engel* Court found this practice to be unconstitutional:

> It is no part of the business of government to compose official prayers for any group of the American people to recite as part of a religious program carried on by

[5] *McCollum* v. *Board of Education*, 333 US 203, 209–11 (1948).
[6] Ibid.

> government. … When the power, prestige, and financial support of government [are] placed behind a particular religious belief, the indirect coercive pressure upon religious minorities to conform to the prevailing officially approved religion is plain.[7]

This prohibition on prayer in public schools was controversial in its day, but the Court has maintained and extended it. *Wallace* v. *Jaffree* (1985) struck down a state statute that authorized a moment of silence at the beginning of each school day for "meditation or voluntary prayer," because the legislature had betrayed its "intent to return prayer to the public schools."[8] *Lee* v. *Weisman* (1992) outlawed a local rabbi's prayer at a one-time public middle-school graduation on school premises, arguing that such prayers effectively coerced graduating students to participate in religion.[9] *Santa Fe Independent School District* v. *Doe* (2000) outlawed elected student invocations at public high-school football games, arguing that this policy not only coerced players, cheerleaders, and band members to participate in prayer but also constituted governmental endorsement of religion.[10]

Not only religious teachers and prayers but also sectarian teachings were forbidden in public schools. In *Abington Township School District v. Schempp* (1963), the Court outlawed the reading of ten Bible verses at the beginning of each school day. Either a teacher or a volunteer student would read a biblical text of their choice, with no commentary or discussion allowed. Students whose parents did not consent could refuse to listen or leave the room. After *Engel*, the *Schempp* Court found this an easy case. "[I]t is no defense that the religious practices here may be relatively minor encroachments on the First Amendent," Justice Clark wrote for the Court. "The breach of neutrality that is today a trickling stream may all too soon become a raging torrent." Responding to Justice Stewart's sharply worded dissent that the Court's purported neutrality toward religion effectively established secularism as the religion of the public school, the Court offered a conciliatory word about the objective value and use of religion as a topic of public education:

> [I]t might well be said that one's education is not complete without a study of comparative religion or the history of religion and its relationship to the advancement of civilization. It certainly may be said that the Bible is worthy of study for its literary and historic qualities. Nothing we have said here indicates that such study of the Bible or of religion, when presented objectively as part of a secular program of education, may not be effected consistently with the First Amendment.[11]

While *Schempp* permitted objective instruction of religious topics in appropriate public-school classes, *Edwards* v. *Aguillard* (1987) struck down a state law that

7 370 US 421, 430–32 (1962).
8 472 US 38, 57–60 (1985).
9 505 US 577 (1992).
10 530 US 290 (2000).
11 374 US 203, 221, 226 (1963).

required equal time for "evolution-science" and "creation-science" in science classrooms. This statute, the Court held, betrayed a "discriminatory preference ... to advance the religious viewpoint that a supernatural being created humankind" and "to restructure the science curriculum to conform with a particular religious viewpoint." This was not a proper objective teaching of religion à la *Schempp*. Creation might be a good topic for a course in cosmology or ancient literature, but not for a science course. Separation of church and state also entailed separation of religion and science.[12] Lower courts have used this precedent to outlaw "intelligent design" teachings from public-school science curricula as well.

In *Stone* v. *Graham* (1980), the Court struck down a state statute that authorized the posting of a plaque bearing the Ten Commandments on the wall of each public-school classroom. The plaques were donated and hung by private groups in the community. There was no public reading of the commandments nor any evident mention or endorsement of them by teachers or school officials. Each plaque also bore a small inscription that sought to immunize it from charges of religious establishment: "The secular application of the Ten Commandments is clearly seen in its adoption as the fundamental legal code of Western Civilization and the Common Law of the United States." The Court struck down these displays as violations of the Establishment Clause. These displays were "plainly religious," in the Court's view. The Ten Commandments are sacred in Jewish and Christian circles, and they command "the religious duties of believers." It made no constitutional difference that they were passively displayed, rather than formally read aloud, or that they were privately donated rather than purchased with state money. The very display of the Decalogue in the public-school classroom served only a religious purpose and was thus inherently unconstitutional.[13]

These early Supreme Court separationist cases were focused on the place of religion in public grade schools and high schools. They were predicated on the reality that students were mandated to be in school until the age of sixteen and were young and impressionable. From the mid-1960s forward, however, many state universities adopted comparable policies that limited the place of religion in the university campus, curriculum, and activities – even though their students were voluntary, more mature, and able to make their own choices about religion. Some of these new university policies about strict separation of church and state on campus were adopted as self-protective measures against expensive lawsuits brought under the First Amendment, especially as some lower courts began to order state universities to follow the religion policies of state high schools. Universities in some states were also subject to state constitutions that mandated the separation of religion and education, and these policies were more aggressively enforced by state regulators and courts.

12 482 US 578, 591–93 (1987).
13 449 US 39, 40–41 (1980) (per curiam).

But legal considerations were only part of the motivation for these reforms of higher education. Pushing religion to the edge of the college campus and curriculum also reflected the growing antireligious movements and countercultural sentiments of the American academy in the mid-twentieth century. Included were the "death of God" theology taught in some religion departments and seminaries; Marxist and other critical and deconstructive attacks on traditional religion; and the strong rise of secularization theories of education and public life. It was significant, too, that many of the new cultural and educational leaders of the nation from the 1960s forward had been reared in public schools that taught them that separation of church and state was the distinct and proper American way of engaging religion. Small wonder, then, that, upon reaching adulthood, this generation adopted separation as a guiding maxim of American higher education as well as lower education.

The Rise of Equal Access Cases. These Establishment Clause cases from 1948 to 1987 limiting religion in public-school classes and at official school events remain good law today.[14] But they have garnered ample criticism that has forced important limits on their logic and subsequent policy.[15] One set of critics has lamented the Court's removal of religion from public schools and worked persistently to return prayer and other traditional religious activities to the classroom. These groups are often conservative Christians pressing the broader thesis that America was founded as a Christian nation and must democratically reflect this in its political institutions, including its state schools. A second group of critics has charged the Court with establishing secularism in the public school under the guise of reason and neutrality. These critics argue that the purportedly secular and scientific instruction offered in the public school is just as laden with subjective moral values and ideological beliefs as traditional religious instruction. Drawing a secular/sectarian dividing line in these cases is too simplistic, these critics argue.

A third group of critics, including some specialists in education and child development, have charged that the policy of quarantining public-school students from instruction and experience in religion harms rather than helps them in cultivating the very democratic values and abilities the Court and country are trying to instill and protect in each new generation. Religion, they argue, is not like alcohol, to be avoided until adulthood. Religion is a powerful and perennial force

[14] See the new summary of the law on religious expression in the public schools in Department of Justice, Civil Rights Division, www2.ed.gov/policy/gen/guid/religionandschools/prayer_guidance.html.

[15] See analysis of the relevant literature and cases in Kent Greenawalt, *Does God Belong in Public Schools?* (Princeton, NJ: Princeton University Press, 2005). The First Amendment Center provides valuable insights and materials on religion and education, as does the American Center for School Choice. See, further, Michael D. Waggoner and Nathan C. Walker, eds., *The Oxford Handbook of Religion and American Education* (New York: Oxford University Press, 2016), and a comprehensive recent study by Ashley Berner, *Pluralism and American Public Education: No One Way to School* (New York: Palgrave Macmillan, 2017).

in society, whether for good or ill, and every budding democratic citizen needs to learn from the start to deal with it responsibly. Such education groups have thus developed a range of ambitious curricular forums that seek to introduce religion judiciously into the public-school curriculum in appropriate courses.

Finally, some critics have charged that the Court has used the Establishment Clause to quash rights of free exercise and free speech. Why should students be muzzled in their religious expression as a condition for participating in a school that the state conscripts them to attend at least until the age of sixteen? Why should religious parents be compelled to expose their children to a pervasive learning environment that views their faith and identity as suspect and dangerous? Some critics add an economic argument: that the religious rights of the poor suffer disproportionately, since only students of more well-to-do families can afford to attend private schools, where their religious expression is not so muzzled.

Particularly these last two arguments – the need to educate students about religion and to protect the students' rights to religious expression – have helped to drive the development of a new line of what are called "equal-access" cases. The principal logic of these cases is that religious students and other parties must be given equal access to facilities, forums, and even funds that the public school makes available to similarly situated nonreligious parties. These cases have not changed the longstanding rule that religion is not allowed in the public classroom during instructional time or at official school events. But they have allowed for private religious exercises on school grounds outside of formal instructional time, and they have allowed for extracurricular education on school premises, even if it is religiously motivated and inspired.

These cases were, at first, grounded variously in the Free Speech, Free Exercise, and Equal Protection Clauses, but they are now largely a staple of free-speech jurisprudence alone. Equal-access cases first began in the public university and then worked their way into the public high school and eventually into the public grade school, though the most recent cases have imposed some limits on this equal-access logic in public schools.

Widmar v. *Vincent* (1981) was the opening case in this series. The University of Missouri at Kansas City, a state university, had a policy of opening its facilities for voluntary student groups to use outside of formal instructional time. More than a hundred student groups organized themselves in the year at issue, each paying a registration fee of forty-one dollars per semester. One student group, called Cornerstone, met for private religious devotions and local charitable activities. They sought permission to use the university facilities but were denied access, given the university's written policy that the campus could not be used "for purposes of religious worship or religious teaching." Cornerstone appealed, arguing that this policy violated their First Amendment free exercise and free speech rights as well as their Fourteenth Amendment equal protection rights. The university countered that it had a compelling state interest to maintain a "strict separation of church and state," per the state constitution, especially in state schools.[16]

The *Widmar* Court found for the religious student group. When a state university creates a limited public forum open to voluntary student groups, the Court opined, religious groups must be given equal access to that forum. Here the university "has discriminated against student groups and speakers based on their desire to use a generally open forum to engage in religious worship and discussion." Religious speech and association are protected by the First Amendment and can be excluded only if the university can demonstrate that its prohibition serves a "compelling state interest and that it is narrowly drawn to achieve that end." But a general desire to keep a strict separation of church and state was not a sufficiently compelling state interest. The values of "equal treatment and access" outweighed the hypothetical dangers of a religious establishment.[17]

The *Widmar* Court explicitly limited its holding to the public university, arguing that university students, unlike public high-school and grade-school students, were more mature and discerning and, after the age of sixteen, were not required by school attendance laws to be there. The following week, the Court let stand a federal circuit court opinion that refused to extend the *Widmar* holding into public high schools.[18] In response, Congress passed the Equal Access Act of 1984, which extended the *Widmar* principle to public high schools that received federal funding. The act provided that any such high school that opened its facilities to some students for voluntary after-school activities would have to give religious students equal access to these facilities. The religious students' activities, however, had to be completely voluntary and free from school endorsement or participation. In *Westside Community Schools* v. *Mergens* (1990), the Court upheld the Equal Access Act against an Establishment Clause challenge, holding that Congress had legitimately protected the rights of religious students to "equal treatment" and "equal protection."[19]

In subsequent cases involving lower schools, the Court rooted this equal-access right more clearly in the First Amendment Free Speech Clause. *Lamb's Chapel* v. *Center Moriches Union Free School District* (1993) involved a public school that opened its facilities to various "social, civic, recreational, and political uses" organized by voluntary groups in the community and held after hours without student involvement. The school banned an otherwise qualified Evangelical group because they wanted to show a film series on traditional family values. Citing *Widmar*, the *Lamb's Chapel* Court held that it was viewpoint discrimination to deny this group

16 454 US 263, 270, 273 (1981). The Court later upheld the constitutionality of charging these flat fees, even to religious groups, finding no prior restraint on free exercise of religion. See *Board of Regents of University of Wisconsin System* v. *Southworth*, 529 US 217 (2000).

17 Ibid.

18 *Brandon* v. *Bd. of Educ. of Guilderland Central School Dist.*, 635 F.2d 971 (2d Cir. 1980), *cert. denied*, 454 US 1123 (1981).

19 496 US 226, 248–50 (1990).

equal access to the facilities just because their film had a religious inspiration.[20] Similarly, *Good News Club* v. *Milford Central School* (2001) held that a public grade school that opened its facilities to licensed private groups to run after-school programs for students with parental permission could not exclude a group whose instruction came "from a religious viewpoint."[21]

In *Rosenberger* v. *Rector and Visitors of the University of Virginia* (1995), a sharply divided Court extended this equal-access principle to the distribution of state funds. The University of Virginia encouraged student groups to organize themselves for extracurricular activities and register with the university. Student groups were required to petition for the right to be recognized as such a registered group. Once registered, they could apply for monies from a general student activity fund to help defray costs of printing and activities. A Christian group sought reimbursement for the costs to print an overtly religious newspaper called *Wide Awake: A Christian Perspective at the University of Virginia*. The university denied their request since it violated the school's policy not to fund "any activity 'that primarily promotes or manifests a particular belief in or about a deity or an ultimate reality.'" The *Wide Awake* group appealed, claiming that this discriminatory treatment violated their free-speech rights.[22]

The *Rosenberger* Court held for the students. Writing for the Court, Justice Kennedy said that the state university policy improperly "selects for disfavored treatment those student journalistic efforts with religious editorial viewpoints." Denying funding to this otherwise qualified student group "is based upon viewpoint discrimination not unlike the discrimination the school district relied upon in *Lamb's Chapel* and that we found invalid." The constitutional principle of equal access applies as much to state university funding as to state university facilities, the Court held.

> Vital First Amendment speech principles are at stake here. The first danger to liberty lies in granting the State the power to examine publications to determine whether or not they are based on some ultimate idea and if so for the State to classify them [as religious]. The second, and corollary, danger is to speech from the chilling of individual thought and expression. That danger is especially real in the University setting, where the State acts against a background and tradition of thought and experiment that is at the center of our intellectual and philosophic tradition. ... For the University, by regulation, to cast disapproval on particular viewpoints of its students risks the suppression of free speech and creative inquiry in one of the vital centers for the nation's intellectual life, its college and university campuses.[23]

20 508 US 384, 387, 394 (1993).
21 533 US 98, 112–14 (2001).
22 515 US 819 (1995).
23 515 US at 831–32, 836–37.

In *Christian Legal Society* v. *Martinez* (2010), however, the Court made clear that this equal-access logic has limits, even on university campuses. Hastings College of Law, a state law school in California, officially recognizes all voluntary student groups through a formal Registered Student Organization (RSO) program. Officially recognized student groups receive access to school funds and certain facilities and communication channels that are foreclosed to nonregistered groups. To qualify for RSO recognition, however, a group must comply with the school's nondiscrimination policy, based on state civil rights laws, which bars discrimination on the basis of religion and sexual orientation, among other grounds. A group of law students sought to form a chapter of the Christian Legal Society (CLS) at the law school. Like all CLS groups in the country, this group required its members to sign a statement of faith and to live in accordance with prescribed principles; the group excluded anyone with religious beliefs contrary to the statement of faith and anyone who engaged in "unrepentant homosexual conduct." Hastings regarded this CLS policy as discrimination based on religion and sexual orientation and thus denied the group's application for official RSO status. CLS filed suit, claiming violations of their rights to free speech, expressive association, and the free exercise of religion.[24]

A 5–4 *Martinez* Court, led by Justice Ginsburg, held for Hastings. The Court combined the CLS's claims to free speech and free association into one and subjected them to "a less restrictive limited-public-forum analysis" than the stricter scrutiny regime of *Widmar* and its progeny. Here, the Court said, the law school was only "dangling the carrot of subsidy, not wielding the stick of prohibition." Unlike the *Widmar* students, the CLS students could certainly meet on the Hastings campus and could use the school's chalk boards and bulletin boards, as well as their own social media to communicate. Unlike the *Rosenberger* students, the CLS students were not singled out for special prohibitions because of their Christian perspective. They were denied RSO status, and its attendant special funds and other benefits, simply because they violated Hasting's general nondiscrimination policy. It is "hard to imagine a more viewpoint-neutral policy than one requiring *all* student groups to accept *all* comers."[25]

GOVERNMENT AND RELIGIOUS EDUCATION

The place of religion in public schools is one major set of issues the Court has addressed under the First Amendment Establishment Clause. The role of government in private religious schools is the other set of issues. These latter issues, particularly questions of government funding and support for religious schools, were hotly contested in the states long before the Supreme Court got actively involved. By 1921, thirty-five states had passed state constitutional amendments that

[24] 561 US 661 (2010).

[25] 561 US at 683, 692, 697.

barred state funding of religious schools.[26] Moreover, in some states, various anti-Catholic and self-professed secularist groups pushed hard to eliminate religious schools altogether and to give public schools a monopoly on education.

In response, the Court developed a general argument about the place of private religious schools in modern society, and the role that government could play in them. Private schools of all sorts, the Court repeatedly held, are viable and valuable alternatives to public schools. Private *religious* schools, moreover, allow parents to educate their students in their own religious tradition, a right which they must enjoy without discrimination or prejudice. Given that public education must be secular under the Establishment Clause, private education may be religious under the Free Exercise Clause. To be accredited, all private schools must meet minimum educational standards. They must teach reading, writing, and arithmetic, history, geography, social studies, and the like, so that their graduates are not culturally or intellectually handicapped as budding democratic citizens. Objections to these baseline requirements by schools or parents on the basis of the Free Exercise Clause are of little avail. But private schools may teach these subjects from a religious perspective and add religious instruction and activities beyond them. They may favor teachers and students who share their faith. Religious schools also are presumptively entitled to the same government services available to public schools – so long as those services are not used for core religious activities.

The Supreme Court developed and applied this accommodationist logic from 1925 to 1971, abruptly reversed course in favor of strict separationism from 1971 to 1985, and since then has returned to a new variant of accommodationist logic framed in terms of equal access and equal treatment that it recently grounded in the First Amendment Free Exercise Clause.

Accommodation of Religious Education. The most important early religious-school case was *Pierce* v. *Society of Sisters* (1925). Oregon had passed a law mandating that all eligible students must attend public elementary and high schools. The law sought to eliminate Catholic and other private religious schools and to give new impetus to the development of the state's public schools. Local private Catholic schools challenged the law as a violation of the educational rights of the parents, children, schools, and teachers alike. The *Pierce* Court agreed and struck down the Oregon law. "The fundamental theory of liberty," the Court opined, "excludes any general power of the state to standardize its children by forcing them to accept instruction from public teachers only." It also forecloses "unwarranted compulsion" of "present and future patrons" of the religious schools.[27] Extending the *Pierce* holding, *Farrington* v. *Tokushige* (1927) held that states could not impose unduly

26 See a tabular summary in Witte and Nichols, *Religion and the American Constitutional Experiment*, Appendix 2, and summary of the issues and literature in ibid., 103–07.

27 268 US 510 (1925).

intrusive and stringent accreditation and regulatory requirements on religious private schools.[28] And *Cochran* v. *Board of Education* (1930) upheld a state policy of supplying basic textbooks to all students, including religious-school students.[29]

This accommodation of religious schools and students continued into the early 1970s. *Everson* v. *Board of Education* (1947), though offering sweeping dicta on the wall of separation between church and state, still held that states could provide school bus transportation to religious and public school children alike or reimburse the parents for the costs of using school bus transportation. "[C]utting off church schools [and their students] from these services, so separate and indisputably marked off from the religious function, would make it far more difficult for the schools to operate," Justice Black wrote for the *Everson* Court. "But such obviously is not the purpose of the First Amendment. The Amendment requires the State to be neutral in its relations with groups of religious believers and non-believers; it does not require the state to be their adversary."[30]

The Court struck a similar tone in *Board of Education* v. *Allen* (1968). The State of New York had a policy of lending prescribed textbooks in science, mathematics, and other secular subjects to all students in the state, whether attending public or private schools. Many of the private-school recipients of the textbooks were religious schools. A taxpayer challenged the policy as a violation of the Establishment Clause. Citing *Cochran*, the *Allen* Court rejected this claim, emphasizing that it was the students and parents, not the religious schools, who directly benefited.[31]

The Court continued this accommodationist tone in a trio of cases upholding government funding for construction of buildings at religious colleges and universities. In *Tilton* v. *Richardson* (1971), the Court rebuffed a challenge to a federal grant program that supported construction of library, science, and arts buildings at four church-related colleges. The grants were made as part of the federal Higher Education Facilities Act (1963), which sponsored all manner of new buildings at public and private colleges and universities throughout the nation. Chief Justice Burger wrote for the plurality: "The Act itself was carefully drafted to ensure that the federally subsidized facilities would be devoted to the secular and not the religious functions of the recipient institution." This feature, together with the reality that most funding was directed to state, not religious, universities and colleges, was sufficient to ensure the Act's constitutionality.[32] In *Hunt* v. *McNair* (1973), the Court upheld a state program of funding the construction of similar secular buildings at various universities within the state, including a religiously chartered college.[33] Again in *Roemer* v. *Board of Public Works* (1977), the Court upheld

28 273 US 284 (1927).
29 281 US 370 (1930).
30 330 US at 16, 18.
31 392 US 236, 243–44 (1968).
32 403 US 672, 679–82 (1971).
33 413 US 734 (1973).

a state construction grant program that included five church-related schools among its seventeen grant recipients. The *Roemer* Court counseled against too zealous an application of the principle of separation of church and state, given the reality and reach of the modern welfare state:

> A system of government that makes itself felt as pervasively as ours could hardly be expected never to cross paths with the church. In fact, our State and Federal Governments impose certain burdens upon, and impart certain benefits to, virtually all our activities, and religious activity is no exception. The Court has enforced a scrupulous neutrality by the State, as among religions, and also as between religious and other activities, but a hermetic separation of the two is an impossibility [and] it has never been required. ... [R]eligious institutions need not be quarantined from public benefits that are neutrally available to all. ... [and have] the incidental effect of facilitating religious activity.[34]

The Court stretched its furthest in accommodating religious education in *Wisconsin* v. *Yoder* (1972). Wisconsin, like all states, mandated that able children attend school until the age of sixteen. A community of Old Order Amish, who were dedicated to a simple agrarian life style based on biblical principles, agreed to send their children to grade school – to teach them the basics of reading, writing, and arithmetic that they would need to function in society as adults. But they refused to send their children to high school, lest these children be tempted by worldly concerns and distracted from learning the values and skills they would need to maintain the Amish lifestyle. After they were fined for disobeying school attendance laws, the parents and community leaders filed suit, arguing that the state had violated their free-exercise and parental rights.[35]

The *Yoder* Court agreed and ordered that the Amish parents and students be exempted from full compliance with laws mandating school attendance. The Court was impressed that the Amish "lifestyle" was centuries-old and "not merely a matter of personal preference, but one of deep religious conviction, shared by an organized group, and intimately related to daily living." In the Court's view, compliance with the compulsory school attendance law would pose "a very real threat of undermining the Amish community and religious practice as they exist today; they must either abandon belief and be assimilated into society at large, or be forced to migrate to some other and more tolerant region." To exempt them was not to "establish the Amish religion" but to "accommodate their free exercise rights."[36] This case became a *locus classicus* for the homeschooling options now on offer in most states.

Separation of Church and State. In *Lemon* v. *Kurtzman* (1971), the Supreme Court abruptly reversed course. Drawing on the strict separationist logic of its earlier public-school cases, the *Lemon* Court crafted a three-part test to be used in all future

34 426 US 736, 746 (1977).
35 406 US 205 (1972).
36 406 US at 216–18.

cases arising under the First Amendment Establishment Clause, including those dealing with religious schools. To meet constitutional objections, the Court held, any challenged government law must: (1) have a secular purpose; (2) have a primary effect that neither advances nor inhibits religion; and (3) not foster an excessive entanglement between church and state.[37]

The *Lemon* Court used this three-part test to strike down a state policy that reimbursed Catholic and religious schools for some of the costs of teaching secular subjects that the state prescribed. The state policy was restricted to religious schools that served students from lower-income families, and the reimbursements were limited to 15 percent of the costs. The *Lemon* Court held that this policy fostered an "excessive entanglement between church and state." The Catholic schools in question were notably religious, the Court held – closely allied with nearby parish churches, filled with religious symbols, and staffed primarily by nuns who were under "religious control and discipline." "[A] dedicated religious person, teaching at a school affiliated with his or her faith and operated to inculcate its tenets, will inevitably experience great difficulty in remaining religiously neutral." She will be tempted to teach secular subjects with a religious orientation in violation of state policy. "A comprehensive, discriminating, and continuing state surveillance will inevitably be required to ensure that these restrictions are obeyed and the First Amendment otherwise obeyed." This is precisely the kind of excessive entanglement between church and state that the First Amendment Establishment Clause outlaws.[38]

Lemon left open the question whether the state could give aid directly to religious students or to their parents – as the Court had allowed in earlier cases. Two years later, the Court closed this door tightly. In *Committee for Public Education* v. *Nyquist* (1973)[39] and *Sloan* v. *Lemon* (1973),[40] the Court struck down state policies that allowed low-income parents to seek reimbursements from the state for some of the costs of religious-school tuition. *Nyquist* further struck down a state policy that allowed low-income parents to take tax deductions for the costs of sending their children to private schools. In *Nyquist*, Justice Powell characterized such policies as just another "of the ingenious plans of channeling state aid to sectarian schools." Responding to the state argument that "grants to parents, unlike grants to [religious] institutions, respect the 'wall of separation' required by the Constitution," the Court declared that "the [primary] effect of the aid is unmistakably to provide desired financial support for non-public, sectarian institutions."[41]

Lemon also left open the question whether the state could give textbooks, educational materials, or other aid to religious schools for teaching mandatory secular

37 403 US 602 (1971)
38 403 US at 619–22.
39 413 US 756 (1973).
40 413 US 825 (1973).
41 413 US at 783, 785.

subjects or administering state-mandated tests and other programs. The Court struck down most such policies in a long series of cases culminating in *Grand Rapids School District* v. *Ball* (1985)[42] and *Aguilar* v. *Felton* (1985).[43] These cases, and their ample extension by lower courts, were all designed to create a high wall of separation between church and state, and between public- and private-school facilities, funds, teachers, students, and programs.

Equal Treatment, Freedom of Choice, and State Aid to Religion. The principle of strict separation, however alluring in theory, ultimately proved unworkable in practice. It also raised questions of fairness to religious parents who had to pay both public-school taxes and religious-school tuition if they wished to educate their children in their own faith. Accordingly, the Supreme Court gradually moved back toward greater accommodation and state support for religious education, eventually overriding strong state constitutional prohibitions on funding at least the secular dimensions of religious education and allowing for various forms of state tax relief for families with religious-school students.

The first case in this new series was *Mueller* v. *Allen* (1983). There the Court upheld a Minnesota law that allowed parents of private-school children to claim tax deductions from state income tax for the costs of "tuition, transportation, and textbooks." Ninety-five percent of the private-school children in the state attended religious schools. Most of their parents availed themselves of this tax deduction. A taxpayer in the state challenged the law as an establishment of religion. The *Mueller* Court disagreed. The tax deduction policy, then Justice Rehnquist wrote for the Court, had a secular purpose of supporting quality education, fostered no entanglement between church and state, and had the primary effect of enhancing the educational choices of parents and students. The state aid to sectarian schools "becomes available only as a result of numerous, private choices of individual parents of school-age children." This saves it from constitutional infirmity.[44]

In *Witters* v. *Washington Department of Services for the Blind* (1986), the Court upheld a state program that furnished aid to a student attending a Christian college. The program provided funds "for special education and/or training in the professions, business or trades" for the visually impaired. Money was to be paid directly to eligible recipients, who were entitled to use the funds to pursue education in the professional schools of their choice. Witters's condition qualified him for the funds. His profession of choice was the Christian ministry, and he sought funds to attend a Christian college in preparation. The state agency denied funding on grounds that this was direct funding of religious education in violation of the Establishment Clause. The *Witters* Court disagreed. The policy served a secular purpose of fostering educational and professional choice for all, including the handicapped. It

42 473 US 373 (1985).
43 473 US 402, overruled by *Agostoni* v. *Felton*, 521 US 203 (1997).
44 463 US 388, 394–99 (1983).

involved no entanglement of church and state. Its primary effect was to facilitate this student's professional education, which happened to be religious. This "is not one of 'the ingenious plans for channeling state aid to sectarian schools,'" Justice Marshall wrote for the Court. "It creates no financial incentive for students to undertake sectarian education. It does not provide greater or broader benefits for recipients who apply their aid to religious education. … In this case, the fact that aid goes to individuals means that the decision to support religious education is made by the individual not by the State."[45]

In *Zobrest* v. *Catalina Foothills School District* (1993), the Court extended this logic from a college student to a high-school student. Both federal and state disability acts required that a hearing-impaired student be furnished with a sign-language interpreter, paid for by the state, to accompany him or her to classes. James Zobrest's hearing impairment qualified him for an interpreter's services. After going to a public grade school where the state furnished these services, he enrolled at a Catholic high school. The state now refused to furnish him with an interpreter, on grounds that this would violate the *Lemon* rule prohibiting direct aid to a religious school. Moreover, the state argued, the presence of a state-employed interpreter in a Catholic high school would foster an excessive entanglement between church and state. Following *Mueller* and *Witters*, the *Zobrest* Court found for the student and upheld the act as "a neutral government program dispensing aid not to schools but to handicapped children."[46]

In *Mitchell* v. *Helms* (2000), the Court upheld the constitutionality of direct government aid to the secular functions of religious schools. The Education Consolidation and Improvement Act (1981) channeled federal funds to state and local education agencies for the purchase of various educational materials and equipment to be distributed to all local schools for "secular, neutral, and nonideological" programs. Louisiana distributed materials and equipment to public and private schools in the state, including Catholic private schools, following statutory procedures and formulae. Local taxpayers sued, arguing that "direct aid" to such "pervasively sectarian" schools constituted an establishment of religion. The *Mitchell* Court upheld the program. The law did not advance religion; indeed, it was overtly "secular, neutral, and nonideological." Nor did it define its recipients by reference to religion; all accredited public and private schools and students were eligible. Moreover, there was no excessive entanglement between religious and governmental officials in the administration of the program. This was no establishment of religion but a neutral program on its face and, as applied, designed to enhance all the nation's schools.[47]

In *Zelman* v. *Simmons-Harris* (2002), the Court further upheld a school voucher program that the State of Ohio had adopted to address a "crisis of magnitude" in its Cleveland public school system. The program gave parents a choice to leave their

45 474 US 481, 488 (1986).
46 509 US 1, 13–14 (1993).
47 530 US 793, 810 (2000).

children in the local Cleveland public school district or to enroll them in another public or private school that participated in the school voucher program. For parents who chose to send their children to a participating private school, the program provided a voucher to help defray tuition costs, but parents had to make copayments according to their means. Some 82 percent of the private schools participating in the voucher program were religiously affiliated; 96 percent of the students who used vouchers enrolled in these private religious schools.[48] Local taxpayers challenged this as a form of direct state aid to religious schools, including their religious education.

The *Zelman* Court upheld the voucher program. It was enacted for a "valid secular purpose of providing educational assistance to poor children in a demonstrably failing public school system," Chief Justice Rehnquist wrote for a sharply divided Court. The primary effect of the program was not to advance religion but to enhance educational choice for poor students and parents. "Where a government aid program is *neutral* with respect to religion, and provides assistance directly to a *broad class of citizens*, who, in turn, direct government aid to religious schools wholly as a result of their own genuine and independent *private choice*," there is no establishment of religion. "The incidental advancement of a religious mission, or the perceived endorsement of a religious message is reasonably attributable to the individual, not the government, whose role ends with the disbursement of the funds."[49]

Free Exercise and Equal Access. These last five cases – *Mueller*, *Witters*, *Zobrest*, *Mitchell*, and *Zelman* – all concerned the Establishment Clause. Each held that it was no establishment of religion to allow religious parties to avail themselves of the same statutory rights and benefits made available to everyone else. This was a narrower constitutional logic than the four cases concerning equal access and the place of religion in public schools analyzed earlier – *Widmar*, *Lamb's Chapel*, *Rosenberger*, and *Good News Club*. In the *Widmar* line of cases, the Court held that the equal access of religious parties to public school forums and funds was not only permissible under the Establishment Clause (as the *Mueller* line of cases had also held) but also mandated by the Free Speech Clause (which the *Mueller* line of cases did not require). The results of these two lines of cases are largely the same: religious and nonreligious parties get equality under the law. But the constitutional logic is different. Religious parties claiming equal access rights in public schools are constitutionally entitled to this equal treatment under the Free Speech Clause. Religious parties claiming equal treatment in religious schools are only statutorily entitled to equal treatment under applicable federal or state statutes. But what the legislature gives by statute, it can also take back by statute.

48 536 US 639 (2002).
49 536 US at 652.

That distinction in logic became clear in *Locke* v. *Davey* (2004). *Locke* involved a successor Washington state scholarship program to the one that the Court had addressed in the 1986 *Witters* case. The new scholarship rules at issue in *Locke* provided that state scholarship recipients could attend any accredited college in the state, including a religious college, but they could not major in "devotional theology." Davey qualified for the scholarship and went to a religious college and then declared a double major in business and theology. He thus lost his state scholarship. He argued that the state had thereby violated the First Amendment Free Exercise Clause. The state countered that paying for his scholarship would violate the state's constitutional prohibition on funding religious education. Davey further argued that the payment made to the Christian college was entirely by his private choice, just like the payments in *Zelman* and *Witters*. The state countered that it should not have to *pay* Davey for the *free* exercise of his religion.

A 7–2 *Locke* Court held for the state, characterizing this as a case that fell "in the joints" between the First Amendment clauses. Chief Justice Rehnquist wrote for the Court that the Free Exercise Clause does not require the state to pay for Davey's scholarship, any more than the Establishment Clause prevents the state from doing so. It was up to the state legislature, not the courts, to decide whether to give, condition, or withhold its funding to religious students. Here, the legislature had applied its own state constitutional prohibition on funding of religious education as narrowly as possible – allowing students to spend their state scholarship funds at religious colleges and to take religion courses, but just not to become theology majors. This was a sensible and well-tailored application of state constitutional law, the Court concluded. It was certainly permissible under the First Amendment and further encouraged by the Tenth Amendment protection of federalism.[50]

In its two most recent cases, however, the Court explicitly anchored the equal-access rights of religious schools, parents, and students in the Free Exercise Clause, effectively limiting *Locke* to its facts. In *Trinity Lutheran Church* v. *Comer* (2017), the state had excluded a church school from a state program that reimbursed schools for the costs of resurfacing their playgrounds with a new rubber surface supplied by the state's recyclers. The Trinity Lutheran Church school had applied on time and easily met all the conditions and criteria to receive the funds, but the state denied their application because of the state constitutional prohibition on funding religious education. The *Trinity Lutheran* court held this to be a violation of the Free Exercise Clause. Chief Justice Roberts distinguished the *Locke* case carefully. "Davey was not denied a scholarship because of who he was; he was denied a scholarship because of what he proposed to do. Here there is no question that Trinity Lutheran was denied a grant simply because of what it is – a church." State laws imposing "special disabilities on the basis of ... religious status" alone are permissible only if the state has a "compelling interest" for doing so. The state's general concern about

50 540 US 712 (2004).

violating its state constitutional prohibition on religious establishment was not compelling enough.[51]

A footnote in *Trinity Lutheran* limited this holding to its facts. In *Espinoza* v. *Montana Department of Revenue* (2020), however, the Court widened this reading of the free-exercise right to equal access for religious and nonreligious parties. In this case, the State of Montana offered its citizens state tax credits if they made donations to nonprofit organizations that awarded scholarships for private-school tuition. The state program, however, would not allow scholarships to go to religious-school students, since the state constitution prohibited all state aid to religious education. Three mothers whose children could not get scholarships to attend a Christian school filed suit under the Free Exercise Clause, claiming that this exclusion constituted discrimination against them and the religious schools. The *Espinoza* Court agreed. The state's "interest in creating greater separation of church and State than the Federal Constitution requires 'cannot qualify as compelling' in the face of the infringement of free exercise here."[52]

Labor and Employment in Religious Schools. The First Amendment requires that religious organizations, including religious schools, be given room to carry out their unique missions and functions. This is partly because religious organizations are places where many individuals manifest their free-exercise rights. But the First Amendment "gives special solicitude to the rights of religious organizations" as such, the Court noted recently, protecting a "religious group's right to shape its own faith and mission," and "bar[ring] the government from interfering" with its internal decisions over membership and leadership.[53]

Reflecting this basic teaching of "religious autonomy," as it is called, legislatures often exempt religious employers from various labor, employment, and civil rights laws. The best-known example is Section 702 of Title VII of the Civil Rights Act of 1964, an act that generally prohibits employment discrimination based on "race, color, religion, sex, or national origin." Section 702, known as the "ministerial exception" provision, provides that the federal prohibition on religious discrimination does not apply to "any religious corporation, association, educational institution, or society" that hires employees of a particular religion to perform work connected with the activities of that particular religious group.[54]

The core cases where Section 702 applies are easy. A synagogue does not have to hire a Baptist minister to serve as its rabbi or read the Torah. The Catholic Church

51 582 US ___, 137 S. Ct. 2012 (2017).

52 140 S. Ct. 2246 (2020). See also *Arizona Christian School Tuition Organization* v. *Winn*, 563 US 125 (2011) (holding that taxpayers lacked standing to bring an Establishment Clause challenge to a state law that provided tax credits to other state residents who contributed to "student tuition organizations" that would then provide scholarships to students attending private schools, including religious schools).

53 *Hosanna-Tabor Evangelical Lutheran Church and School* v. EEOC, 565 US 171, 132 S. Ct. 694, 706 (2012).

54 Civil Rights Act of 1964 § 702(a), 42 USC § 2000e-1(a) (2012).

does not have to hire a Lutheran pastor to serve as its bishop, abbot, or school principal. A denominational Christian seminary can dismiss a dean or professor who converts to Islam. The marginal cases raise harder questions. Does the *ministerial* exception apply to nonclerical or nonordained employees of the religious organization, such as teachers, secretaries, groundskeepers, suppliers, or janitors? What if the religious line-drawing by the religious employer adversely affects a party who is part of an otherwise protected class under the Civil Rights Act? Do women, say, who are denied ordination or religious leadership positions because the church teaches male-only apostolic succession have a sex discrimination claim under the Civil Rights Act? How about African Americans who are excluded from attending predominantly white schools because of a biblical understanding that the races be separate? Or what of same-sex parties who are denied or removed from leadership, employment, or membership because a religious group teaches that homosexuality is sinful? More generally, is this special protection for religious autonomy over employment issues constitutional – let alone wise – given some of the recent financial and sexual scandals of religious organizations and their leaders?

The Supreme Court has provided only limited guidance to address these hard questions, although it has strongly affirmed the constitutionality of the ministerial exception. In *National Labor Relations Board* v. *Catholic Bishop* (1979), the Court held that the National Labor Relations Act (NLRA) did not grant the National Labor Relations Board (NLRB) power to certify unions for lay teachers in religious schools. Siding with the religious schools, and sidestepping the constitutional questions raised, the Court resolved this case statutorily, finding no "clear expression of Congress' intent to bring teachers in church-operated schools within the jurisdiction of the NLRB."[55]

In *Presiding Bishop* v. *Amos* (1987), the Court upheld Section 702 against an Establishment Clause challenge and further allowed its application to a nonclerical employee. Amos was a building engineer for a gymnasium open to the public and owned and operated by the local Latter-Day Saints Church. He was dismissed from his position because he was no longer a member in good standing of that church. He sued, claiming religious discrimination against him. The church defended its decision by invoking the ministerial exception. Amos argued that he was not a minister but an engineer, and thus the ministerial exception did not apply. Moreover, he argued, Section 702 violated the Establishment Clause because it unduly favored religious employers and employment over all others. Why should a public gym run by a church be able to religiously discriminate against an engineer when an identical public gym run by a local corporation cannot do so? The *Amos* Court held for the church, concluding that the Establishment Clause does not forbid Congress from allowing religious organizations to hire members only of their own faith for both secular and religious jobs. It was no establishment of religion for

[55] 440 US 490, 507 (1979).

Congress to give more protection to religious employers than might otherwise be required by the Constitution. Such "benevolent neutrality" is not an "unlawful fostering of religion."[56]

These early precedents led several lower courts to give ample deference to religious schools, colleges, and universities to set their own standards of admission, employment, and discipline. In *Hosanna-Tabor Evangelical Lutheran Church and School* v. *EEOC* (2012), the Court reinforced this deference by grounding the ministerial exception "in the Religion Clauses of the First Amendment." Hosanna-Tabor was a church that operated a small school for students in kindergarten through eighth grade. Cheryl Perich was a "called" teacher in the school. To be a called rather than a "lay" teacher, she had completed theological studies at a religious college, been endorsed by a local church district, passed an oral examination, and performed various spiritual functions in the school, including leading chapel and teaching Bible. In her fifth year of teaching, Perich became ill and took disability leave. The school filled her position with a lay teacher. Perich recovered and notified the school of her intent to return. The school did not want her back. At a congregational meeting, the church voted to release her from her called teacher status and pay a portion of her health insurance premiums in exchange for her resignation. Perich refused to resign. Instead, she produced a doctor's note saying she was healthy, and then showed up for work. School administrators refused to allow her back. Perich then threatened to sue. In response, the school board and congregation revoked her call and fired her on grounds of "insubordination and disruptive behavior" and breach of the church's commitment to internal dispute resolution. Perich filed a claim with the Equal Employment Opportunity Commission (EEOC), alleging that she had been wrongly terminated in violation of the nonretaliation provisions of the Americans with Disabilities Act.

In a unanimous opinion by Chief Justice Roberts, the Court held for Hosanna-Tabor. "The Establishment Clause prevents the Government from appointing ministers," Roberts wrote, "and the Free Exercise Clause prevents it from interfering with the freedom of religious groups to select their own." To force a church to "accept or retain an unwanted minister, or punish[] a church for failing to do so" would "interfere with the internal governance of the church." This would violate the Free Exercise Clause, "which protects a religious group's right to shape its faith and mission through its appointments." Further, it would violate the Establishment Clause by involving the government in "ecclesiastical decisions" over the polity, property, membership, and leadership of the church, all of which were forbidden to courts. The Court accepted Hosanna-Tabor's characterization of Perich as a called teacher who fit into the ministerial exception. The Court also refused to second-guess the church's stated religious reason for firing Perich – that she had violated its

[56] 483 US 327, 330, 334 (1987) (quoting *Walz*, 397 US at 669, and *Hobbie* v. *Unemployment Commission*, 480 US 136, 145 [1987]).

commitment to internal dispute resolution. Such "a pretext inquiry," Justice Alito wrote in concurrence, stood in tension with "principles of religious autonomy." Moreover, the church could exercise its autonomy both "for religious reasons" and for attendant secular reasons.[57]

The Court held similarly in its most recent case, *Our Lady of Guadalupe School* v. *Morrissey-Berru* (2020). This case involved two private Catholic schools under the Archbishopric of Los Angeles. Each school was committed to "religious instruction, worship, and personal modeling of the faith" and held its teachers to Catholic standards. Agnes Morrissey-Berru and Kristin Beil were both lay teachers on annual contracts. Both had some religious training and taught religion courses at their schools. They worshipped and prayed with their students each day, and they counseled and catechized them in the Catholic faith. Both were discharged for underperformance. Both sued. Morrissey-Berru claimed age discrimination because she had been replaced by a younger teacher. Biel claimed retaliatory firing because she had requested a leave of absence to undergo breast cancer treatment. The schools claimed they were protected in their decisions by the ministerial exception. The teachers countered that they were not ministers, they were lay people, with only modest religious training. They did not hold themselves out as ministers, and indeed could not be ministers since the Catholic Church ordained only males as ministers. The Supreme Court held for the schools, citing *Hosanna-Tabor* as dispositive. These two teachers performed even more "ministerial" functions in their schools than Cheryl Perich had performed at Hosanna-Tabor, the Court found. That left decisions about their employment status within the jurisdiction of the schools and diocese.[58]

Limits on Religious Autonomy. The right of religious schools and other religious organizations to engage in such religious line-drawing is not unlimited, however. *Bob Jones University* v. *United States* (1983) was an early case in point. This case involved a conservative Christian university that challenged the revocation of its federal tax-exempt status. Until 1971, the university completely excluded African Americans from its student body; from 1971 to 1975, it accepted married African American applicants only if they were married to another African American. This policy stemmed from the university's religious beliefs that interracial dating and marriage were unbiblical; in their view, God created separate races that must remain separate. In 1970, the Internal Revenue Service (IRS) concluded that it could no longer legally justify granting tax-exempt status to any private religious schools that practiced racial discrimination. The IRS notified Bob Jones University of its change in policy and its intent to remove the university's tax-exempt status unless the school changed its policies. When the university persisted in its racial line-drawing, the IRS removed its tax-exempt status – thus exposing the university to hefty new income-tax

57 565 US 171 (2012).
58 591 US __ (2020).

liability and shutting it off from tax-deductible donations. The university sued the IRS, arguing violations of the Free Exercise Clause.[59]

The Court held for the IRS. Chief Justice Burger made clear that tax exemption was a privilege, not a right, and that the IRS has the authority to revoke the university's tax-exempt status: "[A] declaration that a given institution is not 'charitable'" and therefore not tax-exempt can be made when there is "no doubt that the activity involved is contrary to a fundamental public policy." Given the long series of statutes and cases that have sought to remove the badges of slavery and the ravages of prejudice against Blacks in American history, "there can no longer be any doubt that racial discrimination in education violates deeply and widely accepted views of elementary justice."[60]

This old precedent has come back into conversation since the Supreme Court's case of *Obergefell* v. *Hodges* (2015)[61] declared the constitutional right to same-sex marriage, and the case of *Bostock* v. *Clayton County* (2020)[62] found that discrimination against gay or transgender workers constituted sex discrimination under Title VII of the Civil Rights Act. Some religious schools and seminaries are theologically opposed to same-sex or trans-sex persons, activities, and couples. The question is whether exclusion of those parties from admission, membership, employment, leadership, or other benefits at the religious school is a form of protected religious line-drawing or unprotected discrimination on the basis of sex. Even if viewed as protected religious discrimination, could a local, state, or even national government revoke a school's tax-exempt status or other government benefits or funding as a result – à la *Bob Jones University* or *Christian Legal Society* v. *Martinez*? These issues are now being tested in legislatures and courts. We will take up some of these questions in the next chapter on tax exemption of religious property.

SUMMARY AND CONCLUSIONS

America operates with a basic three-tiered system of education: (1) public elementary schools, high schools and state universities and other institutions of higher learning; (2) private (religious) lower schools, colleges, and universities; and (3) various forms of home schools. Cutting across these three tiers, a few states and cities have experimented with charter schools, magnet schools, and community schools that combine public and private funding and staffing to offer innovative forms of lower education. Some states offer vouchers and tax relief to enhance educational choice for parents and students in primary and secondary schools. Federal and state scholarship and loan programs are available to public and private university

59 461 US 574 (1983).
60 461 US at 592, 595–96, 604.
61 576 US 644 (2015).
62 590 US __ (2020); 140 S. Ct. 1731 (2020).

students.[63] But the three-tiered structure of American education has been largely stable for the past two generations. The vast majority of government funds for education go to public schools and universities, and the vast majority of American students attend these public schools, even though students in private lower schools and some home schools do demonstrably better on various measures of academic performance and social well-being.

Before the twentieth century, individual states largely governed American schooling, taking a wide range of approaches to the place of religion in public schools and the role of government in religious schools. Since 1925, however, the US Supreme Court has been actively involved in shaping American education, devoting nearly a third of its First Amendment religious freedom cases to issues of religion and education. These cases have not always followed clean logical lines, and the Court has sometimes digressed and occasionally reversed itself. But the Court gradually settled on several constitutional principles. While government has the power to mandate basic education for all children, parents have the right to choose public, private, or homeschool education for their minor children, and government may now facilitate that choice through vouchers and tax relief for private-school students. While the First Amendment forbids most forms of religion in public schools, it protects most forms of religion in private schools. While the First Amendment forbids government from funding the core religious activities of private schools, it permits delivery of general governmental services, subsidies, scholarships, and tax breaks to public and private schools, teachers, and students alike. While the First Amendment forbids public-school teachers and outsiders from offering religious instruction and expression in public-school classes and at formal school functions, it permits public-school students to engage in private religious expression and protects these students from coerced religious activities. The amendment further requires that religious parties have equal access to public facilities, forums, and funds that are open to their nonreligious peers.

Two decades ago, the Supreme Court seemed content with this constitutional arrangement, and ready to leave many questions of religious freedom and education to statutes and the states, reflecting the Court's ample appetite at the time for separation of powers and federalism. Federal statutes, such as Section 702 of the Civil Rights Act, the Equal Access Act, the Religious Freedom Restoration Act, and many others, were thought to provide ample protection of religious freedom, including in the education field. With softened standards of review under both the First Amendment Free Exercise and Establishment Clauses, state and local governments were able to engage in greater local experimentation in their schools,

63 See overview of current options in Stephen D. Sugarman, "Is It Unconstitutional to Prohibit Faith-Based Schools from Becoming Charter Schools," *Journal of Law and Religion* 32 (2017), 227–62. For caveats, see Benjamin S. Hillman, "Is There a Place for Religious Charter Schools?," *Yale Law Journal* 118 (2008), 554; Martha Minow, "Confronting the Seduction of Choice: Law, Education and American Pluralism," *Yale Law Journal* 120 (2011), 814.

following the logic of federalism. Many states, however, building on nineteenth-century state constitutional restrictions on religious funding and twenty-first-century attacks on religious freedom, began to provide far less protection for religious freedom, particularly when religious interests were juxtaposed to other fundamental rights.

In response, the Supreme Court of late has again weighed in heavily in favor of religious freedom, including in the area of education. The Court has issued fourteen major cases on religious freedom from 2010 to 2020, including five major cases protecting religious parties in education: *Winn*, *Hosanna-Tabor*, *Trinity Lutheran*, *Espinoza*, and *Our Lady of Guadalupe*. These cases have strengthened free exercise, free speech, and statutory protections of religion in education, and have relaxed traditional limits on government actions and funding for religious schools, parents, and students. Public schools now provide more protections for voluntary religious expression by students than they once did. Religious schools and students have more government access and support than they once did. And religious-school authorities have been newly confirmed in their autonomy to govern their own members and leaders.

7

Tax Exemption of Religious Property

Historical Anomaly or Valid Constitutional Practice?

The cases concerning religious freedom and education that we saw in the last chapter illustrate one complex set of issues under the First Amendment guarantees of religious freedom. These issues have inspired a century-long run of seventy-four US Supreme Court cases – and counting. By comparison, tax exemption of religious property seems like a rather prosaic topic, featuring only one Supreme Court case. What it might lack in political intrigue, however, this nitty-gritty issue makes up for in raising some of the hardest questions to confront the American experiment in religious liberty from colonial days until today.[1]

First, tax exemptions for religious properties highlight the tensions between modern American federal and state laws. Property registration, taxation, and exemption have been, since the beginning of the republic, the exclusive prerogative of the fifty individual states (save in times of war or emergency).[2] By 1940, every state had detailed statutes, and thirty-three states had constitutional guarantees of tax

[1] This chapter builds on and updates my early article: John Witte, Jr., "Tax Exemption of Church Property: Historical Anomaly or Valid Constitutional Practice?" *Southern California Law Review* 64 (1991), 363–415. The revision and update in this chapter owe much to the searching analysis of Edward M. Gaffney, Jr., "Exemption of Religious Organizations from State and Local Taxation," in James Serritella, et al., eds. *Religious Organizations and the State: A Study of Identity, Liberty, and Law* (Durham, NC: Carolina Academic Press, 2006), 459–514. For recent comprehensive updates on the law of religious property exemption, see William Bassett, W. Cole Durham, and Robert Smith, *Religious Organizations and the Law* (St. Paul, MN: West Group, 2016–20), chap. 33 (§§ 33.1–27); Edward Zelinsky, *Taxing the Church: Religion, Exemptions, Entanglement and the Constitution* (Oxford: Oxford University Press, 2017), esp. 25–43; Richard R. Hammar, 2019 *Church and Clergy Tax Guide* (Carol Stream, IL: Christianity Today, 2019). See also the earlier authoritative article of Arvo van Alstyne, "Tax Exemption of Church Property," *Ohio State Law Review* 20 (1959), 461–507 and Carl Zollman, "Tax Exemptions of American Church Property," *Michigan Law Review* 14 (1915–16), 37–47, 646–57.

[2] George Benson et al., *The American Property Tax: Its History, Administration, and Economic Impact* (Claremont, CA: Claremont Colleges' Printing Service, 1965), 11–12. This is not the case with income taxation, which the Sixteenth Amendment empowers Congress to collect. The Court has addressed five religious-liberty cases challenging federal income taxation, all wins for the federal government. See *United States* v. *American Friends*, 419 US 7 (1974) (upholding taxation of conscientious objectors to military taxes); *United States* v. *Lee*, 455 US 252 (1982) (denying free-exercise exemption from social-security taxes for Amish); *Bob Jones University* v. *United States*, 461 US 574 (1983) (upholding the Internal Revenue Service's decision to remove tax-exempt status of religious university engaged in

exemption for religious properties – sometimes after hard-fought state battles, as we saw illustrated in the Massachusetts story in Chapter 4. These state constitutional provisions on tax exemption ranged widely. Some states restricted tax exemptions only to actual worship centers that were regularly used and owned by properly incorporated religious bodies – conditions that, in practice, made it difficult for Catholics, Jews, and new religious faiths to acquire exemptions. Other states granted exemptions to all religious properties, regardless of their use, ownership, or size, and in practice granted exemptions to any religious group that applied for them in good faith. Most states fell between these extremes, the exact parameters of each state's law often the product of decades of intense local lobbying, legislation, and litigation.

In the 1940s, when *Cantwell* and *Everson* first applied the First Amendment religion clauses to the states, the federal courts became an attractive new forum for these disputes, and the First Amendment an attractive new norm to adduce. Groups that were denied tax exemptions for their religious properties filed actions claiming that the state violated their free-exercise rights. Parties opposed to such exemptions filed actions claiming that such state laws constituted an establishment of religion. Scores of such cases were filed in state and federal courts in the 1940s and later. Three cases were appealed unsuccessfully to the Supreme Court in the 1950s and 1960s.[3] How could or should the Court craft a general constitutional law on these diverse and divisive local issues? Were they subject to the same general rules that the Court and Congress had developed for federal income-tax exemptions, or did federalism commend other rules?

Second, questions of tax exemption highlight the tension that has emerged between the religion clauses of the First Amendment under some lines of judicial interpretation. The Establishment Clause forbids government from imparting special benefits to religious groups. The Free Exercise Clause forbids government from imposing special burdens on religious groups. Neither the exemption nor the taxation of religious property appears to satisfy the principles of both clauses. To exempt religious property, while taxing that of nonreligious groups, appears to violate the "no special benefit" mandate of the Establishment Clause. To tax religious property, while exempting that of other nonprofit groups, appears to violate the "no special burden" mandate of the Free Exercise Clause. The controversy thus seems to fall between the First Amendment religion clauses.[4]

racial discrimination); *Hernandez* v. *Commissioner of Internal Revenue*, 490 US 680 (1989) (upholding denial of charitable deduction for contribution in return for religious services); *Davis* v. *United States*, 495 US 472 (1990) (same). See also *Gibbons* v. *District of Columbia*, 116 US 404 (1886) (upholding Congress's property tax on vacant property in Washington, DC, owned by church).

3 See *Lundberg* v. *County of Alameda*, 46 Cal. 2d 644 (1956), app. dism. sub nom. *Heisey* v. *Alameda County*, 352 US 921 (1956); *General Finance Corp.* v. *Archetto*, 93 RI 392 (1961), app. dism. 369 US 423 (1962); *Murray* v. *Comptroller of the Treasury*, 241 Md. 383 (1966), cert. den. 385 US 816 (1966).

4 Gaffney, "Exemption of Religious Organizations," 469–501. Boris Bittker, "Churches, Taxes, and the Constitution," *Yale Law Journal* 78 (1969), 1285–310, updated in Boris Bittker, Scott Idleman, and Frank Ravitch, *Religion and State in American Law* (Cambridge: Cambridge University Press, 2015), 414–50; Erika Lietzan, "Tax Exemptions and the Establishment Clause," *Syracuse Law Review* 49 (1999), 971–1071.

Third, tax exemption of religious property raises squarely the question that the founders left largely open – how to define religion at law. Under most state laws, religious tax exemptions are given to *religious* properties, to properties devoted to *religious* uses, and/or owned by *religious* parties. Proof of religion is thus unavoidable under such provisions.[5] Historically, the issue was considered largely a matter of common sense and local consensus; few definitions of religion were offered in statutes, let alone in state constitutions. In historical practice, the question was whether to set the legal line of religion at Protestantism, Christianity, or theism, and that question was initially resolved almost county by county, commissioner by commissioner, when it came to property tax exemptions. The exponential rise of new or newly prominent religious groups in recent decades, however, has tested the edges, and efficacy, of these traditional religion-based tax exemptions. How is the law to decide on the tax-exempt status of the properties of Scientologists, Wiccans, the Unification Church, ethical clubs, faith families, communitarian religions, personality cults, nontheistic faiths, and any number of the thousand-plus religious groups in America today – together with their parsonages, monasteries, schools, charities, mission stations, retreat centers, youth camps, recreation centers, publishing houses, restaurants, retirement homes, and the like, especially if they are all gathered on one campus. If all such new groups receive tax exemptions for all their properties, does this not place an increasingly disproportionate burden on the remaining nonreligious properties? If all such new groups are denied tax exemption for their properties, does this not unduly favor those traditional religions that receive tax exemptions?[6]

Finally, tax exemption of religious property illustrates broader questions of the propriety of religious exemptions altogether. As we saw in Chapter 5, modern critics now regularly challenge religiously based exemptions from general obligations and neutral laws as unnecessary, unfair, even dangerous in our increasingly postreligious or secular age. Why should religious parties and groups be excused from compliance with general laws and commandments that everyone else must abide? Isn't that a form of religious favoritism contrary to the Establishment Clause? Why, especially, should churches and other religious groups enjoy exemptions when they impose discriminatory harm on third parties – like the Black students in *Bob Jones University*, or the gay couple in *Masterpiece Cakeshop*, or the disabled teachers in *Hosanna-Tabor* and *Our Lady of Guadalupe School*?[7] Couldn't – indeed, shouldn't – these organizations at

[5] For definitions of religion in state property tax cases, see Witte, "Tax Exemption," 401–08; in federal income-tax law, see Grant M. Newman, "The Taxation of Religious Organizations in America," *Harvard Journal of Law and Public Policy* 42 (2019), 681–710; Terry L. Slye, "Rendering unto Caesar: Defining 'Religion' for Purposes of Administering Religion-Based Exemptions," *Harvard Journal of Law and Public Policy* 6 (1983), 219–94.

[6] Zelinsky, *Taxing the Church*; Symposium, "Whether Tax Exemptions for Religious Organizations Violate the First Amendment," *Cumberland Law Review* 22 (1991), 467–680.

[7] See discussion of these cases in Chapter 6. See detailed sources and discussion in Samuel D. Brunson and David J. Herzig, "A Diachronic Approach to Bob Jones: Religious Tax Exemption After Obergefell," *Indiana Law Review* 92 (2017), 1175–219, updated in Samuel D. Brunson, *God and the*

least have all their tax exemptions limited or canceled as a consequence?[8] More to point, don't religious property tax exemptions create pervasive and material harm for all their neighbors, whose property taxes go up to compensate for the lost tax revenue from the tax-exempt property? Thomas Jefferson said famously, "it neither picks my pocket nor breaks my leg . . . for my neighbor to say there are twenty gods, or no god."[9] But religious tax exemptions do "pick my pocket," critics argue, if my property taxes go up because of my neighbor's religious choices, or my property value goes down because of the extra noise, traffic, parking problems, and more that a bustling congregation inflicts on my neighborhood.[10]

The US Supreme Court has only once addressed the constitutionality of state tax exemptions for religious property.[11] In *Walz* v. *Tax Commission* (1970), the Court charted a "course between the two Religion Clauses" and upheld a New York law, typical of laws in other states, that exempts "real or personal property used exclusively for religious, educational or charitable purposes as defined by law and owned by any [nonprofit] corporation or association organized or conducted exclusively for one or more of such purposes." In an 8–1 opinion by Chief Justice Burger, the Court upheld the New York law with arguments from neutrality, separationism, and history.[12]

First, the Court declared, such exemptions are accorded in a "neutral manner" not only to religious groups but also to a broad class of charitable, educational, social service, and other nonprofit groups. The exemption affords these groups only "indirect" support, not a direct subsidy.[13] Such neutrally allocated, indirect support neither establishes religious groups nor "converts" them "into arms of the state."

Second, the Court declared, such exemptions foster the separation of church and state. Taxation, by contrast, would "tend to expand" government involvement in church matters through tax valuations and assessments of, and government liens and

IRS: Accommodating Religious Practice in United States Tax Law (Cambridge: Cambridge University Press, 2018).

8 See, e.g., Johnny Rex Buckles, "The Sexual Integrity of Religious Schools and Tax Exemption," *Harvard Journal of Law and Public Policy* 40 (2017), 255–319.

9 Thomas Jefferson, "Notes on the State of Virginia," in Saul K. Padover, ed. *The Complete Jefferson*, repr. ed. (New York: Books for Libraries Press, 1969), 673–76.

10 See, for example, Paul Matzko, "The Hidden Costs of Tax Exemption," *Christianity Today* (Jan. 6, 2020).

11 In *Camps Newfound/Owatonna* v. *Town of Harrison*, 117 S. Ct. 1590 (1997), the Court addressed religious property exemptions under the Commerce Clause of Article I. A camp operated for children of the Christian Science faith was denied a state property tax exemption because the camp served primarily nonresidents of Maine. The Court struck down the law, and its application to this camp, as an unconstitutional violation of the dormant Commerce Clause – an "unjustified discrimination" against interstate commerce.

12 397 US 664 (1970).

13 In *Walz*, 397 US at 675, the Court wrote: "The grant of a tax exemption is not sponsorship since the government does not transfer part of its revenue to churches but simply abstains from demanding that the church support the state." But in *Regan* v. *Taxation with Representation*, 461 US 540, 544 (1983), the Court wrote: "A tax exemption has much the same effect as a cash grant to the organization of the amount it would have to pay on its income."

foreclosures on, religious property. The creation of such new channels of cooperation and confrontation would cause too "excessive [an] entanglement" between church and state to be countenanced by the no-establishment clause.

Third, the Court declared, tax exemptions of religious property are the product of an "unbroken" history that "covers our entire national existence and indeed predates it." Such exemptions were customarily accorded by the colonists. They have been sanctioned by Congress and state legislatures for more than two centuries. They have not "led to" an established religion but have "operated affirmatively to help guarantee the free exercise of all forms of religious belief." To disinter a practice so "deeply embedded" in our culture and so widely accepted by "common consent" requires a more compelling case. From these arguments, the Court concluded that tax exemptions of religious property, while neither prohibited by the Establishment Clause nor required by the Free Exercise Clause, are, nonetheless, constitutionally permissible.[14]

The Court has repeated this *Walz* rationale in several subsequent cases involving income- and sales-tax exemptions, generally leaving such questions to legislative judgment rather than constitutional decision-making.[15] Religious tax exemptions of any sort are neither required by the Free Exercise Clause nor prohibited by the Establishment Clause. "The collection and payment of [a] generally applicable tax," the Court declared in 1990, "imposes no constitutionally significant burden on [an organization's] religious practices and beliefs. The Free Exercise Clause accordingly does not require the State to grant appellant an exemption from its generally applicable ... tax."[16] But if a legislature does choose to exempt a religious property or organization, it must follow the *Walz* course of "benevolent neutrality" to survive Establishment Clause scrutiny. As Justice William Brennan put it for the Court in 1989:

> Every tax exemption constitutes a subsidy that affects non-qualifying tax payers, forcing them to become "indirect and vicarious donors." Insofar as that subsidy is conferred upon a wide array of nonsectarian groups as well as religious organizations in pursuit of some legitimate secular end, the fact that religious groups benefit incidentally does not deprive the subsidy of the secular purpose and primary effect mandated by the Establishment Clause.[17]

14 397 US at 674–80 (1970), addressing New York State Constitution (1938), art. 16.1 and New York Real Property Tax Law, sec. 420.1

15 See John W. Whitehead, "Tax Exemption for Religious Organizations: A Historical and Constitutional Analysis," *Cumberland Law Review* 22 (1991), 521–76, 545 ff.; Newman, "The Taxation of Religious Organizations," 681–710.

16 See *Jimmy Swaggart Ministries* v. *Board of Equalization of California*, 493 US 378, 392 (1990). The Court confirmed, narrowly, its earlier cases prohibiting flat taxes for licenses that are a prior restraint on the exercise of religion – "the imposing of a condition on the exercise of constitutionally-protected conduct." Ibid., 385–89.

17 *Texas Monthly, Inc.* v. *Bullock*, 489 US 1, 14–15 (1989) (citations omitted). For careful analysis of these cases and the relationship to the reasoning of the *Walz* case, see Gaffney, "Exemption of Religious Organizations," 469–97.

The result in *Walz* was probably inevitable: what Court would want to outlaw a twenty-five-hundred-year tax exemption tradition affecting millions of acres of religious property in response to one disgruntled state taxpayer who objected? But the *Walz* Court's arguments were not ineluctable. The Court's first argument from neutrality does not address the question whether an exemption given for a *religious* use of property is constitutionally permissible. The Court argues that because the state exempts properties devoted to charitable, educational, and other welfare uses, it is constitutionally permissible also to exempt property devoted to religious uses. The Constitution, however, permits government establishments of charity, education, and social welfare. It uniquely forbids government establishments of religion. That exemptions are accorded in a neutral manner for various nonreligious uses of property, therefore, has little bearing on the question of the constitutionality of exemptions for religious uses of property.

The Court's separationism argument is contrived. The Court divines a list of interactions between church and state that taxation of religious property may occasion – tax valuations, foreclosures, and others. But one can devise a list of interactions that tax exemption does occasion – reapplications for exemption, reviews of past uses, reports on present uses, and others. The Court argues that such interactions will result in an unconstitutional "entanglement" between church and state. But the constitutionality of more intrusive and immediate interactions has been consistently upheld against Establishment Clause challenges, when, for example, religious properties are zoned, religious buildings are landmarked, religious societies are incorporated, religious employers are audited, religious broadcasters and publishers are regulated, religious workplaces are inspected, religious labor practices are scrutinized, intrachurch disputes are adjudicated, and many other instances.[18] The expansion of the forms and functions of the modern state have made such interactions between the state and religious institutions both inevitable and necessary. The incidental and isolated interaction that would result from the taxation of religious property is modest by comparison.

The Court's historical argument depends too heavily upon selective presentation of evidence. The Court asserts that tax exemptions of religious property have been adopted by "common consent" for more than two centuries. But a strong vein of criticism has long accompanied the practice in America. The Court asserts that such exemptions have not "led to" an establishment of religion – that sense of the term "respecting" in the First Amendment call for "no law *respecting* an establishment of religion." Tax exemptions are not "the nose of the camel under the tent," the "first

[18] See John Witte, Jr. and Joel A. Nichols, *Religion and the American Constitutional Experiment*, 4th ed. (Oxford: Oxford University Press, 2016), 222–48; Carl Esbeck, *The Regulation of Religious Organizations as Recipients of Governmental Assistance* (Washington, DC: Center for Public Justice, 1996); *Religious Organizations*, passim. See also *Swaggart Ministries*, 493 US at 395–96, where, in upholding the collection of sale and use taxes in arrears from a religious ministry, the Court said: "The sorts of government entanglement that we have found to violate the Establishment Clause have been far more invasive than the level of contact created by the administration of neutral tax laws."

step on the slippery slope" of establishment as the Court put it.[19] But the real question is whether these exemptions are too "respectful," "reflective," or "redolent" of traditional religious establishments – that sense of the word "respecting" in the First Amendment.[20] After all, from biblical and Greco-Roman times forward, tax exemptions were counted among the privileges of state-established religion, while dissenting religions were taxed, in part to support the established religion. The issue is whether such exemptions have now shed the chrysalis of these earlier establishment policies. The Court adduces numerous examples of earlier tax laws that exempted religious property. But it ignores the variety of *theories* that supported these laws. The Court asserts that such property tax exemption laws "historically reflect the concern of [their] authors" to avoid the "dangers of hostility to religion inherent in the imposition of property taxes." But little evidence from state constitutional and legislative debates on tax exemption supports this assertion.

This chapter traces briefly the history and the current theory and law of religious property tax exemptions in the United States, and reconsiders the constitutionality of such exemptions in light of recent First Amendment opinions and commentaries. I conclude that tax exemptions of religious properties are still constitutionally valid, although I add several other constitutional and cultural arguments for them beyond those offered by *Walz*, and conclude with a word of caution to religious property holders.

TAX EXEMPTION OF RELIGIOUS PROPERTY IN THE PAST

Tax exemption of religious property is an ancient privilege. It has roots in ancient Babylon, Persia, Egypt, and Israel, and has been a perennial feature of the Greek, Roman, and Christian traditions of the West.[21] To be sure, the Western legal tradition has long instructed religious believers to pay their taxes. This was based in part on biblical texts. Jesus answered the provocative question, "Is it lawful to pay taxes to Caesar, or not?" with his famous instruction: "Render . . . to Caesar the things that are Caesar's, and to God the things that are God's."[22] Saint Paul instructed the Christians in Rome to be "subject to the governing authorities . . . not only to avoid God's wrath but also for the sake of conscience. For the same reason you also pay taxes, for the authorities are ministers of God, attending to this very thing. Pay all of them their dues, taxes to whom taxes are due, revenue to whom revenue is due, respect to whom respect is due, honor to whom honor is

19 *Walz*, 397 US at 675.

20 See Chapter 5 on the various possible meanings of "Congress shall make no law *respecting* an establishment of religion."

21 See Philip Adler, *Historical Origin of Tax Exemption of Charitable Property* (Westchester, NY: Westchester County Chamber of Commerce, 1922); Eugen Mack, *Die kirchliche Steuerfreiheit in Deutschland seit der Dekretalengesetzgebung*, repr. ed. (Aalen: Scientia Verlag, 1965); Dean M. Kelley, *Why Churches Should Not Pay Taxes* (New York: Harper & Row, 1977).

22 Matthew 22:17, 21.

due."[23] None of these general obligations to pay taxes, however, fell on religious properties or personnel. The Bible explicitly exempted them. The anchor text is Ezra 7:24, which has echoed loudly over the centuries: "you have no authority to impose taxes, tribute or duty on any of the priests, Levites, musicians, gatekeepers, temple servants or other workers at this house of God."[24]

Modern American laws of tax exemption of religious property are rooted in two more recent traditions: (1) a *common law* tradition, which accorded such exemptions to established churches that discharged certain state burdens; and (2) an *equity law* tradition, which accorded such exemptions to all churches that dispensed certain social benefits.[25] These two traditions have contributed to the widespread development of colonial and then state laws that exempt religious property from taxation. These two traditions were ultimately combined in later nineteenth- and twentieth-century state constitutional and statutory guarantees of tax exemption of religious property that remain in place in most states today. There are, however, strong tensions between these two traditions as well, which manifest themselves in both historical and contemporary property tax exemption laws.

Common Law Sources. The English common law that prevailed in most American colonies treated religion as an affair of law and the established church as an agency of the state. In the course of the sixteenth-century English Reformation, the Tudor monarchs had consolidated their authority over religion and the church and subjected them to comprehensive ecclesiastical laws enforceable by both state and church courts. Many of these laws were adopted or emulated in the American colonies and young states. Tax exemption of religious property was part of this broader set of ecclesiastical laws.[26]

The common law prescribed orthodox doctrine, liturgy, and morality and proscribed various forms of heresy, dissent, and nonconformity. Communicant status in the established church was a condition for citizenship status in the commonwealth. Religious dissenters, if tolerated, were foreclosed from most political and ecclesiastical offices and various social and economic opportunities.

[23] Romans 13:1, 5–7.

[24] Ezra 7:24 (NIV). See also Genesis 47:26 and discussion of these and other texts in Geoffrey Parsons Miller, "Taxation," in Brent A. Strawn, ed., *The Oxford Encyclopedia of the Bible and Law*, 2 vols. (Oxford: Oxford University Press, 2105), 2:356–60.

[25] Witte, "Tax Exemption," 368–80 and updated in Nina J. Crimm and Laurence H. Winer, *Politics, Taxes, and the Pulpit: Provocative First Amendment Conflicts* (Oxford: Oxford University Press, 2010), 72–91. I am using the term "common law" not as an antonym for "statute" but as a generic term to describe the English and the colonial and American customs and statutes enforced by various common law courts. I am using the term "equity" not as a synonym for fairness and justice but as a generic term to describe the English and endemic customs and statutes enforced by equity or chancery courts.

[26] For a comprehensive treatment of post-Reformation ecclesiastical law in England and a convenient collection of relevant ecclesiastical statutes, see Richard Burn, *Ecclesiastical Law*, 6th ed., 4 vols. (London: S. Sweet, 1797); John Godolphin, *Repertorium canonicum, or, An Abridgement of the Ecclesiastical Laws of This Realm, Consistent with the Temporal*, 3rd ed. (London: S. Roycroft, 1687). For detailed primary sources, see Witte, "Tax Exemption," nn. 28–44.

The common law governed the form and function of the established church polity. It delineated the boundaries of the parishes and the location of the churches. It determined the procedures of the vestries and the prerogatives of the consistories. It defined the duties of the clerics and the amount of their compensation. It dictated the form of the church corporation and the disposition of its endowments.

The common law regulated the acquisition and maintenance of the established church's properties. Magistrates were authorized to purchase, seize, or condemn private properties within their domains and to convey them to the established church for meetinghouses, parsonages, cemeteries, and glebes. Stern criminal laws sanctioned interference with the enjoyment of these properties. Special property laws prohibited parties from gaining prescriptive or security interests in them. Magistrates levied taxes for the maintenance of the property and the clergy of the established church – the "tithe rates" to meet general ecclesiastical expenses, the "church rates" to pay for the repair or improvement of existing properties, and a host of minor fees like "window taxes" or "pew rents." These religious taxes, though paid to the established church alone, were often levied on all taxable persons in the commonwealth, regardless of their church affiliation.

The common law also governed the taxation of church and other religious properties. In both England and the colonies, the common law afforded no automatic and unrestricted tax exemption to church properties. All property that lay within the jurisdiction of the Crown and its colonial delegates, including religious property, was considered presumptively taxable at common law, unless it had been specially and specifically exempted by statute. Colonial legislatures readily accorded such exemptions to the properties of political officials and to those of immigrants, indigents, and incapacitated persons.

Three restrictions, however, limited the availability of tax exemptions to colonial church properties. First, only certain types of religious property were considered exemptible at common law. The properties of properly incorporated established churches that were devoted to the appropriate "religious uses" prescribed by ecclesiastical law, such as sanctuaries, chapels, parsonages, glebes, and consecrated cemeteries, were generally exemptible. Established church properties, however, that lay vacant, that were devoted to nonreligious uses, or that were held by unincorporated religious bodies were generally taxable. Properties of dissenting religious groups were usually taxed, regardless of their use. Properties held personally by ministers were taxed in some colonies but exempted in others, with exemptions becoming more popular in the later colonial period, when colonies also exempted the properties held personally by political magistrates.

Second, these established church properties were given general exemptions only from the religious taxes that were levied for their own maintenance and use. To impose such taxes on established church properties would have been but "an idle ceremony."[27] Other property taxes, however – the quit-rents, poll taxes, land taxes, special assessments, hearth taxes, window taxes, and other occasional rates on realty and personalty – often fell on the properties of the established church as much as on all other properties. A universal exemption for these established church properties from all property taxes was the exception, not the rule, in the colonies.

Third, these tax exemptions could be held in abeyance in times of emergency or abandoned altogether if the tax liability imposed on remaining properties in the community proved too onerous. Thus, in times of war, pestilence, poverty, or disaster, established churches and their clergy were expected to contribute to the public coffers regardless of their eligibility for exemption.

This common law pattern of tax exemptions and subsidies could be readily rationalized when the state was responsible to propagate and protect one established religion, to the deprecation or exclusion of all others. Established church corporations were effectively state agencies, their clergy effectively state officials in charge of the state's religious matters. By devoting their properties to the religious uses prescribed by the common law, church corporations and their clergy were discharging the state's responsibility for the established religion. In return, they received tax support, tax exemptions, and other protections and privileges, like other state agencies. Occasionally the clergy themselves also received such privileges, like other state officials. Indeed, the established church parsonage and the local political leader's house sometimes stood side by side in the town square, each exempt from state taxation and supported by state taxes collected from all others.

These privileges could be accorded, however, only if and to the extent that churches adhered to the established religion and devoted their properties to prescribed religious uses. Thus, the properties of dissenting or wayward churches and properties devoted to nonreligious uses were taxable. Privileges also could be accorded only in modest proportion, lest the established church grow ostentatious and opulent at the expense of the state and society, as it had prior to the Reformation. Thus the common law limited closely the scope of exemptions once granted.

Equity Law Sources. The law of equity, applied by English chancery courts and their colonial and early American state analogues, accorded tax exemptions to church properties with a different rationale.[28] Consistent with the common law courts, equity courts treated all religious property as presumptively taxable unless specially exempted by statute. Contrary to the common law courts, however, equity courts exempted church properties from taxation not because of the "religious uses" but because of the "charitable uses" to which they were devoted. Church properties could be exempted at equity only if, and to the extent that, they were used "charitably."

27 Carl F. Zollman, *American Church Law*, repr. ed. (St. Paul, MN: West, 1933), 239.

28 See detailed sources in Witte, "Tax Exemption," 375–80.

A definition of charity was derived from the famous English Statute of Charitable Uses of 1601. The statute regarded as charitable all activities that supported orphans, apprentices, or scholars, that sustained public works (like highways, prisons, and bridges), that subsidized schools and universities, or that succored indigent, ill, incapacitated, elderly, or "decayed" persons.[29] Through interpretation and application of the statute over time, equity courts developed a more general definition of charity as any activity that redounded "to the benefit of an indefinite number of persons, either by bringing their hearts or minds under the influence of education or religion, by relieving their bodies from disease, suffering, or constraint, by assisting them to establish themselves in life, by erecting or maintaining public buildings or works, or by otherwise lessening the burdens of government."[30]

The *effect*, not the intent, of the activity was critical to determining its charitable character. The charitable activity could be motivated by piety or pity; it could be meant to serve religious or secular persons and causes – so long as it yielded a distinctly "public benefit" to a sufficiently "indefinite number of persons." Religion and piety were considered an acceptable species, not a necessary source, of charity and benevolence.

Institutions that devoted their properties to one or more such charitable uses or that had property entrusted to them for such charitable uses received a variety of equitable privileges. Special trust and testamentary doctrines, like the *cy pres* doctrine, which allowed courts to follow the donor's intention so much as possible, enabled them to receive property by deeds and wills that were defective in form and generally unenforceable at common law. Special property rules enabled them to transfer goods and lands to beneficiaries, free from liens, fees, and excises. Special procedural rules allowed them to bring actions that were otherwise barred by the statute of limitations. Special tax rules afforded them both tax subsidies and tax exemptions. They received subsidies from the "poor rates," "education rates," and "charity taxes" that the authorities occasionally levied on the community. They received exemptions from taxes on those portions of their property that were "devoted to charitable uses and other public concernments."[31]

Both the amount of the subsidy and the scope of the exemption received by these charitable institutions were calculated case by case. Overseers, visitors, or commissioners, regulated by the equity courts, periodically visited each charitable institution to assess its performance and to determine its needs. Afterward, they recommended to the equity court each charity's entitlement to subsidy and exemption. It was not unusual for the equity court to afford well-established and well-endowed charities only modest subsidies and minimal exemptions in a given year

[29] 43 Eliz. I. c. 4, repealed in 51 and 52 Vict. c. 42, 13.

[30] *Jackson* v. *Phillips*, 14 Allen (Mass.) 539, 556 (1867).

[31] J. Trumbull and C. Hoadly, eds., *The Public Records of the Colony of Connecticut, 1636–1776* (Hartford, CT: Lockwood & Brainard Company, 1890), 3:158.

but to afford new and impoverished charities plentiful subsidies and plenary exemptions from tax.

This law of equity provided churches with a second basis for receiving tax exemptions for their properties and tax subsidies for their activities. As religious institutions, they could receive the religious tax exemptions and subsidies afforded by the common law. As charitable institutions, they could receive the charitable tax exemptions and subsidies afforded by equity law. Although the exemptions and subsidies afforded by the common law were restricted by definition to established churches, those afforded by equity were available, at least in theory, to all churches.

Established churches in the colonies and early states often served as charitable institutions. Church meetinghouses and chapels were used not only to conduct religious services but also to host town assemblies, political rallies, and public auctions, to hold educational and vocational classes, to maintain census rolls and marriage certificates, to house the community library, and to discharge a number of other public functions. Parsonages were used not only to house the minister's family but also to harbor orphans and widows, the sick and the handicapped, and victims of abuse and disaster. Glebes were farmed not only to sustain the priest and his family but also to support widows, sojourners, and needy members of the community. Moreover, charitable and missionary societies sponsored by the established churches helped to found schools, orphanages, sick houses, and almshouses throughout the colonies and young states. These acts of public charity were vital parts of the established church's ministry and mission in the colonies. In return, the established churches and the charitable institutions that they founded were entitled to receive charitable tax exemptions and subsidies from the equity courts.

Established churches, however, held no monopoly on charitable activity. Many nonestablished churches and private philanthropic groups under their sponsorship were equally active. Dissenting churches often used their meetinghouses and parsonages for night shelters, relief stations, sanctuaries, and places of refuge. Quakers and Catholics were famous in the seventeenth through nineteenth centuries for their diligence in running schools, hospitals, hospices, almshouses, orphanages, poor farms, and workhouses all along the Atlantic seaboard. American Methodists, Scottish Presbyterians, and Irish Catholics formed philanthropic groups to sponsor and subsidize the families of new immigrants and newly emancipated indentured servants. Various religious groups contributed to the founding and later support of some of the great eastern universities and colleges, such as Harvard, William and Mary, Yale, Princeton, Dartmouth, and others, as well as many private lower schools. In return, these nonconformist churches, and the charitable organizations that they established, received tax exemptions and subsidies from the equity courts.

These were the twin legal traditions of religious property tax exemptions. Equity courts accorded tax exemptions to any religious properties that were devoted to charitable uses. Common law courts accorded tax exemptions only to established church properties that were devoted to prescribed religious uses. In some later colonies and early states, the sharp contrasts between these two traditions had begun to soften, particularly as traditional religious establishments gradually gave way and dissenting churches began to gain the right to exemption from religious taxes levied for the established church. But these two English legal systems of common law and equity law were the foundational pillars of the American system of tax exemption.

EARLY STATE CONSTITUTIONAL CHALLENGES

The inherited English and colonial law of tax exemption of religious property continued largely uninterrupted in many of the early American states. A number of the early state constitutions provided simply that "all the laws which have heretofore been adopted, used, and approved . . . and usually practised in the courts of law shall still remain and be in full force, until altered or repealed by the legislature."[32] State legislatures and judiciaries were specifically instructed that "all religious bodies or societies of men heretofore united or incorporated for the advancement of religion or learning, or for other pious or charitable purposes, shall be encouraged and protected in the enjoyment of the privileges, immunities, and estates, which they were accustomed to enjoy."[33] Religious bodies that were previously "united or incorporated" thus received the traditional exemptions afforded by the common law and equity law courts.

Four provisions in the new and revised state constitutions and their amendments, however, became grounds for formidable new challenges to this traditional pattern of tax exemption of religious property during the nineteenth and early twentieth centuries.[34]

First, by 1833, all state constitutions had outlawed formal establishments of religion altogether, or at least the state impositions of religious taxes and other forms of compulsory support for religion. These prohibitions undercut the authority of state officials to support one religion over another, to prescribe religious beliefs, to levy religious taxes, and to govern church polities and properties. Religion was no longer an affair of government and law. The cleric was no longer a public official. The established church was no longer a subsidized state agency. The established church meetinghouse was no longer a governmental or public property.[35]

32 Massachusetts Constitution (1780), part II, chap. VI, art. VI. (1780).

33 Constitution of Pennsylvania (1776), sec. 45.

34 See detailed sources for this section in Witte, "Tax Exemption," 380–86.

35 Sarah Barringer Gordon provides a detailed account of how many of these new state disestablishment policies led to sharp reductions in the size of church properties, the imposition of democratic lay control on congregations and parishes, and the broadening and systematizing of religious incorporation as a condition for gaining protection of institutional religious freedom. Sometimes, the states simply seized older established church properties, too. Sarah Barringer Gordon, "The First Disestablishment: Limits on Church Power and Property Before the Civil War," *University of Pennsylvania Law Review* 162 (2014), 307–72. See analysis and detailed sources in Sarah Barringer Gordon, "Religious Property and Confiscation in the Early Republic," in Daniel

These disestablishment provisions rendered the traditional common law exemptions of religious property vulnerable to attack. The establishment rationale on which these exemptions had been based was no longer available. No other consistent rationale had as yet been offered. A small but persistent group of critics from the 1820s onward thus challenged these common law exemptions as vestiges of religious establishment. Their arguments lie at the heart of the anti-exemption case still today.

Such exemptions, critics argued, favor religious groups over nonreligious groups. To exempt owners of religious properties from "their portion of the cost of state services and protections" is not only to subsidize them but also to penalize the owners of nonreligious properties whose tax burdens are proportionately increased.[36] This form of religious subsidy and support, albeit indirect, cannot be countenanced under the no-establishment provisions of the state constitutions.

Nor can such exemptions be countenanced under state constitutional guarantees of liberty of conscience, these critics continued, for these exemptions force other citizens to pay more taxes to make up for the taxes not collected from religious properties. A simple example illustrates this argument. A town consisting of one thousand plots of property of equal value seeks to collect ten thousand dollars in property taxes. If all properties are taxed, each property holder will have to pay ten dollars in taxes. But if one religious property is exempted from taxation, the remaining 999 property holders must each pay $10.01 (for $9,999.99, and one unlucky citizen tapped to pay that last penny). Why should any one of the remaining 999 taxpayers have to pay an extra penny in taxes to support the exempt religious property – particularly if that taxed property owner is opposed to religion altogether, or at least to the particular religion of the exempted property? Is this not precisely the kind of "continuing and intolerable burden on his pocketbook, his conscience, and his constitutional rights" that James Madison warned about?[37] Is this not a fateful first step down the slippery slope that Madison identified? "The same authority that can force a citizen to pay three pence only of his property for the support of any one establishment, may force him to conform to any other establishment in all cases whatsoever."[38] And this is precisely what is happening here, critics argued, with all citizens forced against their conscience to pay for the establishment of any property that is religious.

J. Hulsebosch and R. B. Bernstein, eds., *Making Legal History: Essyas in Honor of William E. Nelson* (New York: NYU Press, 2013), 13–35. In *Terrett* v. *Taylor*, 13 US (9 Cranch) 43 (1815) held that Virginia could not rescind the properly obtained charter of the Episcopal Church or seize its property.

36 *Orr* v. *Baker*, 4 Ind. 86, 88 (1853).

37 Quoted by *Valley Forge Christian College* v. *American United for Separation of Church and State*, 454 US 464, 509–10 (1982) (Brennan, J. dissenting) (references omitted).

38 James Madison, "Memorial and Remonstrance against Religious Assessments (1785)," para. 3, reprinted in William T. Hutchinson, William M. E. Rachal, and Robert A. Rutland, eds., *The Papers of James Madison* (Chicago: University of Chicago Press, 1962), 8:298.

Furthermore, these critics continued, property tax exemptions favor well-vested, traditional religions over struggling, newer religions. Since properties are taxed according to their value, the "humble congregation in a small wooden church" can enjoy only a fraction of the tax savings enjoyed by "the same-sized congregation in the beautiful hewn palace, with painted windows, frescoed ceilings, and silver mounted pews."[39] The no-establishment provisions, if they permit government benefits to religion at all, mandate uniformity and neutrality in such treatment. The "inequality and disparity" in the benefits afforded religious groups under property tax-exemption laws, therefore, cannot be countenanced.[40]

In addition, critics argued, such exemptions encourage the conflation of church and state. The "silent accumulations of [church] property" occasioned by the laws of tax exemption and religious incorporation, James Madison warned already in 1817, will inevitably result in "encroachments by powerful Ecclesiastical Bodies" upon the public square and the political process.[41] Several decades later, President Ulysses Grant portended similarly that tax exemptions had allowed churches to accumulate such "vast amounts of untaxed property" and to aggrandize such "vast political power" that "sequestration without constitutional authority" and "bloody" confrontation would eventually ensue. "The separation of Church and the State," he said, required that all "legal instruments encouraging ecclesiastical aggrandizement of wealth and power," including tax exemptions, be "expunged."[42]

Second, the inherited tax-exemption laws were challenged by state constitutional mandates to revise or to revoke English statutes. The new state constitutional conventions in the later eighteenth and early nineteenth centuries had initially received and ratified English statutes, without much amendment or emendation. But as American nationalist sentiment became more strident in the nineteenth century, and judicial criticisms of English law grew sharper, state legislatures

39 *Official Report of the Proceedings and Debates of the Kentucky Constitutional Convention* (1890), 2:2425 (statement of Rep. Sachs).

40 Josiah Phillips Quincy, *Tax Exemption: No Excuse for Spoliation* (Boston: Proprietors of "Old and New," 1874), 8.

41 Elizabeth Fleet, "Madison's 'Detached Memoranda' [c. 1817]," *William and Mary Quarterly*, 3rd ser. 3 (1946), 554. Similarly, as fourth president of the United States, Madison accompanied his veto of a bill to incorporate the Protestant Episcopal Church in Alexandria, Virginia, with these words: "1. The bill exceeds the rightful authority to which governments are limited by the essential distinction between civil and religious function. . . . 4. Because the bill vests in the said incorporated church an authority to provide for the support of the poor and the education of poor children of the same, an authority which . . . would be a precedent for giving to religious societies as such a legal agency in carrying into effect a public and civil duty." Reprinted in Gaillard Hunt, ed. *The Writings of James Madison*, 9 vols. (New York: G. P. Putnam's Sons, 1900–10), 8:132–33.

42 Fred L. Israel, ed., *State of the Union Messages of the Presidents, 1790–1966* (New York: Chelsea, 1966), 2:1296. Likewise, President James Garfield commented: "The divorce between church and state ought to be absolute. It ought to be so absolute that no church property anywhere, in any state, or in the nation, should be exempt from equal taxation; if you exempt the property of any church organization, to that extent you impose a tax upon the whole community." Quoted by J. Morton, *Exempting the Churches: An Argument for the Abolition of This Unjust and Unconstitutional Practice* (New York: Truth Seeker, 1915), 63.

began to respond. A number of states appointed committees to review English statutes and precedents that had traditionally governed the colonies and states and to purge those that were found odious or obsolete. Many British statutes survived such purges only in revised form, if at all.

Among them was the English Statute of Charitable Uses of 1601, which traditionally undergirded both the charitable jurisdiction of equity courts and the law of charitable institutions that these courts had helped to devise. Several states thus removed charitable institutions from the jurisdiction of equity courts and relieved those institutions of their traditional equitable privileges, including their property tax exemptions. The special testamentary, procedural, and property privileges previously accorded charities were also removed, and the special tax subsidies and tax exemptions were withdrawn. Some courts also developed strict rules for the formation and functioning of new charitable institutions. Such institutions were required to procure corporate charters, to provide detailed annual reports of their charitable activities, and to limit severely their property and endowment holdings. In several cases, donations and devises to religious charities were invalidated, religious groups were denied charitable corporate charters, and religious functions were deemed "inappropriate" as charitable uses.

Third, the inherited tax exemption laws were challenged by new state constitutional requirements that property taxes be "universally" applied across the states, with a strong presumption in favor of taxation. From the 1850s on, many state constitutional conventions – and often state legislatures, too – thoroughly reformed their property taxation laws. The myriad species of special and sporadic taxes on property inherited from colonial and early state days were consolidated into a general annual tax on real property (land and its improvements) and a general *ad valorem* tax on various forms of personal property or movables. The multiple layers of tax officials and tax offices were merged into more uniform state and municipal tax commissions. The antiquated tax-valuation and tax-assessment lists – yellowed, tattered, and endlessly amended since colonial days – were thoroughly revised. The long lists of tax exemptions and immunities inherited from the colonial period were largely cast aside.

The revised state constitutions now started with the provision that "[t]axation shall be equal and uniform throughout the State, and all property, both real and personal, shall be taxed in proportion to its value."[43] The presumption was that all property was to be universally taxed. Tax exemptions, including those for religious properties, were now clearly an exception to generally applicable levies. They could be granted only if the "public welfare" would be advanced, or if other "good and compelling reasons" could be adduced.

[43] West Virginia Const. (1861/3), art. VIII, sec. 1. See, further, sources in Witte, "Tax Exemption," nn. 77–79.

Finally, and related, the majority of state constitutions added explicit prohibitions against state funding and other forms of state aid to religion. The Nevada Constitution (1864), for example, provided briefly: "No public funds of any kind or character whatever, State, county, or municipal, shall be used for sectarian purpose[s]."[44] Several states echoed the strong language of the 1870 Illinois Constitution:

> Neither the General Assembly nor any county, city, town, township, school district or other public corporation shall ever make any appropriation or pay from any public fund whatever, anything in aid of any church or sectarian purpose, or to help support or sustain any school, academy, seminary, college, university or other literary or scientific institution, controlled by any church or sectarian denomination whatever; nor shall any grant or donation of land, money or other personal property ever be made by the State or any such public corporation to any church or for any sectarian or religious purpose.[45]

The pressing issue became whether religious tax exemptions of any sort, including religious properties, were a form of unconstitutional aid to religion.

THE MODERN THEORY AND LAW OF RELIGIOUS PROPERTY EXEMPTIONS

These formidable challenges helped shape the modern theory and law of tax exemptions of religious property. The modern theory of religious property exemptions did not forsake the common law and equity law traditions of tax exemption. Rather, it fused these two traditions, casting religious property tax exemptions into more generic and inclusive forms. The modern exemption laws inherited from colonial times remained largely in place, but were given more general and generous application to all religious properties, particularly those that offered social or public benefits and discharged state burdens in service of society.

Providing Social Benefits, Relieving State Burdens. The modern theory of tax exemption of religious property was set out in a massive outpouring of judicial opinions, legislative arguments, convention speeches, popular pamphlets, newspaper editorials, printed sermons, and scholarly papers beginning in 1850.[46] Although these sources varied widely in quality and clarity, their basic premises

[44] Const. of Nevada (1864), art. XI.10.

[45] Const. of Illinois (1870), art. VIII.3. See, further, Thomas C. Berg, "Disestablishment from Blaine to *Everson*: Federalism, School Wars, and the Emerging Modern State," in T. Jeremy Gunn and John Witte, Jr., eds., *No Establishment of Religion: America's Original Contribution to Religious Liberty* (Oxford: Oxford University Press, 2012), 307–40; Steven K. Green, *The Bible, the School, and the Constitution: The Clash that Shaped Modern Church-State Doctrine* (Oxford: Oxford University Press, 2012). On the efforts to pass the federal Blaine Amendment, which had comparable restrictions on funding, see Chapter 5 of this book, n. 50.

[46] See detailed sources in Witte, "Tax Exemption," 386–88 and further Bassett et al., *Religious Organizations*, §33.2.

and principles admit of rather short summary. "The policy on which the exemption of religious property is granted," declared the Connecticut Supreme Court, "is simply the encouragement of . . . churches." For churches and other religious bodies serve to the advantage of both society in general and the state in particular. They dispense "social benefits" to the relief of "state burdens."[47]

Proponents of exemptions argued that churches and other religious bodies dispense intangible but invaluable benefits to society through their religious activities. They cultivate public spiritedness. They induce citizens to "benevolence, charity, generosity, love of our fellowman, deference to rank, to age and sex, tenderness to the young, active sympathy for those in trouble and distress, beneficence to the destitute." Without such acts and dispositions, a "truly civil society . . . could not long endure."[48] Churches inculcate public morality. They teach chastity and continence, temperance and modesty, obedience and obligation, respect for the person and property of another. They have internal structures of authority to punish parishioners guilty of immorality. Such moral discipline is "probably of as much value to society in keeping the peace and preserving the rights of property as the most elaborate and expensive police system."[49] Churches enhance neighborhood values. Their "immaculate" buildings and grounds are aesthetically pleasing, attract respected citizens, and promote stability of neighborhood populations.[50] Churches promote democratic principles and practices. They inspire citizens to participate in the political process and to vote for candidates, while they instruct officials on moral principles and social needs. They preach against "injustice by the authorities" and "insurrection by the masses."[51] "Churches and religion, therefore," a Massachusetts Tax Commissioner put it, "make life and property more secure and promote peace, order, and prosperity in the community." Exemptions are thus granted "not that religion may increase . . . but that society may be benefitted."[52]

Churches and other religious bodies not only dispense social benefits through their religious activities, exemption proponents argued; they also discharge state burdens through their charitable activities. They discharge the burdens of education through their religious schools and colleges, educational and vocational programs, libraries, literacy programs, and literature societies. They discharge burdens of social

47 *First Unitarian Society* v. *Hartford*, 66 Conn. 368, 375 (1895).

48 *Trustees of the First Methodist Episcopal Church* v. *City of Atlanta*, 76 Ga. 181, 193 (1886), rev'd. on other grounds, *City of Atlanta* v. *First Presbyterian Church*, 86 Ga. 730, 13 SE 252 (1890).

49 *Commonwealth* v. *Y.M.C.A.*, 116 Ky. 711, 718 (1903).

50 Henry Wilder Foote, *The Taxation of Churches* (Boston: n.p., ca. 1876), 27–30 (pamphlet in Library of Congress).

51 See, for example, *Ward* v. *New Hampshire*, 56 NH 508 (1876); T. Brown, *Some Reasons for the Exemption of Church Property from Taxation* (Rochester, NY: Scantom, Wetmore & Co., 1881), 12.

52 Quoted by Foote, *The Taxation of Churches*, 19–20. See also Albert Taylor Bledsoe, *Shall Georgia Tax Church Property?* (Atlanta, GA: Atlanta Litho and Print, ca. 1897), 5: "It is upon this principle . . . that church property has heretofore been exempted from taxation, viz., that the exemption was worth more to the State than the taxation. Churches are not built for purposes of gain . . . the church is built for the benefit of the public."

welfare through their hostels and hospitals, almshouses and night shelters, orphanages and youth camps, men's groups and women's groups, counseling and crisis centers, retirement homes and elder care. They discharge burdens of foreign aid through their programs for foreign missions, economic development, public health, and disaster relief. Churches must be considered, wrote one exuberant pamphleteer, "the most charitable of charities."[53] Through their voluntary social services, churches and other religious bodies save the state enormous costs that would "otherwise be imposed upon the public ... by general taxation."[54] Tax exemption, proponents concluded, is a suitable quid pro quo for such services.

Neighboring property owners have lower, not higher, taxes as a consequence, continued the pro-exemption argument. To return to our earlier example, the town that thought it needed ten thousand dollars in taxes to do all of its work now needs less in tax revenue because exempt religions are doing part of the work. Indeed, the town probably needs far less than expected, because those religions often do the work more efficiently with volunteers and existing service networks. It's far cheaper for the town to use tax exempt church buildings and their volunteers to provide shelter, food, water, and healthcare in an emergency than to rent a building and hire government workers to take on these tasks. It's cheaper for the town to have tax exempt religious schools providing some of the local education than having to erect another public school building or to hire more public schoolteachers.

Even if the town still decides to collect the full ten thousand dollars in taxes–charging every taxable property the extra penny needed to compensate for the revenue lost from the exempted religious property – a liberty of conscience objection by these property owners will find little sympathy in the courts.[55] Religious pacifists must pay taxes that help to support the military. Fervent Marxists must pay taxes that support a capital economy.[56] Ascetic Amish must pay taxes that support a state social-security system that they cannot in good conscience use.[57] Claims of conscience against payments of general taxes, whether based on religion or on antireligion, are ultimately futile. As the Supreme Court once put it: "Because the broad public interest in maintaining a sound tax system is of such a high order, religious belief in conflict with the payment of taxes affords no basis for resisting the tax."[58]

Proponents of tax exemption made still quicker work of the equality argument – that such tax exemptions give disproportionately large benefits to religions with large property holdings, and disproportionately small benefits to religions with no

53 Ibid.

54 *Y.M.C.A. of Omaha* v. *Douglas County*, 60 Neb. 642, 646 (1896).

55 See liberty of conscience criticisms of tax exemptions, p. 209.

56 See, for example, Judge John T. Noonan, Jr.'s account of a case he heard where a taxpayer made this argument. John T. Noonan, Jr., "The Tensions and the Ideals," in Johan D. van der Vyver and John Witte, Jr. , eds., *Religious Human Rights in Global Perspective: Legal Perspectives* (The Hague: Martinus Nijhoff Publishers, 1996), 596–97.

57 *United States* v. *Lee*, 455 US 252 (1982).

58 Ibid., 260.

property holdings. Such disparity in treatment, critics had long argued, violates the principle of equality of all religions before the law. The easy answer to this argument, proponents replied, is that taxation of religious property would be equally disproportionate, but only in reverse. Religions with large properties would face heavy tax burdens; religions with smaller properties would face lighter tax burdens. The purported violation of the principle of equality would be identical. Equal treatment of religion does not require identical treatment; it requires only treating like religious cases alike.

These new arguments from "state burden" and "social benefits" in favor of religious property tax exemption skillfully blended traditional arguments. Traditional common law theory taught that religious-use exemptions were accorded to properties that discharged state burdens of administering the state's established religion. Traditional equity law theory taught that charitable-use exemptions were accorded to any properties that dispensed social or public benefits. These arguments were now reversed and softened. Religious-use exemptions, no longer justifiable on establishment grounds, were now justified on the basis of the distinct social benefits efficiently dispensed by all religious groups. Charitable-use exemptions, no longer justifiable on unspecified grounds of social benefits, were now justified on the basis of relieving the state of expensive services it would otherwise have to take on, and thereby lowering the taxes that it needs to collect from all others. The new theory of tax exemptions thus captured the traditional arguments but recast them to broaden an unduly narrow category of religious-use exemptions and to narrow an unduly broad category of charitable-use exemptions.

THE NEW LAW OF RELIGIOUS PROPERTY TAX EXEMPTION

This modern theory of religious property exemptions is reflected in modern state laws.[59] Over the past century and more, thirty-four[60] of the fifty states ultimately developed new constitutional provisions that guaranteed property tax exemptions to all religious groups, and these provisions were amplified in intricate state laws and county regulations. The remainder of the states developed systematic statutory schemes that were either mandated by or validated under state constitutions. These new tax-exemption provisions, while still sometimes criticized, were not covert attempts by formerly established religious bodies to seize indirect funding now that they lacked the political power to command direct funding. Rather, tax-exemption provisions were often defended as a better way to ensure non-preferential

[59] For this section, see detailed citations of the constitutional provisions, statutes, and cases on point as of 1990, in Witte, "Tax Exemption," 389–407, updated through 2020 in Bassett et al., *Religious Organizations*, §§33.7–26 and in other sources in n. 1.

[60] In 1940, that stood at thirty-three; the new state of Alaska in 1959 added a state constitutional tax-exemption provision, too.

state support to all religious organizations, rather than preferential state support to those religious groups that had power to extract funding from the legislatures.

Vestiges of Common Law Patterns of Tax Exemption. Consistent with the common law tradition, virtually all state constitutions and statutes exempted properties "devoted to religious uses" or "used for religious purposes." Most states insisted, however, that such property uses be "actual" and "real" or at least "planned" or "in the works." Properties that had been abandoned or merely purchased for distant future religious uses were generally taxable. A hundred-acre tract in the countryside that might someday be used for a satellite church, religious school, or youth camp was still taxed.

Roughly half the states insisted that such properties be owned by a "religious association"; a few states, particularly in earlier decades, insisted further that this religious association be incorporated under state law as a religious corporation. Other states, however, took no account of the religious identity of the property owner, so long as the exempt property was devoted to religious uses. That latter trend has increased in recent years as religious property tax exemptions have become more generous. An individually owned storage building converted into a church and used principally for religious worship is usually now tax exempt; a half century ago, most states would have taxed it.[61]

The definition and delimitation of the phrase "religious use" has always been the subject of considerable legislation and litigation, but here, too, most states today have become more permissive. In early common law regimes of religious establishment, state officials looked to the religious uses prescribed by establishment laws and exercised by the established churches alone. Now, however, states exempt all sanctuaries, worship centers, chapels, and other properties devoted to any form of religious worship services, together with the driveways, walkways, parking lots, and other immediate property necessary for their reasonable use. In recent times, the reach of exempt property has also included private worship centers in secluded cloisters and monasteries, and private chapels in orphanages, hospitals, or schools, so long as some portion of the public is benefited. Most states, however, still require that the property devoted to religious uses must be improved or developed. Agrarian communal religions, open youth camps, or naturalist religions that worship in the designated open countryside generally do not receive religious-use exemptions.

A few states have limited religious-use exemptions to public worship facilities alone, but most states now also exempt properties that support the ministry of the worship center, such as parsonages, education buildings, fellowship halls, and the like – albeit often with limitations on acreage and space. Some states also exempt attached church-run schools, cemeteries, counseling centers, retirement homes,

61 Ibid., §33.14. States make their own judgments about what is a "religious" group, use, or property; 501 (c)(3) religious organizations are not necessarily viewed as religious organizations at state law. See Hilary J. Houston, "Are 501(c) Non-Profit Organizations Subject to Real Property Taxation?" *Tax'n Exempts* 32 (2021), 1–6.

retreat centers, and publication and distribution centers – though the more attenuated the activity from actual religious worship, the stricter the requirements regarding religious ownership and space and acreage. Many of those auxiliary properties, however, can usually be exempt as charitable uses, not religious uses, as we will see in a moment.

A persistent question at the edge of the law of property taxation is how to treat the exemption claims of new or newly prominent religions. While the number of religious adherents has slowly declined in the United States, the number of separate religious groups has rapidly increased, with more than a thousand recognized religious groups in place today.[62] Alongside long-standing Christian, Jewish, Muslim, and Native American religious groups, the country is home to sizable populations of Hindus, Buddhists, Sikhs, Rastafarians, Unification Church members, Christian Scientists, Scientologists, and others. Hundreds of small, highly selective communitarian religions, faith families, ethical clubs, personality cults, and more are also clamoring for religious property exemptions, among other benefits and entitlements. State property tax laws, unlike federal income-tax laws, generally offer no definition of a religious association or a religious use of property. State and federal constitutional laws usually offer only rudimentary and inconsistent definitions of religion.[63] Negotiating the boundary between religion and nonreligion for purposes of deciding the tax status of these groups and their properties has thus been the subject of intense litigation in the state courts.

In evaluating new petitions for tax exemption, state courts have developed four alternative tests for finding "religion."[64] Under a simple *common-sense test*, courts will view the "objective facts" of the petitioner's property uses but studiously avoid inquiry into the petitioner's religious inspirations or motivations. They then make a "common-sense judgment" – a variation on "I know when I see it" – regarding whether such uses are really religious or secular. The *deference test* relies heavily on the petitioner's self-characterization of its religion, with the courts reserving judgment on whether the parties are operating in good faith. The *minimal-theism* test requires applicants to "exhibit the minimal requirements of a religion," including a "sincere and meaningful belief in God occupying in the life of its possessors a place parallel to that occupied by God in traditional religions and dedicat[ion] to the practice of that belief."[65] Finally, a few courts have developed a comprehensive *multifactual analysis test* to evaluate petitions for state property tax exemption, akin to the fifteen-point checklist used by the Internal Revenue Service in judging close cases for religious organization applying for federal income-tax exemption. The

62 Bassett et al., *Religious Organizations*, xi.

63 Slye, "Rendering Unto Caesar"; Edward M. Gaffney, "Governmental Definition of Religion: The Rise and Fall of the IRS Regulations of an Integrated Auxiliary of a Church," *Valparaiso University Law Review* 25 (1991), 203–47.

64 For detailed sources see Witte, "Tax Exemption," 401–07; Bassett et al., *Religious Organizations*, §33.7.

65 *Roberts* v. *Ravenwood Church of Wicca*, 249 Ga. 348, 350 (1982).

factors include the motives for the formation of the religious organization, the presence of a supreme being or something in lieu thereof in the belief system, the presence and sophistication of religious doctrine, the practice and celebration of religious liturgies or rites, the degree of formal religious training required for the religious leaders, the strictures on the ability of members simultaneously to practice other religions, and other factors.[66]

These four tests strike markedly different balances between sophistication of analysis and intrusiveness of inquiry. The deference test avoids intrusive inquiry into the beliefs of the petitioner but does so at the cost of analytical sophistication. The multifactual analytical test affords close analysis of each petition but does so at the cost of religious intrusion. The common-sense test is neither very sophisticated nor every intrusive. The minimal-theism test is both more sophisticated and more intrusive, inquiring into the nature of a petitioner's core religious beliefs.

At this contested edge of religious property tax exemptions, a sequenced combination of tests seems to strike a better balance than any one of these tests standing alone. Most petitions for tax exemption can and should be accepted using the common-sense test or deference test alone. It is when the reasonableness of the petition or the sincerity of the petitioner is in question that commissioners and courts should look more closely. A test for theism, or some evidence of a transcendent good held by the group, is a useful first step in such closer scrutiny, and might well dispose of a case. In still doubtful cases, a closer inquiry using multiple criteria will work if these criteria are applied only prudentially, not mechanically. "Charlatanism" might be "a necessary price to pay for religious freedom" in general.[67] But it is not necessary for the state and society to pay a charlatan with particular privileges reserved to the religious alone.

Furthermore, it must be remembered that the initial determination of tax-exempt status is usually made not by a court in a public proceeding but by a bureaucrat within the state, county, or municipal tax commissioner's office. Some measure of formality and predictability must thus attend these decisions, or they will become subject to bureaucratic caprice. Too wooden or generous an application of such tests can still trigger an appeal to the courts, either by the petitioner who is denied an exemption or by a government office that is denied its tax.

Vestiges of Equity Law Patterns of Tax Exemption. Consistent with the equity law tradition, all states also exempt religious properties that are devoted to charitable, benevolent, or eleemosynary uses or purposes. The traditional equity definition of charity still remains in effect: any use of property that provides public services to a sufficiently indefinite number of persons is considered charitable. The conditions imposed on religious-use exemptions are generally also imposed on charitable-use

66 *Ideal Life Church of Lake Elmo* v. *County of Washington*, 304 N.W. 2d 308 (Minn., 1981).

67 The quote is from *Church of the New Faith* v. *Pay Roll Tax Commissioners* 57 AJLR 785, 791 (1983), quoted and discussed in Peter Cumper, "Religious Liberty in the United Kingdom," in van der Vyver and Witte, *Religious Human Rights*, 222.

exemptions. The charitable use has to be actual and public, and the exempt property usually has to be owned by a charitable association.

Religious associations are eligible for these charitable-use exemptions for their properties if they meet these criteria, and some religious groups use them. Most religious associations are also considered to be charitable associations. Aside from religious worship services, most religious uses of property are also considered to be charitable uses of property. Although the core religious uses and core charitable uses of religious property remain distinct, most religious property uses can be considered at once religious and charitable under state exemption laws. Thus, a variety of uses and improvements of religious property that clearly serve the ministry and mission of a religious association are often exempted under charitable-use categories – the properties occupied and used by church administrative centers, seminaries, Bible societies, missionary societies, religious publishers, church youth camps and retreat centers, parochial schools, Sunday schools, church societies, and many others.

Several states allow for religious associations to mix both religious uses and charitable uses of their properties and to choose either one or both forms of exemption for such uses. Religious-use exemptions are often more attractive, however, since they require only an annual petition for renewal to the local tax assessor – with norms of separation of church and state providing protection against more intrusive bureaucratic entanglement with the state. Charitable-use exemptions not only require such a petition but also subject the association to the regular supervisory jurisdiction of the state.

Several other states require religious associations to decide whether religious or charitable use of their properties was primary or predominant and to petition for exemption of their property based on that use alone. If an association can demonstrate that most of the property is devoted to one such exempt use for the majority of the time, an exemption is granted – even if the property is also put to other incidental exempt and nonexempt uses.

A few states require either exclusive religious use or exclusive charitable use of the exempt property. Under such a wooden classification system, religious organizations have to choose either to truncate or to bifurcate their activities. Organizations that resist such a choice – for reasons of ideology or economics – on occasion are denied exemption altogether.

Many states also permit parties to make incidental nonexempt uses of their properties. Traditionally, many states denied exemptions to religious or charitable properties that in any way mixed exempt and nonexempt uses; even incidental profiteering was fatal to a claim for exemption. Today, courts and legislatures have become far less stringent. Some states allow full exemption so long as the primary use is religious or charitable. Even part-time leases of the property to nonexempt entities and purposes does not jeopardize the exemption. Other states allow property devoted to religious or charitable uses to receive partial exemption based on the percentage of space or time devoted to such exempt uses.

Tax Exemptions of Religious Property in the Future. A half century after the fact, *Walz* v. *Tax Commission* (1970) still seems like a prudent decision, and many lower courts since have repeated its basic holding and logic.[68] State tax exemptions of religious property, the *Walz* Court concluded, while neither proscribed by the Establishment Clause nor prescribed by the Free Exercise Clause, are, nonetheless, constitutionally permissible. State and local taxation and tax-exemption laws, the Court has said since, involve a "play in the joints" between the two religious freedom guarantees of the First Amendment.[69]

Federalism provides one strong argument for this conclusion. Property taxation and exemption have, since the beginning of the republic, been principally state, not federal, affairs. The fifty individual states – sometimes their local county commissions, too – have developed wide-ranging forms of property taxation and exemption, which are closely tailored to local norms and habits. Unlike bigger legal regimes like education, prison life, or military service, which involve inherent coercion and have serious implications for the religious freedom of all citizens nationwide, there is little compelling argument to subject this diverse and divisive set of local property tax laws to a single First Amendment norm enforceable by federal courts. Unduly discriminatory denials of tax exemption for seemingly qualified religious properties can and should still give rise to state and federal free-exercise cases.[70] Unduly generous extensions of tax exemption for seemingly unqualified nonreligious properties can and should still give rise to state and federal establishment challenges.[71] This has been the case for controversial decisions over income tax, sales and use taxes, permit taxes, and more, and this kind of constitutional safety net can apply to serious questions of state property tax exemption, too.[72] But mundane and marginal disputes concerning discretionary decisions over tax exemptions of religious properties should be resolved not by federal courts but by local state tribunals, sensitive to the norms and habits of the local communities.

This ongoing federalist solution does pose risks for those who wish to retain such religious property tax exemptions. A future state could conceivably end all religious property tax exemptions – at least one state is considering such a proposal[73] – and the federal courts would have little to say if they stick to their federalist logic. A county or state might condition a church's property tax exemption on its acceptance, say, of

68 *Religious Organizations*, §§ 33.3; 4.43. For a good recent case upholding the *Walz* rationale, see *Gaylor* v. *Munchin*, 919 F. 3d. 420 (7th Cir. 2019). See critical analysis of the Supreme Court's own treatment of *Walz* and other Supreme Court cases dealing with income, sale, use, and permit taxes in Gaffney, "Exemption of Religious Organizations," 469–97.

69 *Locke* v. *Davey*, 540 US 712, 718 (2004).

70 Gaffney," Exemption of Religious Organizations," 502–03.

71 Compare *Texas Monthly, Inc.* v. *Bullock* (1989) (striking down a state sales tax exemption for religious periodicals alone).

72 See several examples in Crimm and Winer, *Politics, Taxes and the Pulpit*; Zelinsky, *Taxing the Church*.

73 See, e.g., Benjamin Brookstone, "Nebraska's LB 675: The Path to Rescinding Religious Property Tax Exemptions," *Tax Lawyer* 68 (2015), 809–26.

same-sex wedding ceremonies. That church will be hard pressed to win a federal constitutional case unless it can show true religious discrimination in how that policy was made or enforced. The better recourse might well be at the ballot box.[74]

Tradition provides a second strong argument for the *Walz* decision. The *Walz* Court overstated its historical argument by exaggerating the continuity and universality of the tradition of such tax exemptions and by imputing modern concerns to early state legislatures and constitutional conventions that devised tax-exemption policies. But even granting its occasional interruptions, dissenting voices, and shifting theories, the American tradition of tax exemption of religious property has been long held and widely embraced. And when nineteenth- and twentieth-century critics challenged this legal regime for its favoritism, abuses, and dangers, state constitutional conventions and legislatures reformed the law to provide property tax exemptions non-preferentially for almost all faiths, and courts and commissioners developed sturdy equitable measures to resolve hard cases at the margins.

A simple argument from tradition, of course, cannot dispose of a federal constitutional case. But tradition can serve as something of a null hypothesis – to be overcome by strong constitutional arguments rather than discarded by simple invocations of principle. As Oliver Wendell Holmes, Jr. once put it: "If a thing has been practised for two hundred years by common consent, it will need a strong case for the Fourteenth Amendment to affect it."[75] No strong constitutional case has been mustered against the twenty-five-hundred-year tradition of granting tax exemptions for religious property.

Social theory provides a third strong argument for continuing the practice of tax exemption of religious property. The *Walz* Court declared it

> unnecessary to justify the tax exemption on the social welfare services or "good works" that some churches perform for parishioners and others. Churches vary substantially in the scope of such services. ... To give emphasis to so variable an aspect of the work of religious bodies would introduce an element of governmental evaluation and standards as to the worth of particular social welfare programs, thus producing the kind of continuing day-to-day relationships which the policy of neutrality seeks to minimize.[76]

Traditional social-benefit and state-burden theories for tax exemption are thus not litmus tests to determine the eligibility of each individual religious property seeking tax exemption. These theories are instead a rationale for having a general category of exemption for religious properties or properties devoted to religious uses. On the whole, the argument goes, religious uses of property, and charitable uses by religious bodies, dispense a sufficiently unique and valuable form of social benefits and

[74] See further Chapter 6 of this book. I deal with the issue of church solemnization of marriage and its tax-exemption consequences in John Witte, Jr., *Church, State, and Family: Reconciling Traditional Teachings and Modern Liberties* (Cambridge: Cambridge University Press, 2019), 318–28.

[75] *Jackman* v. *Rosenbaum*, 260 US 22, 31 (1922).

[76] *Walz*, 397 US at 674.

discharge a sufficiently large number of expensive state burdens to warrant their inclusion as a separate category of tax exemption. In practice, some religious uses of property are more socially beneficial to a broad public, others less so. The social tasks discharged by one religious property might far outweigh the amount of tax that could have been collected from the property; for other religious properties, this might not be true. But on the whole, the argument goes, society is better off, the state is more efficiently run, and religious bodies are freer to exercise their ministries if their properties are exempt from taxation.[77]

This conclusion is supported by religious-autonomy arguments that the Supreme Court has embraced more fully since *Walz*. "[R]eligious organizations have an interest in autonomy in ordering their internal affairs," Justice Brennan wrote in the 1987 case of *Presiding Bishop* v. *Amos*. In that case and several others since, as we saw in Chapter 6, the Court has affirmed the First Amendment freedom of religious organizations to govern their own membership, mission, morals, employees, polity, property, organizational structure, and more – without state regulation, judicial supervision, or local (retaliatory) taxation. As Justice Brennan, a strong liberal member of the Court in his day, put it further in *Amos*:

> Religion includes important communal elements for most believers. They exercise their religion through religious organizations, and these organizations must be protected by [the Constitution]. . . . For many individuals, religious activity derives meaning in large measure from participation in a larger religious community. Such a community represents an ongoing tradition of shared beliefs, an organic entity not reducible to a mere aggregation of individuals.[78]

Collectively, these First Amendment institutions not only deliver valuable social goods for all members of society but also amplify the First Amendment rights of the individuals who help make them up.[79] Leading First Amendment scholar Paul Horwitz puts this well:

> First Amendment law can[not] be modeled on the romantic vision of a single, self-sufficient speaker arrayed against a monolithic state, like a soapbox speaker facing a line of riot police. In public discourse, speech acts are motivated, refined, transmitted, and debated by a host of institutions. Typically, they are the same recurring institutions: the schools and libraries that educate the speaker, the

77 See further discussion by Martin E. Marty, quoted in Chapter 5, p. 165–66.

78 *Corporation of the Presiding Bishop* v. *Amos*, 483 US 327, 341–42 (Brennan, J. concurring), with discussion in Richard W. Garnett, "Religious Freedom and the Churches: Contemporary Challenges in the United States Today," *Studies in Christian Ethics* 33, no. 2 (2020), 196–97.

79 See Paul Horwitz, *First Amendment Institutions* (Cambridge, MA: Harvard University Press, 2013); Paul Horwitz, "Defending (Religious) Institutionalism," *Virginia Law Review* 99 (2013), 1051–02; Richard W. Garnett, "The Freedom of the Church": (Towards) An Exposition, Translation, and Defense," *Journal of Contemporary Legal Issues* 21 (2013), 33–58; Richard W. Garnett, "Do Churches Matter? Toward an Institutional Understanding of the Religion Clauses," *Villanova Law Review* 53 (2008), 273–96; Jack Balkin, "The Infrastructure of Religious Freedom," *Balkinization*, May 5, 2007, https://balkin.blogspot.com/search?q=infrastructure+of+religious+freedom.

> churches and associations that help inspire her message or supply her with allies, and the news media that convey the message to others and host debates over it. Those institutions play a key role in what we might call the infrastructure of public discourse. Their role is established by tradition but capable of institutional evolution and pluralism. And it is safeguarded not just by top-down state regulation, but also, and crucially, by institutional self-regulatory norms and practices.[80]

"The same thing can and should be said of churches" and other religious groups, writes leading Catholic jurist Richard Garnett:

> No less than the freedoms of speech and press, the freedom of religion requires a strong infrastructure, and religious freedom's institutional dimension – that is, the freedom of the churches – helps to provide it. Like free speech, religious freedom is exercised not only by individuals; like free expression, its securing requires more than protecting a solitary conscience. The freedom of religion is . . . not only lived and experienced through institutions, it is also protected, nourished, and facilitated by them. And so, if we hope to understand well the content and implications of our moral, constitutional, and other legal commitments to religious liberty, we have to appreciate the fact that "religious entities occupy a distinctive place in the constitutional order." And, we must not only acknowledge but take care of this "distinctive place," attending carefully to the health of religious freedom's institutional infrastructure.[81]

Religious tax exemptions are part and product of this constitutional respect for religious group autonomy or First Amendment institutionalism. "The power to tax is the power to destroy" an organization, the Supreme Court wrote already in 1819.[82] And if not to destroy, it is certainly the power to control that organization and its members, makeup, mission, and message. Religious tax exemption is thought to be a safer course, the better way to give religious organizations the distance and autonomy they need to govern their own internal affairs without state interference or review.

This is not to deny that tax-exempt status can come with its own costs and conditions. We just posed a hypothetical case where only churches that celebrate same-sex weddings get local property tax exemptions; that scenario might well start happening in dark-blue (liberal) states or counties in the next few years. But real-life examples are already at hand in the world of federal income-tax exemption. A religious group gets and retains its federal income-tax exempt status only if it desists from political lobbying, which some see as a form of "liberal suppression" of religious speech, especially since the *Citizens United* Supreme Court case opened

80 Horwitz, "Defending (Religious) Institutionalism," 1051–52.

81 Richard W. Garnett, "Religious Freedom and the Churches: Contemporary Challenges in the United States Today," *Studies in Christian Ethics* 32 (2019), 201, quoting in part Ira C. Lupu and Robert W. Tuttle, "The Distinctive Place of Religious Entitles in Our Constitutional Order," *Villanova Law Review* 47 (2002), 37–92.

82 *McCulloch* v. *Maryland*, 17 US 316, 341 (1819): "the power to tax involves the power to destroy."

the floodgates to corporate big money influence, if not control of elections.[83] The 1983 Supreme Court case of *Bob Jones University* v. *United States* further makes clear that a religious school that engages in racial discriminatory admissions decisions can lose its federal income-tax exempt status even if it desists from lobbying. Even with these (potential) costs and conditions, however, most proponents agree that tax exemption for religious property is the better course. And if an individual congregation or religious school or charity wants full freedom to press its political agenda during election season, or to engage in internal religious line drawing based on its religious beliefs, it can forgo its tax exemption and carry on.

SUMMARY AND CONCLUSIONS

Three decades ago, when I was young and naïve, I suggested that a more nuanced understanding of the history of tax exemption of religious property points to a middle way between the wholesale eradication of such exemptions proposed by opponents and the blanket endorsements of exemptions proffered by proponents. Neither group, I argued, recognized sufficiently that modern tax exemptions of religious property are rooted in both common law and equity law. Neither group has seen that tax exemptions were historically granted on account of both the religious uses and the charitable uses to which properties were devoted. Thus, besides the all-or-nothing approaches currently debated, a third alternative presented itself. Tax exemptions for religious properties could be granted not for their religious uses but for their charitable uses. Religious properties would thus be exempted from taxation not because of their internal, cultic, and sacerdotal uses but because of the external, cultural, and social uses to which they are devoted.[84]

In further testimony to my youthful naïveté, I argued that it should be left to the church and not to the state to implement this alternative. Nothing in the First Amendment compelled federal judges to order this reform. Elected state officials had even less incentive to raise this reform, whatever their need for further tax revenues. For tax exemptions have long been regarded as a sign of the state's benevolent neutrality toward religion – "a fit recognition by the state of the sanctity of religion," as one official put it.[85] Taxes would be regarded by many as a sign of the state's malevolent adversity toward religion – a reminder of earlier eras of religious

[83] Philip A. Hamburger, *Liberal Suppression: Section 501(c)(3) and the Taxation of Speech* (Chicago: University of Chicago Press, 2018); Crimm and Winer, *Politics, Taxes, and the Pulpit*; Mark A. Goldfeder and Michelle K. Terry, "To Repeal or Not to Repeal: The Johnson Amendment," *Memphis Law Review* 48 (2017), 209–55; Meghan Ryan, "Can the IRS Silence Religious Organizations?," *Indiana Law Review* 40 (2007), 73–96.

[84] See argument in Witte, "Tax Exemption," 395–415, with apt criticism in Gaffney, "Exemption of Religious Organizations," 466–67; Bassett et al., *Religious Organizations*, §10.1; 33.3.

[85] *Massachusetts State Tax Commission Report* (1897), quoted by D. Robertson, *Should Churches Be Taxed?* (Philadelphia: Westminster Press, 1968), 191. See also John C. Bennett, *Christians and the State* (New York: Scribner, 1958), 234–35 (referring to tax exemptions as "the most remarkable of all forms of aid . . . to religious bodies"); William L. Sperry, *Religion in America* (Cambridge: Cambridge

persecution and a foretaste of religious repression to come. To give the state the power to tax the church would, for many, be tantamount to giving it the power to destroy the church.

The catalyst for reform of religious property exemptions, I thus argued, had to come not from the state but from the church and other religious bodies. Churches must consider the costs of exemption – not so much the incremental financial costs to other taxpayers as the important symbolic costs to themselves. For many people, adherents and antagonists alike, tax exemptions and other legal privileges have rendered contemporary churches and religious bodies too mercenary, too opulent, and too self-indulgent – too intent upon building crystal cathedrals, prayer towers, and theme parks than furnishing soup kitchens, youth houses, and night shelters. The church's voluntary renunciation of one of its privileges would do much to allay the anxieties of its adherents and to parry the attacks of its antagonists.

Though now older and more cynical, I still stand by this recommendation – but with two critical qualifications. First, I argued earlier that a full-scale implementation of this reform should result in the eradication of the religious-use category of property tax exemption altogether. Religious properties would need to qualify for charitable-use exemptions or be subject to taxation. The substantial recent literature on the sociology of religion and First Amendment religious institutionalism persuades me that not all religious uses of property can or should be reduced to charitable uses – and, indeed, that there is great social and public value in religious uses as such.[86] Moreover, the principle of religious pluralism counsels against so radical a tax reform. Religions take a variety of forms, from the world affirmative and socially active to the world avertive and socially ascetic. To restrict tax exemptions only to the former types of religion stands in considerable tension with this principle of religious pluralism.

Second, I earlier put this reform in too stark a terms: churches were either charitable or churlish, in this argument, and shame on the latter. This is too strong, I now realize. There is a place for the sublime sanctuary and the secluded monastery that is not only legally sanctioned but socially salutary. There is a role for the private religious school and the ascetic religious community that is not only socially sanctioned but legally salutary. Not all religious forms, functions, and facilities need to be open and charitable in order to benefit the public; indeed, many would lose their distinctive religious identity and social utility if they were.

That said, a self-imposed ethic of moderation and modesty should still attend a religious body's demands for tax exemption. Not every corner and building on a sweeping church campus is necessarily vital to its ministry. Not every acre of a distant rural summer camp, occasionally occupied by the retired rector or rabbi, can be readily claimed to be religious. Not every storage building, administrative

University Press, 1963), 60. ("The most important governmental recognition of religion made in America is the exemption of church property from taxation.")

86 Bassett et al., *Religious Organizations*, 10.20, n. 1 (criticizing my earlier work for neglecting this point).

office, and residential center in the city operated by the church, temple, or mosque can be deemed equally essential and sacred. When such auxiliary properties and facilities are devoted to charitable uses, a religious body should seize on their exemptions with alacrity. But when such properties and facilities lie largely idle and foreclosed to others, a religious body might do well to render its taxes to our modern-day Caesars.

8

Faith in Strasbourg?

Religious Freedom in the European Court of Human Rights

The religious landscape of Europe has changed dramatically in the past half century. Traditional Christian establishments have been challenged by the growth of religious pluralism and strong new movements of *laïcité* and secularism. Once powerful religious cultures have been shattered by exposures of clerical abuses and financial self-dealing, leading to emptier pews and waning political influence. Once homogeneous European communities are now home to large groups of Muslims, making new demands and sparking strong anti-immigrant movements. The opening of national borders across Eastern and Western Europe has led to massive migration and tense intermixtures of Orthodox, Catholics, Protestants, Jews, Muslims, Buddhists, Confucians, Hindus, Atheists, and Secularists never seen on this scale before. Old constitutions, concordats, and customs that privileged Christian identity and morality have come under increasing attack. A single mention of God in the proposed new European Constitution triggered continent-wide debate. Old Christian Europe is dying and a new religious and political order beginning to form.

These new religious developments have reshaped the law of religious freedom, not only of individual European states[1] but also of the European Court of Human Rights in Strasbourg.[2] Reflecting the transition and tenuousness of European law and religion, the Court has become a hotspot for religious freedom claimants from all over Europe.

The Strasbourg Court has jurisdiction over questions of religious freedom under Article 9 of the European Convention on Human Rights (1950).[3] This provision guarantees each person "freedom of thought, conscience and religion," the right to "change" religion or belief, and "freedom, either alone or in community with others

1 See Norman Doe, *Law and Religion in Europe: A Comparative Introduction* (Oxford: Oxford University Press, 2012).

2 For recent religious freedom cases in the Court of Justice of the European Union, which began in earnest only in 2017, see Chapter 9 of this book and Emma Ahlm, *EU Law and Religion: A Study of How the Court of Justice Has Adjudicated on Religious Matters in Union Law* (PhD Diss., Uppsala Universitet, 2020).

3 Convention for the Protection of Human Rights and Fundamental Freedoms, art. 9(1–2), Nov. 4, 1950, 213 UNTS 230.

and in public or private, to manifest his [or her] religion or belief, in worship, teaching, practice and observance."[4] It took the Court forty-three years to issue its first Article 9 religious freedom case on the merits – in *Kokkinakis* v. *Greece* (1993).[5] Since then, however, the Court has exploded with more than 150 such cases. The Court has generally interpreted Article 9 and related articles broadly to protect the religious freedom of most individuals and groups. But the Court lately has been rather hard on Muslim minorities and conservative Christian claimants alike, as well as on Orthodox majority regimes in Eastern Europe and the former Soviet bloc. By contrast, it has been generous in accommodating self-professed atheists and secularists and deferential to the strong secularization and *laïcité* policies of France, Belgium, Turkey, and other countries, even when those policies target religious minorities. Moreover, the Court has begun to use the concept of state "religious neutrality" in a way that deprecates religious expression in public life and political discourse.

These Article 9 cases have fed European religious freedom scholarship and the global human rights agenda and provided member states with an uninterrupted flow of judgments that progressively unfold the scope and meaning of religious freedom and other fundamental rights. The Strasbourg Court and the European Convention also enjoy a special reputation in the fields of both international law and constitutional law. Scholars of international law regard the Strasbourg Court as "the poster child of international human rights law."[6] Comparative constitutional lawyers find the Court's work appealing because its approach is close to that of national constitutional courts.[7] Indeed, the Court has occasionally described itself as a "constitutional instrument of European public order."[8] Even the US Supreme Court, long (in)-famous for eschewing foreign law in its decisions, has cited the Strasbourg Court's jurisprudence and described it as "authoritative."[9]

This chapter first briefly analyzes recent trends and challenges concerning religion in Europe. It then describes the relevant provisions and procedures of the Strasbourg Court in addressing claims of religious freedom. The bulk of the chapter

4 Ibid. See p. 223 herein for full text and related provisions.

5 *Kokkinakis* v. *Greece*, App. No. 14307/88, 1993 Eur. Ct. H.R. para. 28 (May 25, 1993). See Carolyn Evans, "Pre-*Kokkinakis* Case Law of the European Court of Human Rights: Foreshadowing the Future," in Jeroen Temperman, T. Jeremy Gunn, and Malcolm Evans, eds., *The European Court of Human Rights and the Freedom of Religion or Belief: The 25 Years Since Kokkinakis* (Leiden: Brill, 2019), 13; Paul M. Taylor, *Freedom of Religion: UN and European Human Rights Law and Practice* (Cambridge: Cambridge University Press, 2005).

6 Kai Möller, "From Constitutional to Human Rights: On the Moral Structure of International Human Rights," *Global Constitutionalism* 3 (2014), 373, 398.

7 Andrea Pin, "The Costs and Consequences of Incorrect Citations: European Law in the U.S Supreme Court," *Brooklyn Journal of International Law* 42 (2016), 129, 149.

8 *Loizidou* v. *Turkey* (Preliminary Objections), 310 Eur. Ct. H.R. (ser. A), para. 75 (1995); see Robin C. A. White and Iris Boussiakou, "Separate Opinions in the European Court of Human Rights," *Human Rights Law Review* 9 (2009), 37, 38.

9 *Lawrence* v. *Texas*, 539 US 558, 573, 576 (2003).

analyzes closely the Court's religious freedom cases from three different angles: (1) freedom of thought, conscience, and belief; (2) the regulation of public manifestation of religion; and (3) freedom of religious groups. The conclusion evaluates the many notable advances in religious freedom jurisprudence offered by the Strasbourg Court, but also signals the dangers to religious freedom suggested by some of the most recent cases.

RELIGION IN EUROPE TODAY

The place of religion in Europe has generated some of the most intractable controversies in recent decades,[10] and it has shaped the narrative of religious freedom and the jurisprudence of the Strasbourg Court. The Court has jurisdiction over the Council of Europe, which comprises forty-seven member states and 900 million people (not just the twenty-seven countries and 430 million people within the smaller European Union, now made smaller still by Brexit). The Council of Europe includes Western European countries, some with strong and longstanding Roman Catholic and Protestant populations if not religious establishments, others with strong modern movements of secularism and *laïcité*.[11] It includes Greece, Eastern Europe, the Russian Federation, and former Soviet countries like Armenia, Azerbaijan, Georgia, and Ukraine, each with strong Orthodox Christian populations along with smaller communities of Catholic, Protestant, Islamic, Jewish, and other minorities and many professed atheists and nonbelievers.[12] The Council of Europe also includes Turkey, with its Islamic majority.[13]

Four new factors have made religion a hotter topic in Europe of late and religious freedom a more urgent issue: (1) shifts in European religious demography; (2) debates about Europe's religious heritage; (3) the rise of Islam; and (4) various scandals within European churches.

First, European politics and culture have experienced a rapid new awakening of religion in the past generation. "With the disappearance of the East-West divide, which had pushed all other conflicts into the background" during the Cold War from 1945 to 1990, writes Dieter Grimm, "religion and religious communities reappeared on the public scene and began to insist more vigorously on respect for their beliefs and on living according to the commandments

[10] Julie Ringelheim, "State Religious Neutrality as a Common European Standard? Reappraising the European Court of Human Rights Approach," *Oxford Journal of Law and Religion* 6 (2017), 24, 25.

[11] Lorenzo Zucca, A *Secular Europe: Law and Religion in the European Constitutional Landscape* (Oxford: Oxford: Oxford University Press, 2012), 4.

[12] 47 Member States, Council of Europe, www.coe.int/en/web/portal/47-members-states; Pew Forum, "Many Countries Favor Specific Religions, Officially or Unofficially," Oct. 3, 2017, www.pewforum.org/2017/10/03/many-countries-favor-specific-religions-officially-or-unofficially/

[13] W. Cole Durham, Jr., Rik Torfs, and David M. Kirkham, eds., *Islam, Europe, and Emerging Legal Issues* (London: Taylor and Francis, 2016).

of their creed."[14] This insistence has given birth to the "re-politicization of religion"[15] throughout Europe, with both old and many new religious players participating. The freedom of movement guaranteed by European Union treaties has mobilized people of different cultures and faiths to move to other European countries, seeking new homes, new work, better schools, cleaner cities, and more generous welfare. Moreover, the geographical expansion of the Council of Europe into the former Soviet republics and Turkey, and the porousness of its borders has transformed the religious makeup of member states. Orthodox Christians living in Eastern Europe, for example, have relocated in great numbers to the United Kingdom and Western Europe to fill the new jobs that have opened in countries with aging and waning local populations.[16] Secularized Scandinavians have moved to more traditional southern European Christian countries and have rebelled against the religious cultures and customs of their new homes.[17] Evangelical missionary churches have moved into long-closed East European and former Soviet lands and met with strong local opposition as they have sought to create new churches, schools, charities, and publishing houses, and to proselytize door to door and in public streets, squares, and parks. Anti-Semitism is again on the rise throughout Europe, with attacks on synagogues and on Jewish interests both in Europe and in the Middle East.[18] New émigrés from the Indian subcontinent and the Pacific Rim have brought strong forms of Hinduism, Buddhism, Confucianism, and other Asian religions to European cities and neighborhoods.[19]

While Brexit and COVID-19 put a temporary halt to some of this religious movement, it has already produced vast new religious pluralism in European

[14] Dieter Grimm, "Conflicts Between General Laws and Religious Norms," in Susanna Mancini and Michel Rosenfeld, eds., *Constitutional Secularism in an Age of Religious Revival* (Oxford: Oxford University Press, 2014), 3–13.

[15] Ibid., 3.

[16] See, e.g., recent studies by the European Union, the Council of Europe, and the European Parliament: https://ec.europa.eu/info/strategy/priorities-2019-2024/new-push-european-democracy/impact-demographic-change-europe_en; https://cor.europa.eu/en/engage/studies/Documents/The%20impact%20of%20demographic%20change%20on%20European%20regions/Impact_demographic_change_european_regions.pdf; https://ec.europa.eu/futurium/en/system/files/ged/eprs-briefing-633160-demographic-trends-eu-regions-final.pdf. See further Vera Hanewinkel, "EU Internal Migration Before and During The Economic and Financial Crisis – An Overview," Policy Brief No. 20 (Focus Migration, Germany), Feb. 2013.

[17] The famous case of the crucifix in Italian public schools started when Ms. Lautsi, a Finnish mother with secular views living in Italy, challenged the Italian practice of having the crucifix displayed in classrooms. *Lautsi* v. *Italy*, 2011-III Eur. Ct. H.R. 61.

[18] Bojan Pancevski, "One in Four Europeans Holds Anti-Semitic Views, Survey Shows," *The Wall Street Journal*, Nov. 21, 2019, www.wsj.com/articles/one-in-four-europeans-holds-anti-semitic-views-survey-shows-11574339097.

[19] "How Religious Commitment Varies by Country Among People of All Ages," Pew Forum, June 13, 2018, www.pewforum.org/2018/06/13/how-religious-commitment-varies-by-country-among-people-of-all-ages/.

lands and attendant conflicts that have clogged local courts and regulators. Supranational courts, with more detached views on religious freedom, have become more attractive to these new or newly arrived faiths, particularly religious and cultural minorities seeking accommodations for themselves or removals of the religious establishments around them. The Strasbourg Court has been the most influential and active such supranational court – although the Court of Justice of the European Union has begun to weigh in heavily on religious freedom, too, threatening to become "the new boss of religious freedom" in Europe, as we will see Chapter 9.

The second factor making religious freedom more urgent is the heated debates over the public visibility and role of religion within the European Union and the broader Council of Europe. Even the more homogeneous European Union – the collection of twenty-seven mostly Western European states within the broader collection of forty-seven states in the Council of Europe – has struggled to define its constitutional identity, including whether and how to take account of its religious heritage and diversity.[20] That struggle culminated in the early 2000s, when the member states debated intensely a proposed EU Constitution. The first draft constitution referenced Europe's religious tradition in the preamble, raising significant controversy. Some advocates wanted explicit recognition of Europe's long Christian heritage and the indisputable contributions of churches to the development of European culture; others wanted no mention of religion at all, to avoid partisanship and to underscore the EU's neutrality toward religion. The drafters sought a *via media* that recognized the variety of religious heritages and constitutional arrangements on religion within the member states, while establishing a common framework for EU government. That move, too, raised controversy. In the end, the final proposed constitution dropped all references to Christianity and any other religions. This led to inevitable charges that the EU now preferred secularism over religious pluralism, and political expediency over historical authenticity.[21] The EU Constitution was not ratified when put to a vote in 2005, and the European Union has since tabled debates about the EU Constitution, including its religious foundations and dimensions. But any new talk of constitution for the European Union, let alone the broader Council of Europe, will no doubt raise this issue sharply anew.

[20] Brent F. Nelsen and James L. Guth, *Religion and the Struggle for European Union: Confessional Culture and the Limits of Integration* (Washington, DC: Georgetown University Press, 2015), 66–110; Patrick Pasture, *Imagining European Unity since 1000 AD* (Basingstoke: Palgrave MacMillan, 2015), 204.

[21] See "Preamble of the Treaty Establishing a Constitution for Europe, Dec. 16, 2004," OJ 2004 No. C310, p. 3: "DRAWING INSPIRATION from the cultural, religious and humanist inheritance of Europe, from which have developed the universal values of the inviolable and inalienable rights of the human person, freedom, democracy, equality and the rule of law." See discussion in Joseph H. H. Weiler, "A Christian Europe? Europe and Christianity: Rules of Commitment," *European View* 6 (2007), 143–50; Jonathan Chaplin and Gary Wilson, eds., *God and the EU: Faith in the European Project* (London: Routledge, 2017); Andrea Pin, "Does Europe Need Neutrality? The Old Continent in Search of Identity," *Brigham Young University Law Review* (2014), 605, 605–6, 615.

A third factor bringing religious freedom to the fore is the recent rise of Islam in Western Europe, with attendant religious and cultural controversy. For more than a decade, the EU has demurred on Turkey's accession to the EU, in no small part because of deep worries over the compatibility of Turkey's majority "Islamic values" with the "European values" of existing member states.[22] These worries about Islam have been exacerbated by bloody terrorist attacks by Islamists in France, Spain, Germany, England, Austria, and many places beyond Europe; by ongoing struggles with ISIS, the Taliban, and other extremist Islamist groups in the Middle East and their agents abroad; and by repeated controversies over blasphemy, polygamy, civil unrest, labor disputes, and neighborhood segregation of Muslim immigrants in some member states, especially in France, Germany, Belgium, Denmark, and the Netherlands.[23] Since 2015, the massive wave of Muslim refugees and immigrants from war-torn nations of the Middle East and northern Africa coming to European lands, with their open borders, has fueled strong anti-immigration policies and harsh anti-Islamic rhetoric and political movements.

Finally, the grave sex scandals in various churches have put Christianity back on its heels and back into the glaring media spotlight. Catholic churches in Ireland, Germany, the Netherlands, Austria, Spain, Poland, and elsewhere have all been rocked by recent state reports, criminal indictments, and lawsuits about decades of widespread pedophilia by delinquent priests and cover-ups by complicit bishops – all committed under the thick veil of corporate religious freedom.[24] Protestants in various lands also now face charges of sexual and physical abuses by their clergy and other church leaders against wives, children, parishioners, clients, and students.[25] This exposure of the underside of Christianity has led a number of academics and politicians to question seriously the wisdom and safety of maintaining the time-honored human rights principle of recognizing the autonomy of religious groups – and the Court of Justice of the European Union has introduced strong limits on religious employers in several recent cases.[26]

22 Ibid., 618.

23 See Giles Merritt, *Slippery Slope: Europe's Troubled Future* (Oxford: Oxford University Press, 2016), 199; Susanna Mancini, "The Tempting of Europe, The Political Seduction of the Cross: A Schmittian Reading of Christianity and Islam in European Constitutionalism," in Mancini and Rosenfeld, *Constitutional Secularism*, 11, 111–13.

24 See, e.g., Nik Martin, "German Catholic Church 'Needs Urgent Reform,'" *Deutsche Welle* (Feb. 3, 2019), https://p.dw.com/p/3Ce6m; "Poland's Catholic Church Admits Clergy Sexually Abused Hundreds of Children," *Deutsche Welle* (Mar. 14, 2019), https://p.dw.com/p/3F5dV; Ralf Sotscheck, "Pope Francis in Ireland Draws Large Crowd, Protests," *Deutsche Welle* (Aug. 25, 2018), https://p.dw.com/p/33jbq; "Vatican Set to Issue Guidelines on Pedophile Priests," *News.com* (Apr. 10, 2010), www.news.com.au/world/vatican-set-to-issue-guidelines-on-pedophile-priests/news-story/25c18a9da3fdb2d2024da1b11ae2f890.

25 Michael Martin, "Protestant Churches Grapple With Growing Sexual Abuse Crisis," on *Tell Me More, NPR News* (May 23, 2014), www.npr.org/2014/05/23/315129859/sex-abuse-allegations-getting-protestant-churches-to-come-clean?t=1579600456400.

26 See Chapter 9, p. 269–75.

Together, the new debates over the ongoing roles and rights of traditional Christian religions, the new challenges posed by intense religious pluralism and movement, the rise of Islam and Islamic extremists, and the exposure of church abuses have put religion at the heart of Europe's political narratives and legal controversies. All this has accelerated the pace of religious freedom litigation in the Strasbourg Court.

RELIGIOUS FREEDOM CLAIMS IN THE EUROPEAN COURT OF HUMAN RIGHTS

The most important guarantee of religious freedom enforced by the Strasbourg Court is Article 9 of the European Convention:

> 1. Everyone has the right to freedom of thought, conscience and religion; this right includes freedom to change his religion or belief and freedom, either alone or in community with others and in public or private, to manifest his religion or belief, in worship, teaching, practice and observance.
> 2. Freedom to manifest one's religion or beliefs shall be subject only to such limitations as are prescribed by law and are necessary in a democratic society in the interests of public safety, for the protection of public order, health or morals, or for the protection of the rights and freedoms of others.[27]

An important Protocol on Article 9 adds that "the State shall respect the right of parents to ensure such education and teaching in conformity with their own religious and philosophical convictions."[28] Complementing these protections, the Convention also protects other rights and freedoms that have religious dimensions. Included are the right to one's own private religious practices (Article 8); freedom of religious and antireligious expression (Article 10), and freedoms of religious assembly and association (Article 11). The Convention also prohibits religious and other forms of discrimination (Article 14).

As with other international human rights instruments, the European Convention has no formal prohibition of establishments of religion equivalent to the First Amendment of the US Constitution, thereby leaving the European Catholic, Anglican, Lutheran, and Reformed establishments of religion untouched.[29] The European Convention also lacks a separate, explicit provision governing the relations of religious communities and the state, and it thus contemplates a wide range of constitutional and legal arrangements, including professed policies of secularism

[27] Convention for the Protection of Human Rights and Fundamental Freedoms, art. 9(1–2).

[28] Protocol to the Convention for the Protection of Human Rights and Fundamental Freedoms art. 2, opened for signature Mar. 20, 1952, 213 UNTS 262 (entered into force May 18, 1954), hereafter Convention Protocol No. 1.

[29] See Doe, *Law and Religion in Europe*. But cf. Jeroen Temperman, *State-Religion Relationships and Human Rights Law: Towards a Right to Religiously Neutral Governance* (Leiden: Brill, 2010), arguing that contemporary human rights norms imply limits on state-religion identification.

in places like France and Belgium as well as bilateral concordats between the Holy See and several European nations.[30]

While the Convention's religious freedom guarantees have always held ample promise for litigants, they were largely a dead letter for the first forty years, generating little sturdy case law on the merits before the *Kokkinakis* case of 1993.[31] Since then, the Court has issued judgments on the merits in some 150 cases involving religious freedom, including almost a score in the form of Grand Chamber judgments that carry weighty authority. The Court has developed a nuanced jurisprudence of religious freedom. It emphasizes that religion is "one of the most vital elements that go to make up the identity of believers and their conception of life."[32] It appreciates that religious culture and pluralism are vital for "the society as a whole."[33] Moreover, the Court has distilled the crucial aspects of religious freedom – namely, freedom to believe, to manifest one's religion, and to associate for religious purposes – thereby identifying the individual and collective components of religion.[34] Despite the initial individualist focus of the European Convention when it was passed in 1950, the Court of late has emphasized that:

> [T]he autonomous existence of religious communities is indispensable for pluralism in a democratic society and is thus an issue at the very heart of the protection which Article 9 affords. The State's duty of neutrality and impartiality, as defined in the [Court's] case-law, is incompatible with any power on the State's part to assess the legitimacy of religious beliefs.[35]

The Strasbourg Court, however, has surprisingly weak legal authority. Individuals usually file claims in the Court against their home state only after exhausting all their existing domestic remedies in their home state. Their claim is that the member state has failed to comply with the Convention and has violated their rights.[36] A new

30 See W. Cole Durham, Jr., "Patterns of Religion-State Relations," in John Witte, Jr. and M. Christian Green, eds., *in Religion and Human Rights: An Introduction* (Oxford: Oxford University Press, 2012), 360–78.

31 The European Court of Human Rights and its predecessors have found at least fifty-nine violations of Article 9 – the first in 1993 and most of them in the past decade. See European Court of Human Rights, Overview: 1959–2014 ECHR, Council of Europe, Feb. 1, 6–7, 2015, www.echr.coe.int/Documents/Overview_19592014_ENG.pdf. On the early case law, see Malcolm D. Evans, Peter Petkoff, and Julian Rivers, eds., *The Changing Nature of Religious Rights Under International Law* (Oxford: Oxford University Press, 2015); Carolyn Evans, *Freedom of Religion Under the European Convention on Human Rights* (Oxford: Oxford University Press, 2001); T. Jeremy Gunn, "Adjudicating Rights of Conscience Under the European Convention on Human Rights," in Johan D. van der Vyver and John Witte, Jr., eds., *Religious Human Rights in Global Perspective: Legal Perspective* (The Hague: Martinus Nijhoff, 1996), 305–37.

32 *Jehovah's Witnesses of Moscow* v. *Russia*, App. No. 302/02, para. 99, June 10, 2010, http://hudoc.echr.coe.int/eng?i=001-99221.

33 Christopher McCrudden, "Religion, Human Rights, Equality and the Public Sphere," *Ecclesiastical Law Journal* 13 (2011), 26, 32.

34 Ibid., 27.

35 *Jehovah's Witnesses of Moscow*, App. No. 302/02, para. 99 (2010).

36 Convention for the Protection of Human Rights and Fundamental Freedoms, art. 34.

protocol allows the initial trial courts of member states to request a preliminary opinion from the Court on the correct interpretation of a Convention right that might be at issue.[37] But not many member states have adhered to this protocol, and it is hard to foresee what its impact will be.[38] Almost all religious freedom cases before the Court have gone through the entire and often lengthy appeal process in domestic courts before the cases are finally filed in Strasbourg.

Even if the Court finds a violation of rights, the effects of its rulings are weak. States that are party to the European Convention have a specific obligation to comply with the Court's rulings and to remove the reasons for injustice as far as possible. But a state's compliance with the Court's rulings is basically left to its good will, and many member states have ignored the Court's rulings with legal impunity. Unlike the final judgments of the highest national courts, which are binding and will be enforced by coercion if necessary, the Strasbourg Court's cases produce only soft laws that depend on persuasion, not command, and on a willingness of member states to change their practice or reform their laws to protect their reputations for being respectful of human rights, including rights to religious freedom.[39]

Even as soft law, however, the Court's jurisprudence has high respect both within and beyond the Council of Europe. Some member state legislatures and courts do reform and apply their laws in accordance with the Court's rulings, and its general principles and protections of religious freedom are often regarded as exemplary.[40] Article 9 cases and related cases have fed European scholarship and the global human rights agenda and have provided member states with an uninterrupted flow of judgments that progressively unfold the scope and meaning of religious freedom and other fundamental rights.

The Strasbourg Court has touched on Article 9 in nearly 950 cases. Since 1993, 150 of these cases have produced judgments on the merits of religious freedom.[41] Together, these cases have held, on the one hand, that (1) freedom of religion, freedom from religion, and freedom to manifest one's religion are presumptively protected for all peaceable parties, including professed atheists and secular humanists; (2) such rights inhere in all human beings, no matter their citizenship or any other legal status; and (3) religious organizations have their rights protected under the European Convention and enjoy a level of religious autonomy from the state.

37 Protocol No. 16 to the Convention for the Protection of Human Rights and Fundamental Freedoms, art. 1, opened for signature Oct. 2, 2013, CETS No. 214 (entered into force Aug. 1, 2018), hereafter Convention Protocol No. 16.

38 Council of Europe, Details on Treaty No. 214, www.coe.int/en/web/conventions/full-list/-/conventions/treaty/214 (showing that only ten countries have ratified the protocol).

39 Janneke Gerards, "The European Court of Human Rights and the National Courts: Giving Shape to the Notion of 'Shared Responsibility,'" in Jenneke Gerards and Joseph Fleuren, eds., *Implementation of the European Convention on Human Rights and of the Judgments of the ECtHR in National Case-Law: A Comparative Analysis* (Cambridge: Intersentia, 2014), 22–28.

40 Courtney Hillebrecht, *Domestic Politics and International Human Rights Tribunals: The Problem of Compliance* (Cambridge: Cambridge University Press, 2014).

41 HUDOC Database, https://hudoc.echr.coe.int/eng#%20.

On the other hand, however, (4) religious freedom is not necessarily privileged above any other fundamental rights, and exemptions can be restricted when they cause third-party harm; (5) claims of religious freedom usually lose when the Court grants a "margin of appreciation" to member states; and (6) those losses have fallen disproportionately of late on newly arrived Muslims and traditional Christians who have fallen out of cultural step.

THE MAIN CASES ON RIGHTS OF THOUGHT, CONSCIENCE, AND BELIEF

Article 9 of the European Convention protects not just religion but also thought, conscience, and belief.[42] Like other national and international tribunals, the Strasbourg Court has used this more expansive language to provide "religious freedom" protections to theists and nontheists, atheists and agnostics, free thinkers and skeptics, and new religions and ancient traditions alike. The Court has placed a high premium on religious pluralism as a fundamental good for democratic societies, and has insisted that conflicts between religions, or between religion and nonreligion, be resolved in a way that tolerates all peaceable forms of religion and belief in the community. As the Court put it in 2007: "[T]he role of the authorities in such circumstances is not to remove the cause of tension by eliminating pluralism, but to ensure that the competing groups tolerate each other. This State role is conducive to public order, religious harmony and tolerance in a democratic society."[43] In a 2013 case, the Court stressed further "the positive obligation on the State authorities to secure the rights under Article 9," even when they are being violated by another private party rather than by the State.[44]

Article 9 further protects a person's right both to hold religious beliefs in private and to manifest those beliefs peaceably in public. The Court has treated the "internal right to believe" much as Western national courts have treated liberty of conscience.[45] Several Court cases have made clear that this right includes each person's right to accept, reject, or change their thoughts, beliefs, or religious affiliation without involvement, inducement, or impediment of the state.[46] Article 9 thus protects persons from pressure to reveal their religious identity or beliefs to the

42 See also the International Covenant on Civil and Political Rights, art. 18, adopted Dec. 19, 1966, 999 UNTS 171 (entered into force Mar. 23, 1976), providing similar protections; Convention for the Protection of Human Rights and Fundamental Freedoms, art. 9(1).

43 *Members of the Gldani Congregation* v. *Georgia*, Eur. Ct. H.R., para. 132 (2007), http://hudoc.echr.coe.int/eng?i=001-80395 (*citing Refah Partisi [the Welfare Party]* v. *Turkey*, 2003-II Eur. Ct. H. R. 267; *Serif* v. *Greece*, 1999-IX Eur. Ct. H.R. 73); see also *Kuznetsov* v. *Russia*, Eur. Ct. H.R., para. 62 (2007), http://hudoc.echr.coe.int/eng?i=001-78982 (finding an Article 9 violation for a state's failure to prosecute officials who had illegally broken up a Jehovah's Witness Sunday worship service).

44 *Eweida* v. *United Kingdom*, 2013-I Eur. Ct. H.R. 215, 254, para. 84.

45 See European Parliament Research Service, Freedom of Conscience Around the World: Briefing, European Parliament (2019), www.europarl.europa.eu/RegData/etudes/BRIE/2019/642277/EPRS_BRI(2019)642277_EN.pdf.

46 *Kokkinakis* v. *Greece*, 260-A Eur. Ct. H.R. (ser. A), paras. 56, 74 (1993).

state,[47] safeguards military personnel from being forced to discuss religion with superior officers,[48] and guards persons from being forced to swear a religious oath in order to take political office, to testify in court, or to receive a state benefit or professional license.[49] As the Court put it in 2010, "State authorities are not entitled to intervene in the sphere of an individual's freedom of conscience and to seek to discover his or her religious beliefs or oblige him or her to disclose such beliefs."[50]

Conscientious Objection and the Military. Many European countries now use their own constitutional guarantees of liberty of conscience and the internal right to believe as grounds for granting pacifists exemption from compulsory military service.[51] An explicit right to conscientious objection, however, was not included in Article 9 of the 1950 Convention, nor was it included in the 1948 Universal Declaration of Human Rights, whose guarantee of religious freedom was largely echoed in the Convention. Conscientious objection to military service was a vexed human rights topic in the immediate aftermath of the two world wars, and it only gradually came to be recognized by individual states.[52] The European Convention itself, while prohibiting forced labor in general in Article 4, made clear that it was not forced labor for the state to mandate "any service of a military character or, in case of conscientious objectors in countries where they are recognized, service exacted instead of compulsory military service."[53] Only in 1993 did the United Nations Human Rights Committee first declare that "the obligation to use lethal force may seriously conflict with the freedom of conscience and the right to manifest one's religion or belief."[54] The committee urged all nation states to recognize this right "by law or practice," ensuring that "there shall be no differentiation among conscientious objectors on the basis of the nature of their particular beliefs [and] … no discrimination against conscientious objectors because they have failed to perform military service."[55]

In *Bayatyan* v. *Armenia* (2011),[56] the Court for the first time read this right into Article 9 of the European Convention. In this case, the Court granted relief to

47 *Işik* v. *Turkey*, 2010-I Eur. Ct. H.R. 341, 356, para. 41.

48 *Larissis* v. *Greece*, 1998-I Eur. Ct. H.R. 329, 362.

49 *Alexandridis* v. *Greece*, Eur. Ct. H.R., paras. 38, 41 (2008), http://hudoc.echr.coe.int/eng?i=001-85189; *Buscarini* v. *San Marino*, 1999-I Eur. Ct. H.R. 605, 616–18, paras. 36, 39–40.

50 *Işik*, 2010-I Eur. Ct. H.R. at 356, para. 41; see also *Dimitras* v. *Greece*, Eur. Ct. H.R., paras. 46, 64 (2010), http://hudoc.echr.coe.int/eng?i=001-99014.

51 Amicus Curiae by Amnesty International Supporting the Right to Conscientious Objection to Military Service, Constitutional Court [Const. Ct.], 2014 Hun-Ga8, 2013Hun-Ga5, 13, 23, and 27, 2012Hun-Ga17 (S. Kor.), www.amnesty.org/download/Documents/8000/pol310012014en.pdf.

52 Dorothy Estrada Tanck, "Civil Resistance in Public International Law," *Anuario Espanol de Derecho Internacional* 35 (2019), 373, 373–77.

53 Convention for the Protection of Human Rights and Fundamental Freedoms, art. 4(3)(b).

54 General Comment Adopted by the Human Rights Committee under Art. 40(4) of the International Covenant on Civil and Political Rights on its Forty-Eighth Session, UN Doc. CCPR/C/21/Rev.1/Add.4, at 4, para. 11 (1993).

55 Ibid.

56 *Bayatyan* v. *Armenia*, 2011-IV Eur. Ct. H.R. 1.

a Jehovah's Witness who was imprisoned for failing to serve in the military upon his conscription; noncombat options were unavailable at the time. "Article 9 did not explicitly refer to a right to conscientious objection," the Court noted, ignoring Article 4's explicit denial of this right. The Court, however, found that "a serious and insurmountable conflict between the obligation to serve in the army and a person's conscience or deeply and genuinely held religious or other belief constituted a conviction or belief of sufficient cogency, seriousness, cohesion, and importance to attract the guarantees of Article 9." It helped the *Bayatyan* Court that "the overwhelming majority" of European state legislatures by that time had already granted conscientious-objection status to pacifists, thereby generating a consensus among the member states. The Court ruled that in the absence of a legislative accommodation by a member state, Article 9 protects the rights of pacifism.[57] The Court ruled similarly in a more recent case, so long as conscientious objections are rooted in religious beliefs[58] and are not political in inspiration.[59]

Conscientious Objection in the Workplace. The Court dealt with conscientious objection in the field of noncompulsory work with the signature case of *Eweida and Others* v. *The United Kingdom* (2013).[60] This ruling involved claims by four different employees who sought accommodation for their religious beliefs and their manifestation in practice. Two of these employees were traditional Christians who claimed freedom of conscience against private and state employers who insisted they work with same-sex parties.[61] In one case, Gary McFarlane worked as a consultant for a national private organization that provided sex therapy. "Directly motivated by his orthodox Christian beliefs about marriage and sexual relationships," he believed that same-sex relations were sinful, and he therefore refused to provide therapy services to same-sex couples. The organization dismissed him, alleging that he had failed to comply with its code of nondiscrimination on the basis of sexual orientation. McFarlane lost his domestic claim that he had been discriminated against on religious grounds, and he thus sued in the Strasbourg Court under Articles 9 and 14 of the Convention. The Court ruled against McFarlane. It did not deny that he had suffered infringement of his Article 9 religious freedom, but it found that, given his employer's explicit policy of nondiscrimination "in securing the rights" of same-sex parties and all others, the state had an ample margin of appreciation to strike a balance in favor of his employer.[62]

57 Ibid., 4–5. See Compilation of Gen. Comments and Gen. Recommendations Adopted by Human Rights Treaty Bodies, International Human Rights Instruments, at 1, 38, para. 11, UN Doc. HRI/GEN/1/Rev.1 (1994).

58 *Papavasilakis* v. *Greece*, Eur. Ct. H.R. (2016), http://hudoc.echr.coe.int/eng?i=001-166850.

59 *Aydemir* v. *Turkey*, Eur. Ct. H.R. (2016), http://hudoc.echr.coe.int/eng?i=001-163940. The Court recently reaffirmed the necessity that the objector substantiate her claim in *Dyagilev* v. *Russia*, App. no. 49972/16 (third section's ruling; an appeal before the Grand Chamber is pending at the moment).

60 *Eweida* v. *United Kingdom*, 2013-I Eur. Ct. H.R. 215 at 223, para. 3.

61 Ibid., 229–36.

62 Ibid., 232–36, 261–62.

The better-known claimant in the *Eweida* case was Lilian Ladele, an employee in a London borough's registrar office.[63] She held "the orthodox Christian view" of heterosexual marriage. Part of her job consisted in registering partnerships for the state. When the state introduced a same-sex domestic partnership option, she determined that her Christian faith prevented her from participating in the establishment of such partnerships. For a time, fellow employees covered for her, but when they stopped, Ladele requested an accommodation from her state employer, who refused. She lost in British courts and took her case to Strasbourg, arguing that the state's failure to accord her a conscientious objection constituted religious discrimination under Articles 9 and 14 of the Convention.[64]

The Strasbourg Court rejected her claim. It recognized that the new policy of registering same-sex partnerships had "a particularly detrimental impact on her because of her religious beliefs." She was fired from a job that she had taken when there was no conflict between those beliefs and her job responsibilities. On the other hand, the Court noted that "the local authority's policy aimed to secure the rights of others," including same-sex parties. In balancing these conflicting rights, the Court concluded that the state deserved an ample margin of appreciation and could fire Ladele with impunity. The upshot of these twin *Eweida* cases is that religious conscience or belief can be protected through exemptions and accommodated, but not if such protection causes harm to third parties in the exercise of their rights.[65]

Squaring religious freedom claims with same-sex rights and liberties has been a difficult exercise for European states, among others, and it is likely to remain so. The old Continent itself is split between liberal Western and more traditional Central and Eastern European perspectives on same-sex matters. The Netherlands was the first country in the world to legalize same-sex marriage, in 2001. Northern Ireland was the latest to do so, in mid-2019. The main holdout in Western Europe is Italy, which belatedly introduced only a civil partnership for same-sex couples in 2016. Most Central and Eastern European countries, by contrast, make no legal provision for same-sex marriage, and a number of them are actively opposed to same-sex unions or activities of any sort.[66] Accommodating the wide array of opinions on same-sex relations and their compatibility with countervailing claims of religious freedom and liberty of conscience will be a formidable challenge for the Strasbourg Court and national courts for years to come, particularly given the hard right turn in the recent politics of Eastern European countries like Poland and Hungary.

Religion and Education. The Court has also repeatedly addressed claims by students and parents seeking freedom from religious coercion in schools in violation

[63] Ibid., 230.

[64] Ibid., 230–31.

[65] Ibid., 230–31, 254–61.

[66] Michael Lipka and David Masci, "Where Europe Stands on Gay Marriage and Civil Unions," Pew Research Center, Oct. 28, 2019, www.pewresearch.org/fact-tank/2019/10/28/where-europe-stands-on-gay-marriage-and-civil-unions/.

of their "thought, conscience, and belief." These cases have had decidedly mixed results. In an early case, *Valsamis* v. *Greece* (1996), the Court provided no relief to a Jehovah's Witness student who was punished for not participating in a school parade celebrating a national holiday in commemoration of Greece's war with Italy.[67] The student claimed conscientious objection to participation in this celebration of warfare. The school had already accommodated his conscientious objections to religious-education classes and to participation in the school's Orthodox mass, but the school did not think he warranted an exemption from the parade. The Court agreed, concluding that participation in a one-time parade, far removed from the field of military battle, did not "offend the applicants' pacifist convictions" enough to warrant an exemption.[68]

In *Konrad and Others* v. *Germany* (2006), the Court rejected the rights claim of parents to homeschool their primary-school-aged children.[69] The Romeikes were conservative Christians who opposed the German public school's liberal sex-education courses, its use of fairy tales with magic and witchcraft, and its tolerance of physical and psychological violence among students. In the absence of available private schools, they wanted to teach their young children at home at their own expense, using much of the same curriculum as state-approved private schools, but with supplemental religious instruction. Germany denied their request, citing its constitutionally based system of mandatory school attendance. The parents appealed on behalf of themselves and their children. They claimed violations of their rights to privacy, equality, and religious freedom under the Convention. They also pointed to the Protocol to Article 9 that explicitly identifies "the right of parents to ensure such education and teaching in conformity with their own religious and philosophical convictions."[70]

The Strasbourg Court ruled for Germany. The Protocol to Article 9, the Court pointed out, begins by saying that "[n]o person shall be denied the right of education." "It is on to this fundamental right that is grafted the right of parents to respect for their religious and philosophical convictions." The child's right to education comes first, and the Romeike children are too young to waive that right or to understand the implications of that waiver for their later democratic capacities. Germany's interest and duty is in protecting each child's right to education and "safeguarding pluralism in education, which is essential for the preservation of the 'democratic society' . . . . In view of the power of the modern State, it is above all through State teaching that this aim must be realized." Germany has determined that in a democratic society, "not only the acquisition of knowledge but also

67 *Valsamis* v. *Greece*, 1996-VI Eur. Ct. H.R. 2312, 2315.

68 Ibid., 2312, 2315, 2323–26; see also *Efstratiou* v. *Greece*, 1996-VI Eur. Ct. H.R. 2347 (finding no violation of Article 9 when a Greek Orthodox school punished a Jehovah's Witness student for her refusal to participate in a parade honoring the military).

69 *Konrad* v. *Germany*, 2006-XIII Eur. Ct. H.R. 355, 360.

70 Ibid., 359–66; Convention Protocol No. 1, art. 2.

integration into and first experiences of society are important goals in primary-school education. ... [T]hose objectives could not be met to the same extent by home education, even if it allowed children to acquire the same standard of knowledge." Moreover, the parents could provide their children with the religious instruction they desire outside of school time. With no European consensus on homeschooling options, the Court concluded, Germany must enjoy a "margin of appreciation" in how best to educate its citizens.[71] The German police thereafter forcibly transported the Romeike children to the public school, and their parents faced fines and potential loss of custody. In response, the family moved to the United States, which has long allowed homeschooling in many of its states.[72]

The Court was more sympathetic to the claims of atheist and agnostic students and their parents who claimed religious coercion in the cases of *Folgerø and Others* v. *Norway* (2007) and *Grzelak* v. *Poland* (2010). *Folgerø* addressed a new Norwegian law requiring all public grade-school and middle-school students to take a course in "Christianity, Religion and Philosophy" (KRL).[73] The law made no exceptions for non-Christian students. Four students, whose families were professed humanists, objected that this policy forced their children into religious instruction the parents could not abide. The Court agreed. It found that the state had not tailored its new law carefully enough to deal with students who had different religious and non-religious backgrounds. "[N]otwithstanding the many laudable legislative purposes" in introducing this course, the Court held, the material was not "conveyed in an objective, critical and pluralistic manner." Moreover, the school's "refusal to grant the applicant parents full exemption from the KRL subject for their children gave rise to a violation" of the parents' rights to raise their child in their own faith, in this case atheism.[74]

Three years later, in *Grzelak*, a public grade-school student in Poland, with agnostic parents, was properly exempted from mandatory religion classes in public school, as the *Folgerø* ruling had demanded.[75] But his only alternative to attending the religion classes was to spend unsupervised time in the school hallway, library, or club. His parents wanted him enrolled in an alternative course in secular ethics. The school refused to offer such a special course for lack of enough teachers, students, and funds. The school further marked his report card with a blank for "religion/ ethics," and calculated his cumulative grade-point average based on fewer credit hours. The Court found that these state actions violated both Articles 9 and 14 (prohibiting religious discrimination) of the Convention, for "[it] brings about

71 Ibid., 364–66.

72 Billy Gage Raley, "Safe at Home: Establishing a Fundamental Right to Homeschooling," *Brigham Young University Education and Law Journal* (2017), 59, 64.

73 *Folgerø* v. *Norway*, 2007-III Eur. Ct. H.R. 51, 58.

74 Ibid. 59, 61, 100, 102.

75 *Grzelak* v. *Poland*, App. No. 7710/02, para. 7, Nov. 22, 2010, http://hudoc.echr.coe.int/eng?i=001-99384.

a situation in which individuals are obliged – directly or indirectly – to reveal that they are nonbelievers."[76]

In *Lautsi* v. *Italy* (2011), however, the Court upheld Italy's longstanding policy of displaying crucifixes in its public-school classrooms despite religious freedom objections.[77] In this case, an atheist mother of two public-school children challenged Italy's policy as a form of coercion of Christian beliefs. She argued that the presence of crucifixes in public schools violated her and her children's rights to religious freedom and to a secular education guaranteed by Article 9 and its Protocol, and other provisions. The Court's Grand Chamber held in favor of Italy. It recognized that the crucifix is a religious symbol, that atheism is a protected religious belief, and that public schools must be religiously neutral and free from religious coercion. But the Court held that the passive display of a crucifix in a public-school classroom by itself was not a form of religious coercion – particularly when students of all faiths were welcome in public schools and were free to wear their own religious symbols. The Court held further that Italy's policy of displaying only the crucifix and no other religious symbol was not a violation of its obligation of religious neutrality, but an acceptable reflection of its majoritarian Catholic culture and history. As Judge Bonello put it in his concurrence, "A court of human rights cannot allow itself to suffer from historical Alzheimer's. It has no right to disregard the cultural continuum of a nation's flow through time, nor to ignore what, over the centuries, has served to mold and define the profile of a people." With European nations widely divided on whether and where to display religious symbols, the Court concluded, Italy must be granted a "margin of appreciation" to decide for itself how and where to maintain its traditions in school.[78]

Coercion and Religious Worship of Prisoners. The Court has further made clear that a prisoner, though more limited in rights than a soldier or student, still has a right to be free from religious coercion and a basic right to peaceable religious worship without recrimination or punishment.[79] The Court reiterated this longstanding position in the Grand Chamber case of *Mozer* v. *the Republic of Moldova and Russia* (2016), holding that prison authorities who had, for no stated reason, refused to allow a pastor and parents to visit a prisoner violated the Article 9 rights of the prisoner to exercise his faith in "community with others."[80]

76 Ibid. 7, 12, 18, 22–25, 72, 87.

77 *Lautsi* v. *Italy*, 2011-III Eur. Ct. H.R. 61, 63–64.

78 Ibid. 63, 68, 95–97, 103, 110; see also Andrea Pin, "Public Schools, the Italian Crucifix, and the European Court of Human Rights: The Italian Separation of Church and State," *Emory International Law Review* 25 (2011), 95, 97–98 (exploring the conflict in *Lautsi* between the Court's position and the Italian court's position on the relationship between church and state).

79 *Poltoratskiy* v. *Ukraine*, 2003-V Eur Ct. H.R. 89, 129.

80 *Mozer* v. *Republic of Moldova*, App. No. 11138/10, paras. 197–99, Feb. 23, 2016, http://hudoc.echr.coe.int/eng?i=001-161055.

The Court held similarly in *Korostelev* v. *Russia* (2020), in protecting Korostelev, a Muslim held in a Russian penitentiary in solitary confinement.[81] Prison officials subjected him to repeated reprimands for getting up from his bed to pray at night during the holy month of Ramadan. That conduct, officials argued, breached prison rules that required that detainees remain in their beds at night. The Russian government later argued that detainees had not only the right but also the duty to sleep at night. The Court, however, found that Russia had violated Mr. Korostelev's freedom of conscience and worship under Article 9, as the limitation and reprimands that he suffered were not "necessary in a democratic society," as the Article requires.[82]

Not all such restrictions on prisoners, however, constitute coercion. In *Süveges* v. *Hungary* (2016), for example, the Court held that the authorities' refusal to allow a person under house arrest to attend a weekly worship service outside his home was not a violation of Article 9.[83] In this case, the Court concluded, the restriction was prescribed by law, pursued a stated legitimate purpose of safety and security, was proportionate to that purpose, and was necessary in a democratic society. After all, this claimant could still worship in his home with coreligionists and religious leaders coming to him, as they do with others who are shut in because of injury, infirmity, or other limits on their movement. Here, the balance between state interests and private rights tipped in favor of the state.[84]

CASES ON REGULATION OF THE PUBLIC MANIFESTATION OF RELIGION

Article 9 of the European Convention protects not only the internal right to believe but also the external right to "manifest one's beliefs in public through worship, teaching, practice, and observance." Articles 10 and 14 offer complementary guarantees of freedom of expression and freedom of association, respectively. Article 9 further makes clear that the right to "manifest one's religion [in public]" is subject to regulation "in the interests of public safety, for the protection of public order, health or morals, or for the protection of the rights and freedoms of others." When a party claims interference with, violation of, or a burden on Article 9 and related rights, the Court will assess (1) whether there is, in fact, interference with that right; (2) whether this interference was based on law, rather than an arbitrary judgment; and (3) whether the interference was necessary in a democratic society. This last point is judged by whether the law (a) corresponds to a pressing social need; (b) is proportionate to the aim pursued; and (c) is justified by relevant, sufficient, or pressing reasons.[85]

81 App. No. 29290/10, Dec. 8, 2020, http://hudoc.echr.coe.int/eng?i=001-202429.
82 Ibid. 65, 82.
83 *Süveges* v. *Hungary*, App. No. 50255/12, Feb. 5, 2016, http://hudoc.echr.coe.int/eng?i=001-159764.
84 Ibid., 147, 151–57.
85 See European Court of Human Rights, Guide on Article 9 of the European Convention on Human Rights: Freedom of Thought, Conscience, and Religion, 2015, www.echr.coe.int/Documents/Guide_Art_9_ENG.pdf.

Proselytism and Its Legal Limits . In its first Article 9 case on the merits, *Kokkinakis* v. *Greece* (1993), the Strasbourg Court upheld one's right to share one's faith, despite a Greek criminal law that prohibited proselytism.[86] A Jehovah's Witness, peaceably discussing his faith with a local Orthodox woman, was arrested and convicted under this statute. He appealed, and the Court found in his favor. Article 9, the Court reasoned, explicitly protects "freedom to manifest one's religion … in community with others" through "words and deeds" that express one's "religious convictions." The article protects "the right to try to convince one's neighbour, for example through 'teaching.'" If that were not the case, Article 9's "'freedom to change [one's] religion or belief' … would be likely to remain a dead letter." The state may regulate missionary activity for the sake of security and protection of the rights of others. It may also outlaw "activities offering material or social advantages with a view to gaining new members for a Church or exerting improper pressure on people in distress or in need; [or] the use of violence or brainwashing." These factors, however, were not present in *Kokkinakis*, so he prevailed.[87]

By contrast, in *Larissis* v. *Greece*, five years later, the Court found no violation of the Article 9 rights of military officers convicted for proselytizing their military subordinates.[88] The officers were Pentecostal Christians who repeatedly engaged their Greek Orthodox subordinates in theological discussions while on duty, sent and read them sundry biblical and religious texts, and invited them repeatedly to visit or join the Pentecostal church, which one of the subordinates eventually accepted, to the dismay of his family. The officers were convicted of the crime of proselytism, defined by Greek law as "any direct or indirect attempt to intrude on the religious beliefs of a person of a different religious persuasion (*eterodoxos*) with the aim of undermining those beliefs." The officers were given brief prison sentences, which were later commuted to fines so long as the officers desisted from such behavior in the future. The officers claimed violations, inter alia, of their Article 9 rights. The Court held for Greece. It noted that the military's "hierarchical structures … colour every aspect of the relations between military personnel, making it difficult for a subordinate to rebuff the approaches of an individual of superior rank or to withdraw from a conversation initiated by him." What might seem like "an innocuous exchange of ideas which the recipient is free to accept or reject," in civilian life, might in the military be "a form of harassment or the application of undue pressure in abuse of power." The Court further noted that, in this case, the light punishments imposed on the officers were "more preventative than punitive in nature," making Greece's law a proportionate and justified burden on the religious freedom of the officers.[89]

Larissis was an unusual case of military officers exploiting their superiority to proselytize their minority faith among subordinates who belonged to the faith of the

86 *Kokkinakis* v. *Greece*, 260-A Eur. Ct. H.R. (ser. A, 1993).
87 Ibid., 3, 13, 17, paras. 48–49.
88 *Larissis* v. *Greece*, App. No. 23372/94, Feb. 24, 1998, http://hudoc.echr.coe.int/eng?i=001-58139.
89 Ibid., 7, 16, 27, 36, 51, 54, 78.

majority. But the problem of proselytism is much wider in Europe, encompassing also peer-to-peer relationships. It has remained a perennial issue, particularly in Orthodox lands that prohibit evangelization of any who have been baptized as Orthodox; in Muslim communities that regard conversion out of Islam as a (capital) crime of apostasy; and in former Soviet republics unaccustomed to competing with Western missionaries in an open "marketplace of religious ideas."[90] The Strasbourg Court and European national courts have continued to allow general restrictions on the time, place, and manner of proselytizing that are necessary, proportionate, and applied without discrimination against any religion.[91] But the Court has repeatedly made clear since *Kokkinakis* that religious rights of proselytizers are violated by categorical criminal bans on all missionary activity, by prosecution, retention, and detention for preaching, or by patently discriminatory licensing or registration provisions for proselytizing faiths.[92]

Holy Days and Salary. The Strasbourg Court generally has held against religious minorities who seek Article 9 accommodations to observe their holy days. While individual member states are free to adopt and apply their own laws governing religious holidays and Sabbath days, their citizens have no prima facie right to observe their holidays. Thus, in *Kosteski* v. *The Former Yugoslav Republic of Macedonia* (2006), a Muslim employee was fined for taking a day off to celebrate a Muslim religious holiday/festival without giving notice to his employer.[93] He alleged violation of his Article 9 rights to engage in religious worship. The Court rejected these claims, arguing that his attendance at the religious festival was not a clear act of religious worship; moreover, the ostensibly religious nature of the festival did not justify Kosteski's failure to notify his employer that he planned to miss work.[94]

Six years later, in *Sessa* v. *Italy*, a Jewish lawyer objected to a court order that scheduled a hearing date on his major religious holiday of Yom Kippur without granting a continuance in a case where he served as counsel.[95] The Court found no Article 9 violation, arguing that the judge was acting reasonably to vindicate the public's right to the proper administration of justice, and the lawyer could have arranged for substitute counsel at the hearing.[96]

90 See John Witte, Jr. and Richard C. Martin, eds., *Sharing the Book: Religious Perspectives on the Rights and Wrongs of Proselytism*, repr. ed. (Eugene, OR: Wipf & Stock, 2008); John Witte, Jr., "A Primer on the Rights and Wrongs of Proselytism," *Cumberland Law Review* 31 (2001), 619–30.

91 Tad Stahnke, "Proselytism and the Freedom to Change Religion in International Human Rights Law," *Brigham Young University Law Review* (1999), 251, 326.

92 *Nasirov* v. *Azerbaijan*, App. No. 58717/10, paras. 59–60 (2020), http://hudoc.echr.coe.int/eng?i=001-201088 (citing *Kokkinakis* v. *Greece*, App. No. 14307/88, para. 31 [1993]).

93 *Kosteski* v. *Macedonia*, App. No. 55170/00, paras. 3, 8, 9, Apr. 13, 2006, http://hudoc.echr.coe.int/eng?i=001-73342.

94 Ibid., paras. 12, 39.

95 *Sessa* v. *Italy*, 2012-III Eur. Ct. H.R. 165, 167.

96 Ibid., 174.

Religious Dress Cases. The Strasbourg Court has weighed in heavily on oft contested issues of religious dress and ornamentation in public. Until very recently, the Court has interpreted Article 9 to allow states to impose a series of restrictions on Muslim women who wore headscarves in manifestation of their religion but contrary to public-school dress codes. In each case, the Court sided with the member state against the Muslim petitioner, granting the state ample margins of appreciation to regulate this controversial issue of Muslim female apparel. Other, more recent Article 9 cases involving religious apparel, however, have been more successful.

In *Dahlab* v. *Switzerland*, a state elementary schoolteacher, newly converted to Islam from Catholicism, was banned from wearing a headscarf when she taught her classes.[97] She claimed violation of her Article 9 rights. The government countered by highlighting the value of maintaining secularism in a public school that was open to young students from various traditions. Invoking the margin of appreciation doctrine, the Court determined that this school dress code and its application to Dahlab were necessary and proportionate, and dismissed her claim that the state had violated Article 9. The Court recognized that it was "very difficult to assess the impact that a powerful external symbol such as the wearing of a headscarf may have on the freedom of conscience and religion of very young children." But the Court worried "that the wearing of a headscarf might have some kind of proselytizing effect," especially since the teacher was acting as "a representative of the State." Moreover, the Court continued in rather explicit anti-Islamic tones, the headscarf "appear[ed] to be imposed on women by a precept which is laid down in the Koran and which, as the Federal Court noted, is hard to square with the principle of gender equality." It was "therefore ... difficult to reconcile the wearing of an Islamic headscarf with the message of tolerance, respect for others and, above all, equality and nondiscrimination that all teachers in a democratic society must convey to their pupils."

> Accordingly, weighing the right of a teacher to manifest her religion against the need to protect pupils by preserving religious harmony, the Court considers that, in the circumstances of the case and having regard, above all, to the tender age of the children for whom the applicant was responsible as a representative of the State, the Geneva authorities did not exceed their margin of appreciation and that the measure they took was therefore not unreasonable.[98]

Dahlab was only the first of a series of decisions upholding bans on wearing the Islamic headscarf in public. In several more recent cases, the Court largely abandoned its proselytization-based rationale and displayed an increasingly hostile attitude toward the public wearing of this garment. In *Şahin* v. *Turkey*, for example, an

97 *Dahlab* v. *Switzerland*, 2001-V Eur. Ct. H.R. 447, 449.

98 Ibid., 451–52, 463; see also *Kurtulmuş* v. *Turkey*, 2006-II Eur. Ct. H.R. 297, 306–7 (declaring inadmissible an Article 9 objection by a Muslim university professor who was prohibited from wearing her Islamic headscarf in the exercise of her functions).

Islamic medical student at Istanbul University was forbidden to take certain courses and exams because she was wearing a headscarf, contrary to state rules governing dress.[99] When the university brought disciplinary actions against her, she filed an Article 9 claim. The Court sided with Turkey, and again granted a margin of appreciation to the Turkish constitutional and cultural ideals of gender equality and state secularism. "The principle of secularism," the Court noted, created "a modern public society in which equality was guaranteed to all citizens without distinction on grounds of religion, denomination or sex." This principle made possible "[s]ignificant advances in women's rights," including "equality of treatment in education, the introduction of a ban on polygamy," and "the presence of women in public life and their active participation in society. Consequently, the ideas that women should be freed from religious constraints and that society should be modernised had a common origin." Since secularism is "one of the fundamental principles of the Turkish state," and since this principle is "in harmony with the rule of law and respect for human rights," religious "attitude[s]" and actions to the contrary "will not enjoy the protection of Article 9."[100]

The Court continued on this path in *Dogru* v. *France*.[101] There, a Muslim girl refused to follow her public school's dress code that required her to take off her headscarf during physical education classes and sports events. Dismayed by the breach of its rules and the tensions it caused among the other students, the school initiated disciplinary action against her. When she persisted in her claim to wear her headscarf in all public settings, the school offered to teach her through a correspondence program. She and her parents rejected this, so she was expelled from the school. She claimed violation of her Article 9 rights. The Court again held for the state, and again accorded France an ample margin of appreciation for its state policy of secularism.[102]

In its most recent case on this point, *Osmanoğlu* v. *Switzerland*, the Court also ruled against two Muslim girls whose parents challenged a Swiss public school's compulsory swimming lessons, which had boys and girls swimming together in the same pool.[103] The parents claimed that mixed-gender swimming violated their and their daughters' Article 9 rights, and they refused to send their nine- and eleven-year-old daughters to swimming lessons. Although school authorities offered to let the girls wear burkinis and change clothes in a private dressing room, the parents insisted that mixed-gender swimming – even before puberty – contradicted their religious belief and practice,

99 *Şahin* v. *Turkey*, 2005-XI Eur. Ct. H.R. 173, 181, para. 17.

100 Ibid., 182–86, 204–6.

101 *Dogru* v. *France*, App. No. 27058/05, Dec. 4, 2008, http://hudoc.echr.coe.int/eng?i=001-90039.

102 Ibid., 7–11, 33, 77; see also *Köse* v. *Turkey*, 2006-II Eur. Ct. H.R. 339, 359 (declaring inadmissible claims under Article 9 and its Protocol against Turkey's general prohibition against wearing an Islamic headscarf in school); *Kervanci* v. *France*, App. No. 31645/04, paras. 7, 8, 78, Dec. 4, 2008, http://hudoc.echr.coe.int/eng?i=001-90048 (finding no Article 9 violation when a twelve-year-old applicant was expelled for nonparticipation in school sports activities when she would not remove her headscarf).

103 *Osmanoğlu* v. *Switzerland*, App. No. 29086/12, paras. 9, 106, Jan. 10, 2017, http://hudoc.echr.coe.int/eng?i=001-170436.

since their daughters were preparing to observe Muslim customs of female modesty as adults. Moreover, the girls were already taking private swimming lessons. Thus, the parents sought a full exemption from the program. The Court, however, determined that, although the swimming program interfered to some degree with the applicants' ability to manifest their religious beliefs, it also advanced legitimate public goals beyond teaching children to swim, including, most notably, fostering socioeconomic inclusiveness and integration among a diverse student body. Insofar as Swiss authorities had also offered reasonable accommodations, the program did not violate the parties' Article 9 rights but fell within the margin of appreciation for state decision-making about the best forms of education.[104]

The Court has also accepted alternative logics to support other state restrictions on public displays of religious apparel. Twice the Court rejected Article 9 complaints by airline passengers who were forced to remove religious apparel during airport security checks. Safety concerns clearly outweighed Article 9 rights, the Court stated.[105] In *Mann Singh* v. *France*, the Court upheld France's decision to withhold a driver's license from a Sikh who refused to remove his turban for his picture on the license.[106] France's public-safety concerns again outweighed the applicant's genuine religious interest in wearing his turban at all times in public, the Court concluded.[107]

Similarly, in S.A.S. v. *France*, the Court upheld France's controversial ban on full-face coverings in public against a claim by a devout Muslim who wore the niqab and burqa as expressions of her "religious, personal and cultural faith."[108] The Court recognized that the ban interfered with her religion, and it rejected France's arguments that the ban was justified because it promoted the rights of women, protected safety and security, and respected the dignity and equality of men and women alike. Instead, the Court now embraced France's tertiary argument that the ban ensured and promoted "respect for the minimum requirements of life in society" – namely, face-to-face communication. "[T]he face plays an important role in social interaction," the Court reasoned, and "individuals who are present in places open to all may not wish to see practices or attitudes developing there which would fundamentally call into question the possibility of open interpersonal relationships, which, by virtue of an established consensus, forms an indispensable element of community life."[109] The Court held similarly in subsequent French and Belgian cases.[110]

104 Ibid., 9, 17, 33, 57, 66, 95–96 105–06.

105 *El Morsli* v. *France*, App. No. 15585/06, para. 1, Mar. 4, 2008, http://hudoc.echr.coe.int/eng?i=001-117860 (Muslim with headscarf); *Phull* v. *France*, 2005-I Eur. Ct. H.R. 409, 415 (Sikh with turban).

106 *Mann Singh* v. *France*, App. No. 24479/07, Nov. 13, 2008, http://hudoc.echr.coe.int/eng?i=001-89848.

107 Ibid.

108 S.A.S. v. *France*, 2014-III Eur. Ct. H.R. 341, 353–54, para. 12.

109 Ibid., 345, 355, 358–59, 367–71.

110 *Ebrahimian* v. *France*, 2015-VIII Eur. Ct. H.R. 99; *Belcacemi* v. *Belgium*, App. No. 37798/13, July 11, 2017, http://hudoc.echr.coe.int/eng?i=001-175636; *Dakir* v. *Belgium*, App. No. 4619/12, para. 68, July 11, 2017, http://hudoc.echr.coe.int/eng?i=001-175660. A third relevant case, *Barik Edidi* v. *Spain*, App. No. 21780/13, Apr. 26, 2016, http://hudoc.echr.coe.int/eng?i=001-163303, was dismissed

In a few recent cases, however, the Court has become more sympathetic to Article 9 claims involving religious clothing and ornamentation. In *Ahmet Arslan* v. *Turkey* (2010), the Court found that Turkey had violated Article 9 rights by arresting a group of Muslims for wearing, on a public street, traditional religious garb, including a turban, baggy trousers, a tunic, and a stick.[111] Local antiterrorism laws prohibited such dress, except during religious ceremonies and on public holy days. The Court stated that restrictions on religious dress are permissible if they are explicitly designed to protect the state principle of secularism in a democratic society, or to prevent disorder or violation of the rights of others. But without such rationales, this antiterrorism law was neither a necessary nor a proportionate limitation on such religious dress in public.[112]

Likewise, in *Eweida and Others* v. *The United Kingdom* (2013), the Court upheld the right of Nadia Eweida, a check-in staff member for British Airways, to wear at work a small necklace with a crucifix that reflected her Coptic Christian faith.[113] When British Airways introduced a more rigid policy that prohibited religious symbols, she refused to remove or hide the necklace. She was suspended. Later, British Airways amended its policy, and she returned to work. She then sued to recover the income lost while suspended. After losing in British courts, she filed her case in Strasbourg. The Court held in favor of Eweida, arguing that her "insistence on wearing a cross visibly at work was motivated by her desire to bear witness to her Christian faith," and that "there is no evidence of any real encroachment on the interests of others." It found that the interference of British Airways with Eweida's religious freedom was disproportionate, especially since the company had a history of permitting turbans and hijabs and had shifting policies on religious apparel. It is notable in this case that UK law was silent on the right to wear religious clothing or symbols in the workplace, and it was her private employer, not the government, that had imposed the restriction. Nonetheless, the Court chose to "consider the issues in terms of the positive obligation on the State authorities to secure the rights under Article 9," even in the private sector. The Court balanced the concerns for danger, security, safety, or the rights of others against her right to wear a small cross, and ruled in favor of the flight attendant.[114]

In *Hamidović* v. *Bosnia and Herzegovina* (2018), a divided Court upheld the right of a Muslim defendant, indicted for a terroristic attack on the United States embassy, to wear his skullcap in a criminal court.[115] The presiding trial judge had repeatedly ordered the defendant to remove the skullcap, in accordance with local court rules

for the failure to exhaust domestic remedies after the applicant failed to lodge her appeal before the domestic court in time. Ibid., paras. 46–49. The court could not therefore examine her other grounds of appeal including the alleged violation of Article 9. This case concerned the Article 9 rights of a lawyer to wear her hijab in a Spanish courtroom while representing her clients. Ibid., para. 30.

111 *Arslan* v. *Turkey*, App. No. 41135/98, Feb. 23, 2010, http://hudoc.echr.coe.int/eng?i=001-97535.

112 Ibid., 21, 43, 52.

113 *Eweida*, 2013-I Eur. Ct. H.R., at 218.

114 Ibid. 226–28, 254–57. In a companion case, the Court upheld a hospital decision to prohibit a geriatric nurse from wearing her cross on duty in order to protect health and safety on the ward. Ibid., 259.

115 *Hamidović* v. *Bosnia and Herzegovina*, App. No. 57792/15, Eur. Ct. H.R., May 3, 2018, http://hudoc.echr.coe.int/eng?i=001-179219.

that defendants were not permitted to have head coverings of any sort in the courtroom. The defendant protested that he wore the skullcap out of religious duty, and he persisted despite the judge's repeated orders and time to reflect on the consequences. Eventually, the court fined the defendant for contempt of court and then imprisoned him for thirty days for not paying the fine. The defendant appealed, citing violations of Articles 9 and 14.

The Strasbourg Court held for the defendant. It distinguished the case from those concerning religious head coverings in the workplace, since this case involved compulsory appearance rather than voluntary employment. The Court saw "no reason to doubt that the applicant's act was motivated by his sincere religious belief ... without any hidden agenda to make a mockery of the trial, incite others to reject secular and democratic values or cause a disturbance. Pluralism, tolerance and broadmindedness are hallmarks of a 'democratic society.'" Punishing the defendant for contempt, the Court argued, "was not necessary in a democratic society," even though the local court generally deserved a wide margin of appreciation.[116] A few months later, in another Article 9 case, the Court held similarly that a Belgian court was not justified in excluding a private Muslim relative of a defendant from visiting a courtroom just because she wore a veil.[117]

CASES ON RELIGIOUS GROUP RIGHTS

Religious Personality, Autonomy, and Legal Limits. Article 9 of the European Convention on Human Rights, along with Article 11 (on freedom of assembly and association), protects religious groups from undue state intrusion, interference, or discriminatory regulation. These articles on their face and as applied by the Strasbourg Court protect religious groups per se, recognizing their rights to legal personality and religious autonomy.[118] Religious groups have rights to maintain their own standards of teaching, practice, membership, and discipline, to devise their own forms of polity and organization, to hold property and lease facilities, to make contracts, to open bank accounts, to hire and pay employees, suppliers, and service providers, to maintain relations with coreligionists at home and abroad, to publish their literature, and to operate worship centers, clerical housing, seminaries, schools, charities, mission groups, hospitals, and cemeteries.[119]

The Court has repeatedly held that member states may not arbitrarily or discriminatorily withhold, withdraw, or condition a religious group's right to acquire legal

116 Ibid., 7–10, 41–43.

117 *Lachiri* v. *Belgium*, App. No. 3413/09, paras. 31–48, Dec. 18, 2018, http://hudoc.echr.coe.int/eng?i=001-186461.

118 Julian Rivers, *The Law of Organized Religions: Between Establishment and Secularism* (Oxford: Oxford University Press, 2010), 53.

119 *Jehovah's Witnesses of Moscow* v. *Russia*, App No. 302/02, 53 Eur. Ct. H.R. Rep. 141, 167–68, para. 102 (2010); *Metropolitan Church of Bessarabia* v. *Moldova*, 2001-XII Eur. Ct. H.R. 81, 113–14, para. 118.

personality,[120] to procure the necessary state licenses for religious marriages, nursery schools, or educational programs for their members,[121] or to receive state funding or other state benefits available to other properly registered religious groups.[122] Nor may the state impose an exorbitant or discriminatory tax on a religious organization that jeopardizes the organization's ability to operate.[123] Moreover, even if a religious group will not or cannot register as a separate legal entity, the state may not prohibit, intervene, or interfere with its collective worship or assembly in private homes or settings.[124] All these state actions, the Court has held, violate Article 9 rights of religion and sometimes violate Article 11 and Article 14 rights of association and nondiscrimination. As the Court stated in 2000:

> [R]eligious communities traditionally and universally exist in the form of organized structures. They abide by rules which are often seen by followers as being of a divine origin. Religious ceremonies have their meaning and sacred value for the believers if they have been conducted by ministers empowered for that purpose in compliance with these rules. The personality of the religious ministers is undoubtedly of importance to every member of the community. Participation in the life of the community is thus a manifestation of one's religion, protected by Article 9.[125]

The Court has placed special emphasis on the autonomy of religious bodies. In a 2013 case, for example, it opined:

> The autonomous existence of religious communities is indispensable for pluralism in a democratic society and is an issue at the very heart of the protection which Article 9 affords. It directly concerns not only the organisation of these communities as such but also the effective enjoyment of the right to freedom of religion by all their active members.[126]

In implementing this principle of religious autonomy, the Court has held that a state may not force a religious group to admit new members,[127] to exclude a member whom the State disfavors, or to retain a member who has departed or dissented from

120 Ibid., 110, 119; *Dimitrova* v. *Bulgaria*, App. No. 15452/07, paras. 25, 31, Feb. 10, 2015, http://hudoc.echr.coe.int/eng?i=001-151006.

121 *Savez Crkava* v. *Croatia*, App. No. 7798/08, para. 58, Dec. 9, 2010, http://hudoc.echr.coe.int/eng?i=001-102173.

122 *Magyar Keresztény Mennonita Egyház* v. *Hungary*, 2014-I Eur. Ct. H.R. 449, 472.

123 *Ass'n les Témoins de Jéhovah* v. *France*, App. No. 8916/05, para. 53, June 30, 2011, http://hudoc.echr.coe.int/eng?i=001-105386.

124 *Masaev* v. *Moldova*, App. No. 6303/05, 57 Eur. H.R. Rep. 185, 191, para. 26 (2013); see also *Cumhuriyetçi Egitim Ve Kültür Merkezi Vakfi* v. *Turkey*, App. No. 32093/10, paras. 9, 52, Feb. 19, 2014, http://hudoc.echr.coe.int/eng?i=001-148275, where the court found a violation of Article 14 combined with Article 9 (and found no need to conduct a separate examination into Article 9). It was a case where Turkey refused to grant the status of a place of worship. Ibid., para. 9.

125 *Hasan* v. *Bulgaria*, 2000-XI Eur. Ct. H.R. 117, 137, para. 62.

126 *Sindicatul "Păstorul cel Bun"* v. *Romania*, 2013-V Eur. Ct. H.R. 41, 63, para. 136 (citing Hasan, 2000-XI Eur. Ct. H.R. at 137, para. 62).

127 *Svyato-Mykhaylivska Parafiya* v. *Ukraine*, App. No. 77703/01, para. 146, June 14, 2007, http://hudoc.echr.coe.int/eng?i=001-81067.

the group's teachings or practices. So long as the group respects the individual's right to leave without impediment or interference, the group's internal authority trumps the individual's right to participate as a member of the group.[128]

The Court has also held that states may not interfere in the resolution of internal disputes over church leadership, force denominations to unite or divide, compel them to accept one religious official over another, or prevent them from amending their internal legal structures or canons.[129] Even in countries that have established churches or favored traditional religions, the Court held in a 2001 case that Article 9

> excludes assessment by the State of the legitimacy of religious beliefs or the ways in which those beliefs are expressed. State measures favouring a particular leader or specific organs of a divided religious community or seeking to compel the community or part of it to place itself, against its will, under a single leadership, would also constitute an infringement of the freedom of religion.[130]

In a later case, the Court stated further: "While it may be necessary for the State to reconcile the interests of the various religions and religious groups that coexist in a democratic society, the State has a duty to remain neutral and impartial in exercising its regulatory authority and in its relations with the various religions, denominations and groups within them."[131]

Despite this insistence on state deference to religious autonomy, the Court has allowed governments to regulate and restrict the activities of registered religious organizations in order "to protect its institutions and citizens."[132] These limitations, the Court has said, "must be used sparingly, as exceptions to the rule" and allowed only for "convincing and compelling reasons" and in cases of "pressing social need."[133] But some limitations have passed muster under Article 9 review. In *Şerife Yiğit* v. *Turkey* (2010), for example, the Court upheld Turkey's law that required couples to marry monogamously in a civil ceremony before a state official.[134] Turkish law does not recognize a religious marriage ceremony as sufficient to create a valid marriage, and the state threatened to imprison any religious official or group who presided over a marriage ceremony without a prior civil

128 *Holy Synod* v. *Bulgaria*, App. Nos. 412/03 and 35677/04, para. 29, Sept. 16, 2010, http://hudoc.echr.coe.int/eng?i=001-100433; *Svyato-Mykhaylivska Parafiya*, App. No. 77703/01, para. 150, June 14, 2007.

129 *Holy Synod*, App. Nos. 412/03 and 35677/04, para. 29, Sept. 16, 2010; *Svyato-Mykhaylivska Parafiya*, Eur. Ct. H.R., para. 150, June 14, 2007; *Hasan*, 2000-XI Eur. Ct. H.R. at 144, para. 86; *Serif* v. *Greece*, 1999-IX Eur. Ct. H.R. 73, 88–89, para. 54.

130 *Metropolitan Church of Bessarabia* v. *Moldova*, 2001-XII Eur. Ct. H.R. 81, 113, para. 117.

131 *Holy Synod*, Eur. Ct. H.R. at para. 119; see also *Magyar Keresztény Mennonita Egyház* v. *Hungary*, 2014-I Eur. Ct. H.R. 449, 475–76, para. 115 (holding that a new Hungarian law that deregistered several longstanding minority churches in the state violated Articles 9 and 11).

132 *Magyar Keresztény*, 2104-I Eur. Ct. H.R., para. 79.

133 Ibid. (quoting *Gorzelik* v. *Poland*, 2004-I Eur. Ct. H.R. 219, 262, paras. 94–95).

134 *Serife Yiğit* v. *Turkey*, App. No. 3976/05, para. 39, Nov. 2, 2010, http://hudoc.echr.coe.int/eng?i=001-101579.

registration of the marriage. The stated purpose of the Turkish law, as the Court saw it, "was to protect women against polygamy. If religious marriages were to be considered lawful[,] all the attendant religious consequences would have to be recognized, for instance the fact that a [Muslim] man could marry four women."[135] In the case of *Ouardiri* v. *Switzerland* (2011), the Court further upheld Switzerland's constitutional amendment prohibiting the building of minarets against the claim that this violated the rights of Muslims to have suitable mosques for public worship.[136] The Court dismissed the claim, arguing that, since the claimant was complaining against a constitutional provision with general applicability, there was no real victim in the case.[137]

But the Court has stepped in with Article 9 protections when local religious communities were victimized by their neighbors and did not receive help from the police or other state authorities. The case of *97 Members of the Gldani Congregation of Jehovah's Witnesses and 4 Others* v. *Georgia* (2007) provides a good illustration.[138] Orthodox Christians had repeatedly attacked and intimidated a local group of Jehovah's Witnesses in an effort to drive them out of the community or force them to convert to Orthodoxy. The Witnesses were repeatedly assaulted and beaten with crosses, whips, and sticks – sometimes resulting in serious injuries. Their literature was burned and their worship services were interrupted. One man was shaved bald and forced to listen to Orthodox prayers designed to convert him. Further, all of these actions were filmed and aired on national television. Local authorities did nothing, despite hearing 784 formal complaints, because they perceived the Witnesses "as a threat to Christian orthodoxy." The Court held that this gross state indifference was a clear violation of the Witnesses' Article 9 rights. It explained that freedom of religion means that one group may not "apply improper pressure on others from a wish to promote one's religious convictions."

> [T]he role of the authorities in such circumstances is not to remove the cause of tension by eliminating pluralism, but to ensure that the competing groups tolerate each other. This State role is conducive to public order, religious harmony and tolerance in a democratic society and can hardly be conceived as being likely to diminish the role of a faith or a Church with which the population of a specific country has historically and culturally been associated.[139]

135 Ibid., 62, 84.

136 See European Court of Human Rights Press Release, Decision on the Admissibility of *Ouardiri* v. *Switzerland* and *Ligue des Musulmans de Suisse and Others* v. *Switzerland,* July 8, 2011, http://hudoc.echr.coe.int/eng-press?i=003-3602217-4080719.

137 Ibid.

138 *Gldani Congregation* v. *Georgia*, App. No. 71156/01, 46 Eur. H.R. Rep. 613, 649, paras. 151–52 (2007).

139 Ibid., 622–26, 646; see also *Kuznetsov* v. *Russia*, App. No. 184/02, 49 Eur. H.R. 355, 369, para. 62 (2007) (finding an Article 9 violation for a state's failure to prosecute officials who had illegally broken up a Jehovah's Witness Sunday worship service).

The Court held similarly in four subsequent cases involving Eastern European lands imposing blatantly discriminatory restrictions on new minority religious groups.[140]

Religious Employers and Labor Rights. The exact line between the autonomous religious and regulable secular dimensions of a religious group has proved hardest to negotiate in cases of labor and employment.[141] The Court has held that the state may not force a church to accept unionization of its clerical and lay employees, since that "would therefore be likely to undermine the Church's traditional hierarchical structure ... [and] create a real risk to the autonomy of the religious community."[142] A state may not force a church to retain the services of a religious-education teacher who publicly opposed its religious doctrines,[143] or a public relations director who committed adultery in violation of church teaching and in breach of his employment contract.[144]

The leading case is *Fernández Martínez* v. *Spain* (2014).[145] Martínez was an ordained priest of the Roman Catholic Church.[146] In 1984, he had sought, but was denied, a dispensation from the obligation of clerical celibacy. The following year he married a woman in a civil ceremony. Together they had five children. In 1991 he was employed in a state-run secondary school of the region of Murcia. He taught Catholic religion and ethics, in pursuance of an agreement or concordat between the Holy See and Spain. Per the agreement, public authorities can assign such teaching posts only to teachers who have been proposed every year by the diocesan bishop.[147]

While Martínez was teaching Catholic religion and ethics, he participated in the activities of an association advocating for married priests. He wrote articles defending his views, and a picture of him and his family was posted in a local newspaper. In 1997, he finally received a papal dispensation from the rules of mandatory clerical celibacy. Within weeks, the local diocese informed the Ministry of Education that it

140 See *Dimitrova* v. *Bulgaria*, App. No. 15452/07, para. 30, Feb. 10, 2015, http://hudoc.echr.coe.int/eng?i=001-151006; *Ass'n for Solidarity with Jehovah's Witnesses* v. *Turkey*, App. Nos. 36915/10 and 8606/13, paras. 3, 108, May 24, 2016, http://hudoc.echr.coe.int/eng?i=001-163107; *Religious Cmty. of Jehovah's Witnesses* v. *Ukraine*, App. No. 21477/10, paras. 55, 57, 59, Sept. 3, 2019, http://hudoc.echr.coe.int/eng?i=001-195539; *Metodiev* v. *Bulgaria*, App. No. 58088/08, para. 48, June 15, 2017, http://hudoc.echr.coe.int/eng?i=001-174412.

141 Daniel Sabbagh, "Discrimination in the Workplace: Toward a Transatlantic Comparison," *Droit et Société* 102 (2019), 321, 331.

142 *Sindicatul "Păstorul cel Bun"* v. *Romania*, 2013-V Eur. Ct. H.R. 41, 68–69, paras. 161–62.

143 *Martínez* v. *Spain*, 2014-II Eur. Ct. H.R. 449, 490–91, paras. 149–50.

144 *Obst* v. *Germany*, App. No. 425/03, para. 51, Sept. 23, 2010, http://hudoc.echr.coe.int/eng?i=001-100463. But cf. *Schüth* v. *Germany*, 2010-V Eur. Ct. H.R. 397, 403, 426, paras. 3, 67 (a case involving an organist in a Catholic Church who was fired for his adultery). Here, the Court said that the pro forma approval of this discharge by the employment tribunal in Germany did not go far enough to protect the organist's right to privacy under Article 8 of the Convention for the Protection of Human Rights and Fundamental Freedoms. Ibid., 399–401.

145 *Martínez*, 2014-II Eur. Ct. H.R. at 449.

146 Ibid., 459, para. 13.

147 Ibid., 459.

had terminated Martínez's assignment,[148] and the ministry duly notified him. The diocese also issued a statement, explaining that it had terminated the contract because of Martínez's marital status, which was now common knowledge and ran the risk of causing "scandal" among the students and their Catholic families.[149]

Martínez sued in state court, citing the right to equality and to privacy, as well as freedom of expression. Having lost, he brought his claim to Strasbourg, complaining that the state had failed to protect his rights under Article 8 of the European Convention, which reads: "Everyone has the right to respect for his private and family life, his home and his correspondence." Martínez lost before both the first Chamber and the Grand Chamber of the Court. A divided Grand Chamber found no violation of Article 8. The limitation imposed on Martínez's rights was in accordance with state law, and his dismissal was consistent with church canon law. The Court found that the limitation was in pursuance of a "legitimate aim" of protecting the freedom "of the Catholic Church, and in particular its autonomy in respect of the choice of persons accredited to teach religious doctrine." The Court found that among the member states, there was no consensus on the scope of religious autonomy, and thus each state party in the Council of Europe had ample discretion to devise and implement its rules and procedures in this field. Finally, the Court noted that religious organizations had a right to expect loyalty from those who, like Martínez, represented them at the societal level. Considering the circumstances of the case and the publicity that the applicant gave to his situation, the Court found that the balance of rights struck in favor of the church was not disproportionate.[150]

SUMMARY AND CONCLUSIONS

Law and religion in Europe have changed dramatically in the past three decades. The European Union's strong commitment to open borders and freedom of movement has boosted the legal integration of Europe, Brexit notwithstanding. The Council of Europe's sweeping embrace of postglasnost Russia and many former Soviet bloc countries as well as Turkey has brought East and West together as never before. The devastating conflicts in the Middle East and the failed promises of the Arab Spring have driven many émigrés to Europe in search of a better life. Many European countries have thus witnessed a massive influx of people of different faiths, ethnicities, and languages from within and beyond Europe. These countries now face mounting pressure to find common ground for the peaceful coexistence of their increasingly diverse societies. The new challenge for Europe is twofold: how to accommodate previously unknown religious practices now claiming religious freedom protections, and how to reconceptualize old Christian traditions and cultures,

148 Ibid., 461, para. 17.

149 Ibid., 460–62.

150 Ibid., 469–70, 486–88, 491.

long protected by local constitutions, concordats, and customs, but now under attack.

The European Court of Human Rights has become a litigation epicenter for resolving these hard challenges, using Article 9 of the 1950 European Convention of Human Rights. The Court has interpreted Article 9 broadly to protect a person's right to hold religious beliefs in private and to manifest those beliefs peaceably in public. It has treated the "internal right to believe" as the right to accept, reject, or change one's thoughts, beliefs, or religious affiliation without involvement, inducement, or impediment of the state. It protects persons from pressure to reveal their religious identity or beliefs to the state, or to discuss religion with military superiors. It protects persons from being forced to swear a religious oath, and it protects the rights of pacifists to conscientious objection to military service and participation. Finally, it protects school children and their parents from religious teaching in state schools, although not from classrooms that include crucifixes.

Not all claims of conscience have won relief. The Court denied conscientious objection exemptions to pacifists whose coreligionists bore arms, whose objections were deemed political rather than religious, or who sought to be excused from a celebratory parade far removed in time and space from the battlefield. In the Court's view, the burden on religion was not heavy enough in those cases to warrant an exemption. Even when there were ample burdens on conscience, the Court sometimes judged the burden on others' rights or on society's values to be too heavy to grant a religious accommodation. The Court did go out of its way to accommodate the humanist parents in *Folgerø* to exempt their children from generic religious instruction in public schools, but it refused to accommodate the Christian Romeikes, who sought to protect their children from the secular liberal teachings of the public schools by homeschooling them. The rights of children to proper state education trumped the parents' right to religion and religious parentage. Similarly, the Court denied relief to Christian private and public employees who claimed conscientious objection from newly enacted employment policies requiring them to serve same-sex couples. The rights of same-sex couples to dignity and equal treatment, the Court concluded, outweighed the conscientious objections of claimants who held traditional Christian views of sexuality.

Protecting the rights of others and the interests of society has also informed the Court's rulings on limits to the right to manifest one's religion in public. The Court has repeated common human rights teachings that the right to manifest religion includes basic rights to peaceable religious worship, speech, press, diet, dress, holiday observance, pilgrimage, parenting, evangelization, charity services, and more.[151] The Court did step in several times to outlaw blatantly discriminatory

[151] See, e.g., OSCE Office for Democratic Institutions and Human Rights, "Freedom of Religion or Belief and Security: Policy Guidance" (2019) for a typical summary of religious freedom protections.

prohibitions on religious worship and proselytizing for Protestant minorities in Eastern European Orthodox majority lands. But the Court has repeatedly upheld blatantly discriminatory prohibitions on Muslim religious apparel in member states dedicated to secularism or *laïcité*, claiming that these were necessary applications of the margin of appreciation for local resolution of disputes, and that Muslim headscarves were demeaning to women and corrosive. It is hard to resist the conclusion that, in the Strasbourg Court, Western secularist states do better than Eastern Orthodox states; mistreated Christians do better than mistreated Muslims; and public nonreligious speech, however provocative, fares better than public religious expression, however discreet.

The Strasbourg Court has been highly protective of the rights of religious groups. It has upheld the rights of religious groups to maintain their own standards of membership and discipline and their own polity and organization, and to engage in their own financial, missionary, educational, and charitable enterprises. The Court has repeatedly held that member states may not arbitrarily or discriminatorily interfere with a religious group's right to legal personality or to procure state licenses necessary for appropriate activities or to receive state benefits available to other religious groups. Nor may the state impose a discriminatory tax or one so exorbitant that it jeopardizes a religious organization's ability to operate.

It is perhaps no surprise that the Court in these cases has urged member states to adopt the principle of neutrality in their treatment of religion, but also has given states a wide margin of appreciation to resolve controversial issues in accordance with local customs and norms. In view of the wide variety of constitutional settings and church–state structures in the forty-seven member states of the Council of Europe, the Court has tried to avoid enforcing one model of religious freedom for all of Europe. The margin of appreciation principle has given individual states ample leeway to implement religious freedom in accordance with local culture and customs – much as the federalism principle in American constitutional law has allowed for diversity among individual American states in their treatment of religion.[152] But in Europe, the principle of a margin of appreciation has sometimes come at the expense of religious minorities – like Muslim women whose religious head coverings were banned, or conservative Christians whose traditional sexual ethics were spurned. Even when the Court rules that a member state has violated Article 9, the Court depends largely on voluntary compliance by the offending state. Some offending states remain indifferent, only compounding the problem of localism.

When the Grand Chamber of the Court in the 2011 *Lautsi* case addressed the question whether crucifixes were permitted in Italian public schools,[153] Professor Joseph Weiler, an Orthodox Jew wearing his yarmulke in the courtroom, defended

[152] See John Witte, Jr. and Joel A. Nichols, *Religion and the American Constitutional Experiment*, 4th ed. (Oxford: Oxford University Press, 2016), 111–16, 143–49.

[153] *Lautsi* v. *Italy*, 2011-III Eur. Ct. H.R. 61.

the continued display of the crucifix despite the objections of atheist parents. Among other things, Weiler warned the Court not to "Americaniz[e]" Europe, by superimposing a neutrality model of religious freedom and church–state relations, akin to what was being enforced in American courts at the time.[154] Ironically, the US Supreme Court has backed away from the neutrality test in its most recent cases, and it might soon abandon this test in favor of a more robust protection of the free exercise of religion, as had been the law before 1990.[155] If that proves true, perhaps the Americanization of Europe might be just what is needed after all, at least in protecting the free exercise of religion.

[154] Oral Submission by Professor J. H. H. Weiler on behalf of Amenia et al. – Third Party Intervening States in the *Lautsi* Case Before the Grand Chamber of the European Court of Human Rights, paras. 5, 7, 17, June 30, 2018.

[155] See, for example, *Hosanna-Tabor Evangelical* v. *E.E.O.C.*, 132 S. Ct. 604 (2012) (holding that the ministerial exemption for religious employment was mandated by the First Amendment Free Exercise and Establishment Clauses, and rejecting the argument that a neutral disability law should be applied); *Masterpiece Cakeshop* v. *Colo. C.R. Comm'n.*, 138 S. Ct. 1719 (2018) (rejecting application of a state civil rights law to a religious freedom claimant, with concurring judges urging rejection of the Smith approach to free-exercise cases).

9

Meet the New Boss of Religious Freedom

The New Cases of the Court of Justice of the European Union

Europe has a new boss of religious freedom – the Court of Justice of the European Union. To be sure, the European Court of Human Rights, sitting in Strasbourg, will continue to hear religious freedom cases from the forty-seven countries in the Council of Europe, as it has in more than 150 cases since 1993.[1] But the Court of Justice, sitting in Luxembourg, now also issues rulings on religious freedom for the subset of twenty-seven countries that form the European Union (the EU). Before the EU ratified its Charter of Fundamental Rights in 2010 (known simply as the EU Charter),[2] the Luxembourg Court said little about rights and freedoms outside the economic sphere. Since then, however, the Court has delivered a dozen landmark rulings on religious freedom, all but one since 2017. Many cases are pending.

While the Strasbourg Court produces soft law that depends upon voluntary compliance by the offending state, the Luxembourg Court's rulings are hard law that binds the entire European Union, preempting all member-state laws to the contrary and guiding future EU and domestic cases. The Luxembourg Court thus has much more legal power than the Strasbourg Court, and its docket of religious freedom cases is thus likely to grow quickly. Since its rulings are good law throughout the EU, religious freedom litigants have used the Luxembourg Court to shape domestic law.[3] A win in Luxembourg is a win at home and in the entire EU. This has incentivized religious freedom litigants, particularly those with broader European interests or constituents, to appeal to EU law and the EU Charter, with the goal of using the Luxembourg Court as leverage to reform religious freedom in the EU.

The Luxembourg Court is thus rapidly emerging as the new boss of religious freedom in Europe, and the world would do well to take notice. Some of the Court's first dozen cases regarding religious freedom have already shaken the EU,

1 See Chapter 8.

2 Charter of Fundamental Rights of the European Union, OJ 2010 No. C83, pp. 389–403.

3 See Elina Paunio, *Legal Certainty in Multilingual EU Law: Language, Discourse and Reasoning at the European Court of Justice* (Farnham: Ashgate, 2013), 59; Morten Rasmussen, "The Origins of a Legal Revolution – The Early History of the European Court of Justice," *Journal of European Integration History* 14 (2008), 77.

and several trends in these cases bear close watching. In particular, the Court has shown a strong preference for policies of "religious neutrality." That policy is intuitively attractive in postmodern, pluralistic, and liberal societies that need to address a number of legal questions. It is already providing more nuanced protection for religious freedom than the aggressive policies of *läicité* and secularization at work in some EU member states. But norms of religious neutrality, when pressed too strongly, can also come at the cost of accommodations for discrete religious minorities, notably Muslims and Jews, who operate outside of the cultural mainstream, or for other parties, including traditional Christians, whose pressing claims of conscience or commandments of faith prevent them from abiding by the state's neutral laws. Furthermore, this neutrality policy has prompted the Court to question the longstanding Western principle of "religious autonomy" that counsels judicial deference to peaceable religious groups to govern their own internal affairs concerning property, polity, employment, and membership. This policy has further led the Court to question longstanding national church–state arrangements in national constitutions and international concordats, particularly those that establish or privilege one or more traditional forms of Christianity. Even without a "no establishment of religion" clause in the EU Charter, these latter cases are beginning to challenge local religious establishments and the free-exercise rights of religious groups. It is too soon to tell whether these early case trends will become the norm, but some EU litigants have taken notice and are bypassing Strasbourg and heading to Luxembourg.[4]

THE COURT OF JUSTICE OF THE EUROPEAN UNION

The Court of Justice of the European Union (the CJEU or Luxembourg Court) is the judicial organ of the EU.[5] Founded in the 1950s, the EU covers only a subset of the forty-seven states and nine hundred million people in the Council of Europe. The EU has only twenty-seven states and 446 million people since Brexit. But included in the EU are most of Europe's biggest countries and economies – Germany, France, Spain, Italy, Austria, Portugal, Sweden, Poland, Finland, and the Benelux countries, among others.[6]

The Luxembourg Court comprises both the General Court and the Court of Justice, with the latter divided into ten chambers and the Grand Chamber for the most important cases. These two tribunals have discrete competence, with the Court of Justice also functioning as a court of appeal from the General Court's judgments. To date, the Court of Justice has decided the religious freedom cases directly, but the General Court may start taking cases if the volume of religious freedom litigation

4 See, generally, The Court of Justice of the European Union, https://curia.europa.eu/jcms/jcms/j_6/en/ (providing access to court reports on current and past cases of the CJEU).

5 It was only in late 2009 that the CJEU took this name; before then, it was called European Court of Justice. European Commission, Court of Justice of European Union (CJEU), https://ec.europa.eu/home-affairs/content/court-justice-european-union-cjeu_en.

6 European Union, EU in Figures, https://europa.eu/european-union/about-eu/figures/living_en.

continues to increase. The Court of Justice normally employs an advocate general (AG), who is a member of the Court, though not a judge. The AG typically submits a written opinion with a detailed explanation of the case and a recommendation of the best interests of the EU in the case. That more elaborated AG opinion often shapes the Court's final judgment, the rulings of which tend to be succinct and issued without dissenting or concurring opinions. The AG's and the Court's opinions spell out EU policy and mandates, leaving local enforcement of EU law to the member states.[7]

The Luxembourg Court operates primarily through a method called the "preliminary procedure." When a domestic judge is confronted with a controversy that involves interpretation of applicable EU law, the judge requests the Court to issue a preliminary ruling on the right interpretation of that law and how it might be implemented. Once this preliminary ruling is issued, the domestic judge resumes the local proceeding and adjudicates according to the Court's direction.[8]

The Luxembourg Court also operates with the principle that EU law is "supreme law" in the Union with "direct effect" in all member states.[9] Thus, when the EU enacts a new law or the Luxembourg Court issues a new ruling, it is immediately binding and enforceable throughout the EU. Legislatures of the member states need not ratify or execute the new EU law through separate enabling legislation, nor may they remove, revise, or replace it with a new domestic statute. Because EU law is supreme, domestic courts of EU member states, in turn, must enforce EU law instead of domestic law when those laws conflict. Domestic courts thus act as de facto lower EU courts in some cases, and the Luxembourg Court acts as something of a de facto supreme court, with power to issue advisory opinions.[10]

NORMS OF RELIGIOUS FREEDOM IN THE EUROPEAN UNION

Protections of religious freedom and other fundamental rights were not part of the Luxembourg Court's original mission or that of its judicial predecessors. The EU was born out of the European Coal and Steel Community, the European Economic

7 European Union, Court of Justice of the European Union (CJEU), https://europa.eu/european-union/about-eu/institutions-bodies/court-justice_en#composition; Statute of the Court of Justice of the European Union, art. 49, https://curia.europa.eu/jcms/upload/docs/application/pdf/2016-08/tra-doc-en-div-c-0000-2016-201606984-05_00.pdf; Court of Justice of the European Union, Court of Justice: Composition of Chambers, https://curia.europa.eu/jcms/jcms/J02_7029/en/.

8 Paul P. Craig and Gráinne de Búrca, *The Evolution of EU Law*, 5th ed. (Oxford: Oxford University Press, 2011), 362, 382; Giulio Itzcovich, "The European Court of Justice," in András Jakab, Arthur Dyevre, and Giulio Itzcovich, eds., *Comparative Constitutional Reasoning* (Cambridge: Cambridge University Press, 2017), 362, 382.

9 Case C-26/62, N.V. *Algemene Transport-en Expeditie Onderneming van Gend & Loos* v. *Nederlandse Administratie der Belastingen* [1963] ECLI:EU:C:1963:1, paras. 2–3.

10 Joseph Weiler, "Deciphering the Political and Legal DNA of European Integration: An Exploratory Essay," in Julie Dickson and Pavlos Eleftheriadis, eds., *Philosophical Foundations of European Union Law* (Oxford: Oxford University Press, 2012), 150, 154–55; Itzcovich, "The European Court of Justice," 280–81.

Community, and the European Agency for Atomic Energy, all vital cooperative arrangements created in the tense and tenuous aftermath of World War II. The Luxembourg Court and its predecessors accordingly focused on building new cooperation and trust among former national enemies, and fostering economic freedom and equal work and business opportunities in increasingly free and unified European community markets.

In the 1990s, however, the EU took on the language and the narrative of rights more directly as part of an effort to revitalize the union's fading legitimacy.[11] Religious freedom was included in this new discussion. The 1997 Treaty of Amsterdam,[12] which helped solidify the EU, first confirmed the principle of deference to the status of churches and other religious organizations in member states. Declaration 11 of the Treaty provided:

> The European Union respects and does not prejudice the status under national law of churches and religious associations or communities in the Member States.
>
> The European Union equally respects the status of philosophical and non-confessional organisations.[13]

After passage of the Treaty of Amsterdam, the EU took a broader interest in the protection of fundamental rights of EU citizens.[14] In 2000, the member states agreed to the Charter of Fundamental Rights of European Union. The Charter was incorporated into the EU Treaty in 2010 and became binding law throughout the union.

The EU Charter includes several provisions covering religious freedom. Article 10 echoes Article 9 of the European Convention of Human Rights, while adding an express clause regarding conscientious objection:

> Everyone has the right to freedom of thought, conscience and religion. This right includes freedom to change religion or belief and freedom, either alone or in community with others and in public or in private, to manifest religion or belief, in worship, teaching, practice and observance.
>
> The right to conscientious objection is recognised, in accordance with the national laws governing the exercise of this right.

Article 14 of the EU Charter protects the freedom of education, including "the right of parents to ensure the education and teaching of their children in conformity with their religious, philosophical and pedagogical convictions." Article 21 outlaws all discrimination, including religious discrimination. Article 22 proclaims that "[t]he

11 Weiler, "Deciphering the Political and Legal DNA," 157.

12 Treaty of Amsterdam amending the Treaty on European Union, Treaties establishing the European Communities and certain related acts, OJ 1997 No. C340, pp. 1–144.

13 Treaty of Amsterdam, Declaration 11, p. 133. See further Gabriela Alexandra Oanta, "The Status of Churches and Philosophical and Non-Confessional Organizations Within the Framework of the European Union Reform," *Lex et Scientia International Journal* 15 (2008), 123.

14 Ian Ward, "Tempted by Rights: The European Union and Its New Charter of Fundamental Rights," *Constitutional Forum* 11 (2011),113 .

Union shall respect cultural, religious and linguistic diversity." In addition to these Charter rights, some EU statutes and regulations also offer religious freedom protections that the Luxembourg Court also enforces, sometimes in tandem with these Charter articles.

Article 52(3) of the EU Charter expressly calls for EU courts to take into account the parallel provisions of the 1950 European Convention of Human Rights.

> In so far as this Charter contains rights which correspond to rights guaranteed by the Convention for the Protection of Human Rights and Fundamental Freedoms, the meaning and scope of those rights shall be the same as those laid down by the said Convention. This provision shall not prevent Union law providing more extensive protection.[15]

Accordingly, in developing its religious freedom jurisprudence, the Luxembourg Court has looked to the Strasbourg Court's interpretation of Article 9 and related provisions of the European Convention. The Luxembourg Court often references relevant case law, sometimes picking up where the Strasbourg Court left off, and then casting its rulings in the hard-law terms with which it operates. The Luxembourg Court, however, considers these Article 9 cases to be probative only, not binding precedents, and it has gone its own way to protect broader EU interests. The Court also takes seriously the Charter directive to offer "more extensive protection" to all the fundamental rights of all EU citizens, sometimes siding with the latter at the cost of religious freedom claimants.[16]

THE EUROPEAN COURT OF JUSTICE CASES ON RELIGIOUS FREEDOM

From 2010 to 2017, the EU Charter's new provisions on religious freedom produced little case law in the Luxembourg Court. Since then, the Court has issued twelve new cases on religious freedom – including landmark cases on the Islamic headscarf,[17] the selection and treatment of employees on religious grounds,[18] tax exemption and aid to religious schools,[19] religious slaughtering,[20] a religiously

15 Charter of Fundamental Rights, art. 52(3), p. 402.

16 Ibid.

17 Case C-157/15, *Samira Achbita and Centrum voor gelijkheid van kansen en voor racismebestrijding* v. *G4S Secure Solutions NV* [2017] ECLI:EU:C:2017:203; Case C-188/15, *Asma Bougnaoui and Association de défense des droits de l'homme (ADDH)* v. *Micropole SA* [2017] ECLI:EU:C:2017:204.

18 Case C-193/17, *Cresco Investigation GmbH* v. *Markus Achatzi* [2019] ECLI:EU:C:2019:43; Case C-68/17, *IR* v. *JQ* [2018] ECLI:EU:C:2018:696; Case C-414/16, *Vera Egenberger v Evangelisches Werk für Diakonie und Entwicklung e.V.* [2018] ECLI:EU:C:2018:257.

19 Case C-74/16, *Congregación de Escuelas Pías Provincia Betania* v. *Ayuntamiento de Getafe* [2017] ECLI:EU:C:2017:496.

20 Case C-497/17, *Oeuvre d'assistance aux bêtes d'abattoirs* v. *Ministre de l'Agriculture et de l'Alimentation and Others* [2019] ECLI:EU:C:2019:137; Case C-426/16, *Liga van Moskeeën en Islamitische Organisaties Provincie Antwerpen and Others* v. *Vlaams Gewest* [2018] ECLI:EU:C:2018:335.

performed Muslim divorce,[21] religious databases,[22] and protections for refugee applicants suffering religious persecution at home.[23]

These cases are usually tied to questions of EU economic rights. The cases on religious freedom in the workplace are all issues of general workplace discrimination.[24] The Muslim divorce case is mostly about the enforcement of another country's judicial decisions within the EU.[25] The cases on ritual slaughtering come under regulations about animal welfare and organic food labeling. The issue of tax exemption for a religious school is a question in part about state aid to religion, which is prohibited under EU law.[26] The controversy about the Jehovah's Witnesses' record-keeping is a case about data protection under EU law.[27] Highly contentious claims of religious freedom are therefore often reviewed indirectly, usually through the prism of economic principles, and without necessary reference to the rights provisions of the EU Charter or the European Convention.

Nonetheless, these decisions affecting religious freedom are of growing importance and attractiveness to some litigants, since they are binding law for all the EU member states and create immediately enforceable rights at the domestic level.[28] The emergence of these cases is somewhat analogous to American developments in the aftermath of the New Deal in the 1930s, particularly when the US Supreme Court began selectively incorporating the Bill of Rights into the Fourteenth Amendment Due Process Clause.[29] On many important matters, federal constitutional law gradually eclipsed local state laws, making litigation in federal courts more attractive than litigation in state courts.[30] This has been notably true for American religious freedom, too, as we saw in Chapter 5. After the Supreme

[21] Case C-372/16, *Soha Sahyouni* v. *Raja Mamisch* [2017] ECLI:EU:C:2017:988.

[22] Case C-25/17, *Tietosuojavaltuutettu* [2018] ECLI:EU:C:2018:551.

[23] Case C-56/17, *Bahtiyar Fathi* v. *Predsedatel na Darzhavna agentsia za bezhantsite* [2018] ECLI:EU:C:2018:803.

[24] Case C-157/15, *Achbita* [2017] ECLI:EU:C:2017:203; Case C-188/15, *Bougnaoui and ADDH* [2017] ECLI:EU:C:2017:204.

[25] Case C-56/17, *Fathi* [2018] ECLI:EU:C:2018:803.

[26] Case C-74/16, *Congregación de Escuelas Pías Provincia Betania* [2017] ECLI:EU:C:2017:496.

[27] Case C-25/17, *Tietosuojavaltuutettu* [2018] ECLI:EU:C:2018:551. This is the least consequential of these cases, which I will not analyze further. In this case, the Court found no violation of religious freedom when a group of Jehovah's Witnesses challenged a Finnish privacy law that prohibited them from keeping unregistered personal data gathered during their door-to-door solicitation. The Witnesses kept a list of contacted people who did not want to be contacted again. An EU directive required that such personal data were subject to the protections of the EU privacy directive, and the Witnesses were not exempt from compliance just because the data were collected as part of their evangelical work. The EU's interest in protecting the privacy of all citizens outweighed the Witnesses' interest in conducting their evangelism without regulatory impediments, the Court concluded.

[28] Congressional Research Service, RS21372, The European Union: Questions and Answers 2 (2019).

[29] Akhil Reed Amar, *The Bill of Rights: Creation and Reconstruction* (New Haven, CT: Yale University Press, 1998), 215–83.

[30] Jeffrey S. Sutton, 51 *Imperfect Solutions: States and the Making of American Constitutional Law* (Oxford: Oxford University Press, 2018), 8, 14.

Court incorporated the First Amendment religious freedom clauses into the Fourteenth Amendment in the 1940s, more than 80 percent of the Court's subsequent 170 religious freedom cases concerned state and local government issues, and roughly half of these cases found local violations.[31] This has all taken place within the explicit federalist framework of American constitutional law and of the First Amendment itself, which says only that "*Congress* shall make no law respecting an establishment of religion or prohibiting the free exercise thereof" (emphasis added).

Just as American litigants came to prefer litigation in federal courts instead of state courts to protect their fundamental rights, so EU litigants are beginning to prefer the Luxembourg Court to their own domestic courts. The supremacy of EU law over national law ensures the effectiveness of the Court's rulings.[32] Their direct effect protects these rights without the mediation of domestic institutions.[33] The EU-wide reach of these decisions makes every case critical. "Ensuring respect for the freedom of religion is not, and was never intended to be, part of the EU's 'core business.'"[34] But religious freedom is becoming more important as the Court of Justice goes about its business.

CASES ON RELIGIOUS DISCRIMINATION IN THE WORKPLACE

Five of the Luxembourg Court's new cases concern religious discrimination in the workplace, and they have produced lengthy and controversial opinions. The cases concern (1) Islamic headscarves worn by private employees, (2) religious affiliation as a prerequisite for working in a religious organization, and (3) differential treatment of employees of different faiths.

The cases turn, in part, on an EU Council directive in 2000 that forbids religious discrimination in employment.[35] The law distinguishes between: (1) "direct" discrimination, "when one person is treated less favourably than another is, has been or would have been treated in a comparable situation," and (2) "indirect" discrimination, "where an apparently neutral provision, criterion or practice would put persons having a particular religion or belief ... at a particular disadvantage compared with other persons." While direct religious discrimination is prohibited, indirect discrimination is permissible as long as it is "justified by a legitimate aim and the means of achieving that aim are appropriate and necessary." EU member states may permit different

[31] John Witte, Jr. and Joel A. Nichols, *Religion and the American Constitutional Experiment*, 4th ed. (Oxford: Oxford University Press, 2016), 303–37 (table of all Supreme Court cases on religious freedom from 1815–2016).

[32] Precedence of European law, EUR-Lex (Jan. 10, 2010), https://eur-lex.europa.eu/legal-content/EN/TXT/HTML/?uri=LEGISSUM:l14548&from=GA.

[33] Itzcovich, "The European Court of Justice," 281.

[34] Philippa Watson and Peter Oliver, "Is the Court of Justice of the European Union Finding Its Religion?," *Fordham International Law Journal* 42 (2019), 872.

[35] Council Directive 2000/78/EC of November 27, 2000, establishing a general framework for equal treatment in employment and occupation, OJ 2000 No. L303, pp. 16–22.

treatment where, "by reason of the nature of the particular occupational activities concerned or of the context in which they are carried out, such a characteristic constitutes a genuine and determining occupational requirement, provided that the objective is legitimate and the requirement is proportionate."[36]

Islamic Headscarf Cases. The Luxembourg Court issued two cases in 2017 on the use of the Islamic headscarf in the private workplace. In both instances, Muslim female employees were ordered to remove the apparel while at work. Both women refused; both lost their jobs; both sued. One lost, one won.

Achbita v. *G4S Secure Solutions* concerned a dispute between a global security company and Samira Achbita, a receptionist in its Belgian branch. She had been employed in the company for a while before she started to wear the hijab, a veil that covered her head, hair, and chest but left her face fully exposed. This new choice of clothing conflicted with the company dress code, which required employees to avoid wearing any visible religious signs or apparel. Her supervisor ordered her to remove her hijab. When Achbita refused, she was fired. She sued her employer in a Belgian court for religious discrimination in violation of the EU Council directive just quoted. The Belgian judge requested the Luxembourg Court for a preliminary ruling on the correct interpretation of the phrasing "direct discrimination" in that directive.[37]

The Court found that the employer's termination was not "direct discrimination," for its neutral dress code did not target any specific religious faith. Nor was it "indirect discrimination," since the company had a stated legitimate interest in pursuing a policy of religious neutrality reflected in its prohibition of visible religious apparel in its workplace. The Court weighed this right to preserve a religiously neutral environment against Achbita's religious claim to wear the Islamic headscarf, and found that the indirect discrimination caused by the dress code was proportionate and therefore lawful.[38]

The *Achbita* Court cited the Strasbourg Court's Article 9 case law to support its ruling that a private employer's consistent general policy of maintaining religious, political, or philosophical neutrality in the private workplace was a legitimate aim under both the European Convention on Human Rights and EU employment law. "An employer's wish to project an image of neutrality" to its employees and customers must outweigh any restriction "imposed on the freedom of religion."[39]

In her opinion, the AG also considered and rejected American case law to the contrary. She referenced *EEOC* v. *Abercrombie & Fitch Stores, Inc.*, a US Supreme Court case in which a Muslim applicant sued a private company for discrimination. According to the plaintiff, Abercrombie had decided not to hire her because of her

36 Ibid., arts. 2 and 4, pp. 18–19.

37 Case C-157/15, *Achbita* [2017] ECLI:EU:C:2017:203, paras. 11, 13, 17, 21.

38 Ibid., paras. 30–32, 35, 40.

39 Ibid., paras. 37–39.

religious expression.[40] More precisely, she argued that Abercrombie, whose dress code forbade all head coverings, feared that she would seek an accommodation to wear the Islamic headscarf under Title VII of the Civil Rights Act of 1964. The Supreme Court held that a violation occurs if an employer makes a religious practice a motivating factor in an employment decision and thus remanded the case for further investigation and litigation. The AG wanted none of this for Europe, arguing that this approach would be unaffordable for employers, who would have to accommodate all employees' religious needs, however expensive or inconvenient.[41]

The *Achbita* Court agreed, allowing private employers to impose a consistent religiously neutral dress code without forcing them to accommodate religious apparel.[42] It is quite striking that religious accommodation was not required in this case. G4S is a global company with six hundred thousand employees. It could easily have found another receptionist and moved Ms. Achbita to another office where local custom readily accommodated headscarves.

The second case, *Bougnaoui* v. *Micropole*, also involved an employee wearing a hijab at work, but here her French employer had no clear dress code or policy on religious apparel. When Micropole hired Ms. Bougnaoui, they told her that "the wearing of an Islamic headscarf might pose a problem when she was in contact with customers of the company." Bougnaoui first wore a bandana; later, a hijab. Neither head covering met with initial objection. Micropole eventually hired her as a design engineer, and she went to work for one of the company's customers at the customer's site. The customer complained to the company that "the wearing of a veil . . . had upset a number of its employees," and requested "no veil next time." Micropole then fired Bougnaoui. The company stated that she had been warned from the beginning of her internship that wearing a veil could become a problem, and that the company retained "discretion . . . as regards the expression of the personal preferences of [the] employees." The company further stated that, during the job interview, Bougnaoui said she had no difficulty respecting "the need for neutrality" when in the presence of customers.[43]

Bougnaoui sued for religious discrimination under EU law, and she won. Distinguishing *Achbita*, the Court now found that Ms. Bougnaoui had been a victim of direct discrimination on religious grounds. She had been dismissed because a company's customer complained about her headscarf. Even though she had been warned about Micropole's neutrality policy, this policy had not been enforced until that customer complained. While EU law permitted employers to place limits on religious dress, it could do so only by showing that it was a "genuine and determining occupational requirement" that was "objectively dictated by the

40 Opinion of Advocate General Kokott in Case C-157/15, *Achbita* [2017] ECLI:EU:C:2016:382, para. 110, referencing *EEOC* v. *Abercrombie & Fitch Stores, Inc.*, 135 US 2031, 2031 (2015).

41 Case C-157/15, *Achbita* [2017] ECLI:EU:C:2017:203, para. 110.

42 Ibid., para. 141.

43 Case C-188/15, *Bougnaoui and ADDH* [2017] ECLI:EU:C:2017:204, paras. 13–14.

nature of the occupational activities concerned or of the context in which they [were] carried out." But this was not the case here. Ms. Bougnaoui was ordered to remove her headscarf not in implementation of the company's neutral dress policy, but only "to take account of the particular wishes of the customer." That did not justify such discrimination.[44]

The AG's opinion in this case raised broader concerns about religious freedom and its appropriate limits. In her view, "discrimination has both a financial impact (because it may touch on a person's ability to earn a living in the employment market) and a moral impact (because it may affect that person's autonomy)."[45] In this case, Bougnaoui simply sought to practice her religion, not to proselytize. The employer could not violate her right to that religious freedom:

> When the employer concludes a contract of employment with an employee, he does not buy that person's soul. He does, however, buy his time. For that reason, I draw a sharp distinction between the freedom to manifest one's religion – whose scope and possible limitation in the employment context are at the heart of the proceedings before the national court – and proselytising on behalf of one's religion. ... It is therefore legitimate for the employer to impose and enforce rules that prohibit proselytising, both to ensure that the work time he has paid for is used for the purposes of his business and to create harmonious working conditions for his workforce.[46]

While opining in favor of Ms. Bougnaoui, the AG again made clear that private and state employers alike could regulate religious apparel in the workplace, particularly full head and partial face coverings.

> Western society regards visual or eye contact as being of fundamental importance in any relationship involving face-to-face communication. ... [A] rule that imposed a prohibition on wearing religious apparel that covers the eyes and face entirely whilst performing a job that involved such contact with customers would be proportionate.[47]

This was a clear echo of S.A.S. v. *France* and other recent Strasbourg Court cases that upheld French and Belgian bans on the niqab and burqa in public.[48] The AG's message was that private employers, too, could use clear and consistent policies to put comparable comprehensive and consistent limits on all religious apparel without violating norms of religious freedom and nondiscrimination.[49]

Litigation about religious dress, particularly head coverings for Muslim women, has been a staple of Strasbourg Court jurisprudence and is likely to become more

44 Ibid., paras. 30–31, 39–41.
45 Opinion of Advocate General Sharpston in Case C-188/15, *Bougnaoui and ADDH* [2016] ECLI:EU:C:2016:553, para. 72.
46 Ibid., para. 73.
47 Ibid., para. 130.
48 See Chapter 8, p. 248.
49 Case C-188/15, *Bougnaoui and ADDH* [2016] ECLI:EU:C:2016:553, para. 30.

prominent in Luxembourg cases, too. The topic is perennially controversial, doubly so today in Europe. Debates about religious apparel pit secularism against religiosity, and cultural majorities against religious minorities. Muslim women's head coverings, in particular, have focused the debates on the place of religion in postreligious cultures, the place of Muslims in Europe after three decades of Islamist violence and unrest, and the place of migrants in once homogeneous lands newly infected with nativism and xenophobia. The Strasbourg Court has been quite deferential to the policies of member states, granting wide margins of appreciation to France, Belgium, and Turkey, even though they clearly targeted the apparel of Muslim women. So far, the Luxembourg Court has allowed restrictions on religious dress only if employers follow a strict neutrality approach. Here neutrality norms have proved more protective of religious freedom, at least in the *Bougnaoui* case.

Religious Affiliation and Employment Discrimination. Three recent judgments have set out the Luxembourg Court's approach to the role of religious affiliation in the workplace. The cases of *Egenberger* v. *Evangelisches Werk für Diakonie und Entwicklung eV* (2018) and *IR* v. *JQ* (2018) concerned whether a religious employer could make religious affiliation either a prerequisite for employment or a ground for termination. *Cresco Investigation GmbH* v. *Markus Achatzi* (2019) addressed a state law that allowed for differences in pay between employees of different faiths.

These three cases must be seen in light of the presumptive special protection of religious autonomy within the EU. The principle of state deference to religious groups was established by the 1997 Treaty of Amsterdam.[50] An EU directive in 2000 affirmed that "Member States may maintain or lay down specific provisions on genuine, legitimate and justified occupational requirements which might be required for carrying out an occupational activity."[51] But the same directive allows that

> in the case of occupational activities within churches and other public or private organisations the ethos of which is based on religion or belief, a difference of treatment based on a person's religion or belief shall not constitute discrimination where, by reason of the nature of these activities or of the context in which they are carried out, a person's religion or belief constitute a genuine, legitimate and justified occupational requirement.[52]

The Luxembourg Court has used these provisions to build its framework for dealing with permissible and impermissible religious line drawing by religious employers. Its cases have been considerably less protective of religious autonomy norms than the general EU Treaty language or the Strasbourg Court's jurisprudence.

50 Treaty of Amsterdam, Declaration 11, p. 133.
51 Council Directive 2000/78/EC, preamble, para. 24, p. 17.
52 Ibid., art. 4(2), p. 19.

In *Egenberger*, a Protestant institution advertised a new job that involved producing a report on the United Nations International Convention on the Elimination of All Forms of Racial Discrimination; ancillary duties included presenting the project to the political world and to the general public.[53] Applicants had to be members of "a Protestant church or a church" belonging to the Working Group of Christian Churches in Germany. Ms. Egenberger applied, although she was not religiously affiliated. After being shortlisted for the job, she was not offered an interview. She sued the Protestant institution in a German court, complaining about the religious affiliation requirement. The German court sent a preliminary ruling request to the Luxembourg Court, asking whether the directive allowed that a religious employer "may itself authoritatively determine whether a particular religion of an applicant … constitutes a genuine, legitimate and justified occupational requirement, having regard to the employer or church's ethos."[54]

In her advisory opinion to the *Egenberger* Court, the AG made clear that EU law respected "the defendant's right to autonomy and self-determination, as protected under Articles 9 and 11 of the ECHR." But the AG did "not support a restriction on judicial review" of the employment decisions of a religious organization. Moreover, while recognizing that EU member states had power to decide religion–state relationships for themselves, she argued that the EU embraces the principle of "value pluralism." This principle entails that "conflicts between differing rights … are resolved through balancing conflicting elements rather than according priority to one over another in a hierarchical fashion." This balancing approach stood in marked contrast with the traditional principle of religious autonomy that gave priority and deference to the rights and interests of religious employers over their employees.[55]

Echoing the AG, the *Egenberger* Court instructed the local court to balance the competing interests and values of religious employers and their (prospective) employees in these cases. The local court had to review the "nature" and "context" of the activities and job responsibilities of the (prospective) employee, and look for the "objectively verifiable existence of a direct link between the occupational requirement imposed by the employer and the activity concerned." An employer's act of religious line drawing could be found lawful only if the religious requirement imposed was "genuine, legitimate and justified." To be found *genuine* required proof that

> professing the religion or belief on which the ethos of the church or organisation is founded must appear necessary because of the importance of the occupational activity in question for the manifestation of that ethos or the exercise by the church or organisation of its right of autonomy.

53 Case C-414/16, *Egenberger* [2018] ECLI:EU:C:2018:257, para. 24.
54 Ibid., paras. 24–27 and 41.
55 Opinion of Advocate General Tanchev in Case C-414/16, *Egenberger* [2017] ECLI:EU:C:2017:851, paras. 56, 68, 100.

To be *legitimate*, the affiliation requirement could "not [be] used to pursue an aim that ha[d] no connection with that ethos or with the exercise by the church or organisation of its right of autonomy." To be *justified*, the

> church or organisation imposing the requirement [had] to show, in the light of the factual circumstances of the case, that the supposed risk of causing harm to its ethos or to its right of autonomy is probable and substantial, so that imposing such a requirement is indeed necessary.

If the religious organization failed any of these requirements, the domestic court would have to provide an appropriate local remedy for the individual suffering religious discrimination.[56]

The *Egenberger* Court was aware that its ruling could alter the national constitutional settlements of church–state relations and erode the strong EU principle of religious autonomy and state deference to a church's decisions about its own employees. The Court, however, stated clearly that general "respect for the status of churches" did not excuse local courts from protecting the fundamental rights of both employers to exercise their religious freedom and employees to be free from religious discrimination or coercion.[57]

While *Egenberger* concerned hiring, *IR* v. *JQ* concerned the firing of an employee by a religious organization. IR was a nonprofit organization, subject to the supervision of the Roman Catholic archbishop of Cologne. Established under German law, IR's purpose was to carry out the work of the Catholic federation of charitable organizations called Caritas, including the operation of its hospitals. IR had to comply with the church's Basic Regulations on Employment Relationships in the Services of the Church (Basic Regulations), which subjected all employees of Catholic institutions to a specific "duty of loyalty." The nature of this duty depended on the employee's religion. Non-Catholics had to "respect the truths and values of the Gospel and to contribute to giving them effect within the organisation." Catholic employees were "expected to recognise *and observe* the principles of Catholic doctrinal and moral teaching ... [and] *conduct themselves in a manner consistent with the principles of Catholic doctrinal and moral teaching*." This latter requirement applied also to "employees performing managerial duties." The Basic Regulations contemplated dismissal as the last resort for employees who did not comply with these requirements for employment.[58]

JQ, a physician, was a member of the Catholic Church. He was employed as the head of a medicine department of an IR hospital and had managerial duties. After he divorced and remarried, he was dismissed by IR for failing to comply with Catholic marital doctrine, which forbids divorce and remarriage. He sued IR in German court, arguing that he had been discriminated against on religious grounds, since

56 Case C-414/16, *Egenberger* [2018] ECLI:EU:C:2018:257, paras. 51–53, 61–67, 79.

57 Ibid., para. 81.

58 Case C-68/17, *IR* [2018] ECLI:EU:C:2018:696, paras. 19–23 (emphasis added).

such actions by a Protestant doctor working in the same hospital would not constitute a legitimate ground for dismissal. The German domestic court asked the Luxembourg Court whether the Catholic Church could prescribe such a code of moral or religious conduct for its IR employees and, more specifically, whether it could differentiate between Catholic employees and all others.[59]

Drawing on the *Egenberger* criteria, the *IR* Court ordered the domestic judge to assess whether the hospital's policy of maintaining different religious standards for its employees was "genuine, legitimate and justified." While again deferring to the local court to make this assessment, the Court opined that adherence to Catholic marriage teachings did "not appear to be necessary for the promotion of IR's ethos" or the doctor's work in practicing medicine or managing his department. In its view, treating Catholic and non-Catholic employees differently is permissible under the EU Directive "only if . . . the religion or belief constitutes an occupational requirement that is genuine, legitimate and justified in the light of the ethos of the church or organisation concerned and is consistent with the principle of proportionality, which is a matter to be determined by the national courts."[60] Armed with these instructions, the German court resumed the proceeding, found that the hospital's loyalty requirement was disproportionate, and therefore ruled in favor of the plaintiff doctor.[61]

Cresco Investigation GmbH v. *Markus Achatzi* is the most recent case in this series on religious affiliation and discrimination in the workplace. Achatzi was an employee of a private company in Austria. Austrian national law recognized Good Friday as a holiday for members of Old Catholic Churches, Evangelical Churches of the Augsburg and Helvetic Confession, and the United Methodist Church. The law stipulated that those church members were exempt from working on Good Friday, but if they did work that day, they would receive double pay.[62]

Achatzi did not belong to any of these religions and therefore could neither take a holiday nor get double pay on Good Friday. He sued in Austrian court for religious discrimination. The Austrian Supreme Court called on the Luxembourg Court to assess whether this differential treatment of employees could be justified either (1) as a permissible form of "indirect discrimination" under the Council directive;[63] or (2) as a case that fit into an exception in the same directive allowing "measures which, although discriminatory in appearance, [were] in fact intended to eliminate or reduce actual instances of inequality that may exist in society."[64] This latter exception allowed for favorable treatment of parties affected by social inequalities. The directive also made clear, however, that any such treatment could not prejudice

59 Ibid., paras. 24–28 and 39.

60 Ibid., paras. 50, 58, and 61.

61 http://juris.bundesarbeitsgericht.de/cgi-bin/rechtsprechung/document.py?Gericht=bag&Art=pm&Datum=2019&anz=11&pos=1&nr=22558&linked=urt.

62 Case C-193/17, *Cresco Investigation* [2019] ECLI:EU:C:2019:43.

63 Council Directive 2000/78/EC, art. 2, pp. 18–19.

64 Ibid., art. 7(1), p. 20.

"measures laid down by national law which, in a democratic society, are necessary for public security, for the maintenance of public order and the prevention of criminal offences, for the protection of health and for the protection of the rights and freedom of others."[65]

The AG saw this as an easy case of religious discrimination. The case did not originate in the employer's religious practices or beliefs, the AG noted, but in a national law that accorded different treatments to members of different faiths. The law could certainly allow some believers to have Good Friday off. The real problem stems from doubling the pay of religiously observant employees for working on a Good Friday, but not giving the same double pay to other employees who worked on the same day. For the AG, the case thus did not fall within the delicate field of religiously motivated exceptions allowed by the Council directive, but instead was a more routine case of impermissible salary discrimination based on religion.[66]

The Court's opinion in this case followed the AG's views rather closely and did not ground the case in concerns of religious freedom. The Court also ruled out any justification for this law under the two exceptions in the Council directive. Ordering double pay only to select believers could not be regarded as reducing social inequality, nor could it be justified on grounds of religious freedom or any other public interest. To the contrary, the law's promise of double pay for work on Good Friday discouraged, rather than encouraged, church members from observing their religion's holy day.[67]

The Court was even more specific here than in prior cases about how it wanted the case to be solved. It called on the Austrian court to provide immediate redress to the complainant. Although the discrimination stemmed from a state statute and not from the employer's discretionary salary policies, the Court concluded that the domestic court must require "a private employer who is subject to such legislation ... also to grant his other employees a public holiday on Good Friday ... and, consequently, to recognise that those employees are entitled to [the daily pay plus the indemnity] where the employer has refused to approve such a request."[68]

Egenberger, *IR*, and *Cresco Investigation* form an important trio of cases on religious discrimination in the workplace. The first two cases, in particular, carve out an important role for the Luxembourg Court as well as for domestic judges in employment cases that involve religiously affiliated institutions. Contrary to cases in the Strasbourg Court and the US Supreme Court that strongly support religious autonomy and judicial deference to religious employers,[69] the Luxembourg Court requires domestic courts to scrutinize whether the religious affiliation and the

65 Ibid., art. 2(5), p. 19.

66 Opinion of Advocate General Bobek in Case C-193/17, *Cresco Investigation* [2018] ECLI:EU:C:2018:614, paras. 41 and 51.

67 Case C-193/17, *Cresco Investigation* [2019] ECLI:EU:C:2019:43, para. 50.

68 Ibid., para. 89.

69 For Strasbourg Court cases, see Chapter 8, p. 250–54. For American cases, see Chapter 6, p. 189–93.

private morality of employees are relevant to their duties; if not, their religious or moral conduct can have no bearing on the employee's status or treatment by their employer.

Egenberger further requires domestic courts to balance the competing interests of the religious institution and a job applicant, using the principle of proportionality. Proportionality is a staple of European court jurisprudence, requiring judges to determine which interests are involved in a case, which one prevails, and to what extent.[70] In these cases of religious employment, the principle compels judges to balance the secular interests, individual rights, and private life choices of an employee or job applicant with a religious institution's loyalty to its religious beliefs and practices. But this balance must now be done without the traditional presumption of religious autonomy for private religious employers along with strong protections for (prospective) employees to leave the religious group or employer without encumbrance or reprisal.

Cresco Investigation virtually rules out any direct or indirect discrimination that is not grounded in public interest, while legitimizing measures that favor persons and groups who suffer from social inequalities. The Luxembourg Court might well begin to favor state measures that protect new or minority religious groups who are more likely to suffer from social discrimination and begin questioning state policies that favor members of longstanding established churches and traditional religious groups. This approach may well have powerful ramifications for EU member states with established or favored Catholic, Lutheran, Anglican, Reformed, or Orthodox Christian faiths.

Cresco Investigation's further insistence that the domestic judge accord relief to the plaintiff notwithstanding contrary domestic legislation on religion may also become important. The Court in effect thereby empowers local judges to override – or at least erode – local laws governing national religious establishments and norms of religious freedom when a local plaintiff proves the discriminatory effects of those traditional local laws. The Court's *IR* and *Egenberger* cases have language to the same effect. There the Court recognized that the German constitution grants ample autonomy to Evangelical churches.[71] But the Court states:

> [A] national court hearing a dispute between two individuals is obliged, where it is not possible for it to interpret the applicable national law in conformity with Article 4(2) of Directive 2000/78, to ensure within its jurisdiction the judicial protection deriving for individuals from Article 21 and 47 of the Charter and to guarantee the full effectiveness of those articles by disapplying, if need be any contrary provision of national law.[72]

[70] Alec Stone Sweet and Jud Mathews, *Proportionality Balancing and Constitutional Governance: A Comparative and Global Approach* (Oxford: Oxford University Press, 2019), 3, 68.

[71] Case C-68/17, *IR* [2018] ECLI:EU:C:2018:696 (holding Article 140 of the Basic Law grants churches "the right of self-determination … to undertake and fulfill the church's mandate and mission").

[72] Case C-414/16, *Egenberger* [2018] ECLI:EU:C:2018:257, para. 82.

This logic has the potential to dismantle significant areas of church autonomy, despite the EU's basic starting rule of deference to local church–state relations, set out in the 1997 Treaty of Amsterdam.

The Luxembourg Court's approach stands in marked contrast to the Strasbourg Court's judgments, which give much stronger protection to religious autonomy, but have only weak mechanisms of enforcement.[73] If present trends continue, the more apt comparison might well become the US Supreme Court's strong reading of the First Amendment Establishment Clause in its cases from 1971 to 1986, which gave minority faiths and those with no faith something of a "heckler's veto" over state laws and policies on religion, no matter how old the laws were or how strong the legislative majority was that supported them.[74]

CASES ON RELIGION AND STATE AID

In *Congregación de Escuelas Pías Provincia Betania* v. *Ayuntamiento de Getafe* (2017), the Luxembourg Court addressed more directly the nature and privileges of established churches and church–state agreements under EU law. The Court again raised caveats that may well become important in future cases.

European Union law expressly prohibits state aid to religion to the extent that such aid distorts free-market competition by favoring religious groups in "certain undertakings or the production of certain goods."[75] The Congregación de Escuela Pías Provincia Betania was a school owned by the Catholic Church and located in the Spanish municipality of Getafe. Given its Catholic ownership, the school was governed by the concordat or agreement between Spain and the Holy See entered into force in 1979, before Spain joined the EU.[76] The agreement accords the Catholic Church in Spain a set of distinct privileges based on its ancient pedigree and presence in the land since the time of the Roman Empire. Such religion–state agreements enjoy general protection under EU law, which is bound to "respect . . . the status under national law of churches and religious associations or communities in the Member States."[77] Another EU provision guarantees that EU laws will not affect a member state's rights or obligations "arising from agreements" that a member state concluded with another country, including the Holy See, before joining the EU, although member states must

[73] See Chapter 8, p. 250–54.

[74] Witte and Nichols, *Religion and the American Constitutional Experiment*, 156–58 (discussing liberal standing rules in Establishment Clause cases), 173–80, 192–96, 209–16 (exploring strict separation cases under the Establishment Clause). The term "heckler's veto" was used by Justice Alito in *Pleasant Grove City* v. *Summum*, 555 US 460, 468 (2009).

[75] Treaty on the Functioning of the European Union (TFEU), OJ 2016 No. C202, art. 107(1), p. 91.

[76] Opinion of Advocate General Kokott in Case C-74/16, *Congregación de Escuelas Pías Provincia Betania* [2017] ECLI:EU:C:2017:135, paras. 9 and 14.

[77] TFEU (2016), art. 17(1), p. 55.

"take all the appropriate steps to eliminate the incompatibilities" between these older agreements and EU law.[78]

In 2011, this Catholic school built a new hall, paying the construction tax to the municipality. The school, however, later submitted a request for a tax refund, reasoning that the agreement between Spain and the Holy See calls for the "complete and permanent exemption from property and capital gains taxes and from income tax and wealth tax in respect of properties of the Catholic Church." The municipality refused to pay the refund, and the school sued in state court. The Spanish judge requested the Luxembourg Court to issue a preliminary ruling on whether the tax exemption for Catholic-owned buildings used for education, rather than worship, violated the EU's prohibition on state aid to religion.[79]

The Court drew heavily from its own precedents to define "state aid to religion," including to religious schools, and gave rather precise guidelines for the domestic court to decide. The Court noted that EU law did not distinguish between the religious and nonreligious nature of the identity, or the for-profit and not-for-profit nature of the undertaking. What was essential to trigger the EU prohibition on state aid to religion was whether the activity was remunerated. "Services [that are] normally provided for remuneration" count as an economic undertaking. But in this case the school was part of the Spanish system of public education and lived off of "public funds," not fees paid by students or parents. This put the school's educational activities outside the scope of the EU prohibition on state aid to religion, the Court concluded. The new hall for which the local construction tax had been levied was intended to serve only the educational purpose of the school and could thus be properly exempt from construction tax.[80]

In its opinion, the Luxembourg Court did not go so far as the AG had proposed. The AG did not confine her reasoning to the tax exemption issue at stake. She explored the potential tensions between EU regulations and Spanish church–state relations, portending major possible changes in later cases. She hypothesized that some tax exemptions accorded by the church–state agreement that benefit economic activities run by Catholic institutions would likely not survive scrutiny. She even envisioned that one day Spain would have to use the dispute-resolution procedures in the agreement between Spain and the Holy See to reconcile its obligations toward the Catholic Church and the EU. The AG forecasted even more gravely: "If, in that way, a solution in conformity with EU law were not achieved within a reasonable space of time, Spain would have to give notice of termination of the Agreement."[81]

78 Ibid., art. 351, p. 196.

79 Opinion of Advocate General Kokott in Case C-74/16, *Congregación de Escuelas Pías Provincia Betania* [2017] ECLI:EU:C:2017:135, paras. 9, 15, 18, and 21.

80 Case C-74/16, *Congregación de Escuelas Pías Provincia Betania* [2017] ECLI:EU:C:2017:496, paras. 43–60.

81 Opinion of Advocate General Kokott in Case C-74/16, *Congregación de Escuelas Pías Provincia Betania* [2017] ECLI:EU:C:2017:135, paras. 88–100.

The AG's prophecy about clashes between state compliance with EU regulations and with church–state agreements is disturbing for those who understand EU integration as a smooth process that does not require its member states to give away their traditions in order to become EU members. Even as stated, however, this case might well have powerful ramifications for future cases about religious freedom. The Court's opinion divided admissible from inadmissible state aid to churches based on whether the church charges money for its tax-exempt services. This has the paradoxical result of favoring wealthy, well-endowed, and state-established churches that receive public funds and thus do need not need to charge their users for educational and other services. But smaller religious groups and new private educational institutions that are still making their way into the public education system will have to pay taxes precisely because they receive no public funds and thus need to charge tuition and other fees to recoup their costs.

CASES ON RITUAL SLAUGHTERING AND ANIMAL WELFARE

The Luxembourg Court has issued three recent cases on religious slaughtering. In all three cases, the Court rejected the religious freedom and equality arguments against local regulations that limited halal and kosher ritual slaughtering. All three cases feature rather blunt dismissal of the claims of discrete religious minorities whose central religious practices were targeted and subordinated to state concerns for animal welfare.

Liga van Moskeeën en Islamitische Organisaties Provincie Antwerpen VZW and Others (2018) concerned a specific provision of a broader regulation on food production from animals.[82] European Union laws require that animals be slaughtered only after stunning them as a way of mitigating the animal's stress, suffering, and pain. However, since halal religious rules require that the animal be awake during slaughtering, EU law carves out an exception, allowing such religious ritual slaughtering so long as it performed in licensed slaughterhouses.[83] The latter requirement was at issue in this case.

The dispute started in Belgian Flanders.[84] On the few days of Eid Al-Adha (the Feast of the Sacrifice), a major Islamic holiday, Islamic ritual slaughtering normally peaked. Until 2015, the Flemish authorities had accommodated the extra demand for halal meat in preparation for the festival by licensing local temporary slaughterhouses for Islamic butchers. In 2015, however, the authorities announced that they would no longer issue approvals for temporary slaughter houses, on the ground that such licenses violated EU rules on the structural and hygiene requirements for all

[82] Council Regulation 1099/2009/EC of September 24, 2009, on the protection of animals at the time of killing, OJ 2009 No. L303, pp. 1–36.

[83] Ibid., arts. 4(1) and (4), p. 9.

[84] Case C-426/16, *Liga van Moskeeën en Islamitische Organisaties Provincie Antwerpen and Others* [2018] ECLI:EU:C:2018:335, paras. 16–18.

slaughterhouses. Flemish Muslim communities sued in state court, claiming that this new denial infringed upon their religious freedom to celebrate the feast properly. Under this new rule, they argued, the only way to meet the peak demand for halal meat would be to build a series of permanent slaughterhouses that would be of no use for the rest of the year.[85] The local judge issued a request for a preliminary ruling whether the EU regulation on ritual slaughtering, as implemented by national legislation, violated Article 9 of the ECHR, Article 10 of the EU Charter, and EU laws prohibiting religious discrimination.[86]

The AG's opinion stipulated that "slaughtering of an animal without stunning on the occasion of the Islamic Feast of the Sacrifice is indeed a religious precept that benefits from the protection of religious freedom." The AG continued, however, that the EU's general law on slaughtering was "perfectly *neutral* and applies to any party that organises slaughtering. Legislation that applies in a neutral manner, *with no connection to religious convictions*, cannot in principle be regarded as a limitation on freedom of religion." Its neutrality means that it does not target religious practices. EU laws have already carved out a religious freedom exception to accommodate religious ritual slaughtering. The issue is whether the requirement that such ritual slaughtering be performed only in approved slaughterhouses was disproportionate to the damage to religious freedom that it created.[87]

The Luxembourg Court held that EU law had done enough "to ensure effective observance of the freedom of religion, in particular of practicing Muslims during the Feast of Sacrifice." Requiring that such ritual slaughtering must be performed in licensed slaughterhouses properly balanced the parties' religious freedom interests with the EU's interest in avoiding "excessive and unnecessary suffering of animals killed." The EU's general slaughtering laws, and the Flemish application of them, thus did not violate any Charter rights. The real challenge, the Court noted, was not to religious freedom but to the financial cost for a local Islamic community in Belgium that might have to set up permanent slaughterhouses for only a few days of their use – although, of course, they could rent out those facilities for the rest of the year.[88]

The 2019 case of *Oeuvre d'assistance aux bêtes d'abattoirs* v. *Ministre de l'Agriculture et de l'Alimentation and Others* also involved halal slaughtering practices.[89] EU law reserved the "organic" label for food that had been produced

[85] Ibid., paras. 3, 16–19, and 70.

[86] Consolidated Version of the Treaty on the Functioning of the European Union, OJ 2012 No. C326, art. 13, p. 54.

[87] Opinion of Advocate General Wahl in Case C-426/16, *Liga van Moskeeën en Islamitische Organisaties Provincie Antwerpen and Others* [2017] ECLI:EU:C:2017:926, paras. 58, 78, 113, and 124.

[88] Case C-426/16, *Liga van Moskeeën en Islamitische Organisaties Provincie Antwerpen and Others* [2018] ECLI:EU:C:2018:335, paras. 56, 59, 65, 70, and 77–78.

[89] Commission Regulation 889/2008/EC of September 5, 2008, laying down detailed rules for the implementation of Regulation No 834/2007, OJ 2008 No. L250, amended by Regulation 271/2010/EU of March 24, 2010, OJ 2010 No. L84, pp. 19–21; Council Regulation 834/2007/EC of June 28, 2007, on organic production and labelling of organic products and repealing Regulation 2092/91/EEC, OJ 2007 No. L189, pp. 1–23.

in accordance with high standards of animal welfare. The issue was whether halal meat could be labeled "organic" when ritual slaughtering was performed without previous stunning, thus causing pain to the animals. The Court ruled that halal ritual slaughtering practices and organic food labeling were irreconcilable. The requirement that animals be stunned was meant to ensure that the animals avoid pain and suffering. Slaughtering without stunning was an exceptional regime, "authorised only by way of derogation in the European Union and solely in order to ensure observance of the freedom of religion," but "insufficient to remove all of the animal's pain, distress and suffering as effectively as slaughter with pre-stunning." Ritual slaughtering did not altogether meet the high requirements of animal welfare that were among the core goals of organic food production and the "organic" logo. While norms of religious freedom were strong enough to allow an exemption from general slaughtering rules, they did not entitle a further exemption from organic food labeling rules.[90]

The 2020 case of *Centraal Israëltisch Consistorie van België and Others*, however, upheld a further discriminatory limit on halal and kosher slaughtering that undercut both the EU's statutory exemptions for religious freedom and the Luxembourg Court's requirement that laws be religiously neutral.[91] This case involved a new Flemish regulation that required Jewish and Muslim butchers, even in their own ritual slaughtering houses, to use a nonlethal form of stunning before cutting the animal's throat and letting it bleed out fully. This form of stunning, Flemish scientific experts opined, would spare the animal the pain and suffering of having its throat cut, but would ensure that the animal would regain consciousness before bleeding to death, as religious ritual laws required. A consortium of Jewish and Muslim litigants argued that this new Flemish law violated their religious freedom rights under EU law, Articles 10, 21, and 22 of the Charter, and Article 9 of the European Convention. The new law specially burdened their core religious rituals; introduced a secular requirement that violated ancient religious laws; obstructed religious butchers from practicing their traditional faith; deprived religious consumers from proper food in the niche market of kosher and halal meat; and discriminatorily targeted the small communities of Jews and Muslims while leaving hunters, fishers, and other sportsmen to kill their captured animals without prior stunning. The claimants further argued that if this regulation, deliberately targeting the heart of a religion's core ritual life, could pass muster under EU laws and the EU Charter, even firmer measures against minority religious practices would likely follow in Belgium and other EU lands.

90 Case C-497/17, *Oeuvre d'assistance aux bêtes d'abattoirs* [2019] ECLI:EU:C:2019:137, paras. 17, 36, and 45–52.

91 Case C-336-19, *Centraal Israëltisch Consistorie van België and Others*, v. *Vlaamse Regering* [2020] ECLI:EU:C:2020:1031, paras. 13, 18–31, 45, 67, 71, 77, and 90-91.

Upon request for a preliminary ruling on EU law from the Belgian constitutional court, the Grand Chamber of the Luxembourg Court upheld the Flemish regulation. The Court held that, as an EU member state, Belgium had power to issue "additional rules designed to ensure greater protection for animals," even if those rules encroached on the EU's stated policy of allowing religious ritual slaughtering without stunning. The Court recognized that Belgium's added rule about stunning did impose "a limitation on the exercise of the right of Jewish and Muslim believers to the freedom to manifest their religion." But this limitation was "permissible," the Court argued. It was properly "prescribed by law," not arbitrarily imposed. It required use of the "most up-to-date method of killing" animals humanely. It had a "legitimate objective of general interest . . . to avoid all avoidable animal suffering." This new rule, moreover, was "appropriate and necessary," prescribing "the least onerous" way of harmonizing state interests in protecting animal welfare and the butchers' interest in protecting their religious freedom. Invoking Article 9 Strasbourg cases, the Luxembourg Court now said that Belgium "deserved a wide margin of appreciation in deciding whether, and to what extent, a limitation of the right to manifest religion or beliefs is 'necessary.'" Similarly, the Court cited EU law that called for "a 'certain flexibility' and 'a certain degree of subsidiarity' to Member States" in how to balance EU laws and local standards of health, morality, and culture.

The Luxembourg Court dismissed quickly the Jewish and Muslim litigants' arguments that this new rule was both religiously discriminatory and disrespectful of religious diversity, in open violation of Articles 21 and 22 of the EU Charter. The Court argued that this was a regulation about slaughtering in licensed slaughtering houses, not about hunting, fishing, or licensed sports activities that are subject to their own relevant EU and local laws. That other areas of the law have different rules does not mean that these slaughtering laws are discriminatory. Moreover, hunting and fishing are recreational; they are not primarily about producing meats, hides, and other animal products sold to consumers. Even if they were, it would be "meaningless" to require hunters and fishers to pursue only animals that were previously stunned.

These three cases, particularly *Liga van Moskeeën* and *Centraal Israëltisch Consistorie*, while narrow in their immediate reach, signal trouble for religious freedom in the EU. The *Liga van Moskeeën* Court stated clearly that, in principle, neutral laws do not infringe upon religious freedom, whatever their impact on religious practices. In its words, "the obligation to use an approved slaughterhouse . . . applies in a general and neutral manner to any party that organises slaughtering of animals and applies irrespective of any connection with a particular religion and thereby concerns in a non-discriminatory manner all producers of meat in the European Union."[92] This approach

[92] Case C-426/16, *Liga van Moskeeën en Islamitische Organisaties Provincie Antwerpen and Others* [2018] ECLI:EU:C:2018:33, para. 61.

sees legislative neutrality as the ideal solution for dealing with the "values pluralism" of European society. While facially neutral rules do not explicitly target religion, in application such neutral laws can impose a substantial burden on religious practices, particularly those of minority or disfavored religions that sometimes need exceptions and exemptions from neutral laws to practice their faith.

Centraal Israëltisch Consistorie is even more worrisome, because it upholds a non-neutral local law that specifically and discriminatorily targets a central religious practice of ritual slaughtering that EU law had accommodated on grounds of religious freedom. The new Belgian law is not neutral; hunters who kill downed animals or landed fish, or private farmers who kill their animals for food or when they are injured, need not stun those animals first. The Court made no effort to investigate whether the new slaughtering rules in fact reflect the most advanced science as Belgium asserts, or to listen to how and why these new rules intrude on religious ritual practice. It made no mention of other Belgian government restrictions against Muslim headscarves and its decades-long vendetta against "dangerous sects."[93] Religious freedom, religious equality, and religious diversity are all fundamental rights explicitly protected by the EU Charter. Animals rights and animal welfare are not mentioned. But this case allows animal rights to trump religious freedom.

Scholars of the US First Amendment know the dangers of reducing religious freedom to a mere guarantee of neutrality, and leaving protections of religious freedom in the hands of local legislatures. The US Supreme Court adopted this local neutrality approach in the 1990 free-exercise case of *Employment Division* v. *Smith.*[94] The case held that a "neutral and generally applicable law" is not a violation of the right to free exercise of religion, no matter how great a burden that law casts on a particular religion or religious practice. The *Smith* case itself deprived a Native American from receiving an unemployment benefit that other religious minorities had received in four prior cases. The *Smith* Court's neutrality approach soon led local legislatures to turn on religious minorities, targeting their ritual slaughtering and other religious practices that were deemed eccentric. Congress and many states responded by passing religious freedom-restoration acts that provided stronger statutory protections and remedies for religious minorities.[95] In *Church of Lukumi Babalu Aye, Inc.* v. *City of Hialeah* (1993), the Supreme Court stepped in and struck down a new local slaughtering law that was similarly pitched as a neutral law protecting safety, hygiene, and animal welfare, but in fact similarly targeted a core religious ritual of a minority community of Santerians.[96] The *Smith*

93 US Dept. of State, Office of International Religious Freedom, "2019 Report on International Religious Freedom: Belgium," www.state.gov/reports/2019-report-on-international-religious-freedom/belgium/.

94 494 US 872, 890 (1990).

95 See Witte and Nichols, *Religion and the American Constitutional Experiment*, 138–49.

96 508 US 520 (1993).

Court had made clear that laws that are not neutral and/or not generally applicable can be justified only if they serve a compelling state interest and follow the least restrictive alternative of achieving that interest. That requirement provides a judicial safety net for religious freedom against bald prejudice, just as statutes have provided a stronger legislative safety net for religious minorities against "the tyranny of the legislative majority."[97] It can only be hoped that both the Luxembourg Court and the European Parliament will take lessons from this American experience.

CASES ON RELIGIOUS PERSECUTION AND INTERNATIONAL PROTECTION

What makes these Jewish and Muslim slaughtering cases so startling is that the Luxembourg Court has been quite generous in offering protection for foreign victims of religious persecution who have sought asylum or refugee protection in the EU. The European refugee crisis, born of massive unrest in the Middle East and beyond, has brought challenges to many EU member states and prompted a pair of cases for the CJEU's docket.

An early 2012 case of *Y and Z*[98] turned on the interpretation of two articles of an EU directive that set standards for the qualification and status of third-country nationals or stateless persons as refugees.[99] Y and Z were the pseudonyms of two Ahmadi worshippers who had fled Pakistan and sought refuge in Germany, where they submitted asylum applications. Local German officials denied their requests. The Ahmadis sued in German court under an EU directive that defined a refugee as "a third country national who, owing to a well-founded fear of being persecuted for reasons of . . . religion . . . is outside the country of nationality and is unable or, owing to such fear, is unwilling to avail himself or herself to the protection of that country."[100] The German court asked whether the directive protected only the "core area of religious freedom, limited to the profession and practice of faith in the areas of the home and neighbourhood," or also the observance of faith in public, even if the applicant could abstain from such practice in public. The court also asked whether the applicant or the religious community had to regard that religious observance to be indispensable or a central aspect of the faith.[101]

The AG's opinion was expansive in articulating the proper grounds and limits of such refugee claims. The AG thought it impossible for the Court to decide what is a central or a peripheral tenet or practice of a faith, what is private, what public, what

97 James Madison's phrase quoted in Chapter 5, p. 157.

98 Joined Cases C-71/11 and 99/11, *Bundesrepublik Deutschland* v. *Y and Z* [2012] ECLI:EU:C:2012:518.

99 Ibid., paras. 80–81; see Council Directive 2004/83/EC of April 29, 2004 on minimum standards for the qualification and status of third-country nationals or stateless persons as refugees or as persons who otherwise need international protection and the content of the protection granted, OJ 2004 No. L304, arts. 2(c) and 9(1)(a), pp. 14, 16.

100 Joined Cases C-71/11 and 99/11, *Y and Z* [2012] ECLI:EU:C:2012:518, paras. 30–32.

101 Ibid., para. 45.

essential, what discretionary. But it recognized the tenuous status of Ahmadis under Pakistani law and majority Muslim teachings. The AG called for "a broad interpretation of freedom of religion, encompassing all components thereof." The AG further thought it essential that officials differentiate cases where a refugee applicant "migrates for personal reasons or to improve his living conditions or social status," from cases "where the individual suffers from a restriction of such severity as to deprive him of his most essential rights and he cannot avail himself of the protection of his country of origin." In the AG's view, EU states could not deny asylum or refugee status to applicants who could avoid persecution only by renouncing their religious practices or concealing their religious identities, for that violated the most essential rights of conscience.[102]

The Luxembourg Court agreed. While not every "interference with the right to religious freedom guaranteed by Article 10(1) of the Charter constitutes an act of persecution requiring the competent authorities to grant refugee status,"[103] the Court reasoned, EU law protects both public and private expressions of religion.[104] Prohibitions on public worship and threats of repression and punishment for those who do not follow the state's established religion can constitute persecution under EU law. What is key is that these are concrete, not theoretical, threats to the individual,[105] and that a public religious practice is of particular salience for the individual seeking refuge.[106]

In *Bahtiyar Fathi* v. *Predsedatel na Darzhavna agentsia za bezhantsite* (2018), the Court clarified how EU states should assess the claims of religious persecution of refugee applicants, now interpreting a new EU directive on refugees.[107] Fathi was an Iranian Kurd who applied for refugee protection while living in Bulgaria, an EU member state. He did not identify as a member of a traditional religious community, nor did he submit evidence of his religious practice. He identified himself simply as a "normal Christian with Protestant leanings." He said he had been questioned and detained by Iranian officials for watching and calling into a program playing on a Christian channel that Iranian law prohibited. During his detention, he confessed his Christian faith. Bulgarian authorities found his story of persecution "implausible," and they rejected his refugee application. Fathi sued in a Bulgarian court, which in turn requested the Luxembourg Court to issue a preliminary ruling on: (1) what type of persecution triggered the right to refugee status, (2) how broad was

102 Opinion of Advocate General Bot in Joined Cases C-71/11 and 99/11, *Y and Z* [2012] ECLI:EU:C:2012:224, paras. 29, 33, 43–45, 106.
103 Joined Cases C-71/11 and 99/11, *Y and Z* [2012] ECLI:EU:C:2012:518, para. 58.
104 Ibid., paras. 62–63.
105 Ibid., para. 69.
106 Ibid., para. 70.
107 Case C-56/17, *Fathi* [2018] ECLI:EU:C:2018:803, paras. 99–101; see Directive 2011/95/EU of the European Parliament and of the Council of December 13, 2011, on standards for the qualification of third-country nationals or stateless persons as beneficiaries of international protection, for a uniform status for refugees or for persons eligible for subsidiary protection, and for the content of the protection granted, OJ 2011 No. L337, pp. 9–26.

the protection of religious belief accorded by EU laws, and (3) how should states judge the veracity of the asylum seeker's claim.[108]

The AG argued that, in light of existing EU law, acts of persecution had to be "sufficiently serious by [their] nature or repetition as to constitute a severe violation of basic human rights." This included legal, administrative, policy, or judicial measures that were discriminatory, as well as punishments and prosecutions that were disproportionate or discriminatory. Not "any interference with the right to religious freedom guaranteed by Article 10(1) of the Charter constitutes an act of persecution requiring the competent authorities to grant refugee status." Only "a severe violation" warranted refugee protection in the EU.[109]

The *Fathi* Court largely agreed. First, the Court stated, the concept of "religion" in the EU directive protecting refugees included public and private expressions of religion, "theistic, non-theistic and atheistic beliefs," and "both 'traditional' religions and other beliefs." It covered "participation in" those various forms of religion "either alone or in community with others, or the abstention from, formal worship, which implie[d] that the fact that a person [wa]s not a member of a religious community [could not], in itself, be decisive in the assessment of that concept." Second, the penalties that a convert would face in case of return to his home country had to be "applied in practice" or consist of a real threat. Third, the claimant had to "duly substantiate his claims as to his alleged religious conversion." The claimant also had to provide "coherent and plausible" statements, without running "counter to available specific and general information relevant to [the] case." Overall, the claimant had to be credible. The *Fathi* Court urged domestic authorities not to take too narrow an approach to the evidence provided by a claimant, but to consider a variety of aspects of the claimant's faith, including his "religious beliefs and how he developed such beliefs, how he understands and lives his faith or atheism, its connection with the doctrinal, ritual or prescriptive aspects of the religion to which he states he is affiliated or from which he intends to distance himself, his possible role in the transmission of his faith or even a combination of religious factors and factors regarding identity, ethnicity or gender."[110]

This pair of cases distills what the state and the refugee applicant owe each other. Under EU law, as interpreted by the Court, the claimant must substantiate the claim that they have been or may be persecuted in their country of origin. The state, in turn, must thoroughly consider what it is about the religious practice or personality of the claimant that has triggered or might trigger religious persecution. This approach is consistent with the Court's general aversion to entering into or making judgments about religious veracity or religious disputes. It also tries to encourage a comprehensive understanding of religious persecution, while shortening the list of

[108] Case C-56/17, *Fathi* [2018] ECLI:EU:C:2018:803, paras. 2–4, 30, 73.

[109] Opinion of Advocate General Mengozzi in Case C-56/17, *Fathi* [2018] ECLI:EU:C:2018:621, para. 52 (citing Directive 2011/95/EU, art. 9).

[110] Case C-56/17, *Fathi* [2018] ECLI:EU:C:2018:803, paras. 77, 80, 83–87, 98.

discriminatory practices that amount to persecution. This approach is also consistent with the EU's interest in balancing the need to shelter persecuted people and to control its borders in the midst of a refugee crisis – to make the EU as safe a place as possible for both foreign refugees escaping religious persecution and local residents enjoying their cultural traditions.

CASE ON RELIGIOUS DIVORCE

The only other significant Luxembourg Court case was *Soha Sahyouni* v. *Raja Mamisch* (2017), which for the first time tackled the issue of enforceability of a religious divorce. The case involved a Syrian couple who were married in 1999 in Syria in the Islamic Court of Homs and later moved to Germany. On May 19, 2013, Mr. Mamish divorced Ms. Sahyouni in accordance with Islamic law. His representative performed the ritual Islamic divorce formula before the Islamic sharia court in Latakia, Syria. The next day, the religious court declared the divorce. Mamish sent the divorce settlement required under Islamic law to Sahyouni, who in turn issued a declaration stating that she was releasing Mamish from any further obligation toward her. This declaration was pronounced in Syria shortly thereafter. Mamish then applied to a German court for recognition of the divorce. Sahyouni, however, objected and asked the German court to declare that the requisites for the recognition of divorce had not been satisfied.[111]

The German court regarded EU law as relevant to the case, and thus suspended the proceedings and submitted a preliminary request to the Luxembourg Court. The request called for interpretation of a few articles of an EU Council regulation that aimed to harmonize the jurisdiction and the recognition and enforcement of judgments in matrimonial matters.[112] The regulation's overall goal was to secure legal certainty, predictability, and flexibility, and to prevent forum shopping by litigants. It set out a series of rules that would make a divorce or legal separation enforceable throughout EU member states, regardless of whether the divorce was in accordance with "the law of a participating Member State." But the regulation made clear that any such divorce had to grant "spouses equal access to divorce or legal separation on grounds of their sex," and could not be "manifestly incompatible with the public policy" of the member state within which it had to be applied.[113] The question in *Sahyouni* was whether the Council regulation also applied to a private divorce, and if so, whether the procedural asymmetry between husband and wife in a private sharia divorce was also compatible with the EU regulation.

The case had strong religious freedom dimensions. The Court had to decide whether a husband's unilateral declaration of divorce duly performed under Islamic

[111] Case C-372/16, *Sahyouni* [2017] ECLI:EU:C:2017:988, paras. 20–23 and 26.

[112] Council Regulation 1259/2010/EU, implementing enhanced cooperation in the area of the law applicable to divorce and legal separation, OJ 2010 No. L343, 10–16.

[113] Ibid., arts. 4, 10, 12, pp. 13–14.

law before a religious tribunal constituted a valid divorce under the EU regulation. If so, Islamic unilateral divorces could be recognized throughout the EU; if not, many EU nationals would be affected. The case was further complicated because the wife had issued a formal statement accepting that her husband had fulfilled his divorce obligations under Islamic law, but then backtracked in her petition to the German court. The Court held that Mamish's unilateral divorce from Sahyouni did not fall within the scope of the regulation and thus did not enjoy the EU's legal protection. The EU regulation calls for "proceedings," "judgments," and "courts." That wording, the Court argued, together with the broader context and policy of the regulation, made clear that it excluded divorces by a religious tribunal that permitted a "unilateral declaration of intent" and without divorce "proceedings" involving both parties.[114]

This case leaves open the question whether unilateral divorces could enjoy the regulation's protection if they are performed in front of a public body or a proper religious court with bilateral proceedings. It does not clarify what distinguishes public authorities from religious authorities. This is a sensitive topic not only for Muslims but also for Jews, Catholics, and some Protestant groups that operate with church courts, faith-based arbitration panels, and other forms of alternative dispute resolution in domestic cases.[115] The Luxembourg Court will likely hear other such cases to clarify the rules and recognition of religious divorces.

SUMMARY AND CONCLUSIONS

Since 2017, the Court of Justice of the European Union sitting in Luxembourg has issued landmark rulings on the rights and limits of Muslim employees to wear religious headscarves in the workplace and the rights of employers to make religious affiliation and conformity a prerequisite for employment or a basis for differential treatment of employees. It has allowed local limits on the rights of religious groups to continue ritual slaughtering because of growing concerns for animal well-being and stricter hygiene standards for organic food labeling. The Court has addressed hard questions of tax exemption and other state aid for religious schools; the rights and limits of refugees alleging religious persecution at home; the limits on state recognition of religious divorces; and the limits that privacy laws impose on missionaries. It also has begun to question longstanding claims of religious autonomy and religion–state arrangements in certain countries, including those that establish or favor traditional forms of Christianity.

[114] Case C-372/16, *Sahyouni* [2017] ECLI:EU:C:2017:988, paras. 26, 39, 41, 45.

[115] Ibid., paras. 39 and 49. See also Michael J. Broyde, *Sharia Tribunals, Rabbinic Courts, and Christian Panels: Religious Arbitration in America and the West* (Oxford: Oxford University Press, 2017); John Witte, Jr., *Church, State, and Family: Reconciling Traditional Teachings and Modern Liberties* (Cambridge: Cambridge University Press, 2019), 300–35 (discussing the role of faith-based arbitration in matrimonial disputes).

These are all highly important symbolic and substantive issues for religious freedom in Europe and beyond. The lengthy opinions by the AGs about the EU's evolving interests in religion and religious freedom contextualize the terser but definitive opinions of the Luxembourg Court. Since this Court has a monopoly on the interpretation of EU law, and since its case law trumps domestic laws when there is conflict, the Court effectively rules supreme in all twenty-seven member states of the EU. Its rulings in individual cases are already proving to be effective in governing religious freedom law in EU lands. Litigants have begun to take notice, triggering a growing wave of religious freedom cases that have reached Luxembourg, usually via requests from local courts about the meaning of EU law in their domestic cases. The more the Luxembourg Court spells out its jurisprudence, the more likely the EU will slowly integrate its treatment of religious freedom.

So far in its first dozen cases, the Luxembourg Court has echoed, and sometimes explicitly followed, the religious freedom jurisprudence of the older and more familiar Strasbourg Court whose opinions we analyzed in Chapter 8. That consistency in approach has aided the integration of European law regarding religious freedom. The Strasbourg Court hears cases from any of the nine hundred million citizens in the forty-seven European states that are part of the Council of Europe (which includes all twenty-seven current member states of the European Union). Since 1993, more than 150 of these cases have involved claims that a state has violated the religious freedom and related guarantees set out in the 1950 European Convention on Human Rights. When the Strasbourg Court finds a state in violation of these guarantees, however, it largely depends on voluntary compliance by the state as well as diplomatic pressure from other states. But when the Luxembourg Court issues an opinion on religious freedom along the same lines as the Strasbourg Court, that helps make the latter's jurisprudence binding in the twenty-seven EU states.

That said, the Luxembourg Court has also begun to carve its own path, which has not always led to favorable treatment of claims of religious freedom. The Court has already shown a strong preference for state policies of "religious neutrality." That policy is intuitively attractive in postmodern, pluralistic, liberal societies to address a number of legal questions. It has already begun to provide more nuanced protection for religious freedom claims than the aggressive policies of *läicité* and secularization at work in some EU member states, to which the Strasbourg Court has generally given an ample "margin of appreciation," despite their encroachments on religion.[116] Noteworthy is the Luxembourg Court's 2017 case of *Bougnaoui v. Micropole*, which protected a French Muslim woman's right to continue to wear her hijab in a private workplace. That case stands in marked contrast to several Strasbourg court cases that have repeatedly rejected rights claims by Muslim women to wear religious apparel in private and public settings.

[116] See Chapter 8, p. 238, 241, 242, 246–48, 257.

On the other hand, norms of religious neutrality, when pressed too strongly, can also come at the cost of accommodations for discrete religious minorities who operate outside of the cultural mainstream, or even majority parties whose pressing claims of conscience or central commandments of faith prevent them from abiding by the state's neutral laws. Minority Muslim litigants lost the four other cases heard so far by the Luxembourg Court, involving religious apparel in the workplace, halal ritual slaughter practices, and religious divorces, each time with the Court noting that the laws or policies in question were "neutral." And the ruling in the *Congregación de Escuelas Pías* tax exemption case that makes remuneration for services the tipping point for application of the EU prohibition of state aid to religion paradoxically privileges wealthy, well-endowed majority churches that have access to state funds over smaller religious groups that depend upon private revenue to survive.

More worrisome is the Court's most recent case of *Centraal Israëltisch Consistorie van België and Others*, which upheld a local legislative limit on ritual slaughtering, a central religious practice and source of halal and kosher food for Muslims and Jews. The local Belgian law was not neutral but discriminatory, and it undermined a general EU law that had accommodated religiously ritual slaughtering in all EU states. Rather than using its familiar neutrality logic, which would have compelled it to strike down this new local law, the Court for the first time called for a "margin of appreciation" for Belgian authorities, a logic that the Strasbourg Court had repeatedly used to uphold discriminatory national laws against religious freedom. This shift in logic was all the more striking since the Court, in *Cresco Investigation*, had just given no margin of appreciation to Austria's longstanding law recognizing Good Friday for Christian workers, and instead upheld the claim from a nonreligious adherent that this law discriminated against him on religious grounds.

Furthermore, the Court's neutrality policy has prompted it to question the longstanding Western principle of religious autonomy, echoed in EU treaties and statutes. So far, however, this questioning has come only in cases dealing with Christian majorities. In cases involving religious minorities, the Court has explicitly abstained from judging internal religious claims, practices, or disputes about Muslim slaughtering and holiday practices, sharia divorce proceedings, or the authenticity of religious conviction or vulnerability of foreign refugee applicants claiming religious persecution at home. In these cases, the Luxembourg Court professed its incompetence to enter the internal religious realm, preferring to judge only the sociological dimensions of religion on neutral criteria.

In cases involving Christian religious majorities, however, the Court has shown more willingness to review and question internal religious practices and decision-making. In *Egenberger*, the Court declared that a private German Protestant diaconal organization could require its new employees to be religiously affiliated only if it could prove that this religious requirement was "genuine, legitimate, and justified" and "proportionate" to the competing secular interests, individual rights, and private life choices of an employee or job applicant. In *IR* v. *JQ*, the Court held that a private Catholic hospital could insist on a "duty of loyalty" to Catholic doctrine and practice from its management staff only if it could prove that the religious affiliation and private morality of an employee were relevant to his particular duties. In *Cresco Investigation*, a private employer could follow a traditional state rule that excused employees from work on Good Friday or gave them double pay to work that day, only if all other employees were treated the same way. In *Congregación de Escuelas Pías*, the Court reviewed rather closely the inner workings of a private Catholic school, and its allocation of space and finances, and the Spanish court in response denied the school's tax exemption despite a specific concordat provision guaranteeing such exemptions. These cases stand in marked contrast to traditional rules that give churches autonomy to govern their own internal affairs concerning property, employment, membership, and more, so long as all parties have the unconditional freedom to leave the church.

In these latter cases, the Luxembourg Court has also begun to probe and question longstanding national church–state arrangements set out in constitutions and concordats, particularly those that establish or privilege one or more traditional forms of Christianity. *Cresco Investigation* challenged Austria's recognition of the traditional Christian religious calendar in setting its workplace regulations. *Congregación de Escuelas Pías* threatened to review Spain's concordat with the Holy See in future cases. *Egenberger* queried the German territories' longstanding practices of church–state cooperation in diaconal and educational matters. These rapid-fire dicta have come despite the opening admonition of the 1997 Treaty of Amsterdam, which solidified the EU on the express principle that "[t]he European Union respects and does not prejudice the status under national law of churches and religious associations or communities in the Member States."

Scholars and advocates who see American-style principles of disestablishment of religion and strict separation of church and state as essential to the enhancement of religious freedom[117] will likely applaud these latter queries by the Luxembourg Court. Those who favor traditional balances between individual religious freedom for all and settled religion–state relations in Europe and other parts of the world will have good reason to watch closely this rapidly evolving case law.

[117] See an excellent recent example in Howard Gillman and Erwin Chemerinsky, *The Religion Clauses: The Case for Separating Church and State* (Oxford: Oxford University Press, 2020).

Concluding Reflections

Toward a Christian Defense of Human Rights and Religious Freedom Today

The foregoing chapters have recounted something of the genesis, exodus, and deuteronomy, if you will, of human rights and religious freedom in the Western legal tradition. We have seen the *genesis* of these rights and liberties in the accounts of human nature and natural order. Many Western writers started with the biblical account of males and females created in the image of God and called to join together in one flesh, to be fruitful and multiply, to have dominion over creatures and things, to have freedom to walk and talk with God, and to have choices to partake of some fruits but not others. Pre-Christian Greco-Roman and post-Christian Enlightenment accounts of origins spoke comparably of humans who are "created equal" in a "state of nature" and vested with natural "blessings of liberty" and "unalienable rights" of life, liberty, property, and the pursuit of happiness.

We have witnessed the *exodus* of these primordial rights and liberties in the gradual development of public, private, penal, and procedural rights and liberties for individuals and groups set out in legal, canonical, and other authoritative texts. Over the course of these chapters, we saw this exodus in the provisional rights and liberties teachings of Mosaic law and their complex Talmudic elaboration; in classical Roman law texts and the global civil law tradition that they inspired; in Magna Carta and the global common law tradition of rights and liberties that took this founding text as axiomatic; in medieval canon law texts on rights and liberties and their remarkable resurgences first in early modern Spain and then in the Catholic reforms of Leo XIII and Vatican II; and in Protestant natural law and natural rights jurisprudence and its massive global spread through publication, colonization, democratic revolution, and constitutional formation. This exodus narrative of the development of rights featured plenty of fits and starts, experiments and transplants, and expansions and abridgements over the centuries, but it gradually yielded an ever growing legal tradition of rights and liberties.

And we have witnessed the *deuteronomy* of rights and liberties in modern times, the powerful new restatement of the 1948 Universal Declaration of Human Rights as a global rebuke to the barbaric slaughter of 60 million people in World War II. Much like earlier groups had done in formulating their national declarations of rights in solidarity against political tyrants, now the peoples of the world rose above their tragic differences and stated anew their commitment to the fundamentals of humanity and community. The Declaration put these fundamental values in the generic and accessible terms of human liberty, dignity, equality, and fraternity. And it gathered from Western and all other legal traditions of the world those rights and liberties that were considered essential to being human and to human wellbeing.

The development and expansion of human rights norms and cultures that followed the Declaration have made human rights a dominant mode of political, legal, and moral discourse in the West today and well beyond. Since the mid-twentieth century, protections and violations of rights have become increasingly prominent issues in international relations and diplomacy. Most nation-states now have detailed bills or recitations of rights in their constitutions and statutes, along with case law interpreting and applying them. The United Nations and various other groups of nation-states have detailed catalogues of rights set out in treaties, declarations, conventions, and covenants. Many Christian denominations and ecumenical groups, alongside other religious groups, have their own declarations and statements on rights and have been instrumental in developing the major international human rights instruments. Thousands of governmental, intergovernmental, and nongovernmental organizations are now dedicated to the defense of rights and liberties around the world, including a large number of Christian and other religious lobbying and litigation groups.

CHRISTIAN CHALLENGES TO MODERN HUMAN RIGHTS

A number of prominent Christian scholars today, however, have argued that the language of rights, though not entirely foreign to Christianity, is, in its modern forms, inconsistent with Christian faith and practice. These critics are usually happy with religious freedom norms and worried about their abridgment, but reticent about the broader values and vocabulary of human rights and liberties.

For example, Stanley Hauerwas, a leading Christian ethicist, argues that rights are conceptually and practically inadequate.[1] He acknowledges that "the appeal to rights has been a means to protect those who have no protection in the world in which we find ourselves." He further recognizes that such appeals have "provided for many a moral identity otherwise unavailable." Yet Hauerwas worries that reflexive and repeated "appeals to rights" "threaten to replace first order moral descriptions in a manner that makes us less able to make the moral discriminations that we depend upon to be morally wise." For example, "If you need a theory of rights to know that

[1] See esp. Stanley Hauerwas, *The Hauerwas Reader* (Durham, NC: Duke University Press, 2009), chaps. 4, 6, 7, 8, 9, 11, 12, 16, 21, 22, 26, 28, 31 with a good summary in Stanley Hauweras, "How to Think Theologically About Rights," *Journal of Law and Religion* 30 (2015), 402–13.

torture is morally wrong," Hauerwas writes, "then something has clearly gone wrong with your moral sensibilities."[2]

Hauerwas seems most troubled by rights that entitle individuals to choose and act in socially unbounded ways. He zeroes in on the definition: of the right "to do everything which injures no one else," as the French revolutionaries put it in their 1791 Declaration, largely repeating classical Roman law texts and their many medieval glosses. For Hauweras, this formulation is at once too abstract and too diffuse to sustain the requisite moral commitments and judgments implicit in the recognition that all persons share a common humanity. "No real society can exist when its citizens' only way of relating is in terms of noninterference" with one another.[3] Quoting Simone Weil, he adds:

> [T]he right to choose divorced from the rules that make life together possible can result in the loss of the enjoyment liberty should provide. That loss means people "must either seek refuge in irresponsibility, puerility, and indifference – a refuge where the most they can find is boredom – or feel themselves weighted down by the responsibility at all times for fear of causing harm to others."[4]

For Hauerwas, human rights and liberties have a contingent and milquetoast quality when placed alongside the stronger moral norms and narratives at the heart of Christian teachings. Rights, he says, may aptly describe a vendor's legal capacity to sell goods, or a bank's ability to make a loan. But much more is needed to convey the gravity of the wrongs of, say, child prostitution, rape, or murder, or the seriousness of the commands to love God, neighbor, and self. Moreover, rights claims inevitably reflect a tone of envy, of grasping, of self-promotion. They thus have only a "mediocre character," reflecting a "vocabulary of middle values" that are simply too weak to account for gross injustices or the serious commands of faith, hope and love. Concepts like "truth, beauty, justice, and compassion" are the stronger and sterner concepts we need for the serious moral and social issues that any community regularly faces. While rights may depend on or refer to deeper moral values and relationships, reflexive appeals to rights are more likely to sidestep engagement with the moral dimensions of social life and replace them with a "shrill nagging of claims and counterclaims, which is both impure and unpractical." Thus, even if rights can play a legitimate role in legal spheres, rights are not morally basic or absolute, and, perhaps surprisingly, they distract us from morality. Rights might be "reminder claims to help us remember the thick moral relationships" that become the Christian life. But Christians would do well to jettison rights from their moral vocabularies per se for fear of cheapening their moral discourse or thinning their moral character.[5]

2 Hauerwas, "How to Think Theologically About Rights," 402–5.

3 Ibid., 403; see also Stanley Hauerwas, *Suffering Presence: Theological Reflections on Medicine, the Mentally Handicapped, and the Church* (Notre Dame: University of Notre Dame Press, 1986), 130.

4 Hauerwas, "How to Think Theologically About Rights," 410.

5 Ibid., 410–13.

Patrick Parkinson, a distinguished Christian jurist, cautions against human rights not because they are morally thin, but because they are, in his view, morally thick. In his native Australia, Parkinson argues, human rights norms come laden with thick liberal values that too often conflict with the religious and moral teachings of Christian churches and other religious institutions. To accept a human rights regime is to risk capitulation to these liberal values, he argues. Several Christian leaders in Australia have thus spoken out against adding a bill of rights to the Australian constitution, which is the only Western constitution without a bill of rights. Australian Christians worry that evolving cultural norms, together with untested provisions about gender and same-sex discrimination, will jeopardize churches in their ability to select their own clergy and teachers, or to enforce traditional moral and religious norms among their members. They worry further that those advocating human rights in Australia "do not take freedom of religion and conscience nearly seriously enough." Other common law lands, Parkinson and others point out, are now facing a sustained argument that religion has no special claim to human rights, and that religious freedom, if protected at all, must take second place to other fundamental human rights claims in the event of conflict.[6]

Subordination of religious freedom to other fundamental rights also concerns leading Catholic legal scholar Helen Alvaré.[7] She is particularly concerned that the robust constitutional norms of sexual liberty, privacy, and autonomy are threatening to eclipse religious liberty in the United States. She points to the ur-case of *Griswold* v. *Connecticut* (1965),[8] in which the US Supreme Court recognized the deeply "private" nature of marital relationships and the decision of married couples to procreate (or not), and thus affirmed the right of married heterosexual couples to have access to contraceptives. In subsequent cases, the Supreme Court expanded privacy rights to unmarried individuals, entitling them to make private decisions about sexual relationships, including the gender of their sexual partner and the use of contraceptives and abortion. The resulting sphere of constitutionally protected privacy, Alvare argues, has gradually come into conflict with norms of religious liberty protected by the First Amendment. When the law mandates that pharmacists or employers must participate in assuring and insuring delivery of contraceptives, or prohibits religious employers from insisting on the sexual morality of their employees, or insists that photographers or bakers service the weddings of same-sex couples – this has a direct and dramatic impact on Roman Catholic institutions and

6 Patrick Parkinson, "Christian Concerns About an Australian Charter of Rights," in Paul Babie and Neville Rochow, eds., *Freedom of Religion Under Bills of Rights* (Adelaide: University of Adelaide Press, 2012), 137–39, 150.

7 Helen M. Alvaré, "Religious Freedom v. Sexual Expression: A Guide," *Journal of Law and Religion* 30 (2015), 475–95; see also Helen M. Alvaré, *Putting Children's Interests First in US Family Law and Policy* (Cambridge: Cambridge University Press, 2019); Helen M. Alvaré, ed., *The Conscience of the Institution* (South Bend, IN: St. Augustine's Press, 2014).

8 *Griswold* v. *Connecticut*, 381 US 479 (1965).

individuals who adhere to the church's official teachings about contraception, abortion, marriage, and sexual expression. These teachings are so deeply bound to Catholic cosmology, Alvare argues, that "coercing Catholics to facilitate opposing practices is tantamount to coercing them to abandon their own religion and to practice another."[9] Arguments like Alvare's have found sympathy in American federal courts of late, and are likely to become more prominent with the recent tilt of the courts to a more conservative jurisprudence.

Robert Franklin, leading expert on the Black church, warns that the American human rights movement is increasingly passing by the very African American communities that were so vital in building the case for the Civil Rights Act of 1964 and the Voting Rights Act of 1965.[10] These two acts ostensibly put an end to the "separate but equal" legal status of racial minorities in the United States, Franklin argues. But, despite the formal equality mandated by these acts, recent studies show startling disparities in America's criminal justice system. Black men make up a disproportionate share of the total prison population in the United States, which ballooned from fewer than 350,000 in 1972 to more than 2.2 million today. Blacks make up only 12 percent of the overall population but constitute 37 percent of the prison population.[11] Roughly one-third of all African American men are currently under the control of state or federal prison systems – either in prison or jail, on probation, or on parole.[12]

Researchers debate the underlying causes of criminal behavior, and the political motivations behind American law enforcement policies such as the "war on drugs," which has led to increased rates of arrest and incarceration.[13] A growing number of scholars, however, see troubling similarities between the modern criminal justice system and the Jim Crow laws in place prior to the mid-twentieth-century civil rights movement. These scholars point out apparent racial biases and dubious practices affecting the enforcement and adjudication of drug-related and other criminal laws.[14] They also point out the increasing scope of "collateral consequences" that are often attached to criminal convictions, including "disenfranchisement, loss of professional licenses, and deportation in the case of aliens, as well as newer penalties such as felon registration and ineligibility for certain public welfare benefits."[15] The

9 Alvare, "Religious Freedom v. Sexual Expression," 477.

10 Robert M. Franklin, "Rehabilitating Democracy: Restoring Civil Rights and Leading the Next Human Rights Revolution," *Journal of Law and Religion* 30 (2015), 414–27.

11 E. Ann Carson, "Prisoners in 2013," Washington, DC: US Dept. of Justice, Office of Justice Programs (Sept. 30, 2014), 16.

12 Michelle Alexander, *The New Jim Crow: Mass Incarceration in the Age of Colorblindness* (New York: New Press, 2010), 9.

13 See, e.g., James Forman, Jr., "Racial Critiques of Mass Incarceration: Beyond the New Jim Crow," *New York University Law Review* 87 (2012), 21–69; George Walters-Sleyon, *Locked Up and Locked Down: Multitude Linger in Limbo* (Bloomington, IN: Xlibris, 2009).

14 Marc Mauer, *Race to Incarcerate*, rev. ed. (New York: New Press, 2006).

15 American Bar Association, "ABA Standards for Criminal Justice, 3rd Edition: Collateral Sanctions and Discretionary Disqualifications of Convicted Persons" (2004), 7–8

disproportionate incarceration and disenfranchisement of racial minorities, and the substantial barriers imposed by the criminal justice system to their rehabilitation and re-entry into their communities have dire implications for racial equality and for the long-term wellbeing of the nation as a whole. Serious rights claims are at stake when criminal penalties contribute to, rather than mitigate, the breakdown of families and other community structures. These issues deserve the sustained attention of, among others, Christian scholars who are interested in fostering a just legal and social order.

Not only racial minorities in the United States, but also religious minorities around the world are facing increased oppression and persecution, even as human rights instruments protecting them have become increasingly detailed and more prominent in international diplomacy and news. A 2009 comprehensive study documented that more than a third of the 198 countries and self-administering territories in the world today have "high" or "very high" levels of religious oppression, sometimes exacerbated by civil war, natural disasters, and foreign invasion that have caused massive humanitarian crises. The countries on this dishonor roll include Iran, Iraq, India, Pakistan, Bangladesh, Sri Lanka, Indonesia, Saudi Arabia, Somalia, Yemen, Sudan, Egypt, Israel, Burma, Rwanda, Burundi, Congo, Chechnya, and Uzbekistan.[16] The most recent annual reports of the US Commission on International Religious Freedom confirms the precarious status of religious minorities in many parts of the world, exacerbated by the rise of ISIS in the Middle East and the escalating oppression of Muslim and Christian minorities in various parts of the world, including Western lands.[17] Western readers may be surprised to learn that Christians are among the most persecuted religious groups around the world today. A 2014 study found that Christians were more widely harassed than the members of any other religious tradition, experiencing social and political hostility in at least 110 countries.[18] These hostilities were carried out by a variety of private groups and governmental entities and included arrests and detentions; desecration of holy sites; denial of visas, corporate charters, and entity status; discrimination in employment, education, and housing; and closures of worship centers, schools, charities, cemeteries, and religious services – let alone outright rape, torture, kidnapping, and slaughter of believers in alarming numbers in war-torn areas of the Middle East and Africa.[19] Even while some Western Christians rest comfortably on their tenured rights and liberties and now question the

[16] The Pew Forum on Religion and Public Life, Global Restrictions on Religion" (Dec. 2009) (www.pewforum.org); Allen D. Hertzke, ed., *The Future of Religious Freedom: Global Challenges* (Oxford: Oxford University Press, 2013).

[17] *Annual Report 2014: 15th Anniversary Retrospective: Renewing the Commitment* (Washington, DC: US Commission on International Religious Freedom, 2014).

[18] See Pew Research Center, January 2014, "Religious Hostilities Reach Six-Year High," 21. By comparison, Muslims were harassed in 109 countries; Jews in 71; "others" (e.g., Sikhs, Zoroastrians, Baha'i) in 40 countries; "folk religionists" in 26 countries; Hindus in 16 countries; Buddhists in 13 countries.

[19] Pew Research Center, January 2014, "Religious Hostilities Reach Six-Year High," 21.

theological validity, moral value, or even social utility of protecting human rights and liberties, many Christians and other religious believers have become increasingly desperate to secure the most basic of human rights protections.

FACING THE CHALLENGES

This is a just a sampling of some of the Christian academic sentiments about human rights and liberties today. These arguments join other attacks on Western rights as a tried and tired experiment that is no longer effective, even a fictional faith whose folly has now been fully exposed.[20] Others have bolstered this claim with cultural critiques – that human rights are instruments of neo-colonization that the West uses to impose its values on the rest, even toxic compounds that are exported abroad to breed cultural conflict, social instability, religious warfare, and thus dependence on the West.[21]

A proper response to all these learned critiques and caveats will require a book or two, which I hope eventually to write. But as a placeholder, allow me to sketch out a provisional response as a Christian jurist and legal historian. While sympathetic with some of these critiques, I submit that rights should remain part of Christian moral, legal, and political discourse, and that Christians should remain part of broader public debates about human rights and public advocacy for their protection and implementation. I agree with Christian skeptics who criticize the utopian idealism of some modern rights advocates, the reduction of rights claims to groundless and self-interested wish lists, the monopoly of rights language in public debates about morality and law, and the dominant liberalism of much contemporary rights talk. I also recognize that Christian believers and churches will inevitably vary in their approaches to human rights – from active involvement in litigation, lobbying, and legislation to quiet provision for the poor, needy, and strangers in their midst. In the church, the Bible reminds us, "[t]here are varieties of gifts, but the same Spirit; and there are varieties of service, but the same Lord."[22]

I further acknowledge that some rights and liberties recognized today are more congenial to scripture, tradition, and Christian experience than others. But a good number of contemporary public, penal, private, and procedural rights have deep roots in the Western Christian tradition and remain worth affirming and advocating. Family laws, for example, protect the reciprocal rights and duties of spouses, parents, and children at different stages of the life cycle. Social welfare rights speak to the

[20] See, e.g., Alasdair MacIntyre, *After Virtue: A Study in Moral Theory* (Notre Dame: University of Notre Dame Press, 1984), 69–70.

[21] See sources collected and critically analyzed from various perspectives in David Little, *Essays on Religion and Human Rights: Ground to Stand On* (Cambridge: Cambridge University Press, 2015); Jenna Reinbold, *Seeing the Myth in Human Rights* (Philadelphia: University of Pennsylvania Press, 2017); David Decosimo, "The New Genealogy of Religious Freedom," *Journal of Law and Religion* 33 (2018), 3–41.

[22] 1 Corinthians 12:4–5 (RSV).

basic human need for food, shelter, health care, and education – especially for vulnerable populations. Laws governing speech and the press protect the rights of persons to speak, preach, and publish. Private laws protect rights to contractual performance, property and inheritance, the safety and integrity of our bodies, relationships, and reputations, along with the procedural means to vindicate these rights when they are threatened or breached. Criminal procedural rights ensure individuals of proper forms of arrest and detention, fair hearings and trials, and just punishments proportionate to specific crimes. Freedom of conscience and the free exercise of religion protect the essential right (and duty) of Christians to love God, neighbor, and self.

When Christians affirm such rights – in defense of themselves or others – they need not abandon their religious and moral traditions, much less defy their duty to love God and neighbor.[23] Stanley Hauerwas is right to warn that rights can become a grammar of greed and grasping, of self-promotion and self-aggrandizement at the cost of one's neighbor and one's relationship to God. But Christians from the start have claimed their rights and freedoms first and foremost in order to discharge the moral duties of the faith. Claiming one's right to worship God, to avoid false gods, to observe the Sabbath, and to use God's name properly enables one to discharge the duties of love owed to God under the First Table of the Decalogue. Claiming one's rights to life, property, and reputation, or to the integrity of one's marriage, family, and household gives one's neighbor the chance to honor the duties of love in the Second Table of the Decalogue – to not murder, steal, or bear false witness; to not dishonor parents or breach marital vows; to not covet, threaten, or violate "anything that is your neighbor's."[24] To insist on these Second Table rights can also be an act of love toward your neighbors, giving them the opportunity and accountability necessary to learn and discharge their moral duties.

Viewed this way, many rights claims are not selfish grasping at all – even if they happen to serve one's own interests. Rights claims can reflect and embody love of God and neighbor. The claims of the poor and needy, the widow and the orphan, the child and the stranger, and the "least" of society are, in part, invitations for others to serve God and neighbor: "As you did it to one of the least of these . . . you did it to me," Jesus said.[25] To insist on the rights of self-defense and the protection and integrity of one's body or loved ones, or to bring private claims and support public prosecution of those who rape, batter, starve, abuse, torture, or kidnap you or your loved ones is, in part, an invitation for others to respect the divine image and "temple of the Lord" that each person embodies.[26] To insist on the right to education and training, and the right to work and earn a fair wage is, in part, an invitation for others to respect God's call to each of us to prepare for and pursue our

23 Luke 10:27.
24 Exodus 20:17.
25 Matthew 25:40.
26 1 Corinthians 3:16.

distinct vocation.[27] To sue for contractual performance, to claim a rightful inheritance, to collect on a debt or insurance claim, to bring an action for discrimination or wrongful discharge from a job serves, in part, to help others to live out the Golden Rule – to do unto others as you would have them do unto you.[28] To petition the government for due process and equal protection; to seek compensation for unjust taxes or unlawful takings or searches of property; or to protest governmental abuse, deprivation, persecution, or violence – all of these are, in part, calls for political officers to live up to the lofty ideals of justice that the Bible ascribes to the political office. To sue for freedoms of speech and press or for the right to vote is, in part, a call for others to respect God's generous calling for each of us to serve as a prophet, priest, and sovereign on this earth. And to insist on your freedom of conscience and free exercise of religion is to force others to respect the prerogatives of God, whose loving relationship with his children cannot be trespassed by any person or institution.

These examples, and many others, demonstrate that human rights are not inherently antithetical to Christianity. They are part of the daily currency of life, law, and love in this earthly realm, damaged and distorted as it inevitably is. Rights and their vindication help the law achieve its basic uses in this life – the civil use of keeping peace, order, and constraint among its citizens even if by force; the theological use of driving one to reflect on one's failings and turn to better ways of living in community; and the educational use of teaching everyone the good works of morality and love that please God, however imperfect and transient that achievement inevitably will be in the present age.[29]

To have and use rights in a fallen world does not mean that Christians must always pursue those rights to their furthest reaches. Just as judges must apply the law equitably, so Christians (and others) must pursue the lawful claim of rights equitably. Christians are often called to turn the other cheek,[30] to forgive debtors,[31] to love enemies,[32] and to settle disputes privately.[33] Such acts of faith can serve important theological and educational "uses" of their own, even without directly engaging the civil law. To love a debtor, defendant, or adversary in such ways is, in part, to "heap burning coals upon his head,"[34] to induce him to respect his neighbor's person and property, and to urge him to reform his actions. To forgive an egregious felon – as Pope John Paul II forgave his would-be assassin,[35] or as the Amish forgave those who

[27] Ephesians 4:1.

[28] Matthew 7:12.

[29] See John Witte, Jr., *God's Joust, God's Justice: Law and Religion in the Western Tradition* (Grand Rapids, MI: Eerdmans, 2006), 263–94.

[30] Luke 6:29.

[31] Matthew 6:12.

[32] Matthew 5:44.

[33] 1 Corinthians 6.

[34] Romans 12:20–21.

[35] Pope John Paul II publicly forgave and requested that Mehmet Ali Ağca be pardoned for an assassination attempt on May 13, 1981.

murdered their school children[36] – is to echo and embody a form of self-sacrifice at the heart of Christian faith.[37] But such acts of faith are atypical precisely because they are exceptions to the usual rules of an earthly order in which laws must be enforced if they are to be effective, and in which rights must be vindicated for the law to fulfill its appropriate civil uses and maintain a basic level of peace and order.

To say that rights are useful within the state and civil society is not necessarily to recommend the same set or reach of rights within the church. The state is a universal sovereign; the church is more limited in its membership and reach. The state has ultimate coercive power over life and limb; the church has only spiritual power over its members. The state's authority is inescapable for those who live within its borders; the church's authority rests on voluntary membership. Against the state, rights and liberties have emerged as powerful ways to protect the dignity of individuals and the integrity of social institutions from the totalitarian tendencies of those who command political authority. Within the state, rights and liberties have also emerged as an expedient means for citizens and institutions to establish boundaries and bonds with their neighbors, to protect and preserve their property and promises, to negotiate and peaceably litigate their differences, and more. Here, rights are common and useful instruments for social order, peace, and predictability.

By contrast, churches operate by different means and measures of fellowship, different norms for keeping order and peace, and different models of authority and submission, love and sacrifice, caring and sharing. Some basic rules and rights of canon law and ecclesiastical structures are comparable to those of the state. After all, churches are legal entities that deal, in part, in contracts and property, labor and employment, incorporation and procedures for leadership and members. But rights are less central to spiritual fellowship.

Finally, to say that human rights are useful and important is not to say that rights constitute a freestanding system of morality, or to render Christian moral and religious teachings superfluous. Some contemporary scholars describe human rights as the new religion and catechism of modern liberalism, invented in the Enlightenment to replace worn out Christian establishments. Indeed, core human rights can take on near-sacred qualities in modern societies. Moreover, ideals like "liberty, equality, and fraternity," or "life, liberty, and property," or "due process and equal protection of the law" often function as powerful normative totems.

Modern human rights norms are better understood, however, as the *ius gentium* of our times – the common law of nations – which a variety of Jewish, Greek, Roman, Patristic, Catholic, Protestant, and Enlightenment movements have historically nurtured in the West, and which today still needs the constant nurture of multiple communities, in the West and beyond. To be sure, many formulations of human

36 Members of the Old Order Amish Community in Barth Township, Pennsylvania publicly forgave the perpetrator of a mass shooting at the West Nickel Mines School after he murdered five young girls, and wounded five more before committing suicide on October 2, 2006.

37 Luke 23:34.

rights today are suffused with the fundamental beliefs and values of modern liberalism, some of which run counter to the cardinal beliefs of various religious traditions, including Christianity. But secular political philosophy does not and should not have a monopoly on the nurture of human rights; indeed, a human rights regime cannot long survive under the exclusive patronage of secular philosophy. For human rights are "middle axioms" of political discourse.[38] They are a means to the ends of justice and the common good. But the norms that rights instantiate depend upon the visions and values of human communities for their content and coherence – or, what the Catholic philosopher Jacques Maritain described as "the scale of values governing [their] exercise and concrete manifestation."[39]

Liberal philosophers have come to realize that religion often plays a key role in public life and political deliberation. A generation ago, theorists of secularization, privatization, and disestablishment commonly insisted that religion had no serious place in public life, and that political deliberation required secular or utilitarian rationality for validity. Many asserted that religion could be consigned to the private sphere where it would slowly but inevitably die out, having outlived its utility. Some scholars have maintained these positions, and this is a dominant teaching of elite liberal media. The subsequent growth and transformations of religions around the world, however, have led many others to question the central hypotheses of secularization theory, to reimagine the place of religion in political processes, and to invite people of faith back to the table of public deliberation. Pluralism now outshines strict secularism as a discursive ideal for modern democracies.

Even some of the most influential proponents of religious privatization and political secularization have accordingly retracted their previous calls to exclude religious norms and idioms from legislative and political discourse. Jürgen Habermas, Richard Rorty, and John Rawls, for example, all affirmed in their later writings that religion can play valuable and legitimate roles in the lawmaking processes of liberal democracies.[40] They acknowledge that deeply held beliefs are not easily bracketed; that efforts to exclude an entire class of moral and metaphysical knowledge is more likely to yield mutual distrust and hostility than social accord; that norms of free speech prohibit banning or discriminating against religion in the public square; and that avowedly secular values are not inherently more objective, in

38 Abdullahi Ahmed An-Na'im, "Towards an Islamic Hermeneutics for Human Rights," in Abdullahi Ahmed An-Na'im, et al., eds., *Human Rights and Religious Values: An Uneasy Relationship?* (Grand Rapids, MI: Eerdmans, 1995), 229–42; Robert P. George, "Response," in Michael Cromartie, ed., *A Preserving Grace: Protestants, Catholics, and Natural Law* (Grand Rapids, MI: Eerdmans, 1997), 157–61.

39 Jacques Maritain, "Introduction," in UNESCO, *Human Rights: Comments and Interpretations* (New York: Columbia University Press, 1949).

40 See, e.g., John Rawls, "The Idea of Public Reason Revisited," *University of Chicago Law Review* 64 (1997), 765; Jürgen Habermas, et al, *An Awareness of What Is Missing: Faith and Reason in a Post-secular Age*, trans. Ciaran Cronin (Cambridge, UK and Malden, MA: Polity Press, 2010); Richard Rorty, "Religion in the Public Square: A Reconsideration," *Journal of Religious Ethics* 31 (2003), 141–49.

an epistemological sense, than their religious counterparts.[41] Secular norms and idioms can serve as useful discursive resources in religiously pluralistic societies. But purging religion altogether from public life is impractical, short-sighted, and often unjust.

Leading Jewish philosopher, Lenn E. Goodman, offers a viable alternative to the arguments about the "naked public square" of a generation or two ago.[42] Goodman argues that social and communal bonds are forged through authentic encounters with the genuine other. Moral truth and political justice are best approximated when persons bring their best arguments, their deepest convictions, and a sense of mutual respect for one another to the conversation. He offers "a simple thesis: that we humans, with all our differences in outlook and tradition, can respect one another and learn from one another's ways, without sharing them or relinquishing the commitments we make our own."[43] With this in mind, Goodman urges that members of pluralistic societies should not censor themselves, privatize or gloss over their differences, or naively romanticize the exotic other while showing contempt for the more familiar domestic other. Nor should persons or groups foist sectarian parochialisms on their unreceptive neighbors. Instead, members of pluralistic societies ought to mine their respective moral traditions – including religious *and* secular moral traditions – for wisdom and insights about how to live together with integrity. "The profit of pluralism," Goodman contends, "is the space it allows for individuals and groups to retain their identity and commitments, not blurring the differences that make all the difference or blunting the seriousness that distinguishes high seriousness from mere entertainment. ... [F]ruitful dialogue demands our knowing something about who we are ourselves, what we believe and care about, and how what is other actually is other."[44]

Thus, for Goodman, discerning the proper scope and substance of moral and legal norms is anything but an abstract thought experiment conducted behind a hypothetical "veil of ignorance." Rather, it is a real, historical process – an actual debate among actual people who have actual lives and actual beliefs, hopes, fears, plans, and needs. "[T]he kind of pluralism I advocate finds its ideal in an ongoing conversation among cultures in all their richness and among individuals in all their uniqueness." When it's done right, such pluralism sharpens a society's values the way a whetstone sharpens a blade. "[I]t is in our big ideas," Goodman explains, "that we humans find ways of integrating thoughts with acts and find structural affinities that

41 See, e.g., Cécile Laborde, *Liberalism's Religion* (Cambridge, MA: Harvard University Press, 2017); Cécile Laborde and Aurélia Bardon, eds., *Religion in Liberal Political Philosophy* (Oxford: Oxford University Press, 2017); Eric Nelson, *The Theology of Liberalism* (Cambridge, MA: Harvard University Press, 2019).

42 The following paragraphs are adapted from Justin J. Latterell and John Witte, Jr., "Law, Religion, and Reason in a Constitutional Democracy: Goodman v. Rawls," *Political Theology* 16 (2015), 543–59.

43 Lenn E. Goodman, *Religious Pluralism and Values in the Public Sphere* (New York: Cambridge University Press, 2014), 1.

44 Ibid., 2–3.

may help us link our local truths to one another. The logic of our commitments stands in relief as the family resemblances in our diverse ways of thought and action come into focus."[45] Such discourse ideally allows religiously diverse persons and groups to learn and evaluate the contours – and limits – of their own moral teachings. Different communities discover which values they hold in common, and which they do not, by exhibiting to one another what they actually believe – not by imagining which values they might hold if they didn't know who they were. In short, the pursuit of justice, both as a concept and as an institutional reality, requires candid and thoroughgoing debates within and between moral communities. "A good government will foster religious thought and expression and promote metaphysical conversation and inquiry, not hide behind a factitious or fictitious scrim of value neutrality."[46] Following Goodman, an appropriate posture for Christian scholars working in pluralistic contexts is one of integrity and reciprocity, boldness and humility. In the spirit of Saint Francis of Assisi, Christian scholars should seek not only to be understood by their non-Christian counterparts, but also to understand and empathize with them.

In order to assume their proper place in public deliberation, political law making, and human rights cultivation, however, Christian believers and churches must embody and exemplify the moral ideas that modern rights and liberties in part reflect and help individuals and institutions to realize. Like other institutions, Christian churches are not immune to the vices of their members and leaders. Yet the gross injustices, negligence, and abuses that infect too many Christian institutions today are inexcusable in light of the divine truths and moral ideals they confess. Think of the clerical abuse of minors. The embezzlement of tithes and gifts. The degradation and mistreatment of women. Indifference to the poor and needy. A lack of compassion in matters of sexual orientation. Racially and economically segregated congregations. Inhospitality toward immigrants and foreigners. Wrath. Greed. Sloth. Pride. Lust. Envy. Gluttony. "Therefore you have no excuse . . . whoever you are, when you judge another," the Bible tells us; "for in passing judgment on [another] you condemn yourself, because you, the judge, are doing the very same things."[47] Our failure as Christians to live up to our own truths and values rightly undercuts our moral authority in the eyes of others. Only by embracing and embodying the truths and values we profess can Christians retain the ability to call out injustices in other social spheres and institutions. Christian communities simply must do more to habitualize, institutionalize, and exemplify respect for basic human rights, especially the rights of vulnerable populations within their midst.

Martin Luther King, Jr. once said that the church "is not the master or the servant of the state, but rather the conscience of the state."[48] When their own houses are in

45 Ibid., 107, 79.

46 Ibid., 101.

47 Romans 2:1

48 Martin Luther King, Jr., "A Knock at Midnight," in James M. Washington, ed., *A Testament of Hope: The Essential Writings of Martin Luther King, Jr.* (San Francisco:, CA Harper and Row, 1986), 501.

good order, churches are well situated to play this important prophetic role. Well-ordered churches, in this sense, make for effective thorns in the sides of complacent societies and states. Healthy and vibrant churches are well situated to serve a number of other important functions within society, too. Christian communities that more fully embody the rights and duties they profess can act as a sort of ballast in otherwise turbulent contexts. Like other religious organizations, they can catalyze social, intellectual, and material exchange among citizens; trigger economic, charitable, and educational impulses; provide healthy checks and counterpoints to social and individual excess; build relationships across racial and ethnic boundaries; diffuse social and political crises and absolutisms by relativizing everyday life and its institutions; transmit cultural traditions, wisdom, and memories; provide leadership and aid amid social crises and natural disasters; form persons in the virtues and skills of civic engagement and shared decision-making processes; provide material aid to the underprivileged and downtrodden; enrich and structure family life and other important relationships; and more.[49] Taken together, these tasks represent a tall order for a community of fallible humans. Yet, as Dr. King reminded his listeners:

> If the church will free itself from the shackles of a deadening status quo, and, recovering its great historic mission, will speak and act fearlessly and insistently in terms of justice and peace, it will enkindle the imagination of mankind and fire the souls of men, imbuing them with a glowing and ardent love for truth, justice, and peace. Men far and near will know the church as a great fellowship of love that provides light and bread for lonely travellers at midnight.[50]

49 See Martin E. Marty, *Politics, Religion, and the Common Good: Advancing a Distinctly American Conversation About Religion's Role in Our Shared Life* (San Francisco, CA: Jossey-Bass, Inc., 2000), esp. chap. 2.

50 King, "A Knock at Midnight."

Index

Printed in the USA
CPSIA information can be obtained
at www.ICGtesting.com
CBHW071621260724
12244CB00007B/786

9 781108 45326